TERROR IN THE BALKANS

TERROR IN THE
BALKANS

German Armies and Partisan Warfare

BEN SHEPHERD

Harvard University Press

Cambridge, Massachusetts · London, England

2012

Library of Congress Cataloging-in-Publication Data

Shepherd, Ben.
Terror in the Balkans : German armies and partisan warfare / Ben Shepherd.
p. cm.
Includes bibliographical references and index.
ISBN 978-0-674-04891-1 (alk. paper)
1. World War, 1939–1945—Yugoslavia. 2. World War, 1939–1945—
Underground movements—Yugoslavia. 3. Yugoslavia—History—Axis occupation,
1941–1945. 4. Germany. Heer—History—World War, 1939–1945. I. Title.
D766.6.S44 2012
940.53'497—dc23 2011048292

Contents

TERROR IN THE BALKANS

Introduction

IN SPRING 1941 the German Wehrmacht, replete with victory over successive opponents across Europe, fell upon the Balkan kingdom of Yugoslavia.[1] The Yugoslav army was overwhelmed within ten days, and an improvised occupation regime swiftly established. But there then erupted a national uprising that later developed into an insurgency as violent and obdurate as any in World War II.[2] It lasted almost the entire duration of the war. It was marked not just by a fearsome campaign against the Axis occupier and ferocious Axis countermeasures, but also by fratricidal slaughter between Yugoslavia's mutually belligerent ethnic groups. It was almost the entire cause of the 1.75 million dead—11 percent of the population—Yugoslavia suffered during World War II.[3]

Hitler and the Wehrmacht retaliated against the uprising with a campaign of hostage-taking and reprisals that was exceptional, even by Nazi standards, in the scale of indiscriminate butchery that it inflicted. There is no better expression of the campaign's intent, and of the historically founded hatred that helped to forge it, than an order issued at its outset by Lieutenant General Franz Boehme,[4] the Wehrmacht's Plenipotentiary Commanding General in Serbia:

1

Your objective is to be achieved in a land where, in 1914, streams of German blood flowed because of the treachery of the Serbs, men and women. You are the avengers of those dead. A deterring example must be established for all of Serbia, one that will have the heaviest impact on the entire population. Anyone who carries out his duty in a lenient manner will be called to account, regardless of rank or position, and tried by a military court.[5]

Though the rising posed a considerable danger to the Axis occupation, the response Boehme was urging went beyond all normal constraints of legality and morality.[6] And Boehme belonged not to the organization with which the worst outrages of Nazi occupation are most often associated—the SS—but to the Wehrmacht. It was this same Wehrmacht that was popularly viewed for decades after World War II as having been a bastion of moral decency, sometimes active resistance, against the Nazi regime's depravities. But Boehme's order is only one example of the vast array of evidence, unearthed over the past four-and-a-half decades, that has demolished the myth of the "clean" Wehrmacht.

The myth retained remarkable durability after 1945. Over the course of World War II, the organs of the Nazi regime inflicted destruction and misery upon the swathe of occupied Europe from the Atlantic to the Urals. The occupied peoples were increasingly deprived of their foodstuffs, economic resources, and human labor, all in the cause of feeding Germany's increasingly voracious war economy. The further east one went, the more harrowing the picture got; here, the Nazis' piratical rampage was exacerbated by their belief that the "racially inferior" Slavic peoples of Eastern Europe were natural slaves, to be decimated and exploited with impunity. None of this is to mention the campaign of terror, and ultimately genocide, waged against those groups Nazi ideology regarded as an existential threat to the German race itself—Communists, Sinti and Roma, and, above all, Jews. Finally, across the continent, the Nazis countered mounting resistance to their economic and ideological dictates with a security campaign ever more indiscriminate in the bloodshed and destruction it inflicted. Indeed, particularly in the Nazi empire's eastern regions, "security needs" were often used as convenient cover for implementing those same dictates even further.[7]

Yet the Wehrmacht, its postwar advocates asserted, was untainted by any involvement in such terror and exploitation.[8] Only during the late 1960s, as West German students took to the streets to challenge an establishment they saw as criminally compromised by its earlier associations with Nazism, did historians begin dismantling the myth of the "clean" Wehrmacht. Now, seventy years after World War II, it can be confidently stated that the Wehrmacht, or its higher command levels at any rate, was complicit, sometimes instrumental, in the barbarities the Third Reich perpetrated across occupied Europe. Yet even though the navy (Kriegsmarine), and certainly the air force (Luftwaffe) were tainted by involvement in Nazi crimes, it was the army (Heer), by far the Wehrmacht's numerically largest branch, whose involvement in such crimes was most extensive. And it was the army that, consequently, has been the focus of the vast majority of studies that have collectively revealed the Wehrmacht's damning record. A picture has emerged of a senior army officer corps that was complicit in the Nazi regime's crimes primarily because complicity suited both its professional ambitions and its ideological convictions.[9]

It is in relation to those ideological convictions that Boehme's order is significant for a second reason. For it is a particularly telling reminder that the origins of those convictions lie further back in history. Many of the reasons why the German army came to support the Nazi regime stemmed from the situation in which the German military found itself after the Great War of 1914 to 1918. During this aftermath, the defeated German army of the old imperial regime, the Kaiserheer, was reduced from a millions-strong body to a defense force one hundred thousand strong, the Reichswehr. The Nazis' pledge, in the years that followed, to tear up the treaty and commit Germany to full-scale rearmament was a pledge Reichswehr officers would find increasingly enticing. It provided them, after all, with an opportunity to pursue their professional ambitions, something which the weak democratic regime governing Germany between 1918 and 1933 clearly could not provide. But there were additional reasons, rooted further back in history, why the army was ready to behave so pitilessly in implementing the Nazi agenda. General Boehme's order alludes to one such reason. The decades-old hatred of the Serbs that it invoked was one of the historic enmities whose toxic effect upon the German army's conduct during World War II is a major concern of this study.

Just how brutally the German army behaved during World War II, and why, are vast, labyrinthine questions. But the counterinsurgency campaign in Yugoslavia, the particular focus of this study, provides revealing insights into those enmities and how they affected soldiers' behavior.

As a force that reacted with excessive harshness when confronted with irregular armed resistance, the German army finds ample company throughout history. Occupation troops have often been inadequately trained and equipped, and have often lacked the numbers needed to administer occupied territory effectively. They can thus easily become brutalized by the fear and frustration they feel at being stationed deep within an unfamiliar country, facing an unseen and often highly mobile enemy ready to employ ruthless and underhand methods against them, encountering a civilian population of at best suspect reliability, and often living and fighting amid the kind of impenetrable terrain that is a haven for irregular fighters and a topographical nightmare for the forces facing them.

In fact, the Communist Partisans who would prove the Germans' most implacable adversary in occupied Yugoslavia often fought in the manner of a conventional army. This mode of fighting found growing favor with the Partisan movement as the war progressed, as its burgeoning size and strength increasingly emboldened it, and required it, to fight in the open.[10] Even so, the Partisans and other insurgent groups in wartime Yugoslavia employed irregular methods for much of the time. The irregular combatants the Germans faced in Yugoslavia during World War II frequently flouted two of the criteria of lawful combatant status laid down in the 1907 Hague Convention: they were often not readily identifiable, and often did not carry arms openly. The Yugoslav Partisans also regularly flouted a third criterion: their maltreatment and murder of German prisoners, and particularly of native collaborators, frequently defied all notions of internationally acceptable conduct.[11]

By the outbreak of World War II, international law made allowances for occupying forces facing irregular opponents. Article 50 of the Hague Convention had no issue with seizing hostages to ensure an occupied

population's good behavior. Such hostage-taking was widespread practice during the interwar years. The convention approved reprisals as
long as they were against civilians who had actually resisted in some way.
But it was silent on whether reprisals should take lethal form, or whether
they should restrict themselves to measures such as financial penalties or
confiscation of property. In any case, the German generals convicted in
the "Hostage Trial" at Nuremberg after World War II were not imprisoned for killing civilians per se—something in which servicemen on both
sides had of course been copiously active, particularly in the air war.
Rather, the generals were imprisoned specifically for conducting reprisals on occupied territory so indiscriminately and disproportionately.[12]

The German army's counterinsurgency campaign in Yugoslavia—a
campaign waged under commanders from both air force and army—was
as brutal as it was not just because of the conditions it faced. This, after
all, was an army whose leadership, due to its ideological sympathies and
careerist calculation, had hitched its wagon to the Nazi star. It sought to
instill within its troops' minds and actions a set of beliefs and attitudes
that, it hoped, would transform them into willing executors of the "Nazi"
way of war. It was also deeply complicit in the campaign the SS and
police waged across Europe to "cleanse" the occupied territories of the
Reich's "ideological enemies." In the course of that campaign, the army
leadership became implicated among other things in that succession of
murderous initiatives from which emerged the Nazis' "Final Solution" to
the "problem" of European Jewry.

What all this entailed when it came to counterinsurgency was that the
troops were expected to single out, victimize, and kill Jews, Communists, and Sinti and Roma, as scapegoats or reprisal victims for insurgent
attacks. The German army leadership sought to propagandize its troops
into believing that such groups were a "security threat." From summer
1941, as the Final Solution accelerated across occupied Europe, the same
rationale was used to justify SS executions of tens of thousands of Jews
and Sinti and Roma in the army's jurisdiction.

More generally, the troops themselves were expected to translate into
practice the National Socialist belief that terror was the answer to any
unrest that arose in occupied territory. This approach was considerably
less evident in German-occupied Western Europe for much of the war.

But the Slavic regions of southeastern and Eastern Europe were a different matter. The particularly harsh occupation policy which the Nazi regime practiced in these regions made resistance more likely from the outset. The often impenetrable terrain of forest, swamp, and mountain that covered much of them was an ideal environment for the development of resistance by armed irregular bands. Once resistance had developed, the "racial backwardness" of the Slavic population whom the Germans believed were providing the insurgents with shelter and supply made it even more likely that the population would suffer ferocious German retaliation. And in the German military, the Nazi approach to counterinsurgency in south-eastern and Eastern Europe found an especially fertile seedbed.

The result was a plethora of directives and measures that were often brutal in the extreme. They encompassed immensely disproportionate reprisal shootings, mass destruction of villages, and the ravaging of vast areas in large-scale mobile operations unleashed less against insurgents than against the civilian population whom the German army believed, rightly or wrongly, was aiding and abetting them. Moreover, after-action reports by German army counterinsurgency units recorded countless operations in which "enemy" death tolls dwarfed both German death tolls and the amounts of enemy weaponry counted. These are clear signs that grievous numbers of noncombatants had perished in these actions. Such death tolls could to some extent be intentionally or unintentionally overinflated.[13] Yet there can be no serious doubt that slaughter of civilians took place on a frequently eye-watering scale. Moreover, some commanders, for reasons of their own, spurred their troops to levels of destruction and carnage even greater than higher command expected of them.

Yet, its brutal nature notwithstanding, the counterinsurgency which the German army prosecuted in these regions did display a saner, more restrained side. As the war dragged on and turned ever more emphatically against Germany, many army officers increasingly realized that they could not rely solely on terror if they wanted to keep their Eastern and south-eastern European territories in line. For one thing, they recognized that, though large-scale mobile operations had their place, no viable long-term counterinsurgency strategy could do without small, well-armed mobile patrols and small-scale garrisons stationed amongst the population susceptible to insurgent influence. More fundamentally still, they saw the need to balance terror, perhaps even supplant it, with more measured policies that actually offered the population something concrete in return for its assistance. Consequently, for instance, they might urge leniency towards insurgent deserters, or redistribution of farmland amongst the occupied rural population. Complementing such initiatives was the army's intermittently effective propaganda machine.

These more constructive efforts were never enough to shift decisively the direction of German counterinsurgency warfare in Eastern and south-eastern Europe. Often, all they succeeded in doing was to confuse the troops with mixed messages. And many officers likely went to such effort not because they were more moral than their colleagues, even though some were, but because they were more sensible. That they went to such effort at all, however, reminds the historian to regard the German army's motives and actions with a nuanced eye.

Yet this too is to understate the complexities this study examines. For it investigates what drove counterinsurgency not at higher command levels, but among units in the field. Historians have produced a compelling picture of high-level army culpability in Nazi crimes. But the question of how far, and why, the bulk of German army personnel actually participated in such outrages remains far from resolved.[14]

This study examines the motivations not of ordinary soldiers, something for which sources are often scant,[15] but of divisional commanders. In the German army as in others, the division was a pivotally important command level. As the smallest combined arms formation capable of independent operations, it was the basic unit of the German army. The division was also the interface between the orders of higher command and units in the field; it filtered the high-level orders that directed the counterinsurgency campaign, and conveyed them, together with orders of its own, to its regiments and other units.

The main source base the middle level generated, the official paperwork of divisions and their subordinate units, is rich and extensive, even though problems of reliability and completeness accompany it.[16] The main types of German army divisional record utilized here are drawn from the divisions' operational files (Ia), quartermaster's files (Ib), and intelligence files

(Ic). These files provide an extensive picture of a division's counterinsurgency effort. Operational files contain orders and reports on both general security matters and particular counterinsurgency operations. The divisional quartermaster was responsible for gathering reports generated by various divisional subsections, including the divisional court, the military police, and offices responsible for transport and supply. Intelligence files detail matters relating to the mood of the population, and to the provision of propaganda and leisure activities to the troops. When it came to assessing the population's mood, the intelligence section relied extensively upon information gathered from native informers. Intelligence section files also contain reports on insurgent groups and activities from civilian informers, and transcripts of interviews with captured insurgents or insurgent deserters; these constituted a source of information on the size, composition, and activities of insurgent forces within a particular division's jurisdiction.[17]

The orders and reports contained within these files together illuminate the immediate circumstances and wider contexts that shaped officers' motivations and conduct. Division-level sources rarely, if ever, state officers' ideological motivations explicitly. However, a considerable amount can be inferred from what officers did, even more so when such sources are used in combination with the types of biographical source this study utilizes.

Before turning to those biographical sources, one further point about divisional records needs making. Divisional records, consisting as they do of sources produced by officers rather than rank-and-file soldiers, provide a much fuller picture of what motivated divisional commanders than of what motivated the ordinary troops. Yet they do convey some idea, through such sources as discipline reports and after-action body counts, of how those soldiers were behaving. It is important to recognize the contribution the records make on this score, and not only because soldiers' behavior is a meaningful focus in its own right. It is important also because how divisional commanders responded to the troops' behavior, or failed to respond, sheds further light on the mind-set of those commanders themselves.

The available biographical sources relating to German army divisional commanders in Yugoslavia generally reveal more about motivation than do equivalent sources for the German army divisional commanders who served in other theaters during World War II. The reason for this is that disproportionate numbers of army personnel who served in Yugoslavia were not actually German in origin, but Austrian. And in the shape of the records of the Austro-Hungarian Royal-Imperial Army of the Great War, there exists a source base that illuminates the personal experiences many senior Austrian officers underwent at a formative time in their lives. Equivalent records for the Imperial German Army were largely destroyed by Allied bombing during World War II.[18]

The Royal-Imperial Army records combine with other source types that provide biographical information on both German and Austrian officers. These include Great War regimental histories; the seven volumes of *Österreich-Ungarns letzter Krieg*, the Austrian official history of the Great War published during the 1930s, which detail the movements and actions of Austro-Hungarian units between 1914 and 1918;[19] and officers' personnel files. These list birthplace, birth date, social background, and service record. They were produced by the Imperial German Army, by the Royal-Imperial Army, by their successor armies during the interwar years, and by the German army under the Third Reich.[20]

Divisional command was not simply a conduit for "the word from on high." It often fashioned the way in which higher-level directives were implemented, in ways that could be far from uniform. Given that the mind-set of divisional commanders could be shaped by a multitude of influences, this is not surprising.

The condition of an occupation division was determined by the state of its troops' supply, training, and equipment; by the terrain it was forced to negotiate; by the striking power, ruthlessness, and elusiveness of the insurgents it faced; and, finally, by its relationship with the occupied population with whom its troops interacted daily. It was this relationship that was perhaps the most important factor of all, as well as the most complex. For it was the population, caught as it was between both sides, whose active and effective cooperation—whether in providing manpower, food, accommodation, or information—was vital to either side's success. And in a region as riven by inter-ethnic conflict as Yugoslavia during World War II, relations between occupier and occupied were complicated even further.

Different divisions were affected by all these phenomena in different ways at different times. While one division, for instance, might lead a humdrum existence in a stagnant occupation backwater, another might be thrown into savage, relentless, and exhausting mobile counterinsurgency operations. Most divisions would experience both states, and other states besides, during their time in the field, and this was bound to affect how their officers and men behaved.

Moreover, different divisional commanders might view their situation, and the myriad factors that determined it, in different ways. The formative life influences that could shape commanders' attitudes and behavior were more varied than just uniformly strong National Socialist belief. Finally, the style of command within the Third Reich, from Hitler downwards, was more open-ended than one might expect. This meant that counterinsurgency directives often resembled not so much clear-cut orders as general guidelines for action. Many such guidelines sought to foster a resourceful, ruthless mentality, combining harshness and initiative, among the troops to whom they were issued. In this way they embodied the National Socialist "leadership principle."[21] But some were sufficiently open-ended for units on the ground to implement them in ways that could be restrained *or* ruthless.

The importance of all these influences, together with the institutional command framework within which they operated, is investigated in the chapters that follow. Chapters 1 to 3 examine how, over decades, successive developments shaped the mind-set of the military institutions which encompassed the commanders who are this study's concern. Some of these developments were connected to that particular theater of war, the Balkans, on which this study focuses. Others had wider historical origins. All had potential to affect the attitudes and behavior of the senior German army officers who would serve in that particular theater during World War II.

This sets the scene for the study's core, in Chapters 4 to 10. These chapters do not provide a comprehensive treatment of the German army's counterinsurgency campaign in Yugoslavia. Rather, by providing case studies of four different divisions between spring 1941 and early 1943,[22] they investigate how a range of middle-level commanders and their units behaved on the ground in different parts of Yugoslavia, and why. They also, particularly in Chapters 4 and 7, illuminate the background developments that shaped the conduct of all sides in the conflict during this period, from the Axis invasion of Yugoslavia onward.

One final point needs making here. On the surface, the years between 1914 and 1945 were a time in which Europe experienced a twenty-year peace, however uneasy, sandwiched between two uniquely destructive wars. But there is another way of viewing these years; a prominent adherent of this school is Eric Hobsbawm, who asserts, "Looking back on the thirty-one years from the assassination of the Austrian Archduke in Sarajevo to the unconditional surrender of Japan, they must be seen as an era of havoc comparable to the Thirty Years' War of the seventeenth century in German History."[23] World War II can thus be seen to have brought the destructive culmination of the bitter national and, even more importantly, ideological rivalries that were first acted out so calamitously during this thirty-year period's opening stages. How far this view accurately encapsulates the period in its entirety is a question over which historians will continue to deliberate. This study contributes to answering that question, by investigating how the mind-set of a particular group of officers evolved throughout the period, and how those officers went on to behave during its cataclysmic final years.

CHAPTER 1

Before the Great War

Changes in the Officer Corps

T HE MEN WHO COMPRISED the officer corps of the army that served under the Third Reich did not share a common heritage. During the years following the German Empire's founding in 1871, the needs of an expanded army—unifying the armies of the kingdoms of Prussia, Saxony, Bavaria, and Württemberg—compelled the German officer corps to dilute its social exclusivity and accept growing numbers of entrants from across the spectrum of the German middle classes. This process accelerated with the continental arms race that preceded the outbreak of the Great War in 1914. Following the Great War, such was the diminished size of the post-1918 Reichswehr that the leadership of the new army was able to restore much of its earlier social exclusivity. But in 1935, Hitler declared the Versailles disarmament clauses dead and announced the Reichswehr's replacement with a vastly enlarged, conscript-based *Heer*, together with a new air force and an expanded navy. Now the officer corps' social base grew once more. Then, from 1938 onward, ethnic Germans outwith the Reich's borders swelled the officer corps even further. The biggest intake came from the German-speaking lands of the old Austro-Hungarian Empire, Germany's erstwhile ally during the Great War. Of these, the biggest intake of all came from the post-1918 Republic of Austria.

The nine generals who are this study's main focus all commanded German army divisions that fought insurgents in Axis-occupied Yugoslavia. All were born between 1880 and 1890, either in the German Reich or in the German-speaking parts of the Austro-Hungarian Empire. All, Reich Germans and German-speaking Austrians alike, belonged to institutions that, during the first years of the twentieth century, were being challenged by powerful forces of social and political change. The forces themselves, and the mix of resistance and accommodation with which the two officer corps responded to them, would increasingly influence the officer corps' character and the attitudes of young men embarking upon service within them. Some of the effects were beneficent; rather more would prove pernicious. Nevertheless, new officers were in no sense already set on an ineluctable path towards National Socialist–style warfare during this period; it was the events of later years that would ensure that particular outcome. But important seeds were planted nonetheless.[1]

The arch-conservatives who headed the imperial German officer corps, whether the general staff or the senior-most field commanders, recognized that a necessarily large, technically proficient Imperial German Army necessitated a large, technically proficient officer corps. It would need to be an officer corps whose members were drawn not just from the centuries-old bastions of service to the Prussian state—the families of Junker aristocrats and landowners, of Protestant clerics, of senior civil servants, and of officers themselves—but from a much wider middle-class social spectrum.[2]

But with expansion came risk. The officer corps saw itself as a bulwark against disruptive and dangerous social change. Traditionally aloof from mainstream society, it had long distrusted the bourgeois middle class, albeit nothing like as intensely as it feared Germany's emerging industrial working class.[3] Though the army leadership could countenance a necessarily expanded officer corps, then, it sought to minimize the dangers of social dilution by drawing its officer candidates from what it regarded as the "desired circles" of middle-class German society. The new emperor, Wilhelm II, elaborated on the concept of "desired circles" in 1890: "In addition to the sons of noble families of the country, and the sons of my loyal officers and civil servants, who according to old tradition constitute the main pillars of the officer corps, I see the future standard-bearers of my army in the sons of those honorable bourgeois families in which love for the king and fatherland and respect for the military and Christian morals are cultivated and handed down."[4]

Southeast of the German Reich lay the multiethnic Austro-Hungarian Empire. Here, Magyars and ethnic German Austrians administered a polyglot empire whose population also comprised Poles, Ruthenes, Czechs, Slovaks, Italians, Rumanians, Croats, Albanians, Serbs, and Jews. There were three separate armies under the Emperor's command— home armies for the Austrian and Hungarian halves of the monarchy, and a more powerful joint army. It was the joint army, properly titled the Royal-Imperial Army, that, in the years before the empire's collapse in 1918, was principal home to all the Austrian-born officers in this study.

Like the German officer corps, the Royal-Imperial Army's officer corps was deeply conservative by tradition, socially selective—though the majority of its personnel came from the families of officers, NCOs, or officials, rather than from traditional aristocratic families—and anxious to remain separate from civil society.[5] But like the German officer corps, it needed to reach some sort of accommodation with the imperatives of change during the late nineteenth and early twentieth centuries. Most pressingly, it needed to try and remedy a serious, ongoing shortage of officers in an army that, due to the empire's relative economic backwardness and the parsimony of the Austrian and Hungarian parliaments, was undersized and underresourced.[6] One partial solution was, again, to open the officer corps to candidates from a wider range of social backgrounds. This drive to greater egalitarianism was further abetted by the system of military schooling open to officer candidates.[7]

Within the Royal-Imperial Army's rank and file, the empire's full ethnic kaleidoscope was properly represented. But within the officer corps, the ethnic Germans dominated—even if this had less to do with their ethnicity as such than with the superior education they enjoyed.[8]

The different branches of both armies maintained a distinct pecking order. Most sought after was the cavalry, followed by the artillery and finally the infantry.[9] For Austro-Hungarian officers particularly, going into the infantry was a lottery, contingent upon a regiment's location, the quality of its officers, and the literacy level of its men. The last of these was contingent upon a unit's ethnic composition; only a fraction of the army's units were monolingual, and of these only a smaller fraction still spoke German.[10]

Equally rigid were the social conditions in which new officers found themselves. While some German officers stationed within the Reich's cosmopolitan urban centers were able to pursue some sort of intellectual existence,[11] the German lieutenant's life was usually deeply conformist. In the Imperial German Army, most officers were still required to train even after receiving their lieutenant's commission, by attending the War School (*Kriegsschule*)—eight months' cram-learning of subjects including battle tactics, weaponry, fortifications, terrain, and military organization.[12] Social life centered on the officers' mess, and socially conservative, aristocratic values governed virtually every aspect of an officer's existence, irrespective of his own social origin.

All this made for an existence that, privileged though it was, was also intensive, narrow, and isolated from society. Not only was there no place in the curriculum in which to instruct officers on the social, political, and economic context of that wider society; such was the narrow pattern of their lives, and the strength of the socially conservative programming to which they were subjected, they were likely to be disinclined to learn about such things anyway.[13] Stunting officers' critical faculties in this way would have ominous implications for their later development.[14]

The Austro-Hungarian officer corps similarly sought to isolate its members from society. Given the army's experience of civilians since 1848—violent revolution that year, frequent ethnic unrest throughout the empire in the decades that followed, parsimonious civilian parliaments, and stifling state bureaucracy—it is small wonder that the army leadership sought to instill within its officers a feeling of aloofness from, indeed aversion to, civilian influences.[15] In one respect at least, however, Austro-Hungarian officers were less straitjacketed than their German colleagues. Thanks to Austria-Hungary's sheer diversity, the course of a Habsburg junior officer's military service exposed him to a far greater variety of peoples and environments than his German counterpart. The historian Gunther Rothenburg elaborates:

The large territorial expanse of the Dual Monarchy, which included
the gentle landscapes of Lower Austria and Bohemia, the mighty
ranges of the Alps and the Carpathians, the rich lands of Slovenia and
the plains of Galicia, the wild forests of Bosnia and Transylvania, as
well as the barren crags of the Dalmatian coast, with garrisons rang-
ing from cities of culture and refinement like Vienna, Budapest, and
Prague, provincial towns like Graz, Agram, or Budweis, to small,
isolated hamlets, gave service in the joint army a special character.
An officer might serve a tour in a big city and find himself during
the next in an isolated fort in Bosnia or in the mud of a small Galician hamlet. Described by one English journalist "as hard-working,
hard-living men," the average Austro-Hungarian regimental officer
was judged the "superior of the average German officer . . . more
intelligent, more readily adaptable, in closer touch with his men, less
given to dissipation, and remarkably free from arrogance."[16]

Rothenburg's English eyewitness is overgeneralizing about the German officer of the period.[17] Yet there is something in the argument that
the German officer's Austro-Hungarian counterpart was, on the whole,
more open-minded. But the argument should not be taken too far. Ultimately, how far an Austro-Hungarian officer chose to absorb a better-
developed worldview was down to him individually. Like his German
counterpart, he could expect no meaningful education on wider social,
political, and economic realities from his superiors.

Within both officer corps, meanwhile, the years before the Great War
portended ominous changes. During the late nineteenth and early twentieth centuries, technical and industrial change made it possible for
major powers to recruit, equip, and supply mass conscript-based armies.
The scale of warfare that the Europe-wide emergence of mass armies
presaged required a hitherto unparalleled degree of technical prowess
and operational planning. This was also an era in which the revolution
in defensive firepower, advances in communication, and the advent of
airpower on the battlefield were transforming warfare fundamentally.[18]

In the new reality these converging elements created, it was incumbent upon the ambitious young officer to gain expertise not just in a traditional branch of the army, but also, eventually, in one of the cutting-edge fields of military planning and technology. The most sought-after route was to qualify as a staff officer. This presented the ambitious young officer with the perfect opportunity to master the entire technical, organizational, and operational foundation upon which the new warfare was based. Only the very ablest officers—many of whom, in the case of the German and Austro-Hungarian officer corps, would eventually fill the Wehrmacht's senior-most positions—were granted such an opportunity. But many other future Wehrmacht officers were at least able to pursue their ambitions further by transferring to one of the rapidly developing technology-oriented branches of their respective armies—airships, machine-gunnery, or battlefield communications, for instance—before, during, or after the Great War.[19]

The emergence of the technically minded military planner would culminate during the interwar years in the advent of the "specialist in mass destruction." This was a badge the Reichswehr officer corps would come to sport with particular pride. But even before the outbreak of the Great War, officers' increasing professional specialization could bring baleful implications. For it encouraged ambitious young officers with new professional preoccupations to work and think in a way more specialized, focused, and intensive than ever before. This discouraged out-of-the-box thinking on military matters. And, more importantly for this study, such narrowness could further deprive an officer of the opportunity to develop societal awareness, political maturity, and general openness to the world.[20] Though increasing professional specialization did not make such an outcome inevitable, it did make it more likely.

All the more likely given some of the still more disturbing developments that were now in train. Whether in Wilhelm II's Germany or in the Austro-Hungarian Empire, brutal worldviews were already emerging across wider society. And such was the level of social and political illiteracy that afflicted both officer corps that a great many officers, though not yet automatic prey to such worldviews, were morally and intellectually ill-equipped to resist them as fully as they might have done.

One of the most influential ideas of the age across Europe, and quite possibly the most noxious, was Social Darwinism. Social Darwinists believed that the struggle between the "superior" and the "inferior," and the extinction or subjugation of the weak in favor of the strong, were the natural order of things not just in the animal kingdom, but in human affairs also. During the 1880s, those who believed it was the Germans themselves who, by dint of their cultural, scientific, and military achievements, occupied the foremost position among all the "races" of humanity, merged into the Pan-German movement.

Pan-Germans in Germany itself clustered around the Pan-German League, and in German-speaking Austria around the Greater German People's Party (GDVP). Both groups drew support from particular middle-class circles. For the Pan-German League it was teachers, civil servants, doctors, lawyers, and other professionals who saw themselves as pillars of social authority and custodians of German culture. For the GDVP it was right-wing university students, and artisans and shopkeepers who felt threatened by technological change.[21]

As the German and Austro-Hungarian officer corps expanded, officers who hailed from such backgrounds became much more numerous. If they did indeed subscribe to Pan-German sentiment, they could not necessarily expect a particularly warm reception in the traditionalistic climate of either officer corps. But this did not mean they would encounter particular hostility either. For this same climate itself contained elements common with Pan-Germanism. One such element was anti-Semitism.

From the 1870s onward, the "science" of Social Darwinism lent Europe's long-established tradition of anti-Semitism an even more sinister, biologically founded aspect. For Pan-Germans it provided a warped basis for the equally warped view that Jews, as non-Germans, should be prevented from "polluting," and thus weakening, the "purity" that was the foundation of the German people's strength. Pan-Germans within the Austro-Hungarian Empire in particular regarded Jews as a spiritual, economic, and biological menace. This view became more buttressed and widespread as thousands of eastern Jews were driven to live in the Austro-Hungarian Empire, particularly in Vienna, by murderous pogroms in Tsarist Russia.[22]

Nevertheless, even if there was considerable latent anti-Semitism within the Habsburg officer corps, there was little active anti-Semitism. This was probably due in no small part to the greater open-mindedness that service across such an ethnically diverse realm afforded. Emperor Franz Josef hugely appreciated the loyalty of all his subjects, Gentile and non-Gentile. Jews were disproportionately prominent, thanks probably to their superior education levels, amongst the army's reserve officers. There were also considerable numbers of Jewish career officers.[23]

But by the eve of the Great War, the Royal-Imperial Army was no longer quite as comfortable a home for Jews as it had been. General Conrad, the chief of the army high command, and Archduke Franz Ferdinand, who as well as heir to the throne was also inspector general of the army, were both self-declared anti-Semites. There was also a glass ceiling, with higher-ranking officers and staff officers counting very few Jews among their number.[24] But it would be wrong to exaggerate the extent to which anti-Semitism was beginning to pervade the officer corps in its entirety.[25] The still relatively benign experience of Jewish soldiers within the Austro-Hungarian army of the Great War would vindicate this view.

North of the border, however, the picture was less benign already. "Anti-Semitism," asserts the historian Martin Kitchen, "was one of the fundamental creeds of the German Officer Corps."[26] As Jews could not be barred by law, they were barred instead on grounds of "character." Jews from a commercial background, for instance, could be excluded for their "undesirable" bourgeois social origins. Typical were the remarks of one German officer in 1911. Responding to Jewish demands for equal treatment in the army, he expressed astonishment at the notion that "the salvation of the Fatherland depended on our accepting a few dozen useless Isidores, Manasses, and Abrahams as confessing Semites in our Officer Corps."[27] Reprehensible as they are, such remarks indicate old-school economic and religious anti-Semitism, not the more venomous, biologically based brand espoused by the Pan-Germans. But such old-school anti-Semitism was widespread and entrenched, and would form a bedrock for that more vicious strain later on.

Also widespread across society, and likewise insinuating itself into both officer corps, was anti-Slavism. The pre–Great War anti-Slavism of the imperial German officer corps was particularly directed against "the East." This is not surprising; it was founded both in centuries-old Russophobia, common to the West generally, and in notions of Germany's "moral mission" to civilize its backward, inferior eastern neighbors.[28] Such notions had grown stronger since the demise of the independent Kingdom of Poland and the influx of millions of Poles into the eastern provinces of Prussia itself.[29] Anti-Slavism grew stronger still in reaction to the expansionist pan-Slavic ideology that increasingly animated the foreign policy of Tsarist Russia, particularly over the Balkans, in the years up to 1914.[30]

In the German officer corps, anti-Slavic views went to the top. In February 1913 Hellmuth von Moltke, chief of the German General Staff, opined to his Austro-Hungarian opposite number, Conrad, that any future war would be "a struggle between Slavs and Teutons" for the preservation of "Germanic culture."[31] Conrad dismissed talk of a race war, reminding Moltke that Slavs comprised 47 percent of the Habsburg Empire's population.[32] But six months on Moltke remained stuck in the same groove, asserting to Conrad that the European war would come "sooner or later," and that it would be "primarily a struggle between Germans and Slavs."[33]

Yet though the Pan-Germans were strongly anti-Slavic, there were other educated bourgeois German circles, circles from which ever more officers were now being drawn, that harbored a different attitude. This attitude, condescending though it was, did acknowledge Russia's contribution to the cultural and intellectual life of Europe. At any rate, it was an attitude certainly more favorable than Moltke's stance.[34] True, new officers harboring such sentiments may well have found them stifled following their admission into the officer corps. But this did not mean they were going to automatically convert to Moltke's strident anti-Slavism. The extent of such anti-Slavism within the German officer corps as a whole, then, should not be overstated.

General Conrad, for his part, was not best-placed to rebuke his German counterpart for anti-Slavism. When he recalled his tour of duty fighting Slavic irregulars in Habsburg-occupied Bosnia between 1878 and

1882, he railed against their "cruelty," "bestiality," and "bloodlust."[35] By the early twentieth century, growing numbers of ethnic Germans within the Habsburg Empire would have sympathized. This was down partly to the advent of biologically based racism during the 1870s and 1880s. It was also down partly, especially after universal suffrage was introduced in 1907, to Pan-Germanism's swelling political mobilization in the face of what many Austrians perceived as "Slav encroachment and Jewish emancipation."[36] But probably the most powerful source of burgeoning anti-Slavism within the empire, and ultimately the most cataclysmic, was the empire's confrontation with Serbia.

During the decade before the Great War, Serbia became a significant Balkan power and an increasingly anti-Habsburg one. In particular, the Balkan Wars of 1912–1913 enabled it to expand its territory considerably. Consequently, pan-Slavists in both Serbia and the Austro-Hungarian Empire regarded one another with growing interest. Eventually, the idea of unifying Serbia with the southern Slavic peoples of the empire— something that would, of course, be fatal to the empire's future—began taking root.[37] Unsurprisingly, those years saw Austrian journalists take an increasingly bellicose line against Serbia; Leopold Mandl, for instance, wrote of the "Austro-phobic putrefaction in the nation" that was the foundation of Serbian foreign policy, and warned that Serbia's goal was "the liberation and reunification of all lands that are inhabited by Serbs"—including those within the Habsburg Empire itself.[38] In 1908, Austria-Hungary almost went to war with Serbia, and Serbia's ally Russia, over the surprise Habsburg annexation of Bosnia. And just as some officers saw the apparently imminent conflagration as a conventional battle between states, others viewed it as a battle between superior Germans and inferior Slavs.[39]

Yet while fear of Serbia and Russia as hostile states was strong, racial contempt for Slavs in the "modern" biological sense did not affect the army's outlook or policy, or its officers' behavior. Indeed, as Conrad indicated in his exchanges with Moltke, generic anti-Slavism was hardly a viable policy for an empire that encompassed such a voluminous number of Slavs itself—not least among the rank and file of its own army. So numerous were the army's Slavic troops that the need for a tolerant, understanding attitude on the part of the army's predominantly German officer corps was clearly a given. Army doctrine encouraged it, Franz Josef himself demanded it, and the vast majority of Habsburg officers practiced it.

Conrad himself was an avowed Social Darwinist—a worldview that significant numbers of officers seem, at least at first sight, to have shared.[40] But Conrad's brand of Social Darwinism thought in terms of strong and weak states rather than strong and weak races. He believed that the Habsburg Empire, were it to survive, must reinvigorate itself with a proactive, aggressive foreign policy against its principal foreign enemies. These enemies, in Conrad's view, were Italy—despite the fact that Italy and Austria-Hungary were officially in alliance—and of course Serbia. Such a policy, Conrad argued, would strengthen the monarchy not just against external enemies, but also against the corrosive effects of ethnic nationalism within the empire. He accordingly promoted it with tireless energy. The historian Holger Herwig writes:

> A glance at Conrad's outpourings during the seven years before 1914 provides insight into his fertile mind. In 1907 Conrad demanded war against "Austria's congenital foes" Italy and Serbia; the next year versus Russia, Serbia, and Italy. In 1909 he counselled military action against Serbia and Montenegro; in 1910 against Italy; and in 1911 versus Italy, Serbia, and Montenegro. The year 1912 saw concentration on the struggle against Russia and Serbia. The next year was especially productive, with military studies readied for conflicts with Albania, Montenegro, Russia, Serbia, and even Russian Poland. The final six months of peace in 1914 saw renewed plans versus Montenegro, Romania, Russia, and Serbia. Each of these years also brought contingency plans against numerous combinations of the above-named powers.[41]

Even though Conrad's Social Darwinism was national rather than biological in character, then, the resulting policy was profoundly bellicose. Such a policy could only be credible, of course, with an army capable of executing it. Conrad tried to get round the lack of resources the army's financial straitjacket imposed, by making the bulk of the army's combat manpower—the infantry—as tough and offensive-minded as possible. Extreme infantry training ensured that Conrad's Social Darwinism impacted directly upon the army's soldiers, as well as upon the foreign and military policy for they were intended to promote. The war games of Conrad's revamped infantry maneuvers awarded the greatest number of points to those units that advanced farthest and seized the greatest number of objectives. This ignored the fact that the revolutionary development of defensive firepower would, come actual war, render such rapid advances impossible. The maneuvers also took the cultivation of strength and the purging of weakness to drastic lengths; so enormous were the distances soldiers were now expected to march that some died from heat exhaustion.[42] The hardening psychological effect upon the officers who underwent and survived this ordeal was likely to make itself felt in future years.

But even the Social Darwinism of Conrad's harsh training regime and the transformation in military spirit it was designed to generate were not omnipotent within the Habsburg office corps. They came up against the entrenched "aristocratic conservatism" that still characterized army culture. Many senior officers, at least, shared the mutaphobic stance of the emperor and the inspector general of the army, and this hindered Conrad's "fresh, radical" approach.[43] The impact of Conrad's Social Darwinism may also have been limited because even many of the officers who were influenced by it may have viewed it not so much as a radical departure, than as a rebranded justification of imperial expansion and the old hierarchical system.[44]

Social Darwinism within the German officer corps enjoyed a much more lethal outlet—Germany's colonial wars against "inferior" peoples in Africa and Asia. The worst example was the Germans' particularly savage suppression of the Herero Rebellion in German Southwest Africa in 1904–1905.[45] The extent to which German soldiers' experience of colonial campaigns further brutalized the imperial German military mindset should not be overstated. The number of troops serving in these campaigns was self-selecting and very small;[46] among other things, it included none of the German-born officers featured in this study. But the army's conduct of colonial campaigns was not a fringe issue; it figured prominently, for example, in the 1907 elections for the German parliament. Defenders of the army's conduct depicted it as a national security issue, and so embedded was military culture in middle-class German circles that politicians from many points of the political spectrum supported the troops unreservedly.[47]

Such clamorous approval could only strengthen the German military's hard-line stance on colonial suppression. But such a stance had a strong base within the German military already. For the ferocity of German colonial warfare was not just a product of Social Darwinist racism. These were wars in which the Germans were fighting not conventional troops, but armed irregulars. The revulsion with which the Imperial German Army regarded such opponents surpassed that exhibited by any other regular army during the decades before 1914. Identifying how durably the army's abhorrence affected the German military mind-set is important to understanding what shaped its conduct of counterinsurgency during World War II. This is an ideal point at which to consider how such abhorrence came about.[48]

The waging of ruthless counterinsurgency colonial warfare, suffused by racist thinking, was far from unique to the German military during the late nineteenth and early twentieth centuries. Armies of all the major European colonial powers, and of the United States, waged successive counterinsurgency campaigns during the decades before 1914, usually against indigenous peoples resisting imperial rule. Such campaigns usually demanded the type of fighting, amid the kinds of conditions, for which conventional troops were not traditionally prepared. The conventional troops ordered to contend with all this were liable to lash out ruthlessly against civilians. This might be out of hatred and distrust, desire to somehow compensate for their own shortcomings, pressure from above for results, or brutalizing fear and frustration. The troops' brutality was also fueled—barring exceptions such as the British campaign against the white Boers in southern Africa between 1899 and 1902—by the racism of the period. Put simply, white soldiers who had imbibed racist attitudes found it easier to kill noncombatants of a darker skin color, and their commanders usually stood ready to encourage them.

Yet the early decades of the twentieth century brought signs that some armies, at least, were beginning to appreciate the benefits of hearts-and-minds measures to counterinsurgency. Behind this was a dawning realization that active support, or at least passive cooperation, could make mounting a successful counterinsurgency campaign considerably easier. It might even be crucial to that campaign's success. Measured treatment of insurgent deserters and prisoners, widespread use of propaganda, and, perhaps most importantly, social and economic measures of practical benefit to the population all rendered valuable service in this cause.[49]

But the German military—some saner heads aside—largely failed to properly appreciate this approach. The corrosive influence of its own particularly harsh counterinsurgency history proved too strong. In Clausewitz, the doyen of Prussian military thinkers, the German military had a particularly strong proponent of the view that encircling and destroying an insurgent adversary was far preferable to a drawn-out, costly "passive" security policy that focused entirely on guarding vital installations and supply routes in occupied territory.[50] But perhaps the development that hardened the German military's attitude most profoundly was its experience of francs-tireurs—irregular French fighters or, directly translated, "free-shooters"[51]—during the Franco-Prussian War of 1870–1871.

During this conflict—the culminating point of Prussia's unification with other German states—the armies of Prussia and its German allies developed a strong "franc-tireur psychosis." This was caused by frequent, often ruthless attacks by armed civilians upon German soldiers in occupied France. Most of the penalties the Germans exacted were less severe than they might have been—heavy fines and destruction of property, rather than mass shootings. But hostage-taking and hostage-shooting did take place, and rare as they were, they set a precedent.[52] For the Prussian military establishment heading the German forces detested with special vehemence any disruption of what it perceived to be the "proper" waging of war—the employment of mobile, technical, and tactical superiority, by coordinated and uniformed field armies in open combat, with the aim of vanquishing the enemy's forces in a swift

battle of annihilation. Of course, the Prussians' fondness for such warfare was founded on the belief that they themselves were the unrivaled
masters of it.[53]

But the particular aversion to irregular warfare which the German
military developed during the Franco-Prussian War and after was also
due to its own limitations. It relied upon the concentration of maximum
force, underpinned by superior tactics and technology, without properly
appreciating those other elements so often essential to concluding a war
successfully. For instance, though the Germans defeated the French field
armies in 1870, it was diplomacy that brought the Franco-Prussian War
to an end the following year. In downplaying the importance not just of
diplomacy, but also of factors such as logistical planning, intelligence,
coordination with civilian agencies, and—in the case of counterinsurgency—sufficient cooperation from the occupied population, the German military was narrow-minded to the point of myopia. Its excessive
reliance, instead, upon a battle of annihilation employing concentrated
maximum force therefore meant that it was actually less well equipped
for counterinsurgency than it might have been. The difficulties it then
encountered would in turn harden its conduct even further—this time
out of frustrated ambition and a desire to compensate for its failure.[54]

Finally, once the German military eventually managed, through
extreme exertion and force, to bring a counterinsurgency campaign
to a successful albeit brutal conclusion, such a "victory" could further entrench its view that "success comes only through terror."[55] It
did not help that German civilian-political agencies lacked the power
granted their counterparts in other countries to check the military's
more brutish inclinations.[56] Particularly during the Great War, moreover, the Germans would defend their actions ever more fiercely, citing
the paramountcy of "military necessity" in the face of the international
criticism and humanitarian lawmaking ranged against them.[57] The
Austro-Hungarians tended to support the German stance, albeit for
different reasons. The Habsburg military associated irregular warfare
with internal revolutionary warfare—something that appalled it to the
utmost after violent insurrection had almost brought about the empire's
downfall in 1848.[58]

By the eve of the Great War, then, the two officer corps were undergoing significant and in part disturbing changes. They were more socially diverse, but also more susceptible to pernicious ideology, and more preoccupied with mastering the technical dimensions of warfare than they had been forty years previously. A further incubator of ruthlessness for the German military was the combating of a particularly despised form of warfare in its colonial campaigns.

But there remained a serious limit to how far these forces were transforming officers' attitudes before 1914. Though unsettling traits were emerging within both officer corps, the sum effect as yet fell very far short of a prototype National Socialist worldview. Quite apart from anything else, both officer corps also subscribed to more benign values. For instance, though many officers' conservatism may not have opened them up to a more broad-minded worldview, the traditional Christian beliefs so often intrinsic to such conservatism might help counter, or at least temper, more radical influences. While the military schooling to which German officers were subjected imbibed an array of malignant tendencies, it also conveyed the importance of good character, self-awareness, and personal responsibility.[59] The multiethnic character of the Austro-Hungarian army, meanwhile, helped its officers retain an outlook characterized by open-minded moderation as well as by more reactionary traits. It would be wrong, therefore, to conclude that a combination of social and political myopia, narrow technical specialization, and emergent Social Darwinism with all it vicious offshoots was having a uniformly nefarious effect upon all officers.

Nevertheless, there are many signs that a base of disturbing tendencies was already forming, and on a widespread basis. It would take a new development, the Great War, to radically harden it.

CHAPTER 2

Forging a Wartime Mentality

The Impact of World War I

W HEN MOST OF EUROPE went to war in summer 1914, following a monthlong diplomatic crisis sparked by the assassination of Franz Ferdinand at the hands of a Bosnian Serb radical, the belief that it would be a quick, glorious affair was not universal. Certainly, many generals did not share it. They were cognizant of just how difficult the revolution in defensive firepower had rendered the business of attack. They were also cognizant of nations' capacity to mobilize, field, and equip conscript armies on a scale so great that it was now infinitely harder to vanquish them in one decisive campaign. Moltke was well aware of how protracted, intense, and perilous to the German Empire's future the war might well prove to be.[1] Similarly, of the approaching conflagration's possible impact upon the Habsburg Empire, Conrad wrote his mistress that "it will be a hopeless struggle, but nevertheless it must be, because such an ancient monarchy and such an ancient army cannot perish ingloriously."[2]

The Great War and its tumultuous aftermath would provide favorable conditions for ruthlessness to flourish and for moderation to wither. The effect should not be exaggerated; the brutalization German and Austro-Hungarian officers underwent did not go unchecked, whether by the more restrained side of their own mind-set or by the more level-headed decrees issued by the commands under which they served. And the progression from the brutalizing ordeal they underwent during these years to the mass violence they helped perpetrate during World War II was not yet inescapable. But the Great War and its aftermath certainly made that calamitous endpoint much more likely.

Germany's Schlieffen Plan, devised a decade before war broke out, envisioned committing the bulk of the German army to the front in the west, in a lightning sweep through Belgium and northern France. The Germans would advance on Paris, with the principal aim of encircling and destroying the French armies in that swift "battle of annihilation" of which the German General Staff deemed itself the unrivalled master. Meanwhile, a small force would be stationed in eastern Prussia to hold off the slower-to-mobilize Russians, until the German armies in the west could be sent eastward to settle accounts there. With German armies thus committed elsewhere, the Austro-Hungarian army was left to finish off Serbia and her diminutive neighboring ally, Montenegro.

Franz Ferdinand had been slain by a Bosnian Serb fanatic with the connivance of pan-Slavic elements in the Serbian army. Desire to avenge his murder, and to expunge Slavic nationalism from the Balkans, drove the Austrian urge for a final reckoning with Serbia. Lieutenant General von Appel, commander of X Austro-Hungarian Army Corps stationed in Sarajevo, proclaimed on August 10, 1914:

> We not only have to win here but also shatter and destroy the Serbo-Montenegrin army—this is the carrier of Russian ideas and propaganda. Above all we must thoroughly wean them of their megalomania and arrogance . . . I have forbidden my officers under pain of punishment with loss of honor to treat with Serbian officers on an equal footing . . . If they are captured . . . they are to be treated like common soldiers . . . for an officer corps that takes into its midst foreign deserters like comrades, tolerates regicide, conspires, and (includes) members of secret societies deserves no other treatment than captured soldiers.[3]

It was not just the Serbian army the Austrians faced, however, but also Serbian irregular fighters—men who, to Austrian eyes, were indistinguishable from the bandits who had inhabited the Balkans' wild, mountainous regions for centuries. The previous chapter pointed out that the Austro-Hungarians' aversion to irregular warfare was only slightly less intense than that of the Germans. And, though there were limits to how far they were prepared to go in suppressing such resistance, Austro-Hungarian troops were ready to employ ferocious brutality when they encountered it.

It was during their first invasion of Serbia, in August 1914, that the Austrians encountered the highest levels of irregular resistance. Some came from ethnic Serbian saboteurs (*Komitadjis*) within the empire's own borders. Some *Komitadjis*, to the Austrians' horror, were women—a forerunner of the armed women (*Flintenweiber*) whose irregular resistance during World War II would particularly revolt the German army's sensibilities. Then, once in Serbia, proliferating stories of the enemy's subterfuge and atrociousness, including reports that Austro-Hungarian soldiers were being mutilated before they were killed, increased the troops' fear and revulsion.[4] Austro-Hungarian countermeasures were fierce in the extreme. General von Appell ordered his officers to make their men aware of "our *moral and numerical superiority* to the point of fanaticism."[5] He also proclaimed that the war would be a "punishing hand" for the "fanatical" leaders of Serbia, and that it would serve as "atonement for the country."[6] In a matter of weeks, around thirty-five hundred Serbian civilians perished in Austro-Hungarian reprisals.[7] Many reprisals, usually in the form of mass public hangings, were directed against the "treasonous" border peoples within the empire itself.[8]

Brutal and excessive though it was, there was a context to this bloodletting. The Serbs themselves, and other Balkan peoples, had been guilty of considerably worse during the Balkan Wars of 1912–1913. Moreover, Serbian and Montenegrin troops attacking Sarajevo in August 1914 committed atrocities against Habsburg civilian subjects.[9] And the Austrians did not comport themselves as viciously as they might have done. Though they sometimes threatened to retaliate against Serbian barbarism by devastating the country and decimating its population, they always pulled back from the brink. This was partly out of practicality, partly because they did not wish to transform the Serbian people into an avenging horde, and partly because they wanted to retain the moral high ground in the eyes of domestic and international opinion. This, then, was never a war of racial extermination, even if ethnic contempt contributed to it. Rather, it was an old-school imperial-style campaign—albeit an extremely harsh one—to preserve order.[10]

Worse was the treatment the Imperial German Army dealt out in its march through Belgium and northern France during the war's opening weeks. Here, German troops overreacted massively to the slightest civilian resistance in the regions of Belgium and northern France through which they were advancing. Indeed, so edgy were the German troops that they even blamed cases of friendly fire on francs-tireurs, and exacted dreadful retaliation accordingly. Over six thousand French and Belgian civilians were shot, bayoneted, or burned indiscriminately. This butchery was synthesized with the mass destruction of buildings and property. The most infamous instance was the destruction of large parts of the Belgian university town of Louvain.[11]

That the Germans lashed out so frequently and ferociously during the war's opening weeks was due not just to their embedded hatred of irregular warfare. It was due also to the fact that the Schlieffen Plan was deeply flawed, indeed—it has been widely argued—beyond the German army's capabilities.[12] Any delay to its completion was bound to frustrate and alarm both generals and troops. And no delay was bound to incense them more than delay caused, supposedly or in fact, by civilian resistance.

The German General Staff did not try to clamp down on the troops' brutality; unsurprisingly, given their traditional view of irregular warfare, they encouraged it. They also believed it would help forge the obduracy of spirit they were seeking to instill in their troops in anticipation of an increasingly likely long war. And just as important to German counterinsurgency warfare's future development was the army's prickly, defensive reaction to worldwide criticism of the atrocities it had committed. Such criticism only hardened the army's already pronounced siege mentality on the issue and fortified its belief that its actions had been justified.[13]

The violence also contained a perhaps even more ominous element. For senior German commanders believed that the French and Belgian francs-tireurs possessed important attributes in common with some of the German Empire's "enemies within." They were Catholic, working class, and, like the population of Alsace-Lorraine—provinces France had been forced to cede to Germany in 1871—pro-French.[14] How far the troops themselves were similarly motivated, given that many were themselves working class or Catholic, is an entirely different question.[15] The point, however, is that the senior officer corps was already advocating a reprisal policy that fused "security" needs with ideological ones. Targeting such groups during the Great War therefore set a sinister precedent. As with them, so with Communists, Jews, and Sinti and Roma—albeit to a far more frightful extent—during World War II.

This does not mean that the German army's brutality in the face of irregular resistance during World War II was inevitably preprogrammed. German ferocity towards Belgian and French civilians in 1914 may have been part of an older tradition. But even with its ideological overtones, it was still only one precedent for the conduct of later wars. Less uniformly ferocious, as will be seen, were the Germans' counterinsurgency operations in the Ukraine in 1918.[16] But developments in later years would ensure that the Franco-Belgian precedent, with its own roots in the German military's long-standing aversion to irregular warfare, would influence the German military considerably during World War II.

It was not only Austrian and German troops who retaliated viciously against subversion real or imagined. Russian forces horribly maltreated civilians, particularly Jews, in those border regions of their empire they deemed of suspect loyalty. They also subjected the population of such regions to scorched earth actions and mass deportations.[17] But the irregular warfare of 1914 to 1918 would have a significant long-term effect upon the Austrian and German militaries. For it would harden the equation between combating insurgents and combating ideological enemies in both militaries' institutional mind-sets. The line that carried this equation through the interwar years into the Third Reich would not be continuous, or ineluctable.[18] But in German counterinsurgency campaigns during World War II, the equation between armed civilians and ideological enemies would be resurrected in many officers' minds and shape their methods accordingly.

By autumn 1914 the war was deadlocked, as the combination of defensive firepower and mass mobilization checked all attempts to achieve rapid, decisive victory. Following this came four years of stalemate and slaughter on all major European battlefronts. The experience marked men in fundamental ways for decades to come.

Of all the battlefronts on which men fought and died during the Great War, it is of course the western front in Belgium and northern France that figures most prominently in the Western imagination. Battles like Verdun, the Somme, and the succession of clashes at Ypres have become bywords for industrial-scale carnage. It was on the western front that the greatest number of men perished, in ways reflecting the new industrialized warfare at its most destructive. Then there were the miserable, sometimes fatal living conditions soldiers endured day to day.[19]

But different men responded to the horrors of the western front in different ways. Some, exemplified by Erich Maria Remarque, author of the best-selling 1929 antiwar novel *All Quiet on the Western Front*, went on to embrace pacifism. But men like Ernst Jünger—whose bellicose memoir of life as an assault troops officer, *Storm of Steel*, gained similar levels of recognition—recalled the experience with a visceral thrill. In one passage Jünger described how:

> the turmoil of our feelings was called forth by rage, alcohol and the thirst for blood . . . As we advanced heavily but irresistibly toward the enemy lines, I was boiling over with a fury which gripped me—it gripped us all—in an inexplicable way. The overpowering desire to kill gave me wings. Rage squeezed bitter tears from my eyes . . . Only the spell of primeval instinct remained.[20]

One extract does not do justice to the complexity of Jünger's many-faceted character over the course of his life. But it does encapsulate the way in which many young German officers imbibed the experience of the western front. In time, many men of a similar outlook to Jünger would become infused with the Social Darwinist belief that the western front was the ultimate test of men's ability to survive. And that, in surviving, they had demonstrated such strength, endurance, and resourcefulness that they constituted nothing less than a new, superior breed of man. Wedded to this belief was their considerable lust for violence.

Yet there was another counterpoint, more commonplace than Remarque's eloquent pacifism, to the fanaticism of Jünger and his ilk. Most German soldiers may not have been turned against war in all its forms by their experience of the western front, but there is ample evidence that many failed to embrace war anything like as enthusiastically as Jünger did.[21] They also often regarded the enemy not through the red mist of battle, but with a fraternal feeling for comrades-in-suffering. Fraternization with the enemy on static sectors of the front alarmed high commands in all armies. Never more so was this the case than when fraternization took the form of "live and let live" arrangements, such as reciprocal warning of impending artillery bombardments.[22] In November 1915, for instance, I Bavarian Army Corps reported that "there have lately been further cases of forbidden dealings with the enemy. The guilty will be punished severely."[23]

It should also be recognized that life on the western front was not one of unremitting horror in any case. Had it been, it is doubtful that many soldiers could have withstood it. Considerable time was spent out of the trenches, be it for rest and refitting or for rear area duties such as road-clearing and requisitioning. None of this detracts from the hellish ordeal which soldiers serving in the trenches endured. But it does demonstrate that the western front was a many-sided experience.[24] All told, then, it would be too simple to assume that German army officers fighting in World War II were irrevocably, brutalizingly scarred by what they had experienced on the western front during the Great War.[25]

The experience of other fronts, and its brutalizing effect upon the men involved, have received considerably less attention from Western historians. Just as on the western front, that effect was not always as uniformly, durably malign as one might expect. Yet malign to a great extent it certainly was, and the immediate and longer-term impact upon officers could be profound indeed.

In the Balkans, all three Austro-Hungarian attempts to vanquish Serbia in 1914—in August, September, and December—were humiliatingly routed by the Serbian army. The spectacle was conveyed by the journalist Egon Erwin Kisch: "the flight had begun and swept us further on. A

routed army—no, an unrestrained horde ran in senseless fright back to
the border. Coach drivers whipped their horses, cannon drivers spurred
and hit theirs, officers and men pushed forward and slithered between
the wagon columns or trudged in road ditches."[26] The scapegoat for all
this was the army's "disloyal" Czech troops. The immediate culprits,
however, were primarily General Conrad, whose plan to split his already
deficient forces against Russia and Serbia was thoroughly unrealistic, and
theater commander General Potiorek, whose cack-handed performance
as commander of the Austro-Hungarian invasion guaranteed ignomini-
ous failure even more surely. More fundamentally, these disasters were
the legacy of decades of atrophy brought about by chronic underfund-
ing and stultifying institutional conservatism.[27] In turn, the campaigns
heaped further humiliation upon the Habsburg Empire.

Only with substantial help from Germany, together with new ally
Bulgaria, did the Austrians finally crush Serbia in autumn 1915, before
carving up its territory with the Bulgarians. And even then, the escape of
the Serbian army through the mountains to the coast, taking with it tens
of thousands of Austro-Hungarian prisoners on a winter death march,
could only stoke Austrian hatred further. The conditions of the march,
culminating in an Allied naval evacuation to Italy, are described in a
letter from a captured Austro-Hungarian medical officer caught up in it:

> (October 1915) . . . And so we marched two days to Prizrend [*sic*:
> probably Prizren in Kosovo]. Here the conditions deteriorated; we
> were assigned to the combat officer prisoners. Each of the officers
> had to carry his own baggage, and we received something to eat plus
> bread only once a day, and that only in principle, and it got worse.
> From Prizren to Dobra we marched across Albania; the weather was
> terrible: wind and rain, we were soaked every day, and were unable
> to sleep for cold. Sometimes we stayed around the fire to sleep in a
> sitting position. Many officers' boots wore out, and they had to con-
> tinue walking barefoot. At Dobra there was nothing to buy but dried
> chestnuts, which was all we had to eat one day.[28]

At Valona, their destination on the coast, they finally received enough
to eat. Even so, "you can imagine that if our officers suffered like this,

how badly the poor soldier prisoners fared. The route was strewn with
the bodies of prisoners who died of cold and hunger ... We have nothing
left, everything is ruined."[29]

The flight, largely intact, of the Serbian army into Allied territory
soon created a focal point for deserters from the southern Slavic units
of the Austro-Hungarian army. Indeed, desertion would in time become
endemic among troops from all the Austro-Hungarian Empire's subject
peoples, as the empire found itself mired in an increasingly unwinna-
ble struggle that devastated its economy and stoked its subject peoples'
desire for peace and independence. This desire, and the epidemic desertion it increasingly spawned, would be exploited by Allied propaganda
to great effect.[30] In September 1918, finally, the Serbian army would be
instrumental in breaking the Macedonian Front—the key military event
that heralded the Austro-Hungarian Empire's complete collapse.[31]

All this—the assassination of Franz Ferdinand, the atrocities of Serbian irregulars, the military humiliations of 1914, the death march of
1915, the corrosive effect the Serbian army's survival continued to have
upon morale within the Austro-Hungarian army, and the Serbian army's
direct role in the empire's disintegration in autumn 1918—made it possible for Wehrmacht commanders to stir Austrian hatred and resentment
of the Serbs during World War II.[32]

Yet here too, it would be wrong to imagine that there was an enduring
thread of continuity between the incubation of hatred in one war and
its murderous channeling in the next. Serbia suffered terrible privations
throughout the war, with a worse loss of life per head of population than
any other combatant nation. As well as the 275,000 men lost in battle,
eight hundred thousand civilians perished from diseases born of wartime privations. [33] And the occupation regime the Austrians imposed
had a fearful impact upon the Serbian population. Much of the country's economic resources were ransacked, its menfolk were deported for
labor in the empire, and its intelligentsia were imprisoned.[34] Nevertheless, Habsburg occupation in Serbia was less piratical and oppressive
than it might have been. For the Austrians did not seek systematically
to ethnically cleanse the Serbian people. Their aims were akin instead
to those of nineteenth-century imperialism, seeking to subject Serbia to
absolutism and decisively weaken the foundations of nationalism within

the country.[35] In 1917, they suppressed a Serbian uprising with considerably less indiscriminate severity than they might have done.[36] Overall, Austria-Hungary's occupation of Serbia was less vicious than Bulgaria's.[37] More needed to happen during the decades that followed, then, to ensure that it was the hateful precedent of 1914–1915, not the somewhat less hateful one of 1916–1918, that would hold greatest sway over Austrian-born officers' behavior in Yugoslavia during World War II.

Another theater in which the Austro-Hungarian army saw action—one that, like the western front, was marked by arduous conditions, and by grueling stalemate interspersed with ruinously costly offensives by both sides—was the Italian front.[38] This theater came into being after Italy entered the war on the Allied side in May 1915. Much of the fighting took place amid terrain that was unforgiving in the extreme, such as the towering Dolomites or the harsh, otherworldly terrain of the Carso plateau.[39] Actual fighting, when it came, was as pitiless as anything on the western front. Captain Abel, an officer of the Austro-Hungarian army, wrote:

> The incoming shells are visible to the naked eye; they look like black sausages. If their effect were not so terrible, the sight of Carso veterans leaping this way and that to avoid the shells would be ridiculous. Not realizing that they must dodge the shells, many of the newcomers are blown up. As soon as the bombardment ends, the Italians rush out of their advance positions—usually very close to our front line—and jump into our trenches.[40]

Disease was a further cross to bear, particularly later in the war as mounting food shortages sapped the troops' physical and psychological strength.[41] In spring 1917 the Austro-Hungarian 43d Rifle Division, among whose officers was a future regimental commander in Yugoslavia, Adalbert Lontschar, was assailed with malaria. Matters were not helped by the almost simultaneous conviction of one of the division's staff doctors, Doctor Popper, for theft.[42] At the beginning of August 1918 the Austro-Hungarian 87th Infantry Regiment—home to a future divisional commander in Yugoslavia, Karl Eglseer—was assailed likewise.[43]

The bitterness of the "White War," as the historian Mark Thompson aptly titles it,[44] also possessed a darker impulse, national and cultural in character. Many Austrian officers shared General Conrad's excoriating assessment of the Italians as the "congenital enemy." This animus had originated in the Wars of Italian Unification during the nineteenth century. It resurged when first Italy refused to enter the Great War on the side of Germany and Austria-Hungary, its partners in the so-called Triple Alliance, in summer 1914, and then entered the war on the opposite side the following spring.[45] It first manifested itself during the Great War when Austro-Hungarian combat aircraft bombarded Venice, then as now one of Italy's most important historical and cultural centers. The historian Alan Kramer likens such actions to the warfare of cultural destruction the Germans perpetrated when they torched the university library in Louvain.[46] Italian civilians, such as those who found themselves under fire from Austro-Hungarian and German artillery at the Battle of Caporetto in 1917, also felt the impact of the Austrians' bitter resolve.[47]

Italian POWs suffered also. Admittedly, this was largely due to general wartime privations, brought about by British naval blockade and by the Central powers' often inept "system" of rationing.[48] But not entirely. For instance, while captive Italian officers need not have expected conditions as wretched as their men's, they were still the subject of their captors' detestation. Thus, for instance, decreed the rear area command of the Austro-Hungarian Fourth Army in August 1915:

> This state [Italy] benefited greatly from our alliance; as an alliance partner, she treacherously stabbed us in the back . . . It is forbidden therefore to engage [captured Italian officers] in normal social interaction such as the shaking of hands or general conversation. By this treatment, captured Italian officers must be made to realize that we despise a state that has behaved itself like Italy has, and that we therefore cannot treat its officers as social equals.[49]

By fostering such odium towards prisoners, on top of the odium Austrians already directed against Italians for their country's sneak declaration of war, orders such as these helped to dehumanize the enemy. It would be going much too far to argue that this was a direct harbinger of the ideologically driven pitilessness officers would display during World War II. Such orders tended to look backward—to more traditional notions of honorable and dishonorable conduct—rather than forward. But at the same time, dehumanizing the enemy in this way still constituted a step down that future path, albeit a relatively small one. It is a further sign that the Italian front, like other Great War battlefronts, engendered some of the radicalization that would motivate many officers later.

Finally, from 1914 through to early 1918, along an immense front from the Baltic to the Black Sea, the German and Austro-Hungarian armies faced the armies of Russia. This front was not characterized by bloody, immobile stalemate in the way of the western or Italian fronts. Here, amid mountains, forests, swamps, and seemingly endless plains, the stalemate was often bloody *and* mobile, with immense advances matched by equally immense retreats. The cumulative strain of war steadily sapped the strength of Russia and, eventually, Austria-Hungary to a terminal degree. Only in early 1918 did the new Bolshevik government in Russia sue for peace, bringing to an end more than three years of ferocious struggle across seemingly limitless terrain, amid sometimes unimaginably harsh environmental conditions.[50] And even after that, soldiers of the Central powers found themselves locked in bitter struggle with Bolshevik forces in many parts of the East.

The war in the East was not characterized by modern, industrially charged carnage of the kind seen on the western front. Instead, it was characterized by savagery and chaos such that the historian Michael Geyer has justifiably described it as "the Wild War."[51] More than any other theater of the Great War, moreover, it was in the East that German and Austrian troops could be brutalized not just by the fighting conditions they endured, but also by their experience of the landscape, of its native population, and of the political forces that convulsed the region as the war continued. In other words, while the East was not necessarily *the* most brutalizing environment in which German and Austrian soldiers served during the Great War, it could certainly brutalize them in particularly diverse ways. For this reason, together with the fact that several officers featured in this study served on the eastern front, the characteristics of this theater of war warrant some space here.

In 1914 many Austro-Hungarian officers contemplated the coming struggle with the Russian army—nicknamed the "Steamroller" by virtue of its alleged ability to overwhelm its opponents with its irresistible size—in a cold sweat. Colonel Brosch of the 1st Tyrolean Kaiserjäger Regiment believed he would witness the final destiny of the Habsburg Empire "not as an uncommitted bystander, but as a resigned combatant who will see the black steamroller, which will obliterate us, approach, but who cannot stop it."[52] But Conrad, ever the aggressor in matters strategic, immediately went over to the attack. And as in Serbia, the Austro-Hungarian army's shortcomings brought disastrous failure and colossal death tolls each time. The Germans, to the detriment of their own plans, were repeatedly forced to divert troops southward to bale the Austrians out. The Austro-Hungarian army had soon decimated and debilitated itself to a point where it resembled a territorial and militia army.[53]

The desperate fighting, the harsh conditions, and the Austrians' increasingly apparent military impotence are all conveyed in the war diary of Karl Eglseer's 87th Infantry Regiment:

> 11/22/14 . . . The Russians penetrated behind the second and third companies, and a violent battle ensued . . . Of the third battalion, only a small fraction was able to break through. A large part was captured by the enemy. At the same time the second battalion, positioned at Werretyczos, was outflanked on the right and driven back after resisting heavily. The regiment fought valiantly, but its weakened position, the excessive distance of the . . . battle groups and the lack of reserves all made a successful defense impossible. The Russians' tactic was, clearly, to penetrate in overwhelming strength through dense terrain into the empty gaps between our (positions) . . . Major Leimser, the third battalion's commander, was captured together with between 12–14 other officers of the regiment . . . Due to the great cold, the heavy snow, and having to spend four nights out in the open, the regiment's fighting capability and supplies were completely exhausted.

> 11/28 . . . Losses from 11/20–11/28/: 2 officers and 10 men dead, 3 officers and 100 men wounded (almost all on 11/20 and 11/22/). 7

officers and 129 men taken prisoner. 11 officers and 655 men missing altogether (including those taken prisoner).

12/21 . . . At 3pm the enemy attacked the right flank of the 47th Infantry Regiment. At the same time, the 87th was comprehensively attacked in overwhelming strength. It was therefore forced at 3pm to withdraw to and re-establish defenses in the previously occupied area of Lazy. Major Seidel's attack was unable to make any impact. There was no support from our own artillery to be detected.

12/24 . . . 5.10pm the order came for heightened vigilance and battle readiness, for the Russians were aiming to surprise us . . . The Russians broke through the second battalion; the first battalion was also compelled to abandon its position. The regiment assembled in the town square at Zmigrod. The panic and fear of the Italian troops[54] . . . weakened discipline so much that the officers were only able to restore it by firing their revolvers into the air. The regiment, particularly the second battalion, had suffered painful losses again. It was later established that its companies had fought stubbornly. Lieutenant Eglseer and Captain von Wanka were caught up in the struggle, wounded badly, and captured. This overwhelming blow seems to have been spearheaded by the enemy's cavalry.[55]

As this diary indicates, the environment was especially pitiless during winter. It was never more so than it was for the Austro-Hungarian troops whom General Conrad committed to a horribly misconceived offensive in the Carpathian Mountains during winter 1914–1915.[56] But the environment could be unforgiving at any time of year, as Private Wilhelm Schulin, serving with the German 26th Infantry Division north of Brest-Litovsk, recounted in summer 1915:

Exertions, privations, very heavy knapsack, neck and shoulder pain from the rifle and long, difficult marches; extremely tired feet and body. Bad roads—either uneven asphalt or deep sand—and always the uneven fields, marching up and down deep furrows. Often in double time, and usually no water or at best stinking water, no bread for days on end.[57]

Despite all this, some German and Austro-Hungarian observers favorably contrasted the eastern front with the industrial slaughter and smaller scale of the western front. They romanticized the notion of a military campaign waged across wild, unspoiled expanses, making greater use of "classic" elements of warfare such as cavalry.[58] But there is little doubt that the region's social and economic backwardness, and its mind-numbing size, often made a profoundly negative impression upon German and Austrian troops.

This impression grew stronger the further the two armies advanced into the territory of the Russian Empire. Crossing into the East, a German military official noted, "I have never seen a border like this, which divided not just two states, but two worlds. As far as the eye could see, nothing but a scene of poverty and *Unkultur*, impossible roads, poor villages and neglected huts and a dirty, ragged population with primitive field agriculture, a total opposite of the blooming German landscape in neighboring Upper Silesia."[59]

The East's scarcely conceivable distances and rudimentary road network also made it considerably harder to supply the troops.[60] The men of the Austro-Hungarian 57th Infantry Division, in an army whose supply capabilities were found severely wanting in any case,[61] were complaining about supply as early as August 4, 1914.[62] Under these conditions, disease was an ever present danger. Among the German army, there were 2.8 sick cases for every one wounded man in the West as against 3.7 sick cases for each wounded man in the East.[63] Indeed, lack of hygiene and the consequent fear of contamination were recurrent themes in accounts of life on the eastern front by all levels of German and Austrian personnel.[64] The III Austro-Hungarian Army Corps was alarmed at the possibility of a cholera outbreak among its men as early as October 1914.[65] In January 1915 Adalbert Lontschar's 43d Austro-Hungarian Rifle Division urged its troops to drink boiled water so as to avoid not just cholera, but typhus and dysentery also.[66] Austro-Hungarian XVII Army Corps, which among its formations counted the 11th Field Artillery Brigade—with which Walter Hinghofer, a future divisional commander in Yugoslavia, was serving as a staff officer—was blighted by something approaching the Seven Plagues. Among other things, it faced a cholera alarm in August 1915,[67] put an entire settlement off-limits when it was hit by typhus in February 1916,[68] and was harried by a visitation of flies in April 1917.[69]

German soldiers in particular often extended their disdain at the region's backwardness to its Slavic population also.[70] At the Great War's start, the German government had some trouble stoking up anti-Russian sentiment among the troops; it had after all been a quarrel involving Russia and Austria-Hungary, not Germany, that had precipitated the entire conflagration in the first place. But Russia's brief, unsuccessful invasion of eastern Prussia in August 1914 presented German propagandists with a great opportunity.[71]

The Russians did not comport themselves like a barbarian horde during this short-lived onslaught. They did, however, plunder and destroy property, and sometimes kill civilians.[72] This was nothing the Germans themselves were not doing in the West, and on a larger and more systematic scale. And there are balanced contemporary German accounts of the invasion acknowledging that many Russian troops behaved correctly during its course.[73] But for many German soldiers already weaned on a measure of anti-Slavism, such brutality as the Russians did deal out in eastern Prussia, together with German propaganda's exploitation of it, seemed to confirm age-old prejudices about the barbaric East. Thus, for instance, did Gottard Heinrici, who would go on to serve as a senior field commander during World War II, accuse the Russians of perpetrating acts of "blind destruction and mindless annihilation of a kind we never would have thought possible."[74]

Perceptions of the "Wild East" became further embedded for German and Austrian troops as the war continued. On November 27, 1914, troops of the Austro-Hungarian III Army Corps, to which Karl Eglseer's 87th Infantry Regiment was subordinate, stumbled upon the bodies of mutilated Austro-Hungarian soldiers in a recently reoccupied village. The Russian troops they had been facing had been Kalmuks from Siberia.[75] In January 1915 the 43d Rifle Division uncovered cases of captured or wounded Austro-Hungarian soldiers being "mutilated and murdered in a bestial manner by Russian soldiers." This time the perpetrators comprised Circassian and Siberian irregulars in part, but also regular Russian troops. It was also alleged, on the basis of statements by Russian prisoners of war, that Habsburg officers in Russian captivity had been brutally mistreated.[76]

Incidents like these, and the sentiments they engendered or strengthened, were hardly going to improve relations between advancing German and Austro-Hungarian troops and the eastern Slavic peoples they were encountering. Nor was the fact that the troops detected "dangerous" levels of Russophile sympathy amongst those peoples. Indeed, they detected it among peoples living within those easternmost reaches of the Habsburg Empire through which they marched, as well as those living within enemy territory.[77]

Nevertheless, higher-level Habsburg formations did seek to avoid antagonizing the population without reason. They strove instead to ensure that their troops regard the population with a discriminating eye. Such, for instance, were commands issued by Lieutenant General Szurmay's corps, to which Adalbert Lontschar's 24th Infantry Regiment was subordinate, in June 1915. Szurmay's orders to tighten security included making village headmen responsible for order with their lives, but they did not include taking hostages. This, Szurmay believed, would be "pointless, and potentially harmful to the innocent."[78] Szurmay intervened against excessive harshness in a further directive around the same time: "Not cruelty, but fair and considerate strictness in the handling of penal and preventative measures, guarantees success without embittering a population well-disposed towards the Crown."[79]

Yet Szurmay's moderation had its limits. For he was concerned here to restrain brutality against the empire's own eastern Slavic subjects; he imposed fewer such restraints once his troops were in enemy territory proper. Here, fear of spies and saboteurs, and of the civilians who might be aiding and abetting them, increased markedly. In February 1916, Austro-Hungarian XVII Corps reported sightings of explosives-armed Russians seeking to destroy railway lines. These Russians, it alleged, had come from a school in Kiev that had been training men and women in explosives techniques before sending them into Austrian-occupied territory.[80] That same month, on the strength of a warning in Polish pinned to a telegraph pole, XVII Corps reported with alarm the presence of twenty-five Cossacks, mostly dressed in Austro-Hungarian uniforms. These, it announced, had been roaming the villages, collecting bread, hay, and oats, together with information on Austrian troop dispositions, from the population.[81] Of course, civilian subterfuge was something with which troops on other fronts had to contend also. But on the eastern front, it could exacerbate racial prejudice that was already there.

Yet these cases remind one that, harsh though the Austro-Hungarian army's conduct could be, it was not waging a racial war in the East any more than in the Balkans. The same could be said, broadly, of the German army. Indeed, many ordinary soldiers left more positive accounts of the peoples they encountered on the eastern front. They often, for instance, eulogized the colorful appearance, pretty girls, and idyllic peasant lifestyle of rural Poland and the Ukraine.[82] But the harshness both armies nonetheless practiced was doubtless nourished further by embedded prejudice towards the Slavs, just as it was by the arduous conditions soldiers in the East had to endure.

The Great War was also a war that, more than any other before, impacted directly upon civilians as well as combatants. Nowhere was this clearer than in the realms of economic procurement and production. On the side of the Central powers, so severe did the resource shortfall against the Allies become that labor, foodstuffs, and other economic materials from occupied Europe became increasingly crucial. Indeed, advancing German and Austro-Hungarian troops were expected to live off the land from the war's first weeks. In the West, for example, II Bavarian Army Corps ordered its troops at the end of September 1914 to "obtain supplies in enemy territory with all means."[83] In February 1915 I Bavarian Army Corps reminded its men that "mildness towards the inhabitants is harshness against our Fatherland."[84] Belgium and northern France would suffer dreadfully from German depredations, particularly when large tracts of their territory were laid to waste by withdrawing or retreating German troops during 1917 and 1918.[85]

In the occupied East, meanwhile, the Germans not only exploited labor and food, but also waged an ideological campaign to "civilize" these "backward" regions to German standards. This was not a blueprint for later Nazi schemes; it was, after all, accompanied by degrees of restraint and cultivation the Nazis never practiced.[86] Even so, the

German occupiers still viewed the region as racially and culturally inferior. Civilians were subjected to profoundly demeaning treatment. More fundamentally, the region fell prey to a campaign of economic exploitation in some ways even more ruthless than the one in the West.[87]

All this was intrinsic to a new kind of warfare that instrumentalized civilians like never before. It also included the terroristic killing of civilians that had taken place in the war's opening weeks. "Necessary" harshness towards civilians was another facet of the Great War that impressed itself upon many officers.[88]

But while systematized exploitation was desired, wild exploitation—the kind that threatened the troops' discipline and longer-term interests—emphatically was not. In time, the subject of military discipline within both the German and Austro-Hungarian armies during the Great War would become of great interest to the German army under the Third Reich. For the army would come to believe that it was the steady erosion of that discipline that had sapped the troops' fighting power and made them more susceptible to the "pernicious" ideology of Bolshevism.

Discipline problems became apparent at the very outset of the campaigns in both East and West. In late August 1914 II Bavarian Army Corps, embroiled in fighting on the Franco-German border, reported that "(despite) the instructions issued in the Corps command of 8/22/14, there are still cases of the rough seizure of inhabitants' private property. The men are to be repeatedly instructed that every unauthorized seizure . . . is to be regarded as *plunder* and, in accordance with judicial military regulations, punished with imprisonment of at least 43 days."[89] In the East, Austro-Hungarian III Corps reported in September of the same year that "lone soldiers, excluded from all regular supply and mostly without or with only very little in the way of cash, have begun to maraud, indeed plunder, and therefore constitute an acute danger to discipline."[90]

By 1916, indiscipline was affecting the troops' general morale, fighting spirit, and respect for superiors. This was a portent of the increasingly widespread erosion of discipline that would afflict the Central powers' armies during the war's final year. By August 1916 I Bavarian Army Corps was describing how "on numerous trips within the corps area, deficient posture, dishevelled dress and poor acknowledgement of superiors became increasingly apparent in the troops marching along the roads."[91] Matters were worse just months later, when in December II Bavarian Army Corps reported mounting cases of self-mutilation.[92] "The robustness of the officers and men has left much to be desired in recent times," the commander of the 11th Austro-Hungarian Field Artillery Brigade, with which Walter Hinghofer was serving, declared in December 1917. "I make all regimental commanders personally responsible for raising military spirit in all our batteries."[93] Indiscipline also made itself felt in other forms; on the Italian front in May 1918, the 14th Austro-Hungarian Infantry Regiment gave vent to its desperation at the rising incidence of venereal disease. "The men are to be strenuously reminded," the regiment directed, "that contracting such diseases is punishable, for it is due to this that men have to withdraw from war service for a long period."[94]

One reason why discipline was deteriorating was increasing lack of supply. This was the inevitable result of the Central powers' material disadvantage at the war's start, the privations caused by the British naval blockade, the ineptitude of German and Austro-Hungarian rationing, and the two powers' inability to exploit their occupied territories more effectively.[95] In October 1918 the 11th Austro-Hungarian Infantry Division, stationed on the Italian front, issued a directive that is worth citing at length for the particularly wretched picture it conveys:

> The men's clothing is in many cases in a desolate state; some are wandering around in tatters. Though divisional command itself recognizes the current difficulties, and that quantity and quality of the available varieties leave a lot to be desired, this cannot be entirely to blame for the often shameful and sleep-inhibiting state of the men's clothing and equipment . . . The division is convinced that many men are selling or squandering items of clothing . . . It is likely that uniforms are being worn out because a large portion of the troops are sleeping fully-clothed at night . . . The men do not undress because they will freeze during the night, but because they have no blanket they freeze anyway. But every man is supposed to have a blanket; whoever does not must have either squandered or sold it, or had it stolen by another soldier to sell on.[96]

Against this backdrop, a further peril to the discipline of both armies emerged—the peril of Bolshevism. Even before the Bolsheviks seized power in Russia in November 1917, the belief that radical revolutionary action from below could bring the conflict to an end was winning increasing currency across war-weary Europe. Indeed in July the German Reichstag, inspired by the Petrograd Soviet's call for peace "without annexations or indemnities," made a similar call itself.[97] Anxious, and not without reason, that Bolshevik-inspired appeals for peace might further sap the resolve of soldiers and civilians alike, the high commands of both the German and Austro-Hungarian armies rapidly came to regard Bolshevism as a bacillus infecting the war effort.[98]

After March 1918 the specter of Bolshevism loomed even larger. That month, in order to end the war and concentrate on defending its precarious hold on power, the new Bolshevik government in Russia finally signed a peace deal with the Central powers at Brest-Litovsk. Hundreds of thousands of German troops, hitherto serving in the East, were now transferred to the western front. Many had fallen under the influence of left-wing ideas, if not always undilutedly Bolshevik ones, following extensive fraternization with Russian troops.[99] Similar numbers of Habsburg POWs returned from Russian prison camps and were reintegrated into the Austro-Hungarian army. The army leadership, already facing acute morale problems amongst soldiers from the empire's subject peoples, believed that many returning POWs had become infected with Bolshevik sentiment. Ironically, even where they were not infected—as was probably the case with the majority—the intrusive "screening process" to which they were subjected served to further embitter many of them against army, regime, and war in any case.[100]

During the months following the Russian Revolution, the Russian Bolsheviks sought, with extreme ruthlessness, to suppress all internal opposition real or imagined. Due to this, and to the savage civil war it waged with anti-Bolshevik forces across Russia, Bolshevism came to be widely seen as a harbinger of violence, chaos, and social and political collapse. It also came to be associated with the Slavic East, wherefrom revolution had first emerged.

The most immediate brutalizing effect upon German and Austrian soldiers was seen among the troops assigned to the occupied East. In the Ukraine, for instance, the Central powers propped up a succession of non-Bolshevik governments throughout 1918, while seeking to exploit the region for its grain and economic resources. Bolsheviks and other radical groups sought to destabilize both the native government and the foreign occupation regime, and desperate bands marauded the countryside for food. Both occupying powers responded with the severest repression. The Bavarian Cavalry Division, for instance, took no prisoners in its fighting against the Bolsheviks. In Taganrog in June 1918 the 52d Württemberg Brigade killed twenty-five hundred prisoners, including not just Bolsheviks, but also civilians, women and children included, from the surrounding area.[101] That said, the Central powers' response to the insurgency was not one of unbridled and unprovoked brutality. German forces in particular, their Austrian comrades more belatedly, increasingly sought to differentiate between insurgents in particular and the population generally. Nor should it be forgotten that the Bolsheviks' own methods could be immensely brutal, even though they did not morally justify the retaliatory killing of women and children.[102]

Bolshevism also came to be associated, due to the ethnic background of many leading Bolsheviks, with Jews.[103] Major Bothmer, a German officer stationed in Russia in 1918, vilified the Jews as the source of all Bolshevik infection there. His diary ghoulishly detailed how he would "just love to see a few hundred of these Jew-boys strung up from the walls of the Kremlin, dying as slowly as possible so as to enhance the effect."[104]

But the Great War was nourishing anti-Semitism well before the Revolution. One reason for this was the troops' encounters with eastern Jews. This was a people whose alien appearance and customs could affront even an assimilated German Jew such as Victor Klemperer. Klemperer described how a visit to a Talmud school in 1918 had "repelled me as if with fists," for the "swirl of people" in these rooms at prayer or recitation of holy texts represented for Klemperer "repellent fanaticism . . . No, I did not belong to these people, even if one proved my blood relation to them a hundred times over . . . I belonged to Europe, to Germany, and I thanked my creator that I was a German."[105] Such views were far from universal; other commentators, such as the Bavarian writer Ludwig Ganghofer, regarded the eastern Jews much more positively. "In amongst the farmers you see groups of Jews in their long black dress," he wrote. "If you need to ask the way or enquire as to some other matter, you are best off approaching one of these lock wearers; they are pleasant and friendly, answer knowledgably, (and) almost always speak good German."[106] It is nevertheless clear that there was widespread contempt towards eastern Jews within the German army.[107]

In Germany itself, anti-Semitism within the popular press reared its head following the first setbacks at the front. Newspapers depicted Jews as cowards, shirkers, and profiteers, and many on the political right hoped to exploit such prejudices for political gain.[108] Lieutenant Colonel Max Bauer, a fanatically anti-Semitic officer, wrote:

> There is a huge sense of outrage at the Jews, and rightly so. If you are in Berlin and go to the Ministry of Commerce or walk down the Tauentzienstraße, you could well believe you were in Jerusalem. Up at the front, by contrast, you hardly ever see any Jews. Virtually every thinking person is outraged that so few are called up, but nothing is done, because going after the Jews, meaning the capital that controls the press and the parliament, is impossible.[109]

In 1916, delusions over the extent of Jewish "shirking" led the German army to implement a demeaning "head count" of its Jewish soldiers. This operation eventually concluded that Jews were after all fulfilling their national duty every bit as much as Gentiles. But not before it had devastated the morale of many loyal, patriotic Jewish soldiers.[110]

The war strengthened anti-Semitism in Austria-Hungary also. Here too, the anti-Semitic press fanned long-standing resentments towards Jews, likewise depicting them as shirkers and black marketeers. One of the "foundations" for these rumors, as in Germany, was the underrepresentation of Jews among the army's rank and file. The simple explanation for this, which the rabble-rousers chose to ignore, was that most rank-and-file soldiers were peasants and most peasants were not Jewish.[111] In Vienna, anti-Semitic contempt was exacerbated by an influx of Galician Jewish refugees fleeing persecution from the Tsar. Their appearance was very different to that of the empire's assimilated Jewish population, and their arrival put immense strain on the capital's already acute housing shortage. There was similar resentment towards eastern Jews arriving in Berlin between 1917 and 1920.[112]

But there was still no simple straight line between this anti-Semitism, however abhorrent, and the deadly anti-Semitism that influenced the conduct of German army units in the service of the Nazis a quarter-century later. Apart from the German army's shameful anti-Semitic head count of 1916, the belligerent anti-Semitism that increasingly contaminated German society during the Great War did not inform German military policy.[113] Jewish soldiers serving in the still relatively enlightened Austro-Hungarian army, meanwhile, were not compelled to suffer any kind of head count; Conrad, his own anti-Semitism notwithstanding, opined that "it does not seem appropriate to draw up statistics on the basis of religious distribution."[114]

In any case, the core reason why the Central powers were losing the war by 1918 was neither the Bolsheviks nor the Jews, but their own military and economic weakness. The weakness had been exacerbated by the increasingly megalomaniac way in which the military dictatorship running the German government since August 1916 was conducting the war.[115] By 1918, against an Allied coalition vastly strengthened by the entry of the United States into the war, the Central powers' deficiencies were mercilessly apparent. The extent of their material privations became especially clear to soldiers participating in Germany's desperate final offensives on the western front in the spring and early summer of that year, when advancing German soldiers stumbled upon veritable treasure troves of supply in captured Allied trenches.[116]

By September the German army was firmly on the defensive, fighting a doomed struggle against an Allied coalition now enjoying the prospect of millions of fresh American troops. There is much to be said for the view that, following the failure of its final offensives, the German army became stricken with levels of disobedience that amounted to a "covert military strike."[117] But in reality, considerable though indiscipline was, its effect was not terminal. For the army's resistance stiffened, albeit ultimately in vain, as the fighting approached German soil.[118] In October

1918 Major General von Endres, commander of I Bavarian Army Corps, sought to rally his troops for the final effort:

> (The enemy's) purpose is clear; he wants to bring the war with all its terror into our beloved Fatherland and bring us to our knees . . . But he will not succeed . . . No Frenchman, Englishman, American or Italian will cross our border. If every man does his duty to the utmost, we will succeed in halting their onslaught and achieve an honorable peace. The Fatherland is in danger; you can save it![119]

Vain though such rallying calls would ultimately prove, the great majority of German soldiers responded to them as the borders of their Fatherland were threatened during the weeks before the Armistice. That they did so would be taken as further proof in interwar military circles that the Imperial German Army had not been vanquished in the field at the end of the Great War. Instead, many would claim, the army had been "stabbed in the back" by defeatist elements at home. This take on events was at odds with the reality of autumn 1918. For the army, if not yet actually defeated militarily, could no longer avoid that inevitable fate—regardless of any temporary stiffening in its resistance or of what happened at home. But the "stab-in-the-back" myth would endure in post-1918 Germany nonetheless.

Meanwhile, following peace with Russia, the only remaining battle-front on which Austro-Hungarian troops remained committed was in Italy. But by now the Royal-Imperial Army's fighting power was so far gone that its last ever offensive, on the River Piave in June 1918, came to naught almost immediately.[120] Over the next few months, what remained of the troops' discipline, and with it the army itself, disintegrated completely.[121] Attempts to stem the flood were in vain. The fact that the new emperor, Karl I, had relaxed army discipline in a misconceived attempt to get his subjects to like him more could only hamper such attempts further.[122] By October the 14th Austro-Hungarian Infantry Regiment was declaring that "the rising instances of desertion . . . give rise to the suspicion that one of the motives to desert (is the belief) that the general spirit of conciliation after the war will prevent such offences from being punished with the full force of the law."[123]

When the Armistice finally came, such was the German army's condition that it was at least able to march home in good order. Not so the miasmic exodus of the Austro-Hungarian army from Italy: "trains overcrowded, some looking from a distance like swarms of bees . . . Every train was fully occupied including the roofs, platforms, bumpers, running-boards, and locomotives. Hundreds of men paid the ultimate price of their haste to return home in tunnels, on sharp turns, and across low railway-bridges."[124] The likely traumatizing effect of this spectacular disintegration upon the officers who witnessed it—among whom, by this time, were nearly all the Austrian-born officers examined in this study[125]—is easy to imagine. All told, bearing witness either to the complete collapse in morale within the Royal-Imperial Army, or to its severe albeit less debilitating erosion within the Imperial German Army, is likely to have increased many former officers' later receptivity to National Socialism. For National Socialist ideology, they would come to believe, had a uniquely strengthening effect upon military morale.

Karl abdicated, and a new democratic republic, christened the Republic of Austria in 1919, was set up. The peace treaties imposed upon Austria and Hungary after the Great War did not merely reduce their territory and armed forces to a fraction of their former size. They also dismembered the entire Austro-Hungarian Empire. Its territory was distributed to neighboring countries already in existence, such as Italy and Rumania, or to countries newly formed—Poland; Czechoslovakia; and the Kingdom of the Serbs, Croats, and Slovenes. Austria itself was reduced to a dwarf state a tenth the size of its former empire. The army's remnants were organized into a People's Army, or *Volkswehr*. The Volkswehr joined forces with militias to confront not just unrest within Austria, but also—with a newly formed Frontier Guard—attempts by some of Austria's neighbors to nip at its borders and seize its territory.[126]

In the popular press and right-wing circles, Jews were scapegoated for the collapse of Austrian power, as well as for the inflation that subsequently crippled the postwar Austrian economy. Anti-Semitism was further buttressed when the loss of Galicia to Poland and the Bukovina to Rumania sparked a fresh wave of Jews into Vienna. Many staunch Austrian Catholics, meanwhile, associated Jews with Marxism.[127]

In Germany, the military dictatorship that since 1916 had run the country to ultimately ruinous effect pinned the blame for defeat upon others—Bolsheviks and pacifists[128] and "cowardly" socialist and liberal politicians. It was these same politicians for whom the military dictatorship made way in autumn 1918, so as to saddle them with the blame for the humiliating peace treaty that was imminent. The wartime military leaders believed such action was justified. For they deluded themselves that it was these groups who had sealed Germany's doom by sowing the seeds of defeatism on the German home front while the army in the field had stood firm. The "stab-in-the-back" myth, which denied the military realities of autumn 1918, would become an article of faith for the political right in Germany, as it would for many army officers, during the years of republican government that succeeded the imperial regime.[129]

Many German officers, front-liners in particular, found defeat in 1918 and the humiliation heaped upon army and nation in its wake almost impossible to endure. Consequently, such men regarded the "guilty" parties—democrats, Bolsheviks, and the Jews whom they synonymized with both—with an especially noxious loathing. Captain von Selchow, visiting Berlin days after the Armistice, wrote that "we passed all sorts of people, the dregs of the city. Jews and deserters—gutter scum, in the vilest sense of the word—now rule Germany. But as far as the Jews are concerned, their day will come, and then woe to them!"[130]

Hatred towards the "enemies of the nation" was transformed into violence during the so-called "Time of Struggle" that engulfed Germany between 1918 and 1920. During this period numerous far left-wing groups, most prominently the Bolshevik-inspired Spartakists, sprang up in cities across Germany in an effort to foment Bolshevik-style revolution. Berlin, Munich, and the Ruhr were just three of the areas in which these forces either tried to seize power, or managed to seize it temporarily, before the new government called in the army and, most notoriously, the Free Corps—right-wing vigilante groups composed largely of former soldiers and idealistic university students—to bloodily crush them. The period also saw army and free corps units take on Polish separatists in Silesia and Posen.[131]

Many free corps units themselves were invited by nascent republican governments in the new Baltic states to provide defense against

Bolshevik Russia. The free corps promptly embarked on a barbaric rampage through the region. They launched their self-styled crusade partly to salvage "ancestral" German territory from Bolshevism, partly for land and booty, and partly out of lust for violence and adventure. It is worth mentioning that the British government, keen to use the free corps against the Bolsheviks, gave their campaign its tacit approval.[132]

The conviction that Germany's very existence was imperiled by infernal forces from within and without, and the savagery of the struggle against them, constituted a further seminal moment in the formative development of many of the men who would hold divisional and other middle-level field commands within the army twenty years later.[133] If anything, the experience may have been even more significant for officers who would go on to command counterinsurgency units during World War II. For, even more so than the real or imagined franc-tireur threat that had confronted German troops in Belgium and northern France during 1914, the left-wing forces whom army and free corps contingents faced on the streets of Germany between 1918 and 1920 were not just an irregular opponent, but an ideological one also. A similar process, albeit less pronounced, may have taken place among officers and soldiers returning to the less severe but still considerable upheaval within Austria during these years.[134]

The years between 1914 and 1920, then, did not just harden and radicalize the military and political systems within which German and Austrian officers operated. They also infused officers themselves with a harsher, more obdurate mentality. The forces that forged this mentality came on many fronts. There were the harsh environments, brutal fighting, and often squalid living conditions on the battlefronts themselves, be it the industrialized war of the western front, the wild war of the eastern front, the seesawing carnage of the Italian front, or the serial humiliations the Austro-Hungarians endured against Serbia. War also saw civilians ruthlessly instrumentalized across all battlefronts, whether through reprisal killings, forced labor, scorched earth, or other means.

And on all battlefronts, albeit to varying degrees, brutality against enemy soldiers or civilians was colored by culture and ideology. This was particularly apparent on the eastern front. It was here that German and Austrian troops came into contact with groups who, if they were not already the subject of opprobrium in the run-up to the Great War, certainly became the subject of it during the war itself—eastern Slavs, eastern Jews, and Bolsheviks. Finally, the combined effect of all these forces would coagulate and flow into officers' embittered reaction to the twin traumas of defeat and postwar chaos.

The legacy that resulted was still not enough to ensure that they would become active and willing agents of National Socialist warfare a quarter of a century later. Quite apart from anything else, the experiences officers underwent during this time were still too varied to make such a ferocious endpoint inevitable. But this six-year period had certainly made that outcome more likely. The process was to be completed during the interwar years and the opening phase of the even more destructive conflict that commenced in 1939.

CHAPTER 3

Bridging Two Hells

The 1920s and 1930s

During the 1920s and early 1930s, neither the German Reichswehr nor the Austrian *Bundesheer*—the diminished successors to, respectively, the Imperial German Army and the Austro-Hungarian Royal-Imperial Army—were ineluctably set on the path that would eventually see them commit to the National Socialist cause. But nothing significant happened during those years to steer them in an ultimately less disastrous direction. Then, from the mid-1930s onward, the Reichswehr, then the Bundesheer after it, became ever more entangled with National Socialism, for the greater part willingly so.[1]

In Germany the new Weimar Republic, though defended by the army in its first moment of danger, held little to endear it to the Reichswehr. Officers' disdain for it was increased by the contempt they themselves had drawn, as members of the "ruling class," during the November Revolution that had ushered the republic in. The best most officers had to say about Weimar was that even an unloved democratic republic was more palatable than a Bolshevik dictatorship.[2] And when the republic had seen fit to fall back on the soldiers in order to suppress the violent left-wing threat to its existence, it had been forced to buy the generals' support. The price was a promise not to intervene "excessively" in the Reichswehr's internal affairs in future.

Thanks to this, the Reichswehr leadership was able to cultivate an identity separate to, and aloof from, both the German government and German society. In this cause it turned its truncated size to its advantage; the successor to the old General Staff, the Troops Office, had far more excuse than its predecessor to be selective in its choice of personnel.[3] Further, the fact that the government's hands were tied also enabled the Troops Office to become experts, albeit only theoretical experts for the time being, in the business of mass destruction.

More emphasis was placed on intellect than before, but with one purpose in mind. The Troops Office ignored the fundamental strategic reasons why Germany had lost the Great War. Instead, it fixated itself even more firmly than its predecessor on achieving victory at the operational and tactical levels.[4] The main means of doing so, the Troops Office believed, was to learn how to harness the new military technologies and techniques, particularly those relating to air and armored forces, to their utmost. The fact that both air and armored power were denied to the Reichswehr by the terms of the Treaty of Versailles was something the Reichswehr found imaginative ways of circumventing—be it practicing armored warfare tactics with wooden bicycle-mounted contraptions, or even furtively visiting the Soviet Union to collaborate clandestinely with the new Red Army.[5] After four years of war followed by crushing defeat, moreover, the officer corps' mind-set was not just more technocratic than before. It was also harder, and its threshold for ruthlessness correspondingly lower.[6]

Officers, bar a few fanatics such as those who backed the farcical Kapp Putsch in 1920,[7] did not try to actively undermine the Weimar Republic during this period. They recognized that, for the moment at least, it must be tolerated as the only governmental system that could stave off nationwide chaos. Instead, they immersed themselves collectively in the business of honing their destructive expertise, and individually in the business of furthering their careers. Both ambitions, of course, went hand in hand. The route to success, now more than ever, was to undergo specialist technical training—and in time, preferably, to impart such training oneself. Better still would be to attain the kind of appointment that provided proper expertise in the entire panoply of military planning and organization. In the days of the old Imperial Army, it was the General Staff that had best afforded such an opportunity. Now, it was the new Reichswehr Ministry.[8] This agenda would, of course, eventually dovetail perfectly with National Socialism's aims for the armed forces.

The Reichswehr's senior officers also hoped they would eventually be able to assure Germany's national strength and greatness by wedding their mastery of technological warfare to the mobilized hearts and minds of German society, both civilian and military. This was a mobilization whose absence, they believed, had caused too many Germans to fall victim to the influence of defeatists, pacifists, and Bolsheviks during the Great War. Weimar, they believed—perhaps not unreasonably, given the republic's fractious party system and its at best uneven popular appeal—was incapable either of providing this popular rallying point or of safeguarding Germany's national interests more generally.[9]

Not all military figures were so averse; indeed in 1928 the Defense Minister, General Groener, sought to reconcile the Reichswehr with the republic.[10] But just one year later, the global economic crisis that followed the collapse of the New York stock exchange fatally entrenched most officers' contempt for Weimar. Barely any country was hit harder by the crisis than Germany. This was a consequence of its massive reliance on US loans to pay off the war reparations that the Treaty of Versailles, a treaty with the Weimar Republic's signature on it, had imposed upon the country. Now more than ever before, the majority of Reichswehr officers believed that the best route to achieving their goals lay not in the republic but in an authoritarian, national conservative government.

But in 1933, following the failure of two short-lived national conservative administrations to govern the country stably in the face of mounting political chaos, the Reichswehr leadership hit upon a more radical solution: alliance with the Nazis.[11] The Reichswehr gave its tacit approval as a cabal of arch-conservative politicians prevailed upon the increasingly doddery State President Hindenburg to award Hitler the chancellorship in January of that year. Behind the conservatives' maneuvering was the tragically misconceived notion of "taming" Hitler once he was in office. This was the culmination of the economic and political corrosion of the Weimar Republic that had been set in train when the global economic

crisis had broken over Germany. Already the corrosion had resulted in
six million unemployed, the lurch of German politics to extremes of left
and right, and frightening levels of social and political unrest. What followed its culmination was, of course, incomparably worse.

The Austrian Bundesheer's goals during the 1920s and early 1930s were
much more prosaic than the Reichswehr's. Partly this was because the
old Royal-Imperial Army had not bequeathed a similarly formidable
technocratic tradition to live up to. The more pressing reason was that
the Bundesheer had no practical choice. Any grand ambitions it might
have harbored were scotched by the sobering economic and political
realities of postwar Austria—realities even more sobering than they were
north of the border. Many officers, facing a squeeze on their pay and
pensions, also resented the new dwarf republic for material reasons.[12]
Then, during the 1920s, War Minister Vaugoin of the governing center-
right Christian Social Party weeded out the—not inconsiderable—left-
wing elements within the army. By 1927 at the latest, the Bundesheer was
solidly loyal to the Christian Socials and their coalition partners, but
deeply ambivalent towards the democratic republic as an institution.[13]
This would of course impact enormously on how it would conduct itself
amid the violent political turmoil that ripped Austria apart during the
early 1930s.

For Austrians, the most catastrophic phase of the global economic crisis, and with it the unfolding political crisis, followed the collapse of the
Vienna Credit Institute in 1931.[14] The elections that followed in April 1932
saw a surge in support for the Austrian Nazis similar to that which their
comrades in Germany were then enjoying.[15] The Christian Social chancellor, Engelbert Dollfuss, was profoundly alarmed at this development.
He saw it as a threat both to Austria's internal stability and, following the
Nazis' ascent to power in Germany, to Austria's national independence.
Dollfuss might have countered the threat by forming an alliance with
the trade unions and the Social Democrats. But the distrust between
socialist left and conservative right, which had been poisoning Austrian
politics since the republic's founding, prompted Dollfuss to dismiss that
option. Instead, he declared the formation of an Austro-fascist Catholic

"corporate state," backed by Mussolini's Italy and led by a new, post-democratic political organization, the Patriotic Front.

The Austrian Nazis, banned as an organization in May 1933, murdered Dollfuss in July 1934. But already Dollfuss had inadvertently hastened the day when the German Nazis would achieve a smooth takeover of the Austrian state. For, by provoking confrontation with the Social Democrats and the trade unions and then crushing them in bloody urban battles—a civil war–type situation for which, arguably, neither side was entirely blameless—he removed what might have been a major bulwark against a Nazi takeover.[16]

During the civil war the Bundesheer stood by the government unwaveringly, suppressing both the Austrian left and the Austrian Nazis with merciless force. Many officers, reeling from the swinging defense budget cuts previous governments had enacted in the wake of the economic crisis, hoped the new regime would expand and improve the army.[17] The majority of senior officers, old-school conservative in outlook and deeply ambivalent towards National Socialism, were concerned above all with safeguarding Austria's national integrity. Even so, there were limits to their patriotism; many senior officers were prepared to contemplate eventual union (*Anschluß*) with National Socialist Germany if it meant keeping "Italy and the Jews" out.[18] Meanwhile sympathy with National Socialism gathered strength, not only among rank-and-file troops but also, in time, among junior officers.[19]

North of the border, meanwhile, the Reichswehr officer corps' sympathy for the Nazi regime already in place was gathering strength also. Many younger officers, in particular, were highly supportive. Some had been hardened and radicalized by their experience of the Great War. Others, too young for wartime service, were anxious to prove their technocratic proficiency in the business of mass destruction.[20] All were aware of the many war veterans—Hitler himself being the most high-profile example—among the Nazis' leadership and rank and file, the enthusiasm the Nazis exuded for all things military, and their clear intention of tearing up the treaty that had so diminished Germany's military capability.[21] Many younger officers, war veterans and otherwise, thus perceived the greatly expanded, technologically enhanced army now in prospect as a means of fulfilling the aspirations not just of the officer corps as a whole, but of their own careers also.[22] They also believed that the Nazi concept of a "national community," embracing all Germans—or at least all Germans of the desired racial and social material—would be a sure means of rallying and unifying the German people, in both civilian and military spheres, for the waging of future wars.[23]

Older, more conservative officers were reassured by Hitler's show of moderation when, in the words of the historian Joachim Fest, he invoked "nationalism, tradition, the Prussian spirit, Western values, or the spirit of the front-line soldier . . . and (stressed) decency, morality, order, Christianity, and all those concepts which went with a conservative idea of the state."[24] They were reassured even more when he eliminated the leaders of the Reichswehr's bitter rival, the Nazis' paramilitary wing, the SA. This murderous act, albeit one committed against a coterie of thugs, became known as the Night of the Long Knives. The Reichswehr leadership not only supported it, but readily facilitated it, by providing weapons to the SS killing squads who did the deed.[25]

Moreover, that majority of officers who as yet remained less enthusiastic than some of their fellows did not yet pay serious heed to Hitler's wilder pronunciations, such as his call for "living space" in the East.[26] When eventually they did take notice, most would do so approvingly. Finally, if most officers did not share the Nazis' anti-Semitism to the same rabid extent, few allowed it to trouble them actively. Indeed the broad thrust of the Nazis' anti-Semitic campaign—with its stress, at this stage, on discrimination and disenfranchisement rather than extermination—found widespread approval among many officers. Army chief General von Fritsch, who regarded himself as a conservative nationalist rather than a Nazi, wrote:

> Soon after (the Great War), I came to the conclusion that three battles would have to be fought and won if Germany was to become powerful again. 1. The fight against the working class, in which Hitler has been victorious; 2. Against the Catholic Church, or to put it better, against ultramontanism; and 3. Against the Jews. We are still in the midst of the last two battles. And the struggle against the Jews

is the hardest. I hope it is clear to people everywhere what a battle it will be.[27]

By now, moreover, the already widespread anti-Semitism within the German officer corps was being hardened by the connections officers drew between Jews and Bolshevism.[28]

The murder of the SA leaders, which took place in June 1934, was followed on Hindenburg's death two months later by Hitler's merging of the offices of president and chancellor in his new position as leader—Führer—and by the army's swearing of a new oath, dedicated not to the state, but to Hitler personally. Most senior officers did not yet anticipate the catastrophic consequences the taking of the oath would eventually have.[29] The oath's introduction was followed in 1935 by Hitler's announcement that Germany would no longer adhere to the disarmament terms of the Versailles Treaty, but would instead embark upon a massive expansion of its armed forces. The years from 1935 onward brought both an enormous, socially diverse intake of new officers, and the reentry into the army of many former officers who had left the service on the inception of the Reichswehr.

The expansion of the officer corps brought large numbers of men from those predominantly middle-class circles—such as small businessmen, small farmers and landowners, and white-collar workers and professionals—who had provided the Nazis with particularly strong electoral support.[30] From that point on the leadership of the new German armed forces, the Wehrmacht, implemented an extensive program of National Socialist indoctrination among conscripts. It also implemented Nazi-style regulations to purge the new force of all "undesirable" social, racial, and political elements.

Over the next three years, Hitler also set about abolishing more of the hated provisions of Versailles—the territorial clauses that had emasculated Germany's borders. But he aimed to go further—by unifying the German-speaking peoples beyond the Reich's borders. These were to be the first stages in a foreign policy plan Hitler had detailed in his writings of the 1920s, aimed ultimately at the total domination of Europe, perhaps even at global power.[31] As a first step, in defiance of Versailles but with no practical opposition from France or Britain when it was taken, German troops reoccupied the demilitarized Rhineland in March 1936. That same year, the Pact of Steel was signed with fascist Italy. This particular development brought Austria's eventual absorption into the Reich significantly closer.

Before the Pact of Steel, the Italian dictator Mussolini had strongly opposed what he saw as an unacceptable extension of German influence into his own backyard. But he was reassured by the new stance on the *Anschluß* question Hitler now adopted; out went misconceived support for botched and bloody coup attempts, in came an "evolutionary" approach intended to integrate Austria gradually and peacefully into the Reich. Dollfuss's successor as Austrian chancellor, Kurt Schuschnigg, reluctantly played along to an extent. He recognized that the absence of effective support against Hitler from Britain, France, and now Italy left him no alternative.[32] At the same time, an unsuccessful attempt by Schuschnigg to crack down further on the Austrian Nazis gave Hitler the leverage to compel Schuschnigg to lift the ban on the party and appoint several of its number to key government positions. Hitler also compelled Schuschnigg to remove the head of the Bundesheer, General Jansa, who had intended military resistance to any future German invasion.[33] Schuschnigg regarded all these developments with mounting anxiety. So too did many Catholic, old-school conservative, senior Bundesheer officers.[34] But many of their younger colleagues increasingly did not.

There are many indications that the Bundesheer would have resisted German invasion had it been ordered to do so.[35] Nevertheless, contact between the Bundesheer and the German army grew increasingly close and cooperative during the years following 1935.[36] Among other things, this caused Bundesheer officers to grow increasingly disgruntled at the two armies' contrasting standards of equipment. From 1936, moreover, National Socialist sympathy was firmly on the rise among the Bundesheer's lower ranks after the Bundesheer aped its northern counterpart by introducing conscription.[37] The debilitating effect of burgeoning National Socialist support upon relations among Bundesheer officers was commented on by a German observer:

One group, up to lieutenant-colonel or thereabouts, thinks National Socialist and pro-Anschluß. Second group thoroughly pro-government. Because of the differences between these political opinions and attitudes, any sense of unity and comradeship within the officer corps is entirely absent. What has taken its place is mutual distrust, spying, and denunciation.[38]

Hitler finally annexed Austria directly, and bloodlessly, in March 1938. He was spurred among other things by Schuschnigg's pledge to hold a national plebiscite in an attempt to settle the question of Austria's independence for good. Across many parts of Austria pro-Nazi officers, under the aegis of the pro-Nazi soldiers' organization, the Circle of National Socialist Soldiers, moved swiftly to neutralize their anti-Nazi colleagues and ensure that the Bundesheer would not intervene against advancing German forces.[39] Schuschnigg was forced to resign and make way for the Austrian Nazi Artur Seyss-Inquart.

Over the months that followed, the Bundesheer was absorbed into the German army as smoothly as Austria, or the Eastern March as it was now renamed, was absorbed into the Reich. Most divisional commanders and many regimental ones—non-Nazi, old-school, and often monarchical in outlook—were removed. The submerging into the German army of the rest of the Bundesheer officer corps, and their troops, then proceeded swiftly. Apart from anything else, this was a comment on the Republic of Austria's failure to cultivate a proper sense of national identity during its nineteen-year existence.[40] From March 1938, then, the German army contained officers from both Germany and Austria, and the story of two officer corps becomes the story of one.

The Anschluß was only the first of Hitler's foreign policy triumphs in 1938. The second came that autumn. After months of international tension, a negotiated settlement at Munich granted the Reich the German-speaking Sudetenland region of neighboring Czechoslovakia. Officers throughout the Wehrmacht, like the population as a whole, were dazzled by Hitler's purported diplomatic brilliance. But though the resolution of the crisis had been peaceful, the consequences for Hitler's relations with the army leadership were anything but.

At the outset of the crisis, Hitler had sought to use the "violation" of the rights of Sudeten Germans by the Czech government as an excuse to smash Czechoslovakia through military action. But then, faced with the prospect of war with Britain and France over the issue, he had been persuaded by his more cautious generals that Germany was not yet ready for such a war, and that it would therefore be prudent to negotiate a way out of the crisis. Now, having acquired the Sudetenland by negotiation, Hitler rued his ever having been swayed by such "timid" counsel. Instead, he concluded that his generals' advice had been wrong, that Britain and France would not have gone to war after all, and that his future foreign policy must always employ the radical brinkmanship that had enabled him to bring the Rhineland and Austria into the German fold. Thus, in a process inaugurated earlier in 1938, those senior officers who were concerned at the destabilizing pace of Hitler's foreign and rearmament policies were replaced or sidelined. That or they simply resigned themselves to the impossibility of challenging a leader whose popularity among the German people was now greater than ever.

Hitler's new measure of control over the armed forces was reflected in a restructuring of the high command system. Out went the old War Ministry; in came two new bodies, the Army High Command (*Oberkommando des Heeres* or OKH), which from June 1941 would be concerned primarily with coordinating the war against the Soviet Union, and the Armed Forces High Command (*Oberkommando der Wehrmacht* or OKW). The OKW was effectively Hitler's personal military office, and would from 1941 be responsible for coordinating the war across the rest of Europe. Hitler's inner military circle now consisted largely of careerists, sycophants, or at best officers who, able though they were, refrained from criticizing Hitler's decisions openly. He now pursued his foreign policy program ever more recklessly. In March 1939, he seized the remaining Czech lands of Bohemia and Moravia. Hitler's next move, against Poland, led directly to war, the dictator wrongly calculating that Britain and France would be deterred from intervening by the cynically utilitarian Nazi-Soviet Pact of August 1939. But while the Germans took one month to vanquish Poland, Britain and France were powerless to intervene.

Many army officers, particularly those originating from eastern Prussia, were eager to settle accounts with Poland.[41] Yet triumphant in the field though the army was, the invasion also exposed the moral degeneration that by now afflicted its leadership and, increasingly, its officer corps more widely. Hitler's speech to his highest commanders on August 22 had set the tone for the way the Polish campaign was to be waged: "Close your hearts to pity. Proceed brutally. Eighty million people must have what is theirs by right. Their existence must be secured. The stronger has the right. (Exercise the) greatest harshness."[42]

Now, after years of growing accommodation with the Nazi regime and burgeoning enthusiasm for its military and ideological policies, the army largely stood by as Nazi murder squads—the *Einsatzgruppen* of the SS-run Security Service (SD)—fanned out behind the advancing troops to "cleanse" Polish territory of "dangerous elements." The Einsatzgruppen were charged with rounding up and liquidating all Poles who might conceivably threaten the German occupation's stability. They netted political figures, the intelligentsia, former army officers, and many Jews. Several thousand individuals, in a portent of far greater slaughter later in the war, were shot en masse.[43]

In failing to protest effectively at these killings, the officer corps of the German army crossed a further moral line. In turn, they emboldened the SS to cross lines even more bestial in the future. A number of army officers did object, but few used moral arguments.[44] Most other protesting officers, whether because they were not morally affronted in the first place or because they perceived that appeals to morality would simply be ignored, objected more mildly on "pragmatic" grounds instead: their fear for the discipline of army troops in the vicinity of the killings or their concern at the damage that might be wrought on the army's "good name" were it to be tainted by association with them. And no protesting officer received any backing whatsoever from the supine head of the army, General von Brauchitsch.

Many officers, meanwhile, did not protest at all. Moreover, whether because their own anti-Slavic and anti-Semitic beliefs were influencing them, because their scruples were diluted by careerism, or because they obsessed over needing to preemptively crush any potential opposition to German occupation, they were liberally bloodying their own hands in the name of "security"—sometimes, indeed, in co-operation with the SS. Any civilian resistance posed to the German invasion of Poland—and of civilian resistance in Poland, in contrast to Belgium and France in 1914, there was plenty—was answered with massively disproportionate reprisals.

German interwar military doctrine, besotted as it was with mobile, technical, and tactical superiority at the front line, had in fact paid relatively little attention to counterinsurgency. But in Poland in 1939, the German army's leadership chose to resurrect that singularly harsh counterinsurgency doctrine that had led German soldiers to commit brutal acts of suppression such as those in German Southwest Africa in 1904–1905 and Belgium and northern France in 1914. That the army leadership acted thus was not simply because German generals were preprogrammed to counter irregular warfare with terror. After all, the Germans' relatively balanced counterinsurgency campaign in the Ukraine in 1918 had demonstrated that they were not thus preprogrammed.

But the senior German officer corps of 1939 was harder and more radical than its predecessor of 1918. It was also enmeshed, for the greater part willingly, in a criminally brutal regime, and extensively shared that regime's ideological contempt for "Slavic races." And brutal counterinsurgency conduct of the Belgium 1914 variety dovetailed perfectly with the Nazis' steadfast belief that terror and suppression were the only sure means of keeping an occupied population in line—particularly if both parties regarded that population as racially inferior.[45] Such sentiments would go on to underpin the German army's counterinsurgency campaigns in both the Soviet Union and Yugoslavia.

The campaign in the West of spring 1940 radicalized virtually all elements of the National Socialist regime. The Wehrmacht achieved in six weeks what the Kaiserheer had failed to achieve in four years—the conclusive defeat of France herself, and the apparent prospect of imminent peace with Britain. The stunning victory, and the euphoric accolade that followed it, combined to infuse Hitler and the Nazi regime with immense hubris. Consequently, when Britain refused to make peace, they believed it well within their capabilities to compel Britain to the negotiating table by defeating her last potential ally on mainland Europe. This potential ally, the small matter of the Nazi-Soviet Pact notwithstanding, was the Soviet Union. Invading the Soviet Union sooner or later had always been a long-standing aim of Hitler's; he believed that the German people's long-term future could only be secured by annihilating the mortal danger the Soviet Union's "Jew-Bolshevik" leadership posed and seizing the country's economic wealth and vast rural spaces. But the aim of sapping Britain's will to resist by defeating the Soviet Union sooner rather than later certainly influenced the timing of his decision to invade.[46]

The army leadership's complicity in the invasion of the Soviet Union, code-named Operation Barbarossa, is the most resonant statement of how far it had by now debased itself, and the army, in the name of National Socialism. Hitler and the leading power blocs of the Third Reich did not regard the attack on the Soviet Union as an ordinary invasion. They conceived it instead as a "war of extermination," one aimed at destroying an entire nation, plundering its resources, annihilating its "Jew-Bolshevik" leadership class, and decimating and enslaving its population. It was a war the army's leadership and senior officer corps broadly supported. By now, they were even more heavily under the influence of Hitler and National Socialism, enthused at the opportunity to provide the ultimate demonstration of their army's fighting prowess, and animated by anti-Semitism, by anti-Slavism and, perhaps above all, by anti-Bolshevism. While this final motive may have been muted by short-term exigencies such as the Reichswehr's erstwhile clandestine collaboration with the Red Army, it was now established as a major driving force.[47] Typical of many generals' views on the eve of the invasion were those of General Erich Hoepner, commander of the Fourth Panzer Group. "The war against the Soviet Union," he wrote early in May 1941, "is an essential component of the German people's struggle for existence. It is the old struggle of the Germans against the Slavs, the defense of European culture against the Muscovite-Asiatic flood, and the repulsion of Judeo-Bolshevism."[48]

The war of extermination against the Soviet Union was also a war into which, through saturation propaganda and ruthless directives, the generals would endeavor to embed their troops.[49] The Barbarossa Decree, issued by the Armed Forces High Command a month before the invasion on May 19 1941, declared that "Bolshevism is the mortal

enemy of the National Socialist German people. It is against this sub-
versive world-view and its carriers that Germany is fighting. This battle
demands ruthless and energetic measures against Bolshevik agitators,
irregulars, saboteurs, and Jews, and the total eradication of any active
or passive resistance."[50]

Ultimately, the hubris that shaped the pitiless conception of the invasion
of the Soviet Union, and indeed the decision to invade in the first place,
would be the Nazi regime's undoing. It would lead it, in its planning
of Barbarossa, to fatally underestimate the Soviet Union's capabilities
and fatally overestimate Germany's own. But in spring 1941, it was the
culmination of a series of developments which had seen the leadership
of the German army become increasingly radicalized and brutalized,
increasingly intertwined with the Nazi regime, and increasingly set on
a course that would implicate it in the regime's worst deeds. It was a
process to which many if not most of the army's senior officer corps,
including those officers who are this study's concern, had become party
sooner or later.

From the years before 1914, through the Great War and the interwar
years, and up to 1941, the forces that eventually brought the army's senior
officer corps to this threshold had been many and varied. By 1941, a succession of developments had ensured that senior officers were now technocratic, ruthlessly utilitarian, and ideologically hardened to an extent
that would have been barely conceivable, if at all, to their late-nineteenth
century predecessors. The merging of the two armies in 1938 and their
assimilation into the Nazi state had accelerated the process. Senior officers now belonged to a body that, as a whole, stood ready to wage a
singularly brutal form of warfare in the service of National Socialism.
Just how far each individual officer was prepared to go in the service of
that cause would be determined by the influences and experiences that
had shaped him over the course of his life. But the strength of conviction now animating the senior officer corps as a whole would manifest
itself with brutal clarity in the campaign the Wehrmacht would conduct
in Yugoslavia that year, just as surely as it would in the Wehrmacht's
campaign against the Soviet Union.

Yet neither the collective mind-set nor the personal attitudes to which officers subscribed fully explain how those officers actually went on to behave. Yugoslavia's topography, the political conditions under which the German occupation regime would operate, and the conditions on the ground in which German army units would find themselves all helped shape the circumstances that would in turn determine how officers' attitudes translated into action. The interplay of all these forces, and the behavior that resulted, are the concern of the book's remaining chapters. The very next chapter outlines the topographical, political, and military backdrop of the Wehrmacht's invasion and occupation of Yugoslavia in 1941.

CHAPTER 4

Invasion and Occupation

Yugoslavia, 1941

I N MARCH 1941, the impending drive into the Soviet Union was delayed by events in a different quarter. The Reich's hapless ally, Italy, had sought to extend its influence in the Balkans since 1939. But so deficient was the Italian army that even the first step, the seizure of Albania in 1939, had gone far from smoothly. Less smoothly still went the course of Italy's next attempted venture, the conquest of Greece.[1] Italy's ongoing failure to subdue the Greeks raised the ominous prospect of Britain propping Greece up and threatening Germany's southeastern flank in the run-up to Barbarossa. This threat needed neutralizing before Barbarossa was launched. Thus began preparations to divert German forces southward into an attack on Greece.

But on March 27, 1941, matters became vastly more complicated. That day, the broadly pro-Axis government of Yugoslavia—the erstwhile Kingdom of the Serbs, Croats, and Slovenes—was toppled in a coup orchestrated by Serbian officers of the Yugoslav air force. The officers were hostile to the Axis, and believed that excessive Croat influence had caused the former government to cozy up to Hitler and Mussolini.[2] Their disgruntlement was partly a symptom of deeper conflicts that had beset the country since its inception at the end of the Great War. Those same conflicts would be catastrophically magnified during the Axis occupation of World War II, and would critically influence that occupation in nearly all its aspects.

The 1921 census records that Serbs—the kingdom's largest ethnic group—Croats, and Slovenes comprised nearly ten million of its twelve million inhabitants. The rest comprised ethnic Germans, Magyars, Macedonians, Albanians, Romanians, Turks, and others. The fault lines were religious as well as ethnic; five and a half million Yugoslavs, including most Serbs, practiced the Orthodox faith, while the Croats comprised the majority of the country's 4.7 million Catholics. There were also 1.3 million Muslims, including Turks and Albanians as well as Bosnian Muslims.[3]

Nineteenth-century nationalism, the centuries-old divide-and-rule tactics of Ottoman and Habsburg rulers, and other cultural, economic, and political forces had generated much mutual resentment between these groups. While the desire for a genuinely harmonious, united southern Slavic state was strong and widespread, then, achieving it in practice was a much greater challenge. An evenhanded, reasonably decentralized constitution might yet have enabled the new kingdom to achieve it.[4] But instead, the Kingdom of the Serbs, Croats, and Slovenes was conceived in a hurry, partly for fear that delay might lead to Bolshevik revolution, as a centralized unitary state.

And it was the Serbs, on account of their military, political, and international clout, who acquired much the greater portion of power within the new state. This could only increase irredentist and separatist tendencies among other ethnic groups, particularly the Croats and Macedonians. It also hindered efforts to tackle the country's manifold economic problems.[5] In 1928, a sequence of events including political assassinations, allegations of governmental corruption, and the diminution of parliament's prestige in the nation's eyes led King Alexander to conclude that the country's problems could not be solved by conventional political means. The following year he dissolved parliament, established a royal dictatorship, and—ostensibly so as to promote the unitary state and supersede all ethnic divisions—renamed the country Yugoslavia.

"Yugoslavism" as a principle held that not one of the kingdom's ethnic groups should excessively dominate the others. But Yugoslav society remained polarized, all the more so as the global economic crisis assailed it and agricultural prices tumbled during the early 1930s.[6] Many Croats believed that Alexander's particular brand of Yugoslavism was merely cover for a subtler imposition of Serb-oriented centralism.[7] One effect of Yugoslavia's polarization, born also of widespread anti-Communism and disdain for "irresolute" liberal democracy, was the emergence of two far-right movements in the country. The Zbor Movement was robustly "Great Serbian" in outlook, seeking to further entrench Serb dominance. In complete contrast, the Croatian Ustasha, whose principal leadership was forced to operate from exile in Italy, was fervently, violently separatist. In 1934, in cahoots with the Internal Macedonian Revolutionary Organization, it assassinated King Alexander himself. This shocking event seems, with hindsight, to portend the slaughterous mushrooming of Yugoslavia's ethnic strife during World War II.

Yet that fate was still not inescapable. With the murdered monarch's son, Peter, still in his minority, Alexander's cousin Prince Paul became regent. Real power, however, lay with the prime minister, Milan Stojadinović. But Stojadinović's successor from February 1939, Dragisa Cvetković, sought to build on previous attempts at compromise between the centralizing and separatist forces by which Yugoslav society was riven.[8] In August 1939, on the back of extensive support in Serbia, he granted the Croats extensive autonomy. To an extent this dug the country out of one hole of ethnic conflict into another, for many ethnic Serbs within the newly formed provinces of Croatia now lost their own autonomy. And many Croats, increasingly desirous of a separate nation, regarded their new self-governing powers as being too little, too late.[9] These conundrums, however, might yet have been resolved.

But the following month, war broke out; though Yugoslavia did not declare itself for either side, it mobilized its army as a precaution and held its breath. This, together with a sudden vacuum in Yugoslavia's political leadership caused by the death or retirement of many leading statesmen, put prospects of further political progress on hold.[10]

Externally, meanwhile, Yugoslavia had become unsettlingly dependent on Nazi Germany. The Yugoslav government's bitter opposition to Communism was bound to palliate any accommodation it might reach with the Nazi regime.[11] As it was, by 1934 Yugoslavia's acute economic vulnerability had drawn it into a restrictive trade agreement with Germany. The League of Nations' failure to condemn Italian collusion in the murder of

King Alexander had eroded the Yugoslav government's faith in the Western powers; further accommodation with Berlin seemed the only alternative offering a measure of security. When Italy invaded Albania in 1939, Italian encroachment on Yugoslav territory seemed sure to follow; this too drew the country closer into Germany's orbit. Germany's supremacy on the European continent following its triumphs of 1939–1940 placed Yugoslavia even more firmly in its shadow. All this, of course, suited the Germans enormously; it seemed to assure them a large economic base and help safeguard their southern flank in advance of Barbarossa. German interests in the region were further advanced when, on March 25, 1941, Yugoslavia joined Germany's Tripartite Pact with Italy and Japan.[12]

For the Germans, then, the 27 March coup was the rudest jolt imaginable. Prince Paul was obliged to leave the country, and Peter, still in his minority, assumed the throne. The new prime minister, Dušan Simović, pledged to maintain good relations with Germany and meet Yugoslavia's obligations under the Tripartite Pact. Yet the coup had been accompanied by demonstrations against the pact, isolated excesses against German institutions and individuals, and other unsettling incidents. The Germans suspected the coup had been orchestrated from London. Certainly the British, though they could have done little if anything to support the coup practically, saw it as an emphatic slap in the face for Hitler's Balkan policy.[13]

Hitler, enraged at the Yugoslavs' "betrayal," fearing for Germany's international prestige, anxious to extinguish all uncertainty in the Balkan theater before Barbarossa, and ignoring Simović's protestations of continued support, vowed to smash Yugoslavia as a military power. Also driving his decision was that long-standing Serbophobic mind-frame peculiar to many Austrians during the earlier decades of the twentieth century. Hitler now resolved on a simultaneous onslaught against Yugoslavia as well as Greece.[14] The invasion of Yugoslavia, launched on April 6, was intended not just to defeat the country militarily, but also to break its spirit of resistance through maximum, terrorizing force.

There was no greater contrast than that between the Serbs' pugnacious defense against the Royal and Imperial Army in 1914, and the half-mobilized, ill-equipped Yugoslav army's almost instant collapse in the face of the German Second and Twelfth Armies, supported by the First Panzer Group and forces from Italy and the Axis satellite of Hungary, in 1941. Dissident Croatian units in the north refused to fight, and indeed some Croatian units sank to fighting soldiers of other ethnic groups in the Yugoslav army instead. Simović fled Belgrade upon its devastating bombardment by the Luftwaffe, and on April 11 a separate Croatian state was declared. Yugoslavia itself surrendered on April 18, two days before Greece. Those Yugoslav forces that did not surrender simply disbanded and went home, or—like the forces fighting around Belgrade—retreated into the mountains.[15]

If Yugoslavia was worth conquering, it was also worth securing. As well as helping to facilitate a secure southern flank for Barbarossa, occupying Yugoslavia provided direct access to the Agram-Belgrade-Niš railway line—the main land route supplying the Axis in Greece, and the main link with Germany's ally Bulgaria. It also provided unbroken access to the River Danube, a major supply line for oil from another Balkan ally, Rumania.[16]

Yet Yugoslavia's geography, as a succession of invaders throughout history had discovered, challenged any occupier. Its mountains were of medium-range height but their fissures, caverns, and general topography were similar to those of higher mountains. They were also difficult to penetrate, particularly in harsh winter conditions.[17] All this, of course, made them a potential haven for irregular resistance.

Because Yugoslavia had never figured in Hitler's long-term plans, he committed minimal German forces to its occupation and left most of the burden to the Italians, the Axis satellites of Bulgaria and Hungary, or collaborationist native administrations.[18] Italy, in fulfillment of its ambitions in the region, was allowed to acquire the most territory. It annexed Western Slovenia and the Dalmatian coast, installing a quisling government in Montenegro and adding Serbian Kosovo to its Albanian possession. Yet Italy, despite its great power pretensions in the Balkans, had been as surprised as the Germans by the turn of events. Indeed, its territorial claims in Yugoslavia were little more than a hastily conceived grab bag.[19] With its defective, overburdened armed forces, Italy's deficiencies as an occupying power soon became apparent.

With King Peter and most of his cabinet ministers having fled to London, Serbia was initially governed by the puppet Aćimović administration. From August 29 onward, however, it would be administered by a German-controlled regime headed by former Yugoslav army general Milan Nedić. Of all the regions of occupied Yugoslavia, it was Serbia that would be saddled with the lowliest position. The fact that most noteworthy Serbian conservatives had fled the country would have impaired any collaborationist Serbian government from the start. As it was, the contempt in which Hitler held the Serbs, and the calculation that suffused the Reich leadership's perception of Balkan power politics, combined to reduce Serbia, in Nazi Foreign Minister Joachim von Ribbentrop's words, "to the smallest limits to prevent . . . conspiracies and intrigues."[20] Thus was the country truncated to an unviable rump state. Yet as the historian Matteo Milazzo, considering the paucity of German occupation troops in Serbia, points out, "what Germany was attempting . . . was the imposition of a Carthaginian peace on Yugoslavia's Serb population which it lacked the strength to enforce."[21]

Disastrous as this state of affairs would soon prove, more disastrous still were the arrangements for governing Croatia. A coastal strip of Croatian territory, renamed the Governorate of Dalmatia and designated Zone I in operational parlance, was to be administered directly by General Vittorio Ambrosio's Italian Second Army. The rest, officially, was to comprise the Independent State of Croatia, or NDH.[22] The NDH was itself divided into three areas. In Zone II, a demilitarized buffer between Italian territory and the rest of the NDH, the NDH was to enjoy civilian administrative power only. Within a strip further inland, Zone III, it was to enjoy military power. Northeast of Zone III was another demarcation line, beyond which lay the German sphere of influence.

The Germans' motives in agreeing to this carve-up were twofold. The first motivation was to give the Croats a power base that would advantage them at the Serbs' expense—a divide-and-rule ploy the Germans had already employed with the Czechs and Slovaks. The second was to place a check on the Italians' territorial designs. This would help ensure that much of the region's valuable economic resources would be controlled by either the Germans themselves or their smaller, more malleable allies—Bulgaria, Hungary, and the NDH itself.[23]

But from the moment Vladko Maček, leader of the Croatian Peasants' Party, rejected German attempts to appoint him head of government, the NDH was set on a calamitous path. For the Axis then gave the job to the Ustasha, and its leader, Ante Pavelić. Favoring Pavelić for their own calculating reasons, the Italians and Germans ignored the fact that his movement enjoyed only limited support among ordinary Croats. Exiled for years in Italy as Pavelić had been, the Italians regarded him as indebted to them. In fact, Pavelić did not feel beholden to the Italians, and believed the eventual, inevitable collapse of the Italian army would give the Ustasha an even freer hand to pursue its ambitions. The Germans, meanwhile, realized they had underestimated the scale of Italian ambitions in the Balkans, and were happy to use the NDH to keep them in check. In addition, Hitler calculated that the Ustasha's steadfast loyalty to the Reich would bring stability to the region.[24]

That calculation would soon prove particularly risible. For that summer, the Ustasha would go on to pursue a course that would spark a catastrophic chain reaction across occupied Yugoslavia. The Ustasha, extolling a fanatical brand of separatism, was resolved to remodel the NDH as a "pure" Catholic Croatian state. This was despite the fact that Croats comprised just over half its 6.5 million inhabitants. The Ustasha's commitment to this ideal was partly a response to the discrimination to which interwar Yugoslavia's Croat population had been subjected by the Serb-dominated government in Belgrade. But the Ustasha's worship of violence—an exploding bomb adorned the movement's symbol—presaged how it would seek to achieve that aim.[25] The Ustasha's Nazi-style racism ensured that any campaign for the NDH's "ethnic purity" would target Jews, and Sinti and Roma, as well as Serbs.[26] Calculation may well have played a role also; vicious campaigns against all three groups could channel the Ustasha's extreme nationalism away from a premature, potentially damaging confrontation with the Italians. More simply, the Ustasha regime was militarily weak, and the Ustasha movement, as a fringe group, enjoyed limited popular support; terror, therefore, was an alternative means of controlling its ethnically disparate population.[27]

The conditions of Axis occupation weakened the new state in other ways also. It was underdeveloped agriculturally.[28] South of the Italian–German demarcation line, it was subjected to demeaning occupation measures by an arrogant, exploitative Italian regime. More generally, both Germans and Italians massively impaired the new state's military, diplomatic, and economic independence.[29]

Yet that same Axis occupation also enabled the Ustasha to pursue its fanatical program free of outside interference. In particular, the puppet government in Serbia, firmly under German control, would be powerless to prevent any action the Ustasha took against the NDH's ethnic Serbs.[30] And the action it had in store for the NDH's Jews would, of course, meet with German approval.

Moreover, the Ustasha did enjoy the crucial support of the nationalistic, anti-Communist Catholic Church in Croatia, even though many individual priests would in time come to abhor the Ustasha's crimes.[31] The Ustasha also benefited from the fact that in 1941 most Croats, after centuries of foreign rule and two decades of internal discrimination, supported the idea of an independent Croatia. Moreover, few among the population yet appreciated the true extent of the new state's subordination to the Axis.[32]

Granted this window of opportunity, the Ustasha moved quickly. Its first step, days after the NDH's foundation, was to legislate to remove from state employment all elements who did not support the ideal of a "pure" Croatian state. This gave it the means to expel Jews, Serbs, and Yugoslav-minded Croats from the state sector. It then stacked the government's administrative offices with its own supporters, irrespective of whether they were even qualified. This would soon infect the workings of the new state with crippling levels of corruption and incompetence. But it also enabled the Ustasha to immediately assimilate the state apparatus with its own party organization and initiate the next phase of its ethnic program. By May, Nazi-style laws were increasingly excluding Jews and Sinti and Roma from the social and economic life of the NDH. The Serbs, much more numerous and potentially much more troublesome, were at this early stage assaulted somewhat less overtly, but no less surely for that.[33] The regime's measures, personified by notices springing up across the NDH proclaiming "No Serbs, Gypsies, Jews, and dogs,"[34] foreshadowed the carnage the Ustasha would soon unleash. The effects of that carnage would in turn ravage the country's population and debilitate the Axis occupation over the following years. At the same time, relations between Germany, Italy, and the NDH would become afflicted by a paralysis that would enfeeble all attempts to remedy this blight.

Germany's own commitment to the occupation was overseen by Field Marshal Wilhelm List, the Athens-based Wehrmacht Commander Southeast. German troops on the ground were thinly spread. In the NDH was stationed one occupation formation, the 718th Infantry Division. In Serbia, under direct German occupation, the somewhat larger German troop presence was headed by the Luftwaffe's General Ludwig von Schröder, whose title was Commander in Serbia. Schröder was to be replaced in late July, following a fatal air crash, by fellow Luftwaffe general Heinrich Danckelmann.[35] Under Serbia Command's direct charge were the static units of occupation administration, divided among four area commands (*Feldkommandanturen*) and smaller district commands (*Kreiskommandanturen*) and local commands (*Ortskommandanturen*). These were directly overseen by Serbia Command's Administrative Office, headed by SS Lieutenant General Harald Turner. Turner's brief also extended to overseeing the collaborationist Serbian government. Serbia Command also exercised direct control, via its Command Staff, over four substandard territorial battalions, poorly equipped and comprising men from older age-groups.[36] More impressive were the forces provided by the SS and police—Einsatzgruppe Yugoslavia of the SD, and later Reserve Police Battalion 64 from the heavily militarized Order Police. These units, alongside the Wehrmacht's own regular military police and Secret Field Police, would be assigned a prominent role in countering sabotage, insurgency, and other forms of subversion.[37]

But the single largest German troop commitment in Serbia, three additional "700–number" infantry divisions—the 704th, 714th, and 717th—was one over which Serbia Command had only indirect control. These, together with the 718th Infantry Division, were directly commanded by the army's LXV Corps, headed by Lieutenant General Paul Bader.[38] The fact that the occupation divisions were not under Serbia

Command's direct charge augured ill for the prospects of effective and coordinated security.

Bader's substandard formations were "Category Fifteen" divisions, raised in spring 1941 specifically for occupation duties. Their commands had been formed in the military districts of Dresden (the 704th), Königsberg (the 714th), and Salzburg in the Eastern March (the 717th and 718th). Correspondingly, the 704th and 714th's infantry regiments were drawn from the old Reich, the 717th's from the Eastern March. Two thirds of the 718th's infantry strength had likewise been raised in the Eastern March.[39] In contrast with the three infantry regiments allocated to a full-strength frontline infantry division, each occupation division in Yugoslavia was allocated just two such regiments. The divisions possessed cycle, reconnaissance, engineer, and signals troops at company strength only; by contrast, frontline infantry divisions commanded entire battalions of such forces. Nor did the occupation divisions possess medium mortars or medium machine-gun companies, or antitank or infantry-gun support. They did possess other forms of artillery, but, unlike frontline divisions, they were allotted an artillery section of circa three batteries, rather than a full regiment.[40] Their mainly reservist personnel hailed from older age-groups, and such training as they had received was incomplete when they arrived in Yugoslavia.[41]

Between May 7 and 24, all four divisions were transported to their new jurisdictions.[42] Initially, they were assigned to guarding rail communications with Greece and Bulgaria. This was an important task, on which the southern flank of Operation Barbarossa and the Axis position in southeast Europe depended, but scarcely arduous in itself. Yet these divisions were destined to provide the bulk of the German security forces in Yugoslavia well into 1942—a task that would become infinitely more arduous. They embodied what was in fact an established approach within the German military—a cut-price military occupation, employing second-rate commanders, the better to resource the army's frontline formations.[43]

The fact that about half the personnel across the four divisions hailed from the Eastern March would bring no particular benefit. That Austrian-born personnel were so numerous was due greatly to the logistical ease of moving troops down to Yugoslavia from the proximate Eastern March. Granted, senior Austrian-born officers would likely bring some regional expertise to their duties, something of which Hitler himself was conscious.[44] Some Austrian officers were proficient in mountain warfare, a specialism that might serve them well in Yugoslavian terrain.[45] But not until 1943 would their units be resourced to anything like the extent required for such a role. The ferocity with which many of them, and their units, would soon be comporting themselves—partly in an attempt to compensate for their many defects—would prove much more telling.

All these formations faced increasingly daunting conditions as 1941 wore on. By summer, they would bear the brunt of a Communist-led uprising, sparked by the campaign of expulsion and killing the Ustasha inaugurated in early June, which threatened to engulf them entirely. The danger the uprising posed grew most severe when the Communists made common cause with a group towards whom, during the interwar years, they had felt only hostility—Serbian nationalist irregular fighters, or "Chetniks."[46] How the German army units on the spot reacted to this threat reveals much about what motivated them.

The travails the 704th Infantry Division faced during 1941, and its response, are the next chapter's main focus.

CHAPTER 5

Islands in an Insurgent Sea

The 704th Infantry Division in Serbia

B RIGADIER GENERAL HEINRICH BOROWSKI, the 704th Infantry
Division's commander, was born in eastern Prussia in 1880 to
the family of a police inspector. He served as an officer in the 1st Field
Artillery Regiment during the Great War, firstly on the western front,
then on the eastern front from April 1915 onward. Aside from a month
serving under the German military administration in Warsaw in September 1915, he remained on the eastern front until January 1917. After
fighting on the western front in 1917 and 1918, he remained a career
officer throughout the interwar years, and commanded two artillery
regiments in succession from 1939 onward.[1] It was a reasonably distinguished career. It was no preparation for the type of warfare he and his
troops would face in Yugoslavia.

For during summer 1941 the 704th Infantry Division would face levels of resistance that threatened not only the Axis occupation structure,
but also the very survival of the division itself. The intense pressures
which the 704th's officers and men faced on the ground, the mind-set
of the military institution to which they belonged, and the perceptions
of their own commander all played a part in determining how they
responded.

Initially, the 704th and the other occupation divisions enjoyed relatively benign circumstances in Yugoslavia. The great majority of the 704th's troops, its main infantry force comprising the 724th and 734th Infantry Regiments, had been born between 1908 and 1913.[2] The division described its equipment as "complete", the makeup of its personnel "good." Its sickness rate was just over 5 percent.[3] As yet, there was little sign of unrest. The 704th was especially well disposed towards the region's "friendly and obliging" Muslim population.[4] In late May, after releasing hostages it had been holding to help ensure the population's good behavior, it detected a further improvement in the popular mood.[5] So relaxed was the atmosphere that in early June the 704th permitted its personnel to bring reliable civilians along to assist on hunting expeditions. They were forbidden to carry weapons, but this suggests German troops had been so at ease with the locals that they had been entrusting them with weapons before.[6] Indeed, the division warned its troops that "social or private relations with the natives may not develop from relations formed in the course of hunting expeditions. Necessary arrangements (for the expeditions) may not be discussed in private homes."[7]

All across Serbia, the Germans were in reasonably sanguine mood that spring. Serbia Command's intelligence section observed that the population "acknowledged German order and the disciplined behaviour of Wehrmacht personnel." It also noted the population's relief that it had not been left at the mercy of the Hungarians,[8] for the particularly brutish behavior of many of the Habsburg Army's Hungarian troops had marked Serbs' collective memory of the last war. Hunger, always likely to turn a subjugated people against its occupiers, was being headed off by food transports laden with flour and sugar. The work of Serbia Command's intelligence section in building up favorable German- and Serbian-language newspapers was just one way in which the Germans sought to exploit this favorable climate.[9]

It helped, of course, that German troops were not yet mishandling the population.[10] Immediately after the invasion, divisional and higher commands ordered the troops to behave correctly and refrain from plunder. The Army High Command declared on April 21 that "requisitions are to be restricted to what is absolutely necessary, and it is essential that they be carried out by officers in exchange for payment or an IOU note . . .

Anyone who, in the course of service, maliciously or willingly damages the population's property will be punished for plunder in accordance with Article 132 of the Military Penal Code."[11] Both command levels also wanted to impress the population with German discipline, the better to dispose the population towards the Germans and win its cooperation.[12]

Such a spectacle apparently belies German counterinsurgency's singularly ferocious image. Yet it was not the France of 1914 providing inspiration here, but the France of 1940. During the campaign in the West that year, and the military occupation that followed, the German army generally treated civilians with considerable restraint.[13] The contrast with its conduct in Poland was startling. Some of the contrast was due to commanders' concerns for their troops' discipline. Much of it was due to the fact that, in Nazi terms, the French were not an inferior race like the Poles. And while the Serbs, as southern Slavs, sat lower on the Nazi racial scale than the French, they sat higher than the Poles. The Germans in Serbia also had a simpler reason to suppress terroristic urges: they had yet to face meaningful resistance. Even officers schooled in German counter-insurgency doctrine were unlikely to rain terror on civilians without first feeling "provoked." They were even less likely to do so when, in contrast to 1914, their superiors were not inciting them.

There was a sinister exception to this picture, one that presaged a campaign of racial mass killing soon to unfold across all Serbia. This campaign would coagulate with similarly murderous "initiatives" across Axis-occupied Europe that summer and autumn. Together, they would culminate in the emergence of the Nazis' "Final Solution" of the "problem" of European Jewry.[14] This was a process which, in Serbia, would become closely intertwined with the Wehrmacht's counter-insurgency campaign.

From the occupation's start, Wehrmacht authorities were instrumental in marking out and discriminating against Serbia's twenty-three thousand Jews.[15] The first steps were piecemeal. But within weeks, the measures being enacted—including dismissal from public and private operations, transfer of goods and property to "Aryan" ownership, ghettoization, forced labor, and the wearing of the yellow star—were being implemented much more systematically.[16] The Wehrmacht inaugurated such measures because they satisfied not just its anti-Semitic proclivities, but also its practical needs. For instance, seizing Jewish property freed up accommodation for its own troops.[17] All branches of the German occupation regime were complicit in these acts. But it was the Wehrmacht Commander in Serbia who not only approved and oversaw all of them, but who also, within weeks of the occupation commencing, had put them on that much more systematic footing.[18] The historian Walter Manoschek writes that "in registering the Jews, marking them out with yellow armbands bearing the inscription 'Jew,' imposing special taxes on them, 'Aryanizing,' imposing trust companies on Jewish firms, excluding them from public life and driving them from society, the German occupiers had concluded the first phase of robbing the Jews in Serbia of their rights and possessions."[19] On May 30, Serbia Command issued a proclamation authorizing similar treatment for Serbia's Sinti and Roma.[20]

In the 704th's jurisdiction, anti-Semitic measures affected not only Serbian Jews, but also several hundred Jewish refugees, mostly from Austria, who were interned in the town of Šabac. In July these Jews were set to work in the area command headquarters, the local hospital, and German officers' private quarters.[21] It was the *Kommandanturen*, rather than the occupation divisions, that had direct responsibility for enacting the relevant measures. In the 704th's jurisdiction in late May, for instance, the town commandant in Valjevo forbade the troops to visit the town's Jewish dentist, and announced that "all Jews in Valjevo and its environs have been instructed by the mayor and the local authorities to wear a yellow armband from 1 June onward."[22]

A letter from Corporal Gerhard Reichert of the 11th Infantry Division conveyed the wretchedness to which the Serbian Jews were already being reduced. He described how "all the Jews have been penned up. In the towns they've even put aside quarters for them, which they're absolutely forbidden to leave. The roads heading out have been blocked off with a tangle of wire, and a guard stands before it. I wouldn't want to be a Jew."[23] Not every soldier followed anti-Semitic dictates as completely as they might have done: in late June, Serbia Command's operations section complained that some troops, housed in formerly Jewish homes earmarked for their accommodation, were still allowing Jews to stay in them.[24] But the corrosive effect of years of anti-Semitic indoctrination of

German soldiers is easy to imagine. Corporal Ludwig Bauer of Supply Battalion 563 demonstrated it when he wrote that "yesterday there was a raid on the Jews where we were; they were all hauled off to the edge of the town. It was really interesting to see what specimens they are. Truly the scum of humanity."[25] The Wehrmacht reinforced the effect by subjecting its troops to ongoing anti-Semitic propaganda; the 704th Infantry Division's troops, for instance, were provided with cinema showings of the anti-Semitic propaganda film *Jud Süss*.[26]

And though the 704th Infantry Division, and the other German occupation divisions operating on Serbian soil, were not directly involved in this first wave of discriminatory measures, they nevertheless helped to facilitate it—simply by allowing the *Kommandanturen* to enact such measures without hindrance or comment. And the 704th's example indicates that the divisions were also seeing to it that their own troops were being conditioned to approve of such measures. This in turn would help provide the psychological preconditions for the occupation divisions' direct involvement in a later, more terrible phase of the persecution of the Serbian Jews. It was this phase, a shift from discrminatory measures to scapegoating Jews for insurgent attacks and victimizing them in mass reprisals, that would become so closely intertwined with the Wehrmacht's security campaign.

And even this early on the 704th Infantry Division, like the German occupiers generally, could be heavy-handed towards the wider Serbian population also. The 704th's divisional command declared early in June "that interference by the population or attacks on Wehrmacht personnel or property (must) be punished on the spot with suitably just but harsh measures."[27] A divisional order of a fortnight later urged the "punishment," by what means it did not specify, of civilians caught with radios.[28] As long as Serbia remained largely quiescent, the troops were not going to interpret such imprecise exhortations as a blank check for brutality. But they might do so were resistance to flare up.

And though insurgent attacks on German personnel were very rare during the occupation's opening weeks, the Germans' reaction to such cases was an ominous straw in the wind. On April 18, the day after Yugoslavia's capitulation, the Waffen-SS Division "Das Reich" executed thirty-six

Serbs in retaliation for the shooting of one of its own men. The shooting of a German officer in the village of Donji Dobrić three days later brought the village's complete destruction and a fierce directive from Field Marshal von Weichs, commander of the Second Army. Weichs ordered that, wherever an armed band appeared, men from that area capable of bearing arms were to be seized and shot, and their corpses hanged for public display, unless they could prove they had no connection with the "bandits." Hostages were to be seized in advance. Then on May 19, Weichs stipulated that in the future one hundred Serbs should be shot for every German soldier who "came to harm" in any Serb attack. As yet, German units in the field chose not to go that far. But Weichs' 1:100 order would soon prove to be the most ominous straw in the wind of all.[29]

And Weichs' use of the term *bandit* is instructive; only in summer 1942 would *Reichsführer*-SS Heinrich Himmler himself order the term to replace *partisan* in official communication.[30] Although the term was frequently being employed by German commands before this date, Weichs and the German army formations serving in Yugoslavia were particularly quick to employ it. It is not only likely that, as with Himmler in 1942, they were seeking to dehumanize the insurgents in their men's eyes. It is also likely that the region's long history of banditry was influencing their perception of the enemy they were facing.

By the eve of the invasion of the Soviet Union the 704th's unease was increasing, as sightings of "bandit" groups grew more frequent. June 20, two days before the invasion, brought reports that irregulars were causing unrest and unsettling the population east of the main Valjevo-Užice road.[31] Some attacks, such as those around the towns of Kačan and Kosjerić, were the work of civilian marauders.[32] Their mere presence stirred the German military's traditional abhorrence of armed civilians. Around the same time LXV Corps urged its divisions to form *Jagdkommandos*, well-equipped and highly mobile "hunter groups." Such units were designed to carry out reconnaissance patrols or larger "hunting expeditions" to locate, pursue, and annihilate irregular groups.[33] Forming viable hunter groups from the paltry forces available would prove difficult in the extreme. But this was what was now expected.

In fact, the potential danger to security was even more serious. So rapidly had the Yugoslav army collapsed that many of its troops had never even been taken prisoner; instead they had simply gone home. In areas where Yugoslav army units had dissolved themselves thus, vast quantities of small arms remained unaccounted for and ripe for seizure by would-be irregulars.[34] Before the invasion of the Soviet Union, the irregular fighters—as distinct from outright bandits or marauders—who were most at large in Yugoslavia were known as Chetniks.

Chetniks had had a centuries-old involvement in the region's conflicts right up to the Great War. By 1918 they enjoyed status as a leading patriotic group, and considerable political influence. By World War II, however, the movement had fragmented. Initial Chetnik attacks on the Axis occupation regime were the work of uncoordinated individual bands. But there were two larger Chetnik groups of note. The first was a stridently pro-Axis group, a few thousand strong, under Kosta Pećanac.[35] The second group, comprising only thirty men initially but soon to expand rapidly,[36] was based in the Ravna Gora region under Draza Mihailović. Mihailović was a colonel of the former Yugoslav army who, in contrast to Pećanac, had resolved to form an anti-Axis underground following Yugoslavia's collapse. Yet he and his forces were able to establish themselves largely because they quietly built up their organization and numbers while keeping their heads down.[37] Thus, crucial as the Mihailović Chetniks' role in the conflict would eventually become, it was not they but the smaller, uncoordinated Chetnik bands who most disrupted the occupation until Barbarossa.

Already then, the remit of the 704th and its fellow divisions was widening beyond guarding railways. June brought their first protestations at their low combat effectiveness. Already at the end of May, XI Corps, a frontline formation on the point of departing Yugoslavia, asserted that the occupation divisions' training was so poor that all other considerations should be subordinate to it. It also asserted that the divisions were too weak to execute even their static security duties effectively.[38] The state of their equipment became parlous also, with all divisions suffering alarming shortages of guns and ammunition.[39]

The rump state of Serbia, with its sixty thousand square kilometers and 3.8 million inhabitants, was occupied by barely twenty-five thousand German military and police personnel—one man, in other words, for every 2.4 square kilometers and 152 inhabitants.[40] Unsurprisingly, the 704th's biggest problem was that its static units were spread far apart, sometimes to company level, and connected only by an often execrable road system. It also lacked sufficient men to operate its horse-drawn transports.[41] Its more southerly units had some access to rail transport but reaped only limited benefit from it. Fierce storms and endemic theft blighted the Serbian postal service. If the telephone system failed too—and the 704th feared it would, given its signals company's paltry resources and personnel—then the division would be wholly reliant on radio.[42]

Meanwhile, boredom and fatigue were already beginning to erode the troops' discipline. At the end of May General Borowski was aghast to observe a column of soldiers marching through a village, some wearing only swimming trunks. He remarked, understatedly, that "images like these damage the troops' standing."[43] On July 21, divisional command was appalled by several cases of soldiers going unpunished after they had failed to get themselves screened following sex with local women.[44] At the end of that month, the latrines in the 704th's jurisdiction were found in an "indescribable condition," with all the threat of infection this posed. The division pledged to punish future infractions by canceling leave.[45]

These were not trivial matters. Officers would have known from their Great War experience of the damage unchecked discipline could wreak upon soldiers' fighting power. And if indiscipline did go unchecked, it could eventually develop into the kind of wild behavior that debilitated relations with the population—relations neither higher command nor divisional command were yet prepared to endanger unnecessarily. General Borowski demanded that plunder cases be thoroughly reported—a clear sign that such cases were increasing.[46] But the troops seem to have ignored him.[47] And discipline problems went wider than the 704th; LXV Corps declared on June 20 that "the tasks of the Category 15 divisions under command of LXV Corps can only be carried out in the long term if the troops' discipline and manner towards the population are *first-class*. Discipline manifests itself in attitude, appearance, and proper recognition of authority."[48] All three were clearly suffering, but "the population must have and *retain* respect for the Wehrmacht."[49]

June 22 brought the German invasion of the Soviet Union, and with it an entirely new dimension to the burgeoning unrest in Yugoslavia. There was an almost immediate call from Stalin for the Europe-wide Communist movement to take up arms in the antifascist struggle.

The Yugoslav Communists, under their leader Josep Broz—"Tito"—numbered eight thousand members in spring 1941. This was not a huge number, but it was dramatically higher than the fifteen hundred they had counted at the end of 1937.[50] The Communists had achieved this growth, despite their prohibition since 1920, thanks to their increased contact with the labor movement, their "popular front" strategy of forging links with bourgeois opposition politicians, and their infiltration of nonpolitical groups such as sports clubs and cultural societies.[51] The Communists were also highly disciplined and, after years of persecution by the Yugoslav police, seasoned in evasion and subterfuge. They would harness these qualities to form and organize the Partisan detachments that would come to embody the Yugoslav Communist movement's military strength.[52] Tito wanted a full-blown uprising both to drive out the occupiers and attain national power for the Communists in postwar Yugoslavia. He also wanted a central staff to lead the uprising. Accordingly, on April 10, 1941, the Central Committee of the Yugoslav Communist Party established a military committee headed by Tito himself.[53] All depended, however, on when the signal to rise up was given by the Soviet Union. Moscow gave it on July 1:

> The hour has struck when Communists are obliged to raise the people in open struggle against the occupiers. Do not lose a single minute organizing Partisan detachments and igniting a Partisan war in the enemy's rear. Set fire to war factories, warehouses, fuel dumps (oil, petrol, etc.), aerodromes; destroy and demolish railways, telegraphs and telephone lines; prohibit the transport of troops and munitions (war materials in general). Organize the peasantry to hide grain, drive livestock into the forests. It is absolutely essential to terrorize the enemy by all means so that he will feel himself inside a besieged fortress.[54]

As a precursor to driving the Axis out of Yugoslavia completely, and as a foundation for a postwar Communist order, Tito sought to establish liberated territories and administer them through people's liberation committees (NOOs). It was in Croatia, with its more advanced industry and labor movement, that the prewar Yugoslav Communist organization had been strongest. Hence, Croats would predominate among the Partisan leadership throughout the war. But Tito came to believe that western Serbia, with its hilly, wooded terrain, Communist-leaning industrial centers, and tradition of resistance to foreign invasion—not to mention the arrival there, over summer 1941, of huge numbers of Serb refugees uprooted by the Ustasha—would be the ideal region in which to commence the revolt.[55] The Communists' hubris was fueled by their belief that the withdrawal of German forces to the East heralded the occupiers' imminent collapse as it had done in 1918, and that the Red Army was about to attack to liberate its "brother Slavs."[56] Yet the Communists could hope neither to cajole nor persuade large sections of the population to revolt unless the conditions the population faced were intolerable. Fortunately for the Communists, however, this was precisely what was now happening.

The uprising erupted in July. It received by far its greatest boost not from the Communists, but from the hundreds of thousands of ethnic Serbs expelled from or fleeing from the atavistic Ustasha savagery now convulsing the NDH.

The Ustasha had been discriminating against Serbs, Jews, and Sinti and Roma since the NDH's founding. By June, it was exploiting freshly passed legislation authorizing lethal measures against purported "enemies of the people and state" to justify the next, far more rabid phase of its ethnic campaign. The Ustasha claimed that the Serbs in the NDH were "squatters," who had been deposited on ancestral Croatian territory by their Ottoman or Habsburg masters and had subjected the Croats to centuries of cruelty. This was a vast oversimplification of a complex, centuries-old interaction between the two peoples. The Ustasha also depicted the Serbs as the bloodstained hatchet men of the Belgrade government during the interwar years, with thousands of Croat deaths on their hands. Granted, Croats had been discriminated against shamefully over the past two decades, and there had been some deadly if small-scale incidents between the two peoples. But claims of a murderous ethnic campaign were grossly exaggerated. Yet rewriting history in this way, the Ustasha believed, would enable it to publicly justify what it was about to unleash. The Ustasha-controlled media and, shamefully, large portions of the Croatian Catholic clergy propagated such distortions enthusiastically.[57]

The Ustasha did not intend committing genocide on the Serbs. It did intend to fatally dislocate Serbian community life within the NDH, exterminating a portion of the Serbs, driving others beyond its borders, and forcibly converting the rest to Roman Catholicism.[58] Thus, from summer 1941 the Ustasha orchestrated the brutal expulsion or barbaric slaughter of whole Serb communities. It also herded thousands more Serbs into newly established concentration camps, mass killing centers in all but name, the most infamous of which was the camp at Jasenovac. By February 1942, the German Foreign Ministry in Agram estimated with some alarm, the Ustasha had butchered approximately three hundred thousand Serbs.[59]

Matters were made worse by the demographic domino effect of Himmler's misconceived attempt to "Germanize" northern Yugoslavia. Hitler and Himmler sought to expel nearly a quarter of a million Slovenes from their homeland to make way for ethnic German settlers there. The Ustasha was willing to make room for them in the NDH, believing this would excuse "legally" expelling even more Serbs to make way for them. The Germans and Croats agreed terms for an "orderly" transfer on June 4, 1941. But the Germans soon realized that the Ustasha was actually expelling up to five times more Serbs into Serbia, under the most brutal and inhuman conditions, than the number of Slovenes arriving in the NDH. In late August the German authorities in Serbia, fearful of the spiraling practical problems and the gathering backlash from the Serbian population, refused to accept any more Serbs from the NDH; some weeks later, Himmler ordered a halt to the Slovene deportations also. But thousands of the Serbs spared expulsion from the NDH would now be massacred by the Ustasha instead.[60]

In Kozara in Bosnia, the Serb uprising actually preceded the Ustasha's murderous campaign. In Montenegro, the revolt was caused by the population's particular grievances against its Italian occupiers. But for the most part, Serbs in the NDH, and many in Serbia itself, rose up in response to the killings to preserve their existence within the bloody ethnic bear pit that was now rapidly evolving. The main revolt spread

between July 7 and 27 from Krupanj in western Serbia, through Montenegro, Slovenia, Croatia, and Bosnia.[61]

Many German and Italian officials were horrified at the Ustasha killings, if not necessarily for moral reasons then certainly because of the
chaos they threatened to unleash. On June 26 Pavelić was prevailed
upon to issue a decree condemning those guilty of "excesses." Yet apart
from the arrest of a few "bad apples," and the execution of fewer still, the
Pavelić regime did nothing.[62] And neither in 1941 nor later did the highest German military and diplomatic representatives in the NDH actually
take decisive action to try to halt the Ustasha.

This was partly because they knew Hitler would not have supported
them. Hitler's own motives for supporting the NDH were power-politi-
cal in part. The NDH was, theoretically, a sovereign state. Being seen to
interfere "excessively" in its affairs might therefore play badly with Germany's other allies. Hitler was also reluctant to offend Italian sensitivi-
ties by intervening too stridently in a region that was, officially, within
the Italian sphere of interest.[63] But Hitler also harbored a distinct soft
spot for the Ustasha. This was partly because of their shared Habsburg
heritage, but primarily because he approved of the Ustasha's extrem-
ism. Indeed, in June 1941 he positively egged Pavelić on, counseling the
Croatian leader to pursue an "intolerant" policy for the next fifty years.[64]
Hitler also valued what he regarded as the Ustasha regime's steadfast
loyalty to Germany. This was a score on which it contrasted with some
other collaborationist regimes, such as the democratic government in
occupied Denmark. Finally, as the war in general became ever more
protracted, Ribbentrop was increasingly loath to present Hitler with
any bad news. He thus concealed from the Führer the full extent of the
mayhem the Ustasha's campaign was spawning.[65] Nor were the two men
whom Hitler had appointed to directly deal with the Pavelić regime best
suited to challenging it effectively.

Hitler had installed Lieutenant General Edmund Glaise von Horstenau, a former Austro-Hungarian officer, as German General in
Agram, charged with representing Wehrmacht interests to the Ustasha
government.[66] Glaise was in fact very critical of the NDH government,
but there were limits to how far he was prepared to act against it. For one
thing, he recognized the benefits the foundation of the new state had

brought to many of his former colleagues from the old Royal and Imperial Army. He was also united with the Croats against the policies of the Italians. In particular, Glaise failed to argue for stronger action, such as replacing the Pavelić regime with a fully empowered Wehrmacht military commander. This was partly for fear that his own position as German General in Agram might become superfluous were Hitler to accept such a recommendation, and partly for fear that he might be sacked were Hitler to reject it. This was something that Glaise, whose private finances were deeply problematic, was especially anxious to avoid. Nor, as time went by, did Glaise harbor any desire to be appointed military commander himself. For he sought to remain sufficiently disassociated from the proliferating war crimes that would, over time, be committed by German troops in the NDH. From 1943 onward, as the tide of war turned against Germany, this concern assumed pressing significance.[67]

The failure of Siegfried Kasche, the German Foreign Ministry's representative in Agram, to challenge the Ustasha effectively is more easily explained. A thuggish SA man, Kasche instinctively approved of the Ustasha's aims and methods and could usually be relied upon to defend the regime at every turn. Glaise recorded that Kasche had once described Croatia as "the purest paradise."[68] As this quotation suggests, Kasche was also somewhat short on gray matter; the main reason he got the job of Foreign Ministry representative was that, like many of Ribbentrop's appointees, he was a useful check on the SS. This was an organization Kasche hated, understandably enough, because it had tried to murder him in the Night of the Long Knives.[69]

Though the Communists did not start the Serb revolt, they seized its reins as best they could. And it was indeed the Communists, not Mihailović's Chetniks, who were best-placed to do this. The cadres that spearheaded Communist efforts to coordinate and control the revolt had ample experience of subterfuge; as Turner's Administrative Office recorded on 23 July, "as soon as the German invasion of Russia was announced on the radio, a large portion of the known Communist functionaries in Belgrade disappeared into the countryside. The police action which was immediately ordered was therefore only able to capture a fraction of them."[70] Students, workers, and artisans comprised the bulk of Communist support in Serbia. Throwing open the Partisan movement to non-Communists, a step the Yugoslav Communists took on August 10, enabled the revolt to take wing even more emphatically.[71] By now the Communists claimed twenty-one Partisan detachments, with eight thousand members, in Serbia alone.[72] An important component of the Partisans' fighting power at this point was the combat-seasoned Spanish Civil War veterans who gravitated to their cause.[73]

The Communists organized their Partisan units into companies, battalions, and larger detachments, with political commissars attached to units of company size and above. In September, they formed the first NOOs in the areas the Partisans had liberated. The largest and most prominent such area was centered on Užice in northwest Serbia. The NOOs were tasked with mobilizing troops and supplies from villages and towns. This made it possible to supply the Partisans, at least much of the time, through orderly requisition and taxation rather than plunder. The NOOs in the "Užice Republic" also redistributed abandoned and sequestered land and property, together with land and property from accused collaborators. By such means, the Partisans not only built vital support among the local peasantry—in addition to the many peasants among the thousands of destitutes and NDH refugees who poured into the region—but also began laying the foundations for revolutionary change. The power of the NOOs in wartime Yugoslavia would eventually extend to managing local agriculture, performing judicial functions, and organizing education.[74]

The Mihailović Chetniks appealed largely to rural Serbs, former Yugoslav army soldiers seeking to avoid a POW camp, and ethnic Serbs who were either fleeing or had been expelled from the NDH.[75] But they faced obstacles to widening their appeal further. In particular, their lack of a cadre system, or of a proper track record of political activism, prevented them from spreading propaganda anything like as effectively as the Communists. Instead, they relied more on simple verbal propaganda and supportive BBC broadcasts.[76] Mihailović also had immense difficulty controlling "his" Chetnik units, compromising a great deal with his commanders in the field and granting them extensive autonomy.[77] The movement's military potential was similarly limited. Its forces were divided into small, loosely organized detachments, with a combined operative strength in autumn 1941 of five to ten thousand fighters, but as late as November only a fraction were capable of engaging in combat.[78] Moreover, the Mihailović Chetniks as a whole suffered, as did the Partisans initially, from chronic shortages of suitable weaponry.[79]

Until early August the Communists directed the revolt at the collaborationist Aćimović government, particularly its gendarmerie, rather than at the Germans.[80] Selecting softer targets inevitably brought the Partisans greater success, and helped the revolt to mushroom rapidly into a national uprising.[81] Initially the forces the Germans themselves committed to combating the rebels directly comprised Einsatzgruppe Yugoslavia and Reserve Police Battalion 64. Wehrmacht troops themselves were only used occasionally.

By early August, however, this was changing. This was not least because, following an attack on a tank on the Valjevo-Užice road in the 704th Infantry Division's jurisdiction, German army troops were themselves now being targeted.[82] The Partisans switched tactics in this way in an effort to gain better-quality weapons, greater recognition from the population, and more fuel for the revolt.[83]

LXV Corps' summer communiqués convey how rapidly the uprising spread. By early August, it reported, Communist bands were "terrorizing" farmers and "robbing" communities, attacking Serbian gendarmerie stations, and firing on lone military vehicles. In the last ten days of August alone, Serbia Command recorded 135 attacks, whether on railways, telephone lines, road bridges, industrial installations, gendarmerie stations and other public offices, or Wehrmacht personnel. Most of the agricultural population, according to Serbia Command, were not actually siding with the "bandits." But nor would they embrace the Wehrmacht unless the troops could overcome their paucity on the ground and establish a lasting, effective presence that protected collaborating civilians against Communist strikes.[84]

Given the revolt's speed and scale, and the view, widespread among Serbs, that revolt against the occupiers was the only means of staying the Ustasha's bloodied hand, it is likely that farmers and rural communities were cooperating more willingly with the Partisans than LXV Corps was acknowledging. Nevertheless, given the Communists' brutality towards reluctant and "suspect" elements during the Montenegrin revolt,[85] LXV Corps' assertions of Partisan ruthlessness are unlikely to have been wide of the mark. Whatever the reality, however, the scale of the uprising alarmed the Germans in the extreme.

The Germans sought to counter the uprising at every level. At the highest level, they disbanded the Aćimović administration. The administration had attempted to quell the uprising in mid-August by appealing to the Serbian people to assist the authorities against the Communist Partisans, and appealing to all rebels to return to their homes within eighteen days. Both pleas proved fruitless. Moreover, there were indications that Pećanac Chetniks had begun deserting to the rebels. On August 29 the recently appointed Commander in Serbia, General Danckelman, had a new Serbian government installed, under the anti-Communist strongman General Nedić.[86]

Nedić, Danckelmann hoped, would command high levels of respect not only among the population generally, but more specifically among those sections of the population, particularly former Yugoslav army officers, who were attracted to the Mihailović Chetniks. But although Nedić held strongly anti-Communist and anti-Semitic views, he was no straightforward quisling, and took some persuading to assume leadership of the new government. He also managed to wring some concessions out of the Germans. For instance, he was permitted to create a new body, the Serbian State Guard, combining the Serbian gendarmerie with several thousand Pećanac Chetniks—transferred to the gendarmerie as auxiliaries—in a seventeen thousand-strong force. He also got General Danckelmann to promise that reprisals would be directed only against the guilty.[87] As the uprising mushroomed, however, the Germans would renege on this particular pledge. While Danckelmann himself may well have been sincere when he made it, his room for maneuver was constrained by his superior in Athens, Field Marshal List. List, for his part, was deeply skeptical as to the merits of engaging the Serbs.[88]

In the field, LXV Corps urgently requested more mobile troops, accompanied by interpreters, "who are to instruct the population that the troops are there to protect the farmers and their property, and therefore expect their help!"[89] Such appeals were part of a wider German propaganda effort during this period; extensive responsibility for propaganda lay with Section S, a branch of the Wehrmacht propaganda department of the Armed Forces High Command. Section S employed newspapers, public speakers, and other propaganda methods to recruit ethnic Germans as auxiliaries. It also oversaw production of propaganda newspapers for Serbian readers.

The section sought to put a positive spin on conditions in the country, opining that, "if the current situation does seem somewhat tense, experience leads one to believe that the Serbs will be profoundly sobered when the sheer scale of the German victory in the East becomes clear."[90] And General Turner's administrative office, though scathing of German propaganda's initial efforts in Serbia, remained optimistic that popular Communist support could be strangled at birth if the Germans cooperated fully with the collaborationist regime. Turner's office thus gave the Serbian Minister of the Interior "an opportunity to develop a truly effective counter-propaganda campaign. Leaflets were distributed, representatives sent into the villages and so on. These actions had great success; it can be claimed that the Serbian population in general has not been swept up by the Communist wave."[91]

But Turner, a particularly keen advocate of engagement with the collaborationist government, and Section S were being too optimistic. The SD, reporting at the end of June, perceived a strong Communist propaganda drive across Serbia: "well over half the population, particularly in Belgrade, has a Soviet-friendly attitude."[92] And Field Marshal List perceived that the revolt was rapidly developing into a full-scale national uprising.[93]

In any case, if the population were to be receptive to Axis propaganda then the Germans had to demonstrate that they could actually defeat the uprising. Having more troops at its disposal, LXV Corps maintained, would enable the occupation divisions to assemble truck-borne hunter groups to take the fight to the rebels. As things stood, the divisions lacked both trucks and men. Most of the available trucks, the Administrative Office maintained in late July, were "mousetraps"; their need to overload in order to transport sufficient troop numbers made them sitting targets. The 717th Infantry Division described the state of its trucks as "wholly inadequate."[94]

In northwest Serbia, where the revolt was strongest, the Germans effectively relinquished control of the villages and countryside—with its craggy mountains, deep river valleys, and impenetrable forests—and concentrated on holding principal towns and patrolling major road and rail links. But in their fear of being overwhelmed they were already exacting fierce reprisals. LXV Corps frantically urged "more hunter groups, bigger operations, brutal and vigorous action, burning of buildings and villages from which Wehrmacht personnel are attacked, ruthless fire in combat, hanging of captured saboteurs."[95] One thousand Serbian citizens had already fallen victim to reprisals by the end of August.[96] Calls from Hitler himself helped drive the killing; on July 24 Serbia Command noted an order "from the Armed Forces High Command, issued via Wehrmacht Command South-East, in which the Führer and Supreme Commander of the Armed Forces voiced his expectation that the Commander in Serbia will extinguish all trouble spots through brutal action and the harshest reprisals."[97]

Initially, the bulk of the executions was carried out by units of Einsatzgruppe Yugoslavia—which, with their small size, usually assigned the actual shooting to men of the Serbian gendarmerie.[98] The principal victims were Communists and male Jews—the next step in that further escalation in the process that would eventually see the Serbian Jews virtually wiped from the land.[99] In one such reprisal, one hundred Jews and twenty-two Communists were executed in Belgrade on July 29, in retaliation for an arson attack on German trucks by a sixteen-year-old Jewish boy.[100] In fact, much of the groundwork for a "targeted" reprisal campaign had been set by the army leadership on the eve of the Balkan campaign. On April 2 General Halder, chief of staff at the Army High Command, had himself directed that the SS and police should seize Jews and Communists in the newly-occupied territory as potential "dangers to security."[101]

Though there undoubtedly was an ideological motive for targeting Jews and Communists as reprisal victims, the Germans had other motives also. Aside from the fact that Communist Partisans were heading the national uprising, there was also a calculating reason for directing reprisals at Jews and Communists. In early August, after Colonel von Stockhausen, the area commandant in Užice, ordered eighty-one Serbs executed in retaliation for the death of one German policeman, the Serbian gendarmerie began refusing to shoot its own people.[102] The Germans feared, at least during the uprising's early stage, that such indiscriminate killing might fatally damage relations with the general population—not to mention waste the lives of potentially useful informers. By contrast, directing reprisals at narrow sections of the population was less likely to provoke damaging protest from the rest of it.[103] Furthermore, as Section S opined, the Germans could still cow the general population anyway—for, by victimizing Jews and Communists, they could also demonstrate their *capacity* for terror.[104]

And to assume that the German administration in Serbia saw Jews and Communists as separate categories of enemy is to miss the point. In Serbia, as in the Soviet Union, German policy *equated* Jews with Communists. Indeed, the SS and police in Serbia judged that labelling Jews as Communists was a convenient, indeed automatic way of justifying their liquidation.[105] And for the Wehrmacht, Section S sought to ingrain the image of the Jew as the enemy among both German personnel and pro-Axis Serbian groups. Its message was that, while the Communist Partisans were the main perpetrators of unrest, it was the Jews who were the puppet-masters of the Communist-led uprising.[106]

Indeed, the Wehrmacht was complicit from the start in seizing and killing Jews and Communists, not to mention considerable numbers of Sinti and Roma, and became more complicit over time. Einsatzgruppe Yugoslavia cooperated especially closely with the administrative office, which, though headed by an SS general, was integral to Serbia Command. The Wehrmacht's own Secret Field Police and Field Gendarmerie, as well as Reserve Police Battalion 64, became directly involved in the killings. German army personnel were given the task of handing over "suspects"—earmarked reprisal victims in all but name—to any one of these bodies. Within the 704th Infantry Division's jurisdiction during July, for instance, the 724th Infantry Regiment reported that it had assisted the Secret Field Police and the Field Gendarmerie in seizing suspected Communists; thirteen were arrested, for example, on the night of July 8.[107]

Some army *Kommandanturen* were already participating in mass executions themselves, as well as directing the SS and police to carry them out.[108] One instance involved the commander of one of the 704th's regiments. On July 18 Brigadier-General Adalbert Lontschar, commander of the 724th Infantry Regiment, was fired upon in his staff car, "Lasalle," in the woods near the village of Razna on a journey back from Valjevo. Three shots went into the car from above, only one of them causing any injury to its occupants. But because the densely wooded terrain prevented the culprits from being seen, the local district command, in cooperation with the SS and police and the Serbian gendarmerie, had fifty-two Jews, Communists, and other individuals shot. This was retaliation for an attack in which no one had actually been killed.[109] And at least one unit of the 724th was already bloodying its own hands substantially; an operation southwest of Užice on August 17 involving the regiment's first company saw fifteen Communists shot in combat and twenty-three executed afterwards, "nineteen of whom were hanged at the railway station in Uzici [*sic*] because they had been supplying bandits in the Gradina (internment) camp with provisions."[110]

On July 17, Einsatzgruppe personnel were distributed as "security advisers" among the army's four area commands. And on August 13, LXV Corps instructed its battalion commanders to assemble mixed hunter groups. These could incorporate personnel not only from the German army, but also from the SS and police, as well as from the Serbian gendarmerie. The establishment of such groups made it more likely still that army personnel, this time from the occupation divisions rather than the *Kommandanturen*, would become more extensively involved in the killing of Jews and Communists.[111]

Nevertheless, establishing just how far the divisions' troops were actually involved in such killing, whether in collusion with other agencies or not, can be far from straightforward. For one thing, the division-level and regional command-level sources for summer 1941 do not specify which hunter groups mixed army and SS and police personnel. Presumably many would indeed have had mixed personnel, simply because of the important role the SS and police played in seizing suspects. Irrespective of the groups' composition, however, it is unclear just how far they were actually targeting or killing Jews and Communists.

This is apparent in a report of 10 October. Here LXV Corps recorded that, between August 14 and September 26, all hunter groups across its subordinate divisions had between them shot thirty-three Communists and arrested another twenty-nine. These Communists, one assumes, were unarmed civilians rather than actual insurgents, because LXV Corps recorded the ninety-three insurgents its hunter groups had reportedly killed under the separate category of "bandits." LXV Corps also distinguished between Communists and "suspects" more generally; the hunter groups, it reported, had arrested one hundred and thirty-eight such persons. [112]

It is distinctly possible that Jews were being mixed in with any or all of these categories. The particularly strong suspicion arises that the hunter groups, in line with the practice of the SS and police in Serbia, were using the term "Communist" as a covering label for Jews.[113] Indeed, this consideration arouses a more general suspicion as to the racial identity of a great many of the "Communists" who were being killed during the summer months.

However, the majority of killing operations which divisional troops carried out—the majority of these, in turn, being the work of those same hunter groups on whom LXV Corps compiled its October 10 report— were smaller than those in which the *Kommandanturen* were involved. This was due, if nothing else, to the easier access to interned Jews and Communists which town- and city-based *Kommandanturen* possessed. Some examples of large-scale reprisals involving the *Kommandanturen* have been cited already. A further example is the actions of the area command in Belgrade during August and September. Over the course of these two months, the area command cooperated with the SS and police in a sequence of major raids on suspect Communists, Communist leaders, and Communist Party offices. On September 29, the day after one such raid, an "attack" on German soldiers in Belgrade—the report makes no mention of whether any German soldier had actually died as a result—brought the execution of one hundred and fifty Communists in reprisal.[114]

Yet by October, the Serbian national uprising having mushroomed alarmingly and German attitudes having hardened further, divisional troops were themselves more extensively involved in the seizing and killing of increasingly large numbers of Jews and Communists.[115] Those summer Wehrmacht decrees that had victimized such groups, directed army units to collude ever more extensively with the SS and police, and already bloodied the hands of some units among both the *Kommandanturen* and the occupation divisions, helped lay the groundwork for this later murderous escalation.

More generally, meanwhile, the 704th Infantry Division, like its fellow divisions, strove ever more desperately to stave off the occupation edifice's collapse. The division had help from Reserve Police Battalion 64, which dispatched a car-borne company to Užice in July.[116] But it faced a thankless task nonetheless. The insurgents were infiltrating and co-opting the population with ease. In late July, for example, Reserve Police Battalion 64 committed a company to no fewer than eleven seek-locate-destroy missions that, launched as they were on the basis of imprecise tip-offs from locals, proved an utter waste of time. The insurgents were invariably able to slip away, and the battalion was certain that civilians had forewarned them.[117] A little later, a battalion of the 724th Infantry Regiment judged that the insurgents "possess an excellent and far-reaching information service which works very rapidly and reliably . . . its timely warnings always make it possible (for the insurgents) to escape encirclement."[118]

Co-opting the population so easily also enabled the Partisans to move undetected within it. LXV Corps reported that a band of Communists had attacked a town by disguising themselves as farmers in order to smuggle their weapons through the marketplace.[119] The Germans' own efforts in intelligence-gathering were limited among other things by the paltry Luftwaffe forces available. There were no operative units in the Yugoslav theater, so Wehrmacht Command Southeast was reduced to imploring the High Command to transfer a Luftwaffe training school to Serbia, even if it was equipped only with primitive machines.[120]

The insurgents also targeted pro-Axis collaborators with ease. So reported the 724th Infantry Regiment on August 20: "the district headman of Guča appeared today in the regimental office . . . He had been a prisoner of war, and would rather be one again than remain district headman in Guča if the Wehrmacht were not there. He claims that the

Serbian gendarmerie commands no respect and is in no fit state to protect the place. He also claims that there are a large number of Communists in Guča itself, and that there are numerous mayors who sympathize with the bandits."[121] More anguished still was the cry for help from the collaborator Danilac Kostić: "I ask the German Wehrmacht and German commander for weapons so I can protect my own life against the red mob and the Communist bands."[122]

Able to secure and harness growing popular support, and unmolested by a German occupation force preoccupied with clinging on to the main transport arteries and urban centers, the Partisans were able to build up their organization across the country. On September 10 Lieutenant Klemm, of the 724th Infantry Regiment's twelfth company, wrote that:

> the enemy clearly no longer consists of isolated bands, but constitutes a well-organized uprising in which the general population, most of whom are well-armed, are taking part. Within the impenetrable landscape, with troops often restricted only to the one road, proper retaliation against a rebellious population is only possible with the help of the Luftwaffe.[123]

And that help, at least to any meaningful degree, had yet to be forthcoming. All this meant, of course, that the Partisans could ravage the occupiers' supply and communications with alacrity. A late August report from District Command (I) 847 in the 704th's jurisdiction, for instance, reported that rebels had blown bridges on the Šabac-Banjani road and over the River Tamnava in Koceljevo, blocked roads between Šabac, Kocekjevo, Ub, and Valjevo, crippled the Šabac-Lesnica-Losnica rail line, and plunged a whole area north and northwest of Šabac into a state of uprising. The district command knew that the cutting of the transport arteries between its towns placed the towns themselves in peril. "The moment this bridge is severed, the entire district command, the town (Šabac) and the area will be cut off from the outside world. If strong forces are not finally deployed and the center of defense shifted to Šabac, the catastrophe could happen any time." The 724th Infantry Regiment saw the danger too; conditions were worsening so much, it reported, that the safety of the troops in Užice and Požega was seriously under threat.

"Previously the bandits were only appearing occasionally and in small numbers," the regiment maintained. "Now they are drawing ever nearer to Užice and Požega. Their strength can often be counted in the hundreds, and their equipment is often better than that of our own troops."[124]

In the face of the escalating chaos, the Germans scrapped a pledge to allow the collaborationist government control of the Serbian gendarmerie. On August 13 LXV Corps announced it was reorganizing the Serbian gendarmerie into large units of fifty to one hundred men under local German army commanders.[125] The 704th Infantry Division wanted the gendarmerie to bear the main burden of the counterinsurgency campaign, with the German army used only sparingly. It urged that the gendarmerie be bolstered by more reliable elements, and receive proper pay and equipment and motor vehicles seized from civilians.[126]

But relying on the Serbian gendarmerie brought its own problems. The 724th Infantry Regiment reported one engagement, albeit from a later time, November 1941, in which the gendarmerie had not suffered the massive losses it was claiming, but had simply withdrawn in disarray. "On our own march back," the regiment recorded, "we encountered only one gendarme, who had disguised himself as a farmer in order to escape."[127] The gendarmerie, the regiment believed, was incapable of resisting the enemy energetically.[128] The gendarmerie was not always the byword for ineptitude that scapegoat-seeking German commanders often painted it as.[129] But the 704th's reliance on it probably reflected not faith on the division's part so much as desperation. The gendarmerie's defects were also recognized higher up the command chain. Major Jersak, Wehrmacht Command Southeast's liaison officer with LXV Corps, had little faith in it: he believed that neither arming it further nor increasing its numbers in particular trouble spots such as Šabac would hinder or halt the uprising.[130]

The occupation divisions were compelled to take the fight to the insurgents somehow or other, then, but it was an immensely difficult task. And as a federal German investigation during the 1970s revealed, it was a task to which at least some of the 704th Infantry Division's senior officers were unequal. In 1972, Max Koehler, from the second company of the first battalion of the 724th Infantry Regiment, was questioned by the Central Office of Land Administration as part of a preliminary investigation, later abandoned, into possible war crimes by that unit. He spoke warmly of his company commander, but described Major König, the battalion commander, as "arrogant and full of himself . . . with a cynical character, the chronic need to push himself to the forefront, and no understanding of the civilian population." The regimental commander, General Lontschar, he described as "pedantic in military matters, and in tactical questions unequal to his rank."[131]

The 704th Infantry Division, like its fellow occupation divisions, was nonetheless obliged to prosecute mobile counterinsurgency operations to the best of its ability. Yet as well as possessing an officer contingent of at best variable quality, the division also possessed insufficient troops to encircle and annihilate the insurgents.[132] Further problems facing encirclement attempts were recounted in mid-August by the 714th Infantry Division: it suffered from a shortage of hand grenades and small-arms ammunition, delays in its rail transport, and unreliable Serbian gendarmerie units.[133] But the 714th was not simply scapegoating the Serbian gendarmerie. Of its own substandard troops it wrote that "sadly (they) do not always recognize how serious the situation is."[134] In the 704th Infantry Division, similarly, the twelfth company of the 724th Infantry Regiment described the *"exhausted and indifferent impression"* its own men were making by late August.[135]

Key to success in smaller counterinsurgency operations were the hunter groups. But the 704th's efforts at forming such groups, like those of LXV Corps' divisions in general, were blighted by problems. In late August, for instance, the 724th Infantry Regiment's first battalion bewailed the fact that, though hunter groups could be assembled quickly, the plundered trucks they had been assigned could not negotiate mountainous winding roads and were plagued by frequent tire and motor failure.[136] The 717th Infantry Division, too, was constantly frustrated at the Partisans' knowledge of the area in which it faced them.[137]

The Germans were still mindful of the lessons in moderation afforded by the French campaign and its aftermath; indeed, their more measured conduct at this time recalls that relatively balanced counterinsurgency campaign the German army had waged in the Ukraine in 1918. Hunter groups were instructed to cultivate the population, not just terrorize it, relying on help from the Serbian gendarmerie and reliable sightings of Partisans by civilians. Though it did order the seizure of hostages, Serbia Command also ordered more nuanced punishments, such as imposing fines and compelling the population to forced labor and security duty. It also stressed that the troops must distinguish between innocent and guilty.[138] In mid-August, the 704th Infantry Division urged that propaganda be used to convince the population of the Wehrmacht's will to win. There was little in the way of a well-resourced propaganda infrastructure to aid this effort. Rather, the division's units were themselves urged to "seek out and realise new opportunities" for propaganda.[139] But at least the intention was there.

And at least some of the 704th's subordinate units were showing restraint. The 734th Infantry Regiment recounted a relatively moderate reprisal its men exacted on August 23. In one house, they found a sackful of rifles and a duplication machine with Communist appeals produced on it, obtained the names of fifteen absent villagers who were known Communists, and ordered the police to burn down three of their homes. This was a harsh measure indeed, but less harsh than an indiscriminate mass shooting.[140]

There were also displays of genuine humanity by the 704th's men. On one occasion a sixteen-year-old who had been shot trying to evade capture had his wounds bound by German soldiers, who left him with two local women to take care of him.[141] Even as late as September, relations with the population could be positively convivial—too convivial, in fact, for divisional command's liking. "There is greater need than ever," it proclaimed on September 16, "for members of the Wehrmacht to keep themselves fully distanced from the Serbian population." The division particularly bemoaned the "unworthy" practice of "sitting round the kitchen table or in private quarters, chatting with Serbs over cups of coffee."[142]

But overall, throughout July and August, in line with the mounting reprisal activity across all Serbia, the 704th Infantry Division exacted a growing death toll of civilians. Some of the killings in its jurisdiction, such as the reprisal carried out by the local district command following the attack on General Lontschar's car near Razna on July 18, were the work of units outwith the division's own command chain.[143] Elsewhere, however, it was the 704th's troops themselves who exacted the death tolls. From the death toll of thirty-eight, cited earlier in this chapter, that the first company of the 724th Infantry Regiment exacted on August 17, only three machine-guns and twelve rifles were seized. The only Axis casualty was an Albanian gendarme shot in the head.[144] On that same day, the regiment had ten farmsteads burned down and another fifteen destroyed by artillery.[145] And in a firefight near the railway station at Dublje, west of Šabac, in late August, men of the eighth company of the 750th Infantry Regiment, temporarily under the 704th Infantry Division's command, killed twenty-five "bandits" at a loss to themselves of just one dead.[146]

It is clear from such instances that not just insurgents, but civilians also, were perishing in ever greater numbers at the 704th Infantry Division's own hands. The 704th might be failing to crush the uprising in its area, then, but it was certainly exacting a mounting death toll. And the fact that it felt increasingly impotent and frustrated may have been one of the very forces fueling its brutality. Indeed, some units were spilling too much blood even for divisional command's liking. While the 704th urged its units to inform the divisional intelligence section if any Serbian officials were suspected of sabotage, contacting Communists, or tolerating illegal activities, it also stressed that Serbian officials generally should not be taken hostage.[147] LXV Corps detected a wider malaise, declaring on August 23 that:

> It is understandable that troops fired upon in the back by Communist bands will cry out for vengeance. This often results in people found in the field being arrested and shot. But in most cases it is not the guilty who are caught, but the innocent, and this only results in the hitherto loyal population being driven into the arms of the bandits by fear or bitterness.[148]

Tellingly, LXV Corps also stressed that it was better that the Serbian gendarmerie or the Serbian authorities apprehend insurgents. Presumably LXV Corps preferred this to leaving the job to German soldiers who might themselves kill informers or other members of the "loyal" population.[149]

It also reminded its troops that the "loyal" population included women also: "It goes without saying that no woman, except when she goes armed against the troops, should under any circumstances be shot without due legal process."[150] Clearly higher Wehrmacht offices were still seeking to keep the general population onside. Similarly, on September 5 Wehrmacht Command Southeast, Field Marshal List's skepticism toward Serb–German collaboration notwithstanding, urged "active, intensified propaganda in the Serbian language with every means available (wireless, leaflets, newspapers, posters and so on) . . . increased use of informers . . . full use of the influence of the Serbian government."[151]

In September the Germans' situation grew even more alarming. For it was now that Tito and Mihailović temporarily made common cause. Mihailović felt he could no longer remain on the sidelines of such a widespread revolt. Tito saw a Partisan–Chetnik alliance as a means of cultivating potential Partisan support among the Serb peasantry and politicians. He also sought to utilize the Chetniks' assistance, at least for a period, in training Partisans. However calculating the two men's motives, the immediate result was that Mihailović's Chetniks now openly joined the revolt.[152] The most important joint Partisan–Chetnik operations were near Krupanj, Valjevo, and Kraljevo, and the epicenter of their cooperation was northwest Serbia. The Germans' increased Luftwaffe support, mainly in the form of Stuka dive bombers, could only achieve so much in the face of them.[153]

The principal town in the 704th's jurisdiction was Valjevo. But, due above all to explosions on the Valjevo-Užice road, the danger to the town's supply was growing daily, and coal stocks were so low that the troops were forced to plunder the coal supply in the munitions factory in Vistad. Meanwhile, every insurgent act of sabotage against roads, railways, and bridges increased the town's isolation.[154] On September 12 General Borowski was forced to fly from Belgrade to the 704th's headquarters in Valjevo because of the insurgent roadblocks crisscrossing the main road.[155] Many of the division's units were also cut off, and some— such as the 724th Infantry Regiment's tenth and eleventh companies, stationed in Krupanj—faced annihilation.

The reports compiled by these two companies convey such a sense of approaching doom, and of the brutalizing fear it spawned, that they are worth recounting at length.

Both companies believed the disaster that befell them in early September could have been foreseen. Eleventh company claimed that "this catastrophe came about because both companies were situated far from the battalion in bandit-infested, difficult terrain. It requires no strategic ability to cut the troops off from all relief and strike at their backs."[156] Particularly when, in the words of tenth company, the "bandits" were obviously so strong:

> Alarming news about the frequency of bandit unrest in the Krupanj area was increasing during the final days before the attack. According to these rumors, 1,000 men had gathered near Kamenica. In Banjevac, a village next door to Krupanj, another 400–500 bandits were said to be active. In the direct vicinity of Krupanj post offices and administrative offices were being plundered. Headmen, truck drivers, and workers who had ignored the bandits' warning were being shot. Small individual Wehrmacht units were being attacked, motorized columns fired upon and observation posts in Bela Orvka and Stolica attacked. Despite all efforts, nothing could be done against the bandits. These events undermined the Wehrmacht's status and reliability in the eyes of the Serbian population.[157]

As a result, the population's support for the insurgents was growing: "in the behavior of the population towards Wehrmacht members, an inner, icy aversion and an all-unifying hatred towards anything German could be felt."[158]

The prelude to the main insurgent attack was a clash on the morning of September 2. This engagement, and the fear that afflicted the troops in Krupanj in its aftermath, are described by tenth company:

> On Monday 9/1 at 22.00, NCO Seifert reported in from the watch at Stolica with the news that the watch had been attacked by a strong bandit group. On 9/2 at 06.00, a commando of five squads led by Lieutenant Rehmer and Lieutenant Halder, together with Medical

NCO Heinrich,[159] set out for Stolica to clarify the situation. On the way, at the north-west exit of Pirstica, the commando encountered a road block (two-deep felled trees, several meters high), which was nevertheless undefended. About 800 meters in front of Stolica the commando encountered an escaped troop from the Stolica watch consisting of two NCOs and eleven men. At the same time, two armed men were observed on the heights south-east of Stolica. The commando opened fire immediately; this was answered with heavy fire from rifles and light machine-guns on the heights either side of the road. Lieutenant Rehmer took two squads onto the slopes east of the road. The enemy could not be seen.

In consequence of the ever more frequent reports that the bandits were massing and that Stolica had been attacked, the company had already been in a state of high alert for the past week. The hospital had been converted into a defensive strongpoint . . . That the population of Krupanj had deliberately fled (from the Germans) was clear from the behavior of the district chief. At 13.00 I entrusted him with providing 20 men for a work detail. The mayor arrived himself and explained that he could not carry this order out, even on pain of being arrested or shot, for the entire population of Krupanj had disappeared into the forest. It is clear from this that the whole population was informed of the attack in advance, and that its behavior indicates that it had been working with the bandits closely.[160]

"On Tuesday 9/2 at 20.45," reported tenth company, "our watch brought in an envoy with an offer to capitulate."[161] This part of the story is best conveyed by eleventh company, which was stationed in the school and received the ultimatum sooner. At eight in the evening a boy had appeared with a note for tenth company from the leader of the Chetnik forces surrounding them: "I demand your unconditional surrender; you are completely encircled, no one will be harmed, you will be held prisoner until the end of the war. If you accept, fire three flares off at 21.00. If you refuse, the attack will resume at this time and you will be slaughtered."[162] Both companies rejected the ultimatum. Then, "on Wednesday night at 00.30 a new attack began. It was a noise from hell, for the volume was doubled in the valley. They bombarded our positions, particularly in the hospital, with grenade launchers."[163]

Tenth company then picks up the story:

At 00.30 on 9/3 the bandits opened up a heavy fire on our five outposts. These pulled back into the hospital buildings. We returned fire, even though all we had to aim at was the flashes from the mouths of the enemy guns. The enemy attacked in this way four times during the night, whereby the final attack, at 06.00, was the heaviest of all. During the day the hospital was subjected to persistent light rifle fire, and even to machine-gun fire from time to time. Sharpshooters fired from a distance of 100 to 200 meters upon doors, windows, and walkways in the hospital. The fire grew heavier when they spotted our men moving around. We could only move by crawling, jumping or dragging ourselves from place to place, and that with the greatest care. It was impossible to leave the building. During the time following the attack on Stolica the men could neither sleep nor relax, but remained in a state of constant alert.[164]

Our machine-gun posts and grenade-launcher post on the south side of the roof had to be abandoned when dawn broke, because the enemy had fired upon them with a 3.7 cm gun ... Our machine-guns took up position by the windows on the third floor of the hospital.

From the day of the first attack it was impossible to prepare warm food for the men, because the kitchens ... were under constant fire. The men received only greatly reduced amounts of cold provisions such as meat conserve, eggs, and iron portions.

In the night Corporal Volmer was wounded with a shot to the head. The next morning NCO Ulrich was wounded in the thigh when relieving a machine-gun post.[165] In addition, three wounded from the Stolica watch lay in the police station.

At the break of darkness the fire attacks began again, bigger than before, and increasing in intensity and duration. Between 23.00 and 24.00 flashes of light were seen in the direction of Stolica and Moievica at fifteen-minute intervals, coming nearer and nearer to Krupanj.

At midnight a worsening of the weather set in with heavy clouds. The moonlight, which had been providing good vision, deteriorated, and at the same time the enemy fire stopped. At 02.00 on 9/3 (sic), in complete darkness, a heavy fire bombardment began, lasting between 30 and 45 minutes. Because nothing could be seen of the enemy, we had to restrict ourselves to laying down machine-gun, rifle, and grenade launcher fire to prevent the enemy from breaking into the buildings. It was established, by firing flares after the exchange was over, that the stretch of ground in front of the hospital was clear of the enemy. But enemy rifle fire continued with varying degrees of intensity.[166]

By evening on September 3, both companies already knew their position was in imminent danger of being overwhelmed, and they burned all their documents as a precaution: "At 22.00 on 9/3 I (Lieutenant Rehmer) burned all secret documents . . . (On the morning of 4 September) the enemy laid down a well-targeted rifle fire on all windows in the hospital. *The only relief for the men came through air support.*" Attacks on the insurgents by Stuka dive bombers the following day provided some respite, but Lieutenant Rehmer himself was wounded, "whereupon I handed over command to Sergeant Kreidel."[167] Eleventh company reported that "Tenth company was unable to take one step outside, and thus spent four days without water. Everyone was on constant alert from daybreak all the way through to the next morning. And so on and so on."[168]

On September 4 both companies realized they had to break out immediately or be destroyed. According to tenth company, "even before the attack, the men were seriously exhausted from almost constant watch with only brief respite. After the attack on Stolica the men knew no more rest at all . . . Lack of sleep, exhaustion and the effect of the events, not to mention the lack of supply and water, put the men in a nervous and overstrained condition. Ammunition was scarce . . . Under these conditions the hospital could have held out at best for one more night and one more day. The promised help never came, and therefore on 4 September a breakout was judged the only remaining option." As a preliminary, all supplies were destroyed.[169] Then, "240 kilograms of explosives blew the hospital sky-high."[170]

Tenth company described what happened next: "The medical officer, Dr. Höhne, remained behind to care for the wounded. Some wounded, including Lieutenant Rehmer, who had been wounded by splinters from a hand grenade, took part in the breakout, and with immense effort were able to prevail." But, "despite the greatest of care, the breakout became scattered into small groups. Sergeant Kreidel headed further east over the steep, rocky mountain face, where he was surprised at a house on the heights by bandits and, according to the troops behind him . . . was shot." Several other soldiers were picked off during this phase. "Of the main group under Captain Seifert, the only men of tenth company to make it through to Valjevo were the wounded Lieutenant Rehmer, five NCOs, and 30 men."[171]

Worse still was the plight of eleventh company. It was held up by mines and other obstacles from the start. Further on its escape route was blocked again, this time by a demolished bridge: "With infernal pleasure the bandits wanted to gloat at our helplessness."[172] The company had to leave its own equipment and wounded behind. "What happened to our wounded I have no idea . . . In the evening at 22.30 we arrived in Valjevo . . . Up until now we are still missing 42 men. How many are dead and wounded cannot yet be established."[173]

One staff officer in LXV Corps greeted this debacle with apoplexy. "The shit the bandits are dealing out is just beyond belief now," he wrote in a private letter. "Today a general told us that two companies (!) have been missing for fourteen days (!!!) Just imagine that!! Two companies taken prisoner!!! With five officers and so on!!! We're searching for them with aircraft, day and night!!! You just want to scream right at the heavens!!!!!"[174] The two companies' assessment was more analytical—and more remarkable for it, considering what they had been through. Eleventh company wrote: "against encirclement from behind we were completely powerless. A probe into such mountainous and forested territory as around Krupanj, Stolica, Zajaca will lead either to no success, because the enemy can escape with ease, or to defeat if the bandits are strong enough. The land is so peppered with ravines that the use of trucks, maybe even tanks, is also fruitless, for the enemy can put down roadblock after roadblock which cannot be removed within a short space of time."[175]

Of the insurgents themselves, tenth company wrote that "the bandits can be thankful for their communications network, which runs quickly from village to village across otherwise impassable terrain. The only effective weapon here is aerial attack. Up to now we have not had this. For people raised in this land there are many opportunities for overcoming weak units with underhand methods."[176] Tenth company concluded that "only harsh measures, without regard for the population, will resurrect the orderly conditions that will re-establish trust in the Wehrmacht."[177]

Between September 6 and 12 1941, the SD reported, insurgents carried out eighty-one attacks on transport, communication, and economic installations, and no fewer than 175 attacks on the Serbian gendarmerie. There were also eleven attacks on Wehrmacht personnel, resulting in thirty men killed, fifteen wounded, and eleven abducted.[178] All this came to a total of two hundred and sixty-seven attacks. Considering that Serbia Command had recorded "only" one hundred and thirty-five attacks as recently as the final week in August, this was a frightening escalation. The 704th's situation was summed up on September 19 by Lieutenant Dollmann of the divisional staff: "We are facing a uniformly led organisation strongly equipped with weapons and means of communication. It benefits from the terrain, it has managed to compel the population to support it. It is inevitably superior to the road-bound forces at our disposal. Only the most ruthless deployment of armored and air force units, against the suspect civilian population (as well as the insurgents), can effect a dramatic change in the situation."[179]

The quotes by Dollmann and the "lost companies" of the 724th Infantry Regiment indicate that, desperate as they were becoming, the 704th Infantry Division's officers were now emphatically eschewing moderation. They were increasingly less inclined to distinguish between innocent and guilty, and increasingly more inclined to view the entire population as a threat. This hardening mind-set presaged the brutal escalation of the German counteroffensive against the Serbian national uprising that autumn.

During summer 1941, the 704th Infantry Division faced an increasingly debilitating situation. It was condemned to ineffectiveness by a manpower policy that vastly underprioritized the security of occupied areas generally, and of the occupied area in which the division itself was operating.

The 704th was already sinking into a more moribund condition before the Serbian national uprising had even begun. Once the uprising was under way, little time elapsed before the division felt in danger of being overwhelmed. Impotence, fear, and frustration all combined to harden the way it conducted itself. The ferocious escalation of the Wehrmacht's counterinsurgency campaign would only really gather pace during autumn 1941, but the 704th's example indicates that the process was already beginning that summer.

Yet much of the groundwork for the divisions' harsh reaction to their circumstances had been laid decades before the Third Reich. The German military had long idolized the swift use of maximum force to achieve victory. So the fact that the 704th Infantry Division commanded little in the way of either swiftness or force was likely to increase its propensity to lash out in brutalized frustration at the dangers it was facing. Indeed all divisional commanders in Serbia, together with their officers and men, probably felt the mocking contrast between their current, wretched situation and the decisive maneuver warfare that was the German military's meat and drink. General Stahl, commander of the 714th Infantry Division, had experienced such warfare as recently as the French campaign. His colleague General Hoffmann, commander of the 717th, had experienced it in Poland in 1939. And all three divisional commanders, Borowski included, were being prevented from experiencing it in the as yet still successful campaign against the Soviet Union.[180]

The particularly brutal approach to counterinsurgency that the German military had periodically displayed during earlier decades, and had resurrected for the Polish campaign, can only have further augmented the growing desire for an immensely harsh response to the uprising. It should also be remembered that the occupation divisions became increasingly involved, if not yet to the same extent as the *Kommandanturen*, in the ever more vicious campaign against Serbia's Jews and Communists. Commanders who willingly involved their units in such a campaign, and in so doing indicated their own anti-Semitic and anti-Bolshevik proclivities, were if anything even more likely to judge that the security situation was one that demanded ferocious retaliation.

Yet though it may seem perverse to point out, the ruthless conduct of the 704th during these summer months needs placing in perspective. During the occupation's initial months, the 704th Infantry Division treated most of the general population—Jews and Communists excepted—with reasonable restraint. Even when the division's conduct did harden, the brutality it dealt out had yet to become as severe as it would that autumn. Moreover, even though the opponent the division faced was of southern Slavic stock, anti-Slavism did not visibly suffuse the division's conduct. There are also signs that the 704th's rank-and-file troops did not subscribe to the tenets of National Socialist ideology or ruthless counterinsurgency doctrine as thoroughly as they might have done. This speaks of the limits to National Socialist indoctrination's ability to brutalize the German army's ordinary soldiery.

Much of the lead for the 704th Infantry Division's relatively restrained behavior towards the general population came from LXV Corps. This formation was very far from being a model of enlightenment. But it did recognize, in contrast with Field Marshal von Weichs' more brutal strictures, that keeping the bulk of the population onside was important. It directed its divisions accordingly, urging the kinds of restraint that constituted "propaganda of deed" and complemented some of Section S's propaganda measures. Even so, given the pressures it faced as the national uprising mushroomed, the 704th, like its fellow divisions, might still have been expected to behave more ferociously than it did. By September 1941 the German occupation troops in Serbia, facing an unconventional and ruthless enemy, resembled islands in an insurgent sea, beleaguered on all sides and facing the prospect of complete collapse without the injection of powerful reinforcements. Such circumstances might have been enough to shift the 704th's brutality up several more gears than they did. That they did not was probably due to particular attitudes held by key officers within the 704th.[181]

But in autumn 1941, Wehrmacht brutality in Serbia escalated spectacularly. This was an escalation to which Wehrmacht commanders, if the 704th Infantry Division is any guide, were by now increasingly predisposed. The results would be calamitous not just for Serbia's Jews, but also for the general population. And some commanders went to singularly ferocious lengths to bring such results about. A particularly powerful example is the 342d Infantry Division.

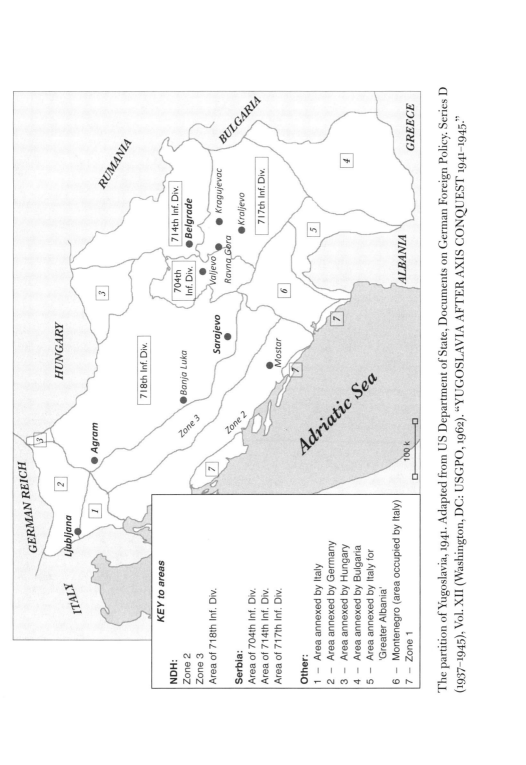

The partition of Yugoslavia, 1941. Adapted from US Department of State, Documents on German Foreign Policy. Series D (1937–1945). Vol. XII (Washington, DC: USGPO, 1962). "YUGOSLAVIA AFTER AXIS CONQUEST 1941–1945."

KEY to areas

NDH:
Zone 2
Zone 3
Area of 718th Inf. Div.

Serbia:
Area of 704th Inf. Div.
Area of 714th Inf. Div.
Area of 717th Inf. Div.

Other:
1 – Area annexed by Italy
2 – Area annexed by Germany
3 – Area annexed by Hungary
4 – Area annexed by Bulgaria
5 – Area annexed by Italy for 'Greater Albania'
6 – Montenegro (area occupied by Italy)
7 – Zone 1

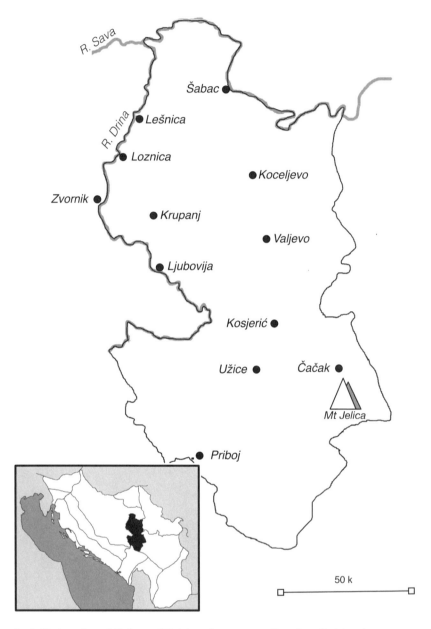

R. Sava

Šabac ●

R. Drina

● Lešnica

● Loznica

● Koceljevo

Zvornik ●

● Krupanj

● Valjevo

● Ljubovija

Kosjerić ●

Užice ●   Čačak ●

Mt Jelica

● Priboj

50 k

Jurisdiction of 704th Infantry Division, August 1941. Based on divisional area map, MFB4/2351, 20294/4, 415.

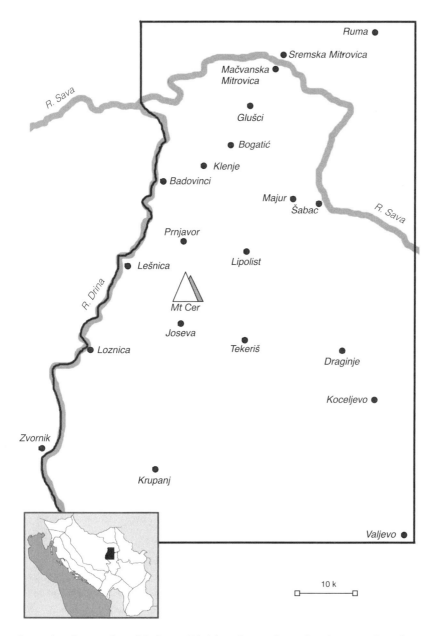

Operational area of 342d Infantry Division, September—October 1941. Based on place names in reports from files of 342d Infantry Division, MFB4/72332–72333.

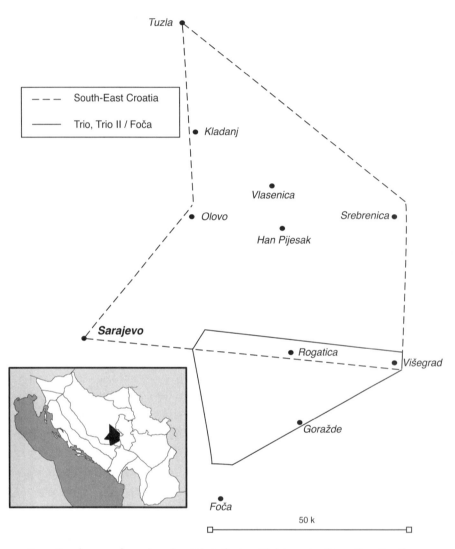

Operational area of 342d and 718th Infantry Divisions in Operation Southeast Croatia, and 718th Infantry Division in Operations Trio I and Trio II/Foča, January–May 1942. Adapted from Klaus Schmider, *Partisanenkrieg in Jugoslawien, 1941–1944* (Hamburg: E. S. Mittler, 2002), 111; place names in reports from files of 718th Infantry Division, MFB4/56155–56158.

Jurisdiction of 718th Infantry Division, January 1943. Based on divisional area map, MFB4/56160, 34404/2, 357.

R. Kupa

Sisak ●

R. Sava

Petrinja ●

Sunja ●

● Glina

Kostajnica ●

Dubica

● Bihać

50 k

Operational area of 369th (Croatian) Infantry Division in Operation White I, January–February 1943. Based on Schmider, *Partisanenkrieg in Jugoslawien, 1941–1944*, 218; 369th Infantry Division area map for White I, MFB4/72341, 30581/13, 559.

Austrian troops guarding Serbian men and women, suspected of firing on Austrian soldiers or harboring weapons, 1915. In 1941 Lieutenant General Franz Boehme, the Plenipotentiary Commanding General in Serbia, invoked the memory of Serbian "atrocities" against Austrian troops during the Great War in order to justify a remarkably brutal campaign to suppress resistance in the country. (Süddeutsche Zeitung Photo)

Jews being assigned to clear rubble in Belgrade, April 1941. This was one of the preliminaries in a process that would see Serbia's male Jewish population virtually wiped out by the end of 1941. The vast majority perished in German reprisals for "bandit" attacks. (Bundesarchiv, Koblenz)

Brigadier General Heinrich Borowski, commander of the 704th Infantry Division. During summer 1941, Borowski's outnumbered and substandard division took the brunt of the Serbian national uprising in its western Serbian jurisdiction. (BArch MSg 109 264)

German soldiers search a village in Macedonia, southern Yugoslavia. Such operations varied greatly in terms of how far they discriminated between insurgents and unarmed civilians. (Süddeutsche Zeitung Photo)

Major General Walter Hinghofer. In autumn 1941, Hinghofer led the 342d Infantry Division as the spearhead of the German counteroffensive against the Serbian national uprising. The division's ferocity exceeded even General Boehme's expectations. (BArch RH7 699)

Brigadier General Paul Hoffmann. As commander of the 717th Infantry Division in October 1941, Hoffmann oversaw one of the most infamous Wehrmacht massacres in the entire Balkan theater. On assuming command of the 342d Infantry Division the following month, however, he began to show more restraint. (BArch RH7 700)

German soldiers in an outpost on the Montenegrin frontier. The photograph gives some idea of the mountainous terrain in which the troops fought. (Süddeutsche Zeitung Photo)

German troops advance through a forest. The danger from insurgents amid such terrain would have been acute. (Bundesarchiv, Koblenz)

Major General Johann Fortner. As commander of the 718th Infantry Division in eastern Bosnia during 1942, Fortner increasingly grasped the importance of winning native hearts and minds in the division's counterinsurgency campaign. By the end of the year, however, the pressures the 718th faced were causing its commitment to wane. (BArch MSg 109 674)

Stuka dive-bombers returning from an anti-Partisan mission in Bosnia. Only in 1943 were sizable Luftwaffe forces committed against the Partisans; in 1942, German ground forces mainly had to rely on dubious support from the Italian and Croatian air forces. (Süddeutsche Zeitung Photo)

Brigadier General Fritz Neidholt, commander of the 369th (Croatian) Infantry Division. Between January and March 1943, Neidholt's German-officered division conducted itself with great brutality during the White operations against the main Partisan stronghold in western Bosnia. (BArch RH7 712)

German soldiers in a village in the NDH, 1943. German anti-Partisan units usually had to make do with tanks plundered from the French. These often proved wholly inadequate for counterinsurgency warfare. (Süddeutsche Zeitung Photo)

German soldiers mingle with Bosnian refugees fleeing the fighting with Partisans, 1943. 1943 saw the largest German anti-Partisan operations in Yugoslavia, with massive loss of civilian life. (Süddeutsche Zeitung Photo)

German troops monitoring Yugoslav civilians, 1943. The Germans consistently lacked the manpower to maintain a sufficiently extensive, permanent presence among the Yugoslav civilian population. (Bundesarchiv, Koblenz)

A column of the National Socialist Motor Corps (NSKK) is ambushed by Partisans. A somewhat sanitized propaganda illustration by the NSKK war journalist Matejko, 1944. (Süddeutsche Zeitung Photo)

The grisly reality: the body of a dead German soldier is carried off by comrades during the winter of 1943-1944. Note that the soldier has been stripped naked; this suggests he was tortured and mutilated by Partisans before being killed. (Bundesarchiv, Koblenz)

Settling Accounts in Blood

The 342d Infantry Division in Serbia

MAJOR GENERAL WALTER HINGHOFER, the 342d Infantry Division's commanding officer, was born to an ethnic German family in Transylvania, in the easternmost part of the Habsburg Empire, in 1884. His father was a senior bank inspector. Hinghofer fought as an artillery officer on the eastern front throughout the entire length of the Great War. He saw uninterrupted duty there for the duration of the fighting from 1914 to 1917. During this period, among other things, he fought in the massive 1915 offensive that took the armies of the Central powers across Russian Poland and into the western Ukraine.[1] He also served as an officer in the Habsburg occupation forces in the Ukraine following the Treaty of Brest-Litovsk. During the interwar years Hinghofer distinguished himself considerably, holding a succession of garrison and brigade commands before becoming an army administrator. In 1934 he joined the Austrian Federal War Ministry. By September 1939 Hinghofer was a brigadier general, serving in a number of staff roles before being promoted again to major general and receiving command of the 342d Infantry Division in July 1941.[2]

Hinghofer's division arrived in Serbia in September 1941. The 342d, later joined by the 113th Infantry Division, was to be the Germans' main counterinsurgency strike force that autumn. It was to bolster the beleaguered German army units already on the ground, execute large mobile operations against the insurgents themselves, and act as the Wehrmacht's main hatchet man in bringing terror to the Serbs. Of all the influences to which Hinghofer was subjected during his earlier life, none seem to have colored his conduct of the campaign more decisively than his eastern front experience during the Great War and, perhaps most decisively of all, his Austrian origins.

The most centrally important figure in the mushrooming ferocity of the autumn security campaign was Lieutenant General Franz Boehme. On September 19, Boehme was assigned the new title of Plenipotentiary Commanding General in Serbia. This position enabled him, aided by the command staff of the German XVIII Corps, to override the split that had hitherto existed between LXV Corps and the Wehrmacht Commander in Serbia.[3] Boehme's appointment was part of a new, radically harsh approach to crushing the Serbian uprising. Officials such as General Danckelmann had advocated a popular anti-Communist front with the Serbs, and sought to distance Nedić from harsh German reprisals. But these men were now sidelined or replaced by hard-liners deeply skeptical as to the potential of Serbo-German cooperation. Danckelmann himself complained at his treatment. But on October 10, on Boehme's recommendation, Field Marshal List sacked him for underestimating the danger posed by the uprising and relying excessively on the Serbian gendarmerie to suppress it.[4]

Boehme and his methods arrived at a critical juncture for the Germans in Serbia. The national uprising surged that month as Mihailović's Chetniks joined forces with the Communist Partisans, and the towns of Užice, Požega, Gornji Milanovac, and Čačak all fell within ten days of one another. This effectively placed all Serbia west of the Belgrade-Kraljevo line in the insurgents' hands. Užice, with its bank and arms factory, was a particularly treasured prize. The Germans fell back to defend the main urban centers and supply lines. Yet their ability to defend even these was dangerously threatened.[5]

On some counts, Boehme pursued a joint approach with Nedić. In line with the Serbian leader's wishes, he ordered the rearming of the Serbian gendarmerie at the end of September. This measure would be vindicated once the gendarmerie began giving a better account of itself as autumn progressed. In late September, Boehme exploited the firm support for the new government shown by the Pećanac Chetniks and the Zbor Movement. He and Nedić agreed a joint role for the Serbian gendarmerie and the Pećanac Chetniks in administering the region south of Belgrade and east of the River Kolubara.[6] Otherwise, however, Boehme firmly repaid the faith in him shown by Field Marshal List—who remained deeply wary of relying on the Serbs themselves to suppress a genuine national uprising—by asserting German control over the counteroffensive.[7]

German reprisals now assumed terrifying dimensions. No longer would they attempt to distinguish between guilty and innocent in the way Nedić had originally persuaded General Danckelmann to agree to. Boehme's September 25 order, quoted at the outset of this study, is worth repeating here. For it encapsulates Boehme's expectations of his men and his invocation of the decades-old anti-Serb hatred with which he sought to inspire them:

> Your objective is to be achieved in a land where, in 1914, streams of German blood flowed because of the treachery of the Serbs, men and women. You are the avengers of those dead. A deterring example must be established for all of Serbia, one that will have the heaviest impact on the entire population. Anyone who carries out his duty in a lenient manner will be called to account, regardless of rank or position, and tried by a military court.[8]

The single order that, more than any other, translated this stance into body counts was Boehme's October 10 directive. This directive stipulated that the troops were to shoot one hundred Serbian hostages for every German killed in the insurgency, and fifty for every German wounded.[9] It thus authorized and systematized levels of bloodletting that Wehrmacht commands might hitherto have considered wild if understandable excesses.[10] Milovan Djilas, one of Tito's lieutenants, recalls how the scale of killing that followed sent a collective shudder through the population:

> It was believed at the time that some 5,000 were executed in Kragujevac, and 1,700 in Kraljevo. These figures grew with time—by

the thousands in both places—though the actual figures have never been confirmed. *Borba*[11] wrote of this but we spoke of it reluctantly, feeling the deathly horror that had seized Serbia. What "reason" did the Germans have for undertaking measures which were then so unthinkable? Was it retaliation, the killing of one hundred Serbs for every dead German, which they proclaimed during the very first days of the occupation? Was it the destruction of Serbia's centers—towns known for their national consciousness and Communist influence? . . . Certainly the Nazis found sufficient justification for crushing the will to resist in a people whom Hitler considered the most politically creative and thus the most dangerous in the Balkans.[12]

Moreover, though the Armed Forces High Command had itself authorized the 1:100 hostage policy in a decree of September 16,[13] Boehme went further. He targeted the bulk of hostage-shootings at Serbian Jews, whom Wehrmacht propaganda already depicted as puppet-masters of the Communist-led uprising. It was not necessarily fanatical ideology that led Boehme to issue his decree—though anti-Semitic and anti-Bolshevik sentiments certainly would have eased the task of issuing it for him. Rather, his actions were determined by his calculation that targeting Jews together with Sinti and Roma, could impress the rest of the population with an object lesson in German terror.[14] Whilst Boehme was not departing radically here from the lethally discriminatory measures which German units had already been enacting in Serbia, he was certainly *escalating* them radically.

Boehme first executed his policy in response to the killing of a group of German soldiers at Topola on October 4. To buttress the policy, Boehme manipulated the details of the attack: when claims that the dead soldiers had been mutilated beforehand were disproved by autopsy, he covered this finding up. Suppressing the facts also enabled Boehme to use the image of cruelly mutilated German soldiers to discourage his troops from surrendering.[15]

It was those Jews and Sinti and Roma who were already interned whom Boehme selected as the principal victims of this intensified reprisal campaign. As they had already been interned en masse, shooting them not only was easier, but would also free up space for the large numbers of genuine rebel suspects whom the Germans would seize as autumn went on. Boehme reckoned with the approval of the Nedić administration and of the SS and police. He also reckoned that the latter's approval would improve the Wehrmacht's general cooperation with it.[16]

Furthermore, as the number of reprisal victims began to spiral, German army units were now ordered to ease the practical burden on the SS and police by shooting increasing numbers of reprisal victims themselves. The worst racially targeted reprisal which army units inflicted was the work of the third battalion of the 433d Infantry Regiment. This unit had been temporarily loaned from the 164th Infantry Division to support the 704th Infantry Division. On 27 October, the battalion shot twenty-two hundred Jews and Sinti and Roma in retaliation for the death of ten German soldiers and the wounding of a further twenty-four in the surrounded town of Valjevo.[17] The "700-number" occupation divisions themselves participated less extensively in such killings, but participate they did; on October 1, for instance, the first battalion of the 724th Infantry Regiment, also subordinate to the 704th Infantry Division, shot sixty-six Jews and Communists.[18] On October 14, meanwhile, the 717th Infantry Division specifically noted its receipt of General Boehme's instructions to seize "Communists, nationalists, democrats, and Jews . . . as hostages."[19]

The killing of Serbian Sinti and Roma in 1941, vicious as it was, was not wholesale.[20] But the killing of Serbian Jews—deadliest of all the Reich's racial enemies in the Nazi world-view—was emphatically wholesale. By the end of the year the entire adult male Jewish population of Serbia had been put to death; the interned women and children would be exterminated in SS-run camps the following year as that organization's Reich Security Main Office finally relieved the Wehrmacht of overall responsibility for the campaign against the Serbian Jews.[21]

From a grisly productionist viewpoint, the extermination of Serbia's male Jews meant that demand for targeted reprisal victims was beginning to outstrip supply. Thus, towards the end of 1941, members of the general Serb population would begin to perish in their thousands also.

On the whole, the "regular" occupation divisions seem to have killed Jews in large numbers somewhat sporadically that autumn. This doe not, of course, absolve them of any condemnation for the still substantial part they played in the extermination of the Serbian Jews. But to grasp the full, devastating extent of the divisions' actions in Serbia in 1941, it is necessary to move from the horrors they visited upon the Serbian Jews, to the horrors they inflicted upon the wider population. It was here that the 342d Infantry Division, more so even than the 700-number divisions, truly came into its own.

The 342d Infantry Division's personnel originated partly from the Twelfth Military District, based around Koblenz in the old Reich, and partly from the Seventeenth Military District around Linz in the Eastern March.[22] It was one of eight Category Fourteen divisions raised that month. These divisions were not among the German army's finest formations. Though they comprised the standard three regiments—the 697th, 698th, and 699th Infantry Regiments in the 342d's case—each regiment comprised twelve companies instead of the usual fourteen. Indeed, according to the division's order of battle for September 28, the 698th possessed only eleven companies.[23] They were also fitted with reduced scales of equipment, and their rank-and-file combat troops fell into the twenty-seven to thirty-two age range. But next to the seven-hundred-number occupation divisions already in Serbia, a Category Fourteen division like the 342d was a fairly strong and effective fighting force. Among other things, it possessed an artillery regiment and an antitank company.[24]

In military terms, the operations the 342d executed that autumn initially brought mixed results at best. But they eventually helped the Wehrmacht to crush the uprising in Serbia and expel its remnants westward. Though the Partisans would eventually find refuge and regroup within the borders of the NDH, the Germans' efforts at least dissipated the immediate danger the Serbian national uprising had posed.

But the 342d Infantry Division is important to this study not so much for its uneven military achievements as for the grisly conduct that accompanied them. Of all the German army divisions on the ground that autumn, the 342d was the one that would convert General Boehme's commandments into the most sanguinary practice.

And this was not just because of the scale of operations which it executed. No German army division on Serbian soil exercised restraint during these months. All carried out terrible reprisals on an enormous scale. But while other divisions followed Boehme's directives, the 342d surpassed them. In its conduct echoed decades-old historical enmities. The enmity that echoed loudest was the one between Austria-Hungary and Serbia.

The 342d commenced its first mobile operation in late September, cleansing the Mačva region, a six-hundred-square-kilometer area west of Šabac between the Rivers Drina and Sava.[25] Advancing into the region from the north enabled the 342d and its forces to form up in Syrmia, an area yet to be affected by the uprising.[26] As well as being a major center of rebel strength, the Germans had an economic motive for targeting the Drina-Sava region—it would enable them to seize valuable agricultural resources from the insurgents. General Boehme's quartermaster's section extolled this resource grab as being for the economic good of the homeland and the occupation troops. It would encompass all the region's livestock, horses, grain, and feed.[27] Three thousand ethnic Germans from Syrmia and the Banat in northern Yugoslavia were employed to seize this prize once the fighting was over.[28]

In cleansing the town of Šabac, which the 342d carried out between September 24 and 27, the division was loaned the second battalion of the 750th Infantry Regiment and a company of Reserve Police Battalion 64.[29] For the operation in the wider region, which took place between September 28 and October 9, the 342d could also count on air reconnaissance and, if they were needed urgently, a limited number of Stuka dive-bombers.[30] Yet the operation was a difficult prospect nonetheless. One reason why the region was such a preeminent rebel center was that the Partisans and Chetniks there, numbering anything between two thousand and ten thousand by German estimates, had been cooperating in joint operations for some time. They were also well organized, well equipped in part, and extensively supported by the population. That all this heightened the challenge for the 342d may help explain why Boehme's orders for the operation were exceptionally harsh.[31]

And exceptionally harsh they were. The SD reported that the entire area between Šabac and Bogatic was to be evacuated. Its menfolk would be brought into concentration camps, to be screened by the SD with the help of the Serbian police. Its women and children were to be driven from their homes, "onto Mount Cer, south-west of Šabac, there to be left to their fate."[32] The operation's general tenor was encapsulated in an order from Boehme himself: "The population . . . between the Drina and Sava has attached itself to the uprising. Women and children are running messages and maintaining the bandits' basis of supply . . . [The area] is to be cleansed by exterminating any bands that appear, so as to deny the bandits the area's supply in the long term."[33] The most noxious passage in Boehme's order conveyed the general's intention that "ruthless measures will set a terrifying example which will, in a short space of time, resonate across all Serbia."[34] Boehme was equally obdurate over the specifics: "any person involved in the fighting in any way is to be seen as a guerrilla and handled accordingly. Any settlement from which German soldiers are fired upon, or in the vicinity of which weapons and munitions are found, is to be burned down."[35] He further added on September 23 that "the shooting of captured and condemned irregulars is to be presented to the population as an exemplary spectacle."[36]

But the 342d was not going to allow Boehme to overshadow it. An order it issued on September 25 was even more ruthless. Hinghofer himself, not the operations section, departed from the usual practice by issuing the order directly. He defined even more sweepingly which sorts of person constituted an irregular, and what they could expect. "Anyone who raises a weapon against the occupier *or* supports corresponding resistance," he declared,

> is an irregular. Accordingly, *every member* of a rebellious band against whom the division fights is to be treated as an *irregular*. The *juridical punishment* of a member of a rebellious band is to be carried out . . . *with execution in every case* . . . Our opponents should be regarded by us without exception as irregulars . . . Only (those) who do not oppose us *in any way* are to be excepted.[37]

Two days later Hinghofer explicitly extended the target group even further. He stipulated that "Serbian officials, police, and gendarmerie are to be disarmed, held as a separate group of prisoners, and then shot."[38] In other words, members of the collaborationist Serbian government and administration were to be regarded with no less suspicion, and treated with no less ferocity, than other civilians. Simply to encounter them in the "bandit-infested" region was to condemn them. Then, on September 29, the division declared that mere suspicion was sufficient grounds for killing anyone: "The night passed quietly, (but) no-one should be fooled by this. Attacks must be reckoned with. Every man encountered in no-man's land is to be shot without delay." "The slightest suspicion" was reason enough for killing prisoners also.[39] Such orders even prompted XVIII Corps itself to advise the 342d to keep a check on its brutality, and at least spare for interrogation those "bandits" who could provide valuable information.[40]

The fate of Šabac itself was sealed once German soldiers "incurred losses" there on September 23.[41] The 342d was ordered by Boehme to sweep up all men in the town aged between fourteen and seventy, put them in a concentration camp north of the Sava, and "immediately shoot *all inhabitants* who participated in the fighting or set themselves against the troops, and all *male inhabitants* in whose homes weapons or munitions were found, from whose homes shots were fired, or who tried to flee arrest."[42] The division's assault on Šabac on September 27 also razed forty houses to the ground and unleashed Stuka attacks on the surrounding villages. Its own losses were minimal—one man killed and one lightly wounded from enemy action, together with a reserve policeman who was killed when his own gun went off.[43]

The men of the town, along with hundreds of Jews hitherto interned in Šabac, were then shunted from camp to camp, first in Šabac, then to Jarak where the 342d's pioneers were in the process of building a new concentration camp, and then back again. This "blood march," as Yugoslav historians have titled it, was preceded by the massacre of eighty prisoners by the 342d for "disobedience," before the division eventually handed responsibility for the remaining prisoners to Reserve Police Battalion 64.[44]

During the final days of September and into October, the 342d exacted a dreadful toll of "enemy" dead throughout the Mačva region. This dwarfed both the hauls of insurgent weaponry the division seized and its own losses. It is clear that many, at least, of the "enemy" dead were unarmed civilians. When the division shot 250 of its prisoners and ordered the 698th Infantry Regiment to obliterate the village and male population of Metković, as retaliation for unspecified "hostile activities," it was an average day's work.[45] The following day, the division shot eighty-four prisoners, from whom only one machine gun and a handful of rifles were seized.[46] Serbian refugees fleeing the division's onslaught were driven onto the anvil of allied Croatian troops on the Drina, and were forced to seek refuge in the islands and woods on and around the river.[47]

Between September 21 and 30 the 342d Infantry Division shot 830 of its eighty-four hundred prisoners. Though it could have shot many more, it is clear that the great majority of those whom it did shoot were unarmed civilians. For here, too, the division counted only a handful of rifles and a couple of machine guns. The 342d itself suffered three dead and twenty wounded.[48] And here too the division was not merely following General Boehme's lead, but also acting on its own initiative. The reprisal ratios General Boehme specified on October 10 were actually less severe than the ratio of Serbs to Germans killed at the division's hands up to that date.[49]

The 342d Infantry Division concluded its initial cleansing of the Mačva region on October 9. The operation had failed to destroy the main insurgent group. The division launched a second, more targeted attack around Mount Cer—to where the insurgents who had eluded it in the Mačva operation had withdrawn—between October 10 and 15, and a third in the direction of Krupanj on October 19 and 20. Again, few weapons were taken but a vast number of shootings took place—4,011, the division reported, across all three operations. This first phase of the 342d's activities in Serbia ended with the relief of Valjevo on October 26.[50]

For the October 10–15 operations, against Mount Cer and its environs, the 342d Infantry Division was further augmented by two companies and two additional platoons from the 202d Panzer Regiment.[51] Infesting this area, the division reckoned, were twenty-five hundred well-equipped Chetniks and up to four thousand generally poorly equipped Communists.[52] The 342d was ordered to annihilate these "bandits" and end the threat they posed to the transport artery of the River Mačva.

Its formations advanced in three groups into the regions of Prnjavor-Zminjak, Klenje-Slepčević-Bogatić, and Vranjska-Šabac. As before, a Stuka bombardment heralded the attack.[53]

The Germans' opponents were set on eluding rather than engaging them, halting only to defend the roadblocks they had erected. The 342d ordered several villages destroyed, declaring that "the villages south of Mount Cer are to be burned. The villages north of Mount Cer are to be burned . . . only Bela Reka and Petkovica are to be spared."[54] It also ordered male villagers sent to the concentration camp at Šabac, and the rest of the inhabitants press-ganged into clearing the roadblocks. During its advance the 342d also obliterated major insurgent strongholds in the monasteries of Radovasnica and Mount Tronosa.[55]

Three days later, the 342d completed the encirclement of the Cer region. But its minuscule haul of prisoners showed that most of the insurgents had escaped again, this time westward. The division surmised that they had gone in the direction either of the Italians, with whom they were likely to try to cut a deal, or of ethnic Serb forces fighting the Ustasha in the NDH.[56]

The 342d then turned on the insurgents in the Jadar region, and their main center in and around Krupanj. Of this group, the division wrote that "the enemy that has surfaced south of the Jadar constitutes not independent groups or isolated pockets, but organized resistance under military-style leadership."[57] Three to four thousand were reportedly gathered in "primeval forest"—perennially ideal country for bandits and irregulars.[58]

The 342d launched its assault on Krupanj on October 19. "Some weeks ago," the 342d's divisional command wrote, referring to the disaster that had befallen the two companies of the 724th Infantry Regiment, "German troops in Krupanj were attacked by overwhelming numbers of insurgents. The division has the task of avenging this attack with every measure of harshness."[59] The division committed its entire strength, intact since the start of operations, aided by two Panzer companies and patrol boats from the Hungarian Danube Flotilla.[60] Within two days, though an unknown number of insurgents had escaped after leveling Krupanj's lead works, the division reported that the town itself had been destroyed. The 342d shot "suspect" inhabitants before it pulled out.[61]

Mass arrests and shootings saturated this attack also. Armed engagements, rare instances aside, did not. Here too, then, the 342d failed to deal the rebels a decisive blow.

But if the 342d's military performance was at best inconsistent during these latter two operations, the butchery it inflicted, much of it on its own initiative, was thoroughly consistent. On October 13, as well as ordering the destruction of numerous villages within the Mount Cer region, it reiterated the command to kill on the slightest suspicion "all those in uniform, as with all civilians encountered in no-man's land, who are suspected of belonging to the insurgency, are to be shot."[62] When it attacked Krupanj, it ordered that "anything found there is to be shot and the place burned down,"[63] and that "every harshness must be visited upon any civilians encountered, for it is known that the enemy does not wear uniform."[64]

Such orders ensured that these operations too inflicted a massively disproportionate tally of "enemy" dead. During the last ten days of October, for example, the 342d lost six men, together with four officers and twenty men wounded. Yet it reported that it had, in turn, killed two hundred of the enemy in combat and shot one hundred after capture—three hundred persons against the thirty-seven guns the division had seized from them.[65] Between October 10 and 19, the 342d reported, its troops had killed 546 insurgents in combat and shot a further 1,081 following their capture—from whom they had recovered just four guns.[66]

Some of the explanations for these massive contrasts do not point to the 342d itself. These are explanations that, indeed, need keeping in mind throughout this study. Insurgents sometimes retrieved or buried the weapons of the fallen before retreating. Some, such as medics, pioneers, and some members of less well-equipped groups generally, would probably have been unarmed anyway. Figures for insurgent dead may also have been inflated for other intentional or unintentional reasons. Yet this is still such a colossal shortfall that the mass shooting of unarmed civilians must account for a very great deal of it.[67]

More grisly still were the 342d's reprisal shootings. Yet they are also more significant, for they highlight even more clearly just how ferocious the division's campaign was becoming. During the Krupanj operation's opening stages the 342d reported that, in reprisal for the killing of one of its officer and seven of its men, and the wounding of a further three officers and twenty-seven men, it planned to execute twenty-three hundred hostages—four hundred of whom it had already shot.[68]

This grim figure corresponded to General Boehme's stipulated reprisal ratios. But then the 342d took things even further. By the time it had relieved Valjevo in late October, it had lost ten dead and thirty-nine wounded; in reprisal, it declared it would shoot one thousand hostages in retaliation for its dead, and 3,950 hostages in retaliation for its wounded. It sharply reminded its troops of Boehme's stipulated 1:100 and 1:50 killing ratios. This was a likely sign that not all the division's rank-and-file soldiers had been administering those ratios as thoroughly as the division wished.[69] But simple calculation reveals that the 342d's command was now actually *exceeding* Boehme's ratios. For it intended to shoot one hundred hostages not just for every one of its dead, but also for every one of its wounded. In fact, by November 11 the division had actually run out of prisoners with which to meet its target.[70]

Clearly then, the need to follow orders was not the only thing powering the butchery which the 342d Infantry Division was inflicting. It should also be remembered that the division had been butchering with particular aplomb for a fortnight *before* Boehme issued his 1:100 reprisal order. Indeed, not content just to outdo Boehme for ruthlessness, Hinghofer also challenged his superior when he felt Boehme was going "soft." Perhaps surprisingly, there was one occasion when Boehme did provide Hinghofer with such grounds.

By October 20 the SD, at Boehme's command, had released over five thousand of the more than twenty-two thousand prisoners who had been incarcerated in the Šabac concentration camp for most of the period since the start of the Drina-Sava operation. Boehme's decision was not prompted by humanity. He acted as he did partly because the Germans needed more native informers and collaborators, and partly because the SD simply had too many prisoners to cope with inside the camp. Hinghofer, however, opined that the action would enable thousands of insurgents, and their accomplices, to disappear undetected among the population and reemerge once the 342d had left the area.[71]

Given the scale of the production-line carnage the 342d was inflicting, it may at first appear obscene to argue that the conditions the division encountered on the ground could have helped to fuel it. Certainly, onerous though the 342d's travails were, they do not even begin to justify bloodletting of such magnitude. Yet their effect, alongside other possible explanations, needs to be considered.

Following the relative failure of the Drina-Sava operation, General Boehme and the 342d Infantry Division were under even greater pressure to produce results. And by the time of the Mount Cer operation, the 342d also faced increasingly arduous conditions. Insurgents frustrated the 342d's advance by razing villages to the ground in "scorched earth" fashion. The division's troops were hindered in their advance by a road system resembling a "baseless mass of mud."[72] They endured a debilitating slog through harsh terrain; slept under canvas in lashing rain, cold, and snow; and lived on invariably cold rations.[73] The 342d's Chetnik opponents, meanwhile, posed an ever greater challenge. Even though between 50 percent and 30 percent of their men were reportedly without arms,[74] they were increasingly well armed overall. At times they turned on their attackers and inflicted significant casualties. The 697th Infantry Regiment faced especially stubborn resistance on September 27, for instance. So too did the 699th Infantry Regiment on October 10.[75]

Together, these conditions gnawed at the troops' resilience. "The troops' state of health can no longer be described as good," the 342d reported on November 12. "The duration and relentlessness of the operations has meant that shoes, uniforms, weaponry, and equipment cannot be brought up to strength or cared for properly . . . The character and duration of the operations (combing, searching, shooting, and living off the land) are beginning to affect the troops' discipline and demeanor badly. The division urgently needs a reasonably long period of peace and quiet in which to re-establish its fighting worth, and immunize its troops against infection and malaria."[76] The 342d also lacked specialist mountain warfare equipment. Finally, though it did not lack for tanks—having acquired two from another unit—they were inferior French models in constant need of maintenance, which the absence of a proper workshop rendered impossible. They were also so loud that they quickly alerted the insurgents to the Germans' imminent approach.[77]

Fighting in such conditions, feeling the pressure from above for results, and frustrated at their failure to capture or kill actual insurgents in large numbers, soldiers were more likely to respond when their commanders exhorted them to ever greater ruthlessness. Indeed, some of the troops were so brutally inclined that their discipline was seriously threatened. Consequently, at different times in September and October, the 342d Infantry Division felt compelled to forbid its troops to plunder, destroy churches, shoot prisoners who could be screened for information, shoot dogs and livestock, seize livestock except on the highest authority, or execute persons outside the domain of the proper legal offices.[78]

And there are signs that some of the 342d's own senior officers could barely keep themselves on a leash, let alone their men. During the 1970s the Federal German Central Office of Land Administration interviewed witnesses for preliminary investigations, later abandoned, into war crimes committed by the 342d Infantry Division. The interviews revealed that Colonel Trüstedt, commander of the 342d's artillery regiment, had been unhealthily fond of alcohol and known to issue orders while under the influence. He had also been a terror to work under; when his subordinates had nicknamed him the "Lion of Mannheim," they had not meant it as a compliment.[79]

But the conditions the 342d experienced do not explain the division's especially ferocious conduct on their own. Units within the permanent German army occupation divisions stationed in Serbia—the 704th, 714th, and 717th Infantry Divisions—had even more reason to lash out in frustration at their circumstances. For the situation their isolated units faced did not just impede them; it could also imperil them. Yet whilst the actions of the some of the units within these divisions were horrendous, neither they nor the division-level orders that spawned them actually went further than General Boehme's dictates. But the 342d Infantry Division's actions did go further.

It is not just the 342d's particular situation that needs examining, then, but also the attitudes that ensured that it would react to them in singularly brutal fashion. The main source of such attitudes lies at the division's apex—divisional command, and particularly General Hinghofer himself.

Divisional command implemented vicious measures not only out of obedience to Boehme, but also according to its own convictions. The quartermaster department's summary at the end of the Drina-Sava operation of September exhibited both a steadfast faith in the efficacy of terror, and a marked indifference to the plight of civilians caught up in the fighting: "It is clear that the population of the Sava-Drina bend, due in part to being terrorized by bandits and Communist groups, has by and large cooperated in the uprising. The division's harsh and vigorous action has seriously weakened its moral power to resist."[80] It also credited the division's use of extreme terror with ensuring suspects' "willingness" to line up to be transported to concentration camps.[81]

Such language oozes the German military's decades-old proclivity for maximum force and terroristic counterinsurgency warfare. The fact that Hinghofer himself had been born in Austria, not Germany, does not detract from this. This is not least because Austrians too had plenty in the way of terroristic counterinsurgency tradition on which to draw.

A divisional command that harbored these convictions so strongly was more likely to lash out excessively at the slightest trouble from armed civilians. And while the 342d's opponents could hardly be described as the "slightest" trouble, nor could they yet be described as truly formidable. Indeed, perhaps because they were attempting to get more reinforcements and equipment put their way, the 342d's officers sometimes overblew the scale of difficulty that they faced. This point needs keeping in mind when considering any report in which a German army counterinsurgency formation loudly protested the parlousness of its condition. For instance, the 342d asserted that the Chetnik forces in the Mount Cer region possessed an excellent communications network. In fact, the Chetniks lacked modern communication equipment and relied almost entirely upon runners and riders.[82] Nor should it be forgotten that the 342d was able to summon Luftwaffe support against the rebels. Stuka attacks could sometimes be hindered by poor visibility, but they provided the 342d with telling offensive impact.[83]

That the 342d Infantry Division's travails were not always as onerous as it made out is a further indication that the principal source of its singular brutality lay elsewhere. Indeed, the divisional files also indicate that the 342d's command was suffused with that anti-Serb prejudice then particularly prevalent among Austrians. The Chetniks, it claimed, did not just employ underhand irregular tactics and avoid direct confrontation; they also responded strongly to "their leaders' constant appeals to the old Serbian tradition of taking up arms in 'small wars' against 'the other.'"[84] The Chetniks' attempts to break out of the division's encirclements, meanwhile, were marked by "fanaticism and desperation."[85]

Given the large gaps in the records of the 714th and 717th Infantry Divisions, it is difficult to be completely certain how far the 342d Infantry Division's attitude differed from theirs. But those 700-number division orders and reports that do survive in archives, material that for the 704th at least is extensive, neither advocate terror nor evince anti-Serbism with the same alacrity as the 342d's. The clearest clues as to the origins of the 342d's particularly obdurate attitude lie with General Hinghofer. Indeed, when Hinghofer was replaced in mid-November, because his superiors doubted his offensive spirit,[86] the 342d began behaving in a manner that, brutal though it continued to be, was less brutal than before.

Hinghofer was not dismissed, but he was required, in mid-November, to swap divisional commands with that of the 717th Infantry Division, hitherto led by Brigadier General Paul Hoffmann. In being shunted from a relatively powerful, mobile Category Fourteen division to a substandard, static Category Fifteen division, Hinghofer was clearly being demoted. And his desperate, ultimately fruitless protest to higher command shows that he knew it.[87]

Some impetus for the division's new approach under General Hoffmann came from above. In late October and early November, Boehme himself, seeing the pragmatic value of greater restraint, displayed further rare flashes of moderation. On October 25 he declared that indiscriminate arrests and persecution would drive the Serbs into the insurgents' arms. He also directed that hostages be seized only from villages known to be centers of the uprising. A week later he directed that, while anyone found carrying a weapon in the operational area was to be shot, those who were unarmed were not.[88]

Hoffmann also invoked an Army High Command directive of October 25, which stated that "the population must be shown clearly that it is pointless to resist the troops and their instruments of power. Harsh conduct is required in guilty or doubtful cases. On the other hand, practical support and good setting of examples are essential to the reestablishment of peace, confidence and trust." And while he reiterated that the troops must conduct themselves harshly, Hoffmann also put new stress on "protecting the population against Communists and against unpermitted attacks on their property from any side [including, presumably, from rank-and-file German troops], help with agriculture through the commitment of personnel and equipment, support over rebuilding of houses, (and) propaganda to promote peace, quiet, and work, as well as defense against disruptive elements."[89] The division now also directed that "suspects are to be taken prisoner if there is no reason to shoot them."[90]

Similarly, units of the 342d taking part in December's Operation Mihailović, launched against the Chetnik leader's headquarters in the Ravna Gora region, did not inflict butchery on anything like the scale of earlier operations. That operation saw twelve enemy dead, and 745 men, seven officers, and two women taken prisoner. Three hundred and seventeen rifles and seven machine guns were seized.[91] Saner attitudes also seemed to be penetrating the subordinate units involved in this particular operation. "The speediest way to achieve success was through ruthless offensive action," reported Antitank Detachment 342. But while it also described the population as "difficult to figure out," it judged it "friendly for the most part."[92] This was new language for the 342d.

The 342d also issued a directive in late November stressing that the best means of improving workers' willingness to toil for the Axis occupation was to protect them from insurgent attack.[93] Reprisals, too, ferocious though they remained, were now less ferocious than before. Under General Hinghofer, a violent assault on a member of the division's personnel would probably have precipitated a reprisal shooting of fifty or even one hundred victims. But under General Hoffmann the 342d's riposte to one such incident, the victim being one Lieutenant Friedrich, was to shoot twenty-five hostages—a brutal act, but less brutal than it might have been—and fine the local population five hundred thousand dinars.[94]

In December, finally, Hoffmann would seek to impress his more measured stance upon his superiors. Serbia Command's war diary for December 11 records that Hoffmann paid a visit that day to recommend that farmers belonging to Mihailović's movement who were not carrying weapons should not be treated as rebels. Hoffmann believed that the farmers had had no other choice but to join Mihailović if they were to avoid having to join the Communists instead. As long as they comported themselves quietly, they should be allowed to go about their work and feel secure in the protection of the German Wehrmacht. Hoffmann also urged that intensified propaganda be employed among the Serbian farmers, particularly on market days.[95]

Much of the impetus behind the division's new approach emanated, then, from divisional command. And the fact that divisional command was now under new management can hardly have been coincidental.

Hinghofer's biography reveals much about what made his approach to counterinsurgency warfare markedly more ferocious than his successor's. In some respects there was little significant difference between Hinghofer's background and those of the other divisional commanders serving in Yugoslavia that autumn. All came from middle-class families; Hinghofer's father had been a senior bank inspector, Hoffmann's a senior postal official, Borowski's a police inspector. General Stahl, commander of the 714th Infantry Division, was perhaps slightly higher on the social scale, his father having been a privy councilor. But all four officers essentially hailed from the families of middle-class petty officials, albeit fairly senior ones.[96] Such professions did not belong to the traditional officer recruitment circles of either army. But they did belong to the "reliable" middle-class circles from which both armies were extensively recruiting by the early twentieth century.

There were also elements of Hinghofer's military career common with those of Borowski, Hoffmann, and Stahl. All were continuing officers, in the Reichswehr or Bundesheer, during the interwar years. Only Hoffmann saw any period of civilian employment. He left the army between November 1932 and March 1935 to work as an official in the area of youth sport and physical training. He also experienced a spell of unemployment between October and December 1933.[97] Further, all four men had spent significant periods serving with a specialist technical branch of the army, a higher-level staff body, or both. In other words, all four had pursued careers to that level of technical and professional specialization that could limit officers' wider social outlook and restrict their vision to perfecting their professional skills. Indeed, both Hoffmann and Hing-hofer had gone even further; each had served in the war ministries of their respective countries during the 1930s.[98]

Yet when it comes to where the four officers served during the Great War, significant differences do emerge. The impact the eastern front could have upon an officer's perceptions was considered in Chapter 2. The fact that Hinghofer served there during the Great War did not in itself distinguish him from his fellow divisional commanders in Serbia. For one thing, Hoffmann himself spent considerable periods on the eastern front during the Great War. After fighting in the initial battles in East Prussia in August 1914, Hoffmann fought on more southerly sectors of the eastern front for lengthy periods between 1915 and 1917. There was a hiatus in 1916 when he was transferred west to fight in the Battle of Verdun. He then served on the western front again throughout 1918. Hoffmann's own ideological convictions may have been particularly strengthened by his experience during the march into the Baltic region and the battle against the Bolsheviks there during 1919.[99] Borowski too served for significant periods in the East, as well as on the western front.[100] Stahl interspersed homeland-based staff posts with active service in military airships and observation balloons on a number of fronts, the eastern front included.[101] But while Borowski's and Hoffmann's Great War service records were less peripatetic than Stahl's, all three men also spent significant, sometimes lengthy periods away from the eastern front.[102] Hinghofer, however, served entirely on the eastern front from 1914 through to 1918.[103]

An officer who had experienced the eastern front in this way, and for this duration, had more time than many to imbibe that particular brew of experiences—the region's hostile environment, its peoples, the nature of the fighting and of the opponents against whom it was being waged—that could render him more susceptible to brutalizing influences later in life. This is not to deny the brutalizing potency of other fronts, not least the western. But it is to re-emphasize the brutalizing potency of the eastern front. Of course, Serbia in 1941 was a different region, populated by a different people, to the eastern theater of the Great War. But in north-west Serbia the 342d Infantry Division contended with a dangerous insurgency, an arduous environment, and a population whose reliability was at best doubtful and at worst non-existent. Such conditions could brutal-ize the view of any commander facing them. They were especially likely to brutalize it if that commander had undergone experiences during the Great War that made him highly susceptible to brutalization already.

Hinghofer may also have been particularly susceptible because, hav-ing served in the Ukraine in 1918, he had already participated in an occupation regime that prosecuted extremely harsh counterinsurgency warfare. The Austro-Hungarian portion of the occupied Ukraine was administered by the Eastern Army, formerly the Austro-Hungarian Sec-ond Army. Both German and Austrian forces faced brutalizing condi-tions in the Ukraine that year. They faced an elusive, resourceful, and ruthless foe—no more ruthless than the Bolsheviks numbered among their opponents. Such opponents were often indistinguishable from the wider civilian population, and the Germans and Austrians had to com-bat them across an area too vast for their own inadequate manpower to master properly. Matters were made worse by the unsuitability of the indigenous administrative personnel on whom the Central powers had to rely, and by their own failure to develop a more coordinated occupa-tion strategy.[104]

And the Austrian forces in the Ukraine were slower than the Germans to develop an approach that sought to genuinely engage the population instead of simply terrorize it. What may have particularly hardened the Austrians' own conduct was their need to stave off a domestic food situ-ation even more desperate than Germany's. Certainly their grain requi-sitioning operation, and the pacification measures that accompanied it, were particularly brutal.[105]

Just how directly involved Hinghofer's 11th Field Artillery Brigade was in suppressing resistance is something that the sources that could be accessed for this study do not reveal. At the very least, however, he would have been acutely aware of the insurgency in the countryside, and the danger it posed both to the Austrian occupation and to personnel such as himself in particular. And if the insurgents could assassinate the German military commander in the Ukraine, Field Marshal von Eichhorn, then no German or Austrian officer was safe.[106]

Hinghofer and Hoffmann also differed on another score. Hoffmann's personal file shows him to have been a man who, in a manner all too uncommon among senior German army officers in Yugoslavia during World War II, possessed an element of moral courage. The key event took place after Hoffmann had been transferred from Yugoslavia to the Ukraine. Here, in September 1943, the Wehrmacht's Ukraine Command judged Hoffmann as lacking the "necessary harshness for the war in the East." Ukraine Command reached this judgment when Hoffmann disobeyed an order to decimate by firing squad a mutinous Turkic unit in German service. The term "to decimate" was meant literally here, inspired by the ancient Roman punishment of executing every tenth legionary in a unit that had mutinied or deserted. Hoffmann refused to carry out the order because, he maintained, he did not wish to impose the moral burden for the killing upon his men. In particular, he did not wish to compel older personnel to do the deed. The incident seems to have effectively finished Hoffmann's military career.[107] He ended the war as commandant of a POW camp.[108]

Courageous though Hoffmann's stand was, it is important to keep it in proportion. Hoffmann was anything but a dove in counterinsurgency matters. Some of his active suggestions to Boehme were anything but enlightened. For instance, on October 10, 1941, while still commanding the 717th Infantry Division, he proposed a package of "Balkan-style" measures to counter the "bandits." His list included forced labor, house burning, hostage-taking and reprisals, and the herding of "idle and loitering" men into concentration camps. Most damningly of all, it was under Hoffmann's leadership that units of the 717th Infantry Division committed killings into the thousands, albeit within the boundaries set by General Boehme, in Kraljevo and Kragujevac. Kragujevac was the work of one battalion, but at Kraljevo Hoffmann himself oversaw proceedings and praised his men fulsomely for their "enthusiastic fulfilment of what was demanded of them."[109]

But Hoffmann's conduct in the Ukraine does show that, at the very least, he was less likely to actually surpass General Boehme's calls for vengeful terror in the way Hinghofer did. This does not amount to anything remotely approaching moral exoneration for his actions in Yugoslavia. But the actions of the 342d under his command, abhorrent as many of them were, fell within the boundaries of Boehme's directives. The 342d's actions under Hinghofer's command did not.

But perhaps the most decisive reason why General Hinghofer combated the 1941 uprising even more truculently than his fellow divisional commanders was that, of all them, he was the only Austrian.[110] Thus, even though Hinghofer himself did not actually serve in Serbia during the Great War—something common to him and General Boehme—he was more likely than his German-born colleagues to feel the decades-old anti-Serb sentiment that Boehme exploited in the cause of crushing the 1941 uprising.[111]

Such are the source limitations that it is impossible to know how wholeheartedly the 342d Infantry Division's rank-and-file troops adhered to Hinghofer's pitiless approach. The fact that many were not Austrian meant that they may not have felt such intense hatred towards the Serbs.[112] Indeed, some did fail to follow their commander's directives as enthusiastically as he would have wished. But the overall record is clear. Of all the German army counterinsurgency divisions fighting in Serbia during 1941, the 342d Infantry Division was the most ferocious by some way. It behaved not just according to directives from above or to the conditions it faced, but also according to its commander's standpoint. Hinghofer's particular pattern of service during the Great War may well have helped incubate his extreme obduracy. He was also Austrian-born, and thus more likely than his German-born fellows to comport himself viciously against the Serbs. This may also help explain why General Borowski's 704th Infantry Division did not comport itself as viciously as it might have in summer 1941.

The behavior of Hoffmann, Borowski, and Stahl needs keeping firmly in perspective. They had no compunction in unleashing their formations upon the Serbian population in autumn 1941 with the full force of General Boehme's directives. Indeed, there is no indication that any of them saw fit even to question those directives. And here it should be remembered that, though it was rare in the extreme for officers to directly question indiscriminately terroristic orders, it could and did happen. Two examples demonstrate this.

In August 1941 the area commandant in Niš, Freiherr von Bothmer, not only objected to indiscriminately shooting innocent Serbs en masse.

He also used moral and legal arguments when he refused to shoot Communists in his custody against whom no wrongdoing had been proved. Even though he acknowledged that they would probably be executed by the SD, he refused to endorse even that action.[113] Then in October the district commandant in Kragujevac, Captain von Bischofshausen, prevailed upon the first battalion of the 724th Infantry Regiment to execute reprisal victims from "Communist-infested" villages, rather than from Kragujevac itself, because "not a single Wehrmacht member or ethnic German has been wounded or shot there."[114] Bischofshausen does not appear to have been acting out of a sense of morality here, though it is possible he was disguising moral objections with pragmatic arguments because he felt such arguments might be more likely to be heeded.[115] Yet whatever his motive, he was showing some grasp, however compromised it may have been, of the need to make some distinction between "guilty" and "innocent."

That relatively junior officers saw fit to question indiscriminate brutality officially—whether on moral, legal, or pragmatic grounds—but divisional commanders did not, suggests that those divisional commanders approved of such methods. After all, Borowski, Hoffmann, and Stahl served in an institution whose leadership had chosen to revive a profoundly harsh strain of counterinsurgency, and which had over the years become suffused by ideological, careerist, and technocratic ruthlessness. The social backgrounds, Great War experiences, and broader career paths of all three men were in many respects similarly conducive to such attitudes. The troops they commanded comported themselves with according ruthlessness in 1941, be it against Jews, Communists, or—most devastatingly—the general population. The difference, however, is that Hinghofer's 342d comported itself with a ruthlessness even more extreme.

As it turned out, General Hoffmann's 342d Infantry Division began tempering its ferocity just as the Germans began landing serious blows upon the Serbian national uprising. By late October, Serbia Command was reporting that German mobile operations against the insurgents were helping to relieve the pressure elsewhere. Rebels and population had been surprised by the ferocity of the German operations and the reprisals that accompanied them.[116] The SD opined that, though there was no room for complacency, the number of rebel attacks had fallen. It also asserted that Boehme's 1:100 order had created "clear guidelines" for the practice of reprisals.[117]

The most serious blow of all was Operation Užice. This operation, involving the 342d together with the temporarily assigned 113th Infantry Division and parts of the 714th, commenced on November 25, a fortnight after the 342d's divisional command had changed hands, and concluded on December 4.[118] The divisional order for the operation conveyed the moderation, albeit moderation blended with harshness, that the 342d had begun to practice under General Hoffmann:

  a) Any burning down (of dwellings) is strictly prohibited and punishable. It is applicable only if arms and ammunition are found or if fire is levelled from houses.
  b) To be shot to death are all men carrying arms, using them or concealing them, women and children (sic), however, only if they actively participate in the fighting. In any case children are to be spared.
  c) All Chetniks and Communists who surrender are to be made prisoners and are to be disarmed.[119]

But Operation Užice's greater importance was military: while the Germans failed to encircle and annihilate the Partisans, they inflicted serious losses and drove Tito's staff southward into Italian-occupied Sandzak.

Yet Operation Užice was successful partly because of wider forces. For one thing the German reprisals, abhorrent as they were, were from September helping to drive a wedge between the Chetniks and the Partisans. Mihailović's already lukewarm commitment to the national uprising thus dwindled further. He was already disheartened by the fact that the Serbian gendarmerie, many of whom had some sympathy with his movement, had been a prime target for the Communists from the uprising's earliest days. He also perceived that the Germans' intransigence towards the Nedić government made it much harder for his own movement to benefit from its earlier contact and communication with that government.[120]

Haunted by the memory of Serbia's trauma during the Great War, the reprisals led Mihailović to conclude that continuing to resist the Germans openly would precipitate Serbia's "national suicide."[121] The reprisals' severity would eventually diminish in effect as the war continued. Indeed, the number of hostages needed to feed them was already beginning to render them unworkable. But they had immense shock effect in autumn 1941.[122] As Milovan Djilas wrote:

> The tragedy gave to Nedić "convincing proof" that the Serbs would be biologically exterminated if they were not submissive and loyal, and to the Chetniks "proof" that the Partisans were prematurely provoking the Germans and thus causing the decimation of Serbs and the destruction of Serbian culture . . . If there was treason, and I hold that there was, it justified itself with biological survival.[123]

But the Germans failed to fully recognize that Operation Užice also succeeded for political reasons. For one thing, it was not just fierce German reprisals that had driven Mihailović to sever his links with the Partisans, but the man's increasing confidence also. Mihailović felt increasingly assured of the active support of the British, and the royal government-in-exile. He first obtained British material aid in November 1941. The government-in-exile, which was almost identical to the Simović administration the March 1941 coup had propelled into power, and which was almost entirely composed of Serbs, backed Mihailović to the hilt. In January 1942, it would appoint him Minister for War. By contrast, the Partisans found themselves extensively frozen out by the British in late 1941, and scolded by Moscow for lacking the constructive coalition mentality necessary for wartime alliances.[124]

But probably the most important reason for the Chetnik–Partisan split was that the two movements' aims fundamentally conflicted. The Chetniks' program went well beyond the agenda of the government-in-exile; they sought not only to restore the old monarchical system, but also to extend Serbian power within Yugoslavia. The most grandiose form this ambition would take was a plan for a "Great Serbia." The blueprint for Great Serbia was proposed in a memorandum produced on June 30, 1941, by Stevan Moljević of the Chetniks' Central National Committee. Great

Serbia would incorporate Bosnia and much of Croatia into a greatly enlarged Serbia, which would then dominate postwar Yugoslavia even more emphatically than before.[125]

The Partisans, by contrast, sought a revolution against the old order and the foundation of a new state based on the principles of Communism and Yugoslavism. Moreover, the Partisans had loudly declared their intent by using the liberated area around Užice as a laboratory for revolutionary measures. NOOs had been rapidly established, for instance, tax and land records burned, and women deployed in the Partisans' ranks. More ominously, the Partisans had eliminated local politicians who had criticized them.[126] All this, of course, rendered impossible anything but the most short-term cooperation between Partisans and Chetniks.

What had united the two movements in 1941, then, was far less important than what divided them. This, more than anything else, guaranteed their split that autumn and their deadly antagonism over the following years. By late October, amid halfhearted and soon-to-be-abandoned attempts by Tito and Mihailović to stave off armed confrontation, Partisan and Chetnik units were openly fighting one another.

There were now opportunities for the Axis to co-opt the Mihailović Chetniks, if only temporarily.[127] Some of Mihailović's forces did come to an arrangement with the Nedić regime. The two parties shared common anti-Communist ground, and many of their leading figures were connected by strong personal links. At the end of November, though there was no formal agreement between the Mihailović movement and the Nedić government, many of Mihailović's commanders aligned their men with Nedić's "legal" Chetnik formations in exchange for official protection.[128] This agreement, and the Mihailović's Chetniks' relative quiescence more generally, would ensure that occupied Serbia, at least, remained comparatively peaceful for the rest of the war.

But the Germans, though their distrust of Mihailović was understandable, missed an opportunity for an active temporary alliance against the Partisans. They believed Mihailović was cooperating with Nedić to play the general and themselves off against one another, and that any approach Mihailović might make to them would be made out of sheer military necessity.[129] Mihailović did indeed approach the Germans in November 1941, following one of his failed meetings with Tito. He requested guns and ammunition in return for his help in "(purging) the Serbian area once and for all of the Communist bands."[130] But the Germans rebuffed him, demanded his unconditional surrender, and then narrowly failed to capture him when they overran his headquarters at Ravna Gora in early December.[131]

Spurned by the Germans, Mihailović's forces within Serbia would now restrict their actions to low-key subversion and sabotage against the occupation. Ostensibly this was so they could await the time when, their strength and organization sufficiently developed, they could rise up in tandem with an Allied invasion. But their closeness to Nedić was embroiling them in a double game, one that would increasingly turn them into de facto collaborators rather than freedom fighters. The implications for their movement, and for Yugoslavia, would be immense.

But in November 1941, the Chetnik–Partisan split offered Boehme one major opportunity. Free now to turn his fire entirely against the Partisans, he shortened his front by concentrating his forces on selected areas. The Partisans, recklessly overconfident following the revolt's early successes, had already played into his hands. They had declared the area around Užice a "free zone" and visibly concentrated their forces there. This, of course, made it much easier for Boehme to target them in a conventional kind of operation. The operation also succeeded for mundane practical reasons: the stripping of the fields during harvesttime deprived the Partisans of a major source of cover.[132]

Though the Partisans were not destroyed outright during Operation Užice, they came close. According to German reports, two thousand Partisans were killed during the operation. And the reports' claim that 2,723 guns were recovered from the Partisan dead indicates that this time it was armed fighters, not defenseless civilians, who had perished in great numbers.[133] The remnant of Tito's force had to flee for its very existence. It seems the 342d Infantry Division only failed to press its pursuit of them for fear of antagonizing the Italians with a probe into their territory. This was probably the closest the Germans ever came to killing or capturing Tito.[134] They would come to rue this lost opportunity at length. Yet for now, the Communist Partisan movement had been dealt a fearful blow. Tito himself even offered to resign on December 7, although the offer was rejected.[135] His main force now comprised only two thousand fighters in the field,[136] for whom the only hope of survival lay in fleeing Serbia for the mountains of the NDH.

General Boehme departed with the staff of XVIII Corps for the eastern front on December 6. His successor, General Bader—who assumed the title Commander in Serbia rather than Plenipotentiary Commanding General—was aware that the insurgency had not been crushed conclusively. He feared that the spring thaw could bring new unrest, particularly given the amount of weapons and munitions still in Serb hands. But for now, in the aftermath of Operation Užice and amid further successful mopping-up operations, Bader surveyed a situation far less perilous than that of three months earlier. He felt sufficiently confident, on December 22, to replace Boehme's now unworkable 1:100 reprisal directive with one that instead stipulated that "only" fifty Serbs should be shot for every German soldier killed.[137]

The Wehrmacht's defeat of the Serbian national uprising of 1941 trumpeted its readiness to employ terror to the utmost. German documents record that, between August 1 and December 5, the Germans killed eleven thousand insurgents in combat and executed nearly twenty-two thousand reprisal victims, at a cost to themselves of fewer than six hundred killed or wounded.[138] But such was the attitude of at least one particular divisional commander, and the life experiences and life influences that had shaped him, that he demonstrated his own ferocity even more emphatically than his fellows demonstrated theirs.

During 1942, however, a rather different picture would emerge from the German army occupation divisions operating in the NDH.

CHAPTER 7

Standing Divided

The Independent State of Croatia, 1942

AT FIRST SIGHT, the prognosis for the Partisans in the NDH at the dawn of 1942 did not look promising.[1] Not only had the Axis expelled them from Serbia. In the NDH, they remained too strongly associated with the Serbian struggle for them to be yet able to extend their appeal to the NDH's Croat and Muslim populations. And such was Chetnik strength in parts of the NDH, particularly eastern Bosnia, that the Partisans also faced a serious challenge for control of the NDH's remaining Serbian population.

Yet the NDH offered the Partisans potentially fertile territory. In the NDH's Croatian regions, they benefited from a strong Communist organization of long standing. They would also benefit, in time, from a particular groundswell of support from the oppressed Croatian population of Italian-occupied Dalmatia.[2] And in Bosnia, the Partisans stood to benefit from a particular combination of rugged terrain, strong Communist organization, and considerable potential support.

In 1931, Bosnia's diverse population of Muslims, Orthodox Serbs, and (predominantly Croat) Catholics stood at just over 2.3 million; this was an increase of almost half a million in just ten years.[3] The increase was due to the rapid expansion of that constituency from which the Bosnian Communists could expect to draw their firmest support, the urban working class. But the rural population, nearly 85 percent of Bosnia's population in total, was potentially fertile ground also.[4] This was due in large part to the Communists' collaboration with the League of Farmers. After defending the rights of Bosnian Serb peasants against Muslim landlords during the interwar years, the League enjoyed a strong following among the ethnic Serbs who in 1931 comprised almost half of Bosnia's rural population.[5]

More generally, the Bosnian Communists' growth had been aided by the interwar expansion of Bosnia's education system. This had brought together different ethnic groupings as well as urban and rural populations. It had also engendered an emerging left-wing intelligentsia, particularly among teachers and university students, from which the Bosnian Communists drew much of their leadership.[6] In the early days of the Axis occupation the Communists sought to appeal to a collective "Bosnian patriotism" among the region's population groups. They stressed the brotherhood of all Bosnians and depicted the struggle against the occupiers as a continuation of the struggle for Bosnian liberation that had been waged against an oppressive, centralizing government in Belgrade during the interwar years.[7]

By the beginning of 1942, the Communists' main strength was in urban areas, western Bosnia, and certain parts of eastern Bosnia. It was in these areas that the nascent Bosnian Partisan movement now developed.[8] Throughout the war, the Serbs would predominate within the Bosnian Partisan rank and file. But in time, Croats and Bosnian Muslims would become more visible also.[9] Yet in the eastern part of Herzegovina, Bosnia's southern region, the Communists were numerically strong but organizationally weak. And among many population circles of eastern Bosnia it was the Chetniks who held sway.[10]

On 25 January 1942, following its expulsion from Serbia and brief hiatus in Sandzak, the remnant of Tito's own Partisan force arrived in Foča in eastern Bosnia.[11] Chetniks and Partisans had been tensely coexisting in eastern Bosnia since the beginning of the Serbian national uprising. The Chetniks here had even paid some lip service to the rights of Croats and Muslims.[12] But here as in Serbia, long-term cooperation was never in prospect. As in Serbia, the leaderships of the two groups here had fundamentally different aims—and already by mid-November 1941, the mere presence of Muslims and Croats in the Bosnian Partisans' ranks was becoming a particular deal-breaker for the Bosnian Chetniks.[13] The breakdown of relations between the two movements in Serbia further removed any incentive to cooperate in eastern Bosnia.[14]

Moreover, from the early days of the Axis occupation, the Chetniks were offered cooperation with the Italians instead. In July 1941, as the interior of the NDH grew increasingly lawless, the Italians sought to improve their Croatian territory's economic security and safeguard its inland communications. Thus, to the Ustasha regime's great alarm, they extended their area of occupation as far as Zone III in the NDH.[15] To avoid overstretching themselves, they began employing Chetnik groups on the ground. They wooed the Bosnian Chetniks with offers of arms and money to fight the Partisans, and wooed Bosnian Serbs more generally by pledging to protect them from the ravages of the Ustasha.[16]

But what Italian protection meant in practice would rapidly become clear—it provided ideal cover for the Chetniks to vent themselves murderously against their Croat and Muslim neighbors. Even without the Ustasha massacres, Bosnian Chetniks felt intense hostility towards the NDH's other ethnic groups. They drew no distinction between the Ustasha and other Croats, and referred to Bosnia's Muslim population as "Turks." This particular antagonism was a legacy not just of centuries-old Muslim–Christian enmity, but also of recent history. Bosnian Muslims in Habsburg service had often behaved savagely towards Serbs during the Great War. During the 1920s, the League of Farmers had defended Bosnian Serb peasants against Muslim landlords, and throughout the interwar years Serb and Muslim political parties had clashed bitterly. All this, and the fact that Bosnia's Muslim population was larger than its Croatian one, meant that Bosnian Serbs if anything hated Muslims even more than they hated Croats.[17]

What the Italians gained in the Chetniks was relief from administrative and security duty, and—they believed—a force they could use to increase their leverage against the NDH. They also believed that, by co-opting the Chetniks, they could drive the Partisans to more brutal lengths and thus isolate them from the general population. But the Italians' machinations would eventually backfire. It was not the Partisans but the Chetniks who would come to alienate many potential supporters, even among the Bosnian Serbs.[18] Partly this was because their quiescence against the occupiers, and their increasingly open collaboration with them, would increasingly cause many among the population to perceive them as Axis stooges. Partly, it was because of the fearful cruelty and massacre to which they subjected the territory's Croat and Muslim populations.

And the Chetniks were not just exacting revenge for Ustasha outrages; indeed, in 1941 the Ustasha killings in eastern Bosnia had been considerably less extensive than elsewhere.[19] Their actions belonged instead to a wider campaign of massacre, expulsion, and subjugation. The Chetniks were conducting it not only to settle local scores but also to provide the foundation of a "Great Serbia." Unlike the Ustasha, the Chetniks lacked the state apparatus, the strong (albeit vicious) ideology, or the practical "expertise" that would have enabled them to conduct this program more thoroughly. But commanders on the spot incited copious mayhem and butchery in those areas they controlled.[20] Mihailović fully supported the expulsions, though it is much less clear how much he knew of, or approved of, the killings that were taking place. But there was little, if anything, he could have done to prevent the killings even if he had wanted to.[21] Horrific as the Chetniks' conduct was, the Partisans would reap long-term benefit from it.

But in January 1942, the Partisans seemed far from gaining the upper hand. For one thing, they faced a difficult balancing act. The mainstay of Partisan rank-and-file manpower, as well as Chetnik manpower, was the Bosnian Serbs. But the Partisans' Communist leadership did not wish to appear too partial to Serb interests for fear of alienating the NDH's Muslim and Croat populations. As yet though, they lacked the resources necessary to properly reeducate their Serb rank and file to embrace Yugoslavism.[22] The result was that rank-and-file Bosnian Serb Partisans could feel as antagonistic towards Muslims as did Bosnian Chetniks. And even if they themselves did not perpetrate massacres against Muslims, they were not above actively enabling the Chetniks to do so.[23]

Yet it was not just rogue Partisan groups, but also the Communist leadership of the Partisan movement whose exercise of terror in early 1942 was stymieing the support levels the movement might otherwise have enjoyed. Already the Communists had lost much ground to the Chetniks in Montenegro because, since the July revolt there, they had spent too little time building popular support and too much time indulging in terroristic class war. They had been eliminating opponents real or perceived with a zeal that not only was excessively ruthless, but had also alienated the wider population. Tito had lambasted the Montenegrin Communists for their actions. But in winter 1941–1942 the Communists, despite losing Serbia also, were again infected with hubris. The cause this time was the Red Army's defeat of the Wehrmacht before Moscow in early December. Certain of the Red Army's imminent triumph, they devoted too much energy to ruthlessly digging out and eliminating supposed fifth columnists. The brutality of this "red terror" increased Chetnik support at the Partisans' expense.[24]

In February, however, the Partisan movement began to change its approach. Tito at last sought an end to violent sectarianism and rigid ideology. The Communist leadership of the Partisan movement was as set as ever on achieving postwar power, but for the duration of the war itself the movement's language and approach would extol the cause of national liberation rather than of class struggle. The Partisan leadership now issued the "Foča Instructions," directing that the movement, and the NOOs it was establishing, work to establish a broad front of popular support. Among other things, NOOs operating on Bosnian territory strove to place the administration of the liberated areas on a more ethnically equitable footing.[25] Tito also recognized that the Partisans could potentially garner mass support simply by conducting themselves in a morally irreproachable fashion towards the general—in other words, non-Chetnik—population. This did not always happen in practice, but it happened more than enough to set the Partisans' behavior apart from that of the Chetniks and Ustasha.[26] The Partisans also sought to increase their appeal to the British, by making great play of Mihailović's "collaboration" with the Axis.[27]

The Partisans also stood to gain from the Chetniks' manifold defects. The Bosnian Chetniks did benefit from their links, using Bosnian Serb refugees as middlemen, with the Nedić regime and Mihailović's "Supreme Command." But this did not make them more coordinated. Led, as many were, by assorted local warlords, they were impervious to anything more than the most fragmentary supervision by the centre.[28] Thus, though

Mihailović sought to co-opt all Chetniks in Yugoslavia, his authority in real terms extended only as far as Serbia. By and large the Bosnian Chetniks were Great Serb in outlook, but concerned first and foremost with their own narrow interests.[29] Squabbles and rivalries between local Chetnik commanders became legion; some turned murderous. And although the Bosnian Chetniks would come to nominally accept Mihailović's leadership, they usually did so only in the hope of acquiring more arms and legitimacy.[30] All this hampered attempts to unify the Chetnik movement, if indeed a movement it was, more effectively.

And if the Mihailović movement encountered obstacles to mobilizing the Bosnian Chetniks effectively, its focus on Serb interests prevented it from gaining broader support. In fact, the Mihailović Chetniks' whole standpoint was rigidly conservative, supporting the monarchy and organized Church but thereby alienating large strands of urban opinion. They also alienated women, failing to utilize them as the Partisans did, whether as fighters in the field or administrative personnel in the areas they controlled. Mihailović and his commanders, though possessing some military ability, were unsuited to developing their movement's political organization and propaganda. Correspondingly, they also underestimated the Partisans' abilities on these counts. The Mihailović movement's leadership compounded its failure to take these weaknesses more seriously by relying too heavily on the Allies and believing that the movement was indispensable to them.[31]

But in early 1942, the Germans were too concerned with the Mihailović Chetniks—whom they perceived as the main threat to security, particularly security of the rail route to Greece—to take the embryonic Partisan movement in the NDH as seriously as they should have. Whether because they were seeking to impress the Allies, or because they simply did not wish to dispense with resistance entirely, some Chetnik groups in both Bosnia and Serbia did persist with sabotage acts during 1942.[32] The Mihailović Chetniks launched a particularly extensive campaign against the railway line to Greece that autumn.[33] But by the end of the year there could be no reasonable doubt that it was the Partisans who were the most rapidly growing threat. The most important effect of the

Germans' misjudgment was that it would not be until 1943 that they would commit genuinely powerful forces to combating them. In 1942, they relied too heavily on their Italian and Ustasha allies to do the job.

The Germans, with their forces committed to the eastern front or spread across occupied Europe, relied on the Italians in Yugoslavia in large part out of necessity. The Italian Second Army comprised a two hundred thousand strong, albeit poorly trained and led, body of manpower, which the Germans believed could provide substantial relief for their own overstretched forces in the region.[34] Another important underpinning of the Italo-German relationship in the Balkans, as elsewhere, was personal and political. Hitler valued his strong personal relationship with Mussolini, their shared worldview, and the Italian dictator's loyalty since enabling the Reich to annex Austria in 1938.[35] Militarily, however, the Germans could hardly have chosen more ineffectual allies.[36] Relations were not helped when, over Loznica on January 23, an Italian combat aircraft accidentally killed four German soldiers and one civilian, and wounded twenty-three soldiers and civilians, despite German troops on the ground frantically firing signal flares and waving Nazi flags.[37]

While the derision with which the Germans in Yugoslavia regarded the Italians is distasteful and not altogether fair, then, it did reflect real military failings on the Italians' part. Lieutenant Peter Geissler, a staff officer with LXV Corps, provided a flavor of such derision in a private letter in 1941: "There's a load of Italian soldiers milling around Belgrade. Never did a people look so unsoldierly in uniform . . . You barely encounter any that don't have their hands in their pockets and a cigarette in their beak. Just as though they were civilians, the little squirts wear neither belts nor side arms . . . Still, we shouldn't talk about the spaghetti eaters like that. They're our allies after all."[38]

In January 1942 General Mario Roatta exchanged his post of Italian army chief of staff with General Ambrosio, and thus became the Italian Second Army's new commander.[39] Roatta tailored his army's counterinsurgency policy to his troops' failings. It was not that the Italians shied away from terror tactics where they deemed them useful. Indeed, they brought with them a brutal tradition of their own from their colonial campaigns in Libya and Abyssinia. Their suppression of the Montenegrin revolt of July 1941 was only marginally less ferocious than the

German reprisal campaign in Serbia that year. But the Italians eventually came to see that, against a Partisan adversary in the mountainous regions of the NDH, brutal colonial-style methods had their limits. The terrain was more arduous, and the enemy—even one as militarily weak as the Partisans still were—too well equipped for the Italians' own substandard troops to take on. And the ruthless determination with which the Partisans pursued their cause made them more impervious than Mihailović to the pressure of mass reprisals.[40]

Instead of relying extensively on force and terror, then, the Italians were much more likely than the Germans to cut deals with other groups antagonistic to the Partisans. Above all, this meant cutting deals with the Chetniks. The Italians were prepared to woo the Chetniks even to the point of becoming complicit in interethnic killing;[41] sometimes they disarmed the Chetniks' rivals in the Muslim militias the better to enable the Chetniks to savage them also.

But there were immense practical failings, not to mention the moral ones, to the Italians' approach. Over time, the Italians' mounting difficulties would lead them to rely ever more heavily on the Chetniks; by February 1943, over twenty thousand Chetniks in the NDH had been organized by the Italians into the Anti-Communist Volunteer Militia (MVAC).[42] The Italians, like the Germans, believed the Chetniks to be better organized and better led than they actually were. Thus, when the Italians disengaged from extensive areas of the NDH and left them to the Chetniks, it was ultimately the Partisans who would occupy the resulting vacuum.[43] But even if the Germans wanted to prevent the Italians from pandering to the Chetniks—and their own stance on the matter would itself prove increasingly ambivalent—they were powerless to do so as long as their military dominance of the Italians in the Balkan theater remained far less complete than it was in others.[44]

An even worse bane for the Germans was the Pavelić regime. In 1941, the regime's barbarism towards Serbs and other groups within the NDH's borders had created perfect conditions for the Serbian national uprising. In 1942, similarly, Ustasha depravities would greatly fuel Partisan support across the NDH.

Again, however, Hitler approved of the Ustasha's actions; the Ustashe, he declared in August 1942, should be allowed to "rage themselves out."[45] Milovan Djilas wrote that "Hitler's invasion unearthed the long pent-up shadows of ages past and gave them a new dress, a new motivation: neighbors who might have lived out their lives side by side were now all of a sudden plundering and annihilating one another."[46] At various times in 1941 and 1942, German administrators did manage to compel Pavelić to place limited checks on the Ustasha's rampage. In April 1942, whether as a fig leaf or as a genuine acknowledgment that the Ustasha could not annihilate NDH Serbdom entirely, Pavelić also announced the formation of a Croatian orthodox church.[47] And such was the spread of Partisan territory by 1943 that the Ustasha's opportunity for massacre and cruelty became increasingly limited. But the damage was largely done, and Partisan support vastly augmented as a result.[48]

The NDH's image as a tool of the Axis, and the parlous state of its economy, would in time erode its limited support amongst the Croatian population also. This would render Croats increasingly susceptible to the Partisan cause.[49] For this, however, it is the Germans and Italians who should shoulder most blame.

While the Germans did not formally annex Croatian territory, the Italians did. This, and the arrogance with which they comported themselves—partly to compensate for their own military inadequacies—disgruntled the population immensely. The Italians also introduced an intrusive, widely resented policy of cultural "Italianization" within the Governorate of Dalmatia. The Germans treated the Croats more tactfully, at least until Italy's surrender to the Allies in 1943. They also took responsibility for equipping the Croatian armed forces, mainly with captured Czech and French weapons. Sometimes they supplied the state with food from German-occupied territory elsewhere. But they ensured they got something in return; they, like the Italians, increasingly saw the NDH as a reservoir of economic resources as the war went on.[50]

Because the NDH was officially a sovereign state, the Germans were unable to control its economy as closely as they could Serbia's. Serbia suffered greater loss of food and labor to the Axis during the war, but the NDH suffered also. By 1944 the Germans would be press-ganging Croatian workers in their hundreds of thousands, and routinely ignoring pledges to maintain decent standards of treatment for them. They also gained a monopoly, or at least a high priority, over the NDH's oil and minerals. Its bauxite mines, for instance, were leased to Germany for the length of the war, and large amounts of plant were dismantled and shipped back to the Reich. Heavy costs for the maintenance of occupation were imposed on the NDH also. To meet them, the Ustasha government printed more money and inflation spiraled.

The Italians inflicted similar woes on the NDH. Italian-controlled areas of the NDH were actually a food deficit region, so they were sometimes forced to import food. That aside, however, their exploitation of the Croatian economy was perhaps even worse than that which the Germans inflicted.[51] They exploited the interior to secure supply sources and routes from inland Croatia and Bosnia. They also zealously procured foodstuffs for their occupation troops and for Dalmatia's Italian population. The Croatian population was not only burdened by economic hardship; it also succumbed to general war weariness, and grew increasingly fearful of being tarred by association with the Ustasha's crimes.[52]

When it came to actually combating Partisans, and Chetniks also, the NDH felt the symptoms of its moribund condition on the front line: in the Croatian army itself.[53] The army could hardly hope for an enthusiastic soldiery drawn from a population harboring at best only marginal enthusiasm for the Ustasha regime. Croatian rank-and-file soldiers suffered shortages in clothing, equipment, suitable arms, and ammunition. Though benefiting initially from the Yugoslav arms the Germans sold to them, they later had to make do with poorer-quality Czech, French, and Polish weaponry. They were also discriminated against by their own government; when it came to allocating equipment or duties, the Ustasha regime consistently favored its own militias. Inevitably, there was deep antagonism between the two institutions.[54] Croatian army troops also endured arrogant and abusive behavior from the German commanders and NCOs with whom their units had to operate. There was also a lack of well-trained officers—the Croatian army's officer corps consisted of elderly former Habsburg officers at senior levels, of Ustashe with inadequate military experience,[55] and of Croats from the old Yugoslav officer corps whose Yugoslav connections provoked their Ustasha colleagues' intense distrust. All this, together with the mounting impact of serial defeats over the next two years, led to increasing Partisan infiltration of the army, epidemic draft dodging, and, in time, to the army's disintegration.[56]

Yet in early 1942 General Bader, the new Commander in Serbia, whose occupation divisions would become increasingly committed in the NDH that year, still hoped the Croats would soon be able to assume full responsibility for their own security.[57] Meanwhile, conscious of his own troops' limitations, he sought alternative ways of achieving some stability. Bader's approach did not rely exclusively on terror. But such constructive engagement as he did pursue was fitful and uneven—hardly helped by a lack of backing from the Armed Forces High Command—and interspersed with sharp bursts of ruthlessness. That ruthlessness would intensify as the year wore on; in October, for instance, Bader came close to praising the 7th Waffen-SS Mountain Division "Prinz Eugen" for its brutal "Balkan method" of burning down any village whose inhabitants looked even slightly suspicious.[58]

And some of Bader's more "constructive" notions were themselves misguided. In early 1942, for instance, he advocated granting much of the territory of eastern Bosnia to Chetniks under Mihailović's representative there, Colonel Jezdemir Dangić. What was misguided was the notion that such a Chetnik administration, even if one overseen by the Germans, could bring stability to the region. Senior German military and diplomatic figures were horrified at the prospect. They feared the effect empowering Dangić might have upon the integrity of the NDH—with which Dangić refused to cooperate—and upon eastern Bosnia's stability more generally. Bader's arguments were not exactly strengthened by the Dangić Chetniks' poor military showing against the Partisans in April.

Ultimately, Hitler vetoed the whole idea. Dangić, who had also curried the Italians' favor, eventually outlived his usefulness to the Axis. That month the Germans arrested him on a return visit to Serbia.[59] The fact that Bader had contemplated relying on Dangić so much in the first place demonstrates not just the imprudence of the general's approach but also, in fairness, the difficulties of achieving a workable state of security in the NDH with the means that were available. Indeed, though the

Armed Forces High Command forbade dealings with Chetniks on April 6, there were cases barely a fortnight later of meetings between individual German units and Chetnik groups.[60]

In any case, the Germans recognized that they would themselves need to make at least some active contribution to the counterinsurgency campaign in the NDH. But such was the paucity of their manpower that they could not hope to resource the kind of sustained campaign that would impose a sufficiently permanent troop presence among the population. Instead, they opted for periodic bouts of brutal offensive action, as and when they judged them necessary, interspersed with Bader's inadequate hearts and minds initiatives. And Lieutenant General Walter Kuntze, who replaced the ailing Field Marshal List at the end of October 1941 as Wehrmacht Commander Southeast, would display little appetite for any measure of constructive engagement.[61] The German counterinsurgency effort of 1942 would reach its gruesome apex during the summer months.

The Germans would have some success with small-scale hunter group operations. But such operations, if they were to enjoy decisive theater-level success, needed far more long-term resourcing than the German high command was prepared to commit. Even so, German commanders on the spot might have made more use of them than they did. Instead, whether due to pressure for more rapid and spectacular results, or to their own predilection for maximum force and maximum terror, they relied all too often on large-scale encirclement operations. Here a designated area was cordoned off. Then, with some troops assigned the task of holding the perimeter to prevent breakouts, the rest advanced to a central point, in theory combing the area for Partisans as they went and vetting the villages for suspect elements. This phase saw the most encounters with insurgents, if any, and the most German casualties. But the designated daily targets were frequently beyond the capabilities of the often insufficient troop numbers committed to such operations.

Thus, all too often, the insurgents and "suspect elements" who were the ostensible target of such operations slipped the cordon. Then the Germans, whether through frustration, pressure from above for results, or the belief that cowing the population was at least one means of combating the insurgents, turned on civilians. But any "benefit" gained from such operations usually proved transitory. Their insufficient manpower rendered the Germans incapable of occupying a recently cleansed area over a lengthier period and ensuring that the insurgents did not reestablish themselves there. This pattern would repeat itself numerous times during the German counterinsurgency campaign in the NDH. Only from 1943, as the Germans refined their tactics and sometimes deployed high-quality formations, such as the 1st Mountain Division and the Prinz Eugen Division, did they achieve some successes.[62]

Despite the so often horrendous civilian casualties such operations inflicted, Wehrmacht commanders sought to distinguish their "good" brand of violence from the "bad" violence of the Ustasha. In the words of the historian Jonathan Gumz, "in the eyes of German staff officers, cool technocrats, not angry men, produced Wehrmacht violence."[63] They saw their own violence as systematic and organized, controlled in such a way as to prevent the troops from degenerating into savagery, and executed in the cause of restoring and maintaining order. Ustasha violence, by contrast, was barbaric, chaotic, and a guarantor of ever greater support for the Partisans amongst those sections of the population who were imperiled by it. Accurate though the Wehrmacht's general assessment of Ustasha violence undoubtedly was, however, Wehrmacht commanders certainly had a vested interest in demonizing it. By contrasting it with their own "proper" terror methods, they could fall back on atavistic Ustasha savagery as an explanation for their own failure to maintain order and stability.[64]

The following two chapters focus mainly upon the 718th Infantry Division. This formation possesses by far the largest source base of any of the German army occupation divisions that operated in the NDH in 1942. It thus offers a particularly rich insight into how a German army division conducted its campaign in the face of the mounting, increasingly intractable challenges which the NDH presented to its German occupiers that year.

CHAPTER 8

Glimmers of Sanity

The 718th Infantry Division in Bosnia

THE 718TH INFANTRY DIVISION was formed in the Eighteenth
Military District in the Eastern March in spring 1941. The units it
commanded—consisting primarily of the 738th and 750th Infantry Regiments and the 668th Artillery Section—originated from the southern
part of the old Reich as well as from the Eastern March.[1] Its commander,
Major General Johann Fortner, was born in Zweibrücken in the Rhineland Palatinate in 1884. He spent the first two years of the Great War with
the 5th Bavarian Infantry Regiment on the western front, before being
captured by the British in September 1916. He served in the police during
the 1920s, before retiring and then later resuming his military career. He
took up a post as a training commander in Landeck, in the Eastern March,
before assuming command of the 718th Infantry Division in May 1941.[2]

The 718th spent the whole of 1942, as well as periods before and after, in
the NDH. It thus not only carried out mobile operations. It also had opportunity between operations to cultivate popular support, through both
restrained conduct and, as far as practicable, propaganda and constructive engagement. This was, after all, the population of a country to which
Germany was officially allied. Nevertheless the 718th did not tread a consistent path during 1942: it sometimes exercised terror more than restraint,
at other times restraint more than terror. What helped shape the division's

behavior at any one time, as with other formations, were the particular circumstances it faced and the particular standpoint of its commander.

Not that any of this was apparent when the 718th began campaigning
that year. Contending with a resourceful opponent, debilitating fighting
conditions, and its own substandard fighting power, it initially reacted
with what was in many ways textbook ruthlessness.

A trio of mobile operations, taking place between mid-January and mid-
February, were the division's introduction to the 1942 counterinsurgency
campaign. These operations were part of a larger effort, titled the "Second
Enemy Offensive" by the Partisans. It employed between thirty thousand
and thirty-five thousand troops, the bulk of whom were provided by the
718th Infantry Division and, for the first operation, by the 342d Infantry
Division also. The latter formation had arrived from Serbia after Bulgar-
ian troops had been deployed there. General Bader, having witnessed
the almost complete destruction of the Partisans in Serbia, now sought
to replicate the feat against the Partisans in eastern Bosnia. But the German forces in Yugoslavia, subordinated as they were to the needs of their
comrades fighting in the Soviet Union, lacked the strength to destroy the
insurgents in eastern Bosnia on their own. Their need instead to rely on
their Croatian and Italian allies would impede the operations' success considerably. But other factors impeded the operations also. Among other
things, the operations took place in temperatures of minus thirty.[3] And the
units prosecuting them, German units included, were seriously lacking in
the kinds of equipment that mountainous, wintry conditions demanded.

The first operation, code-named Southeast Croatia, was the largest
of the three. It took place between January 15 and 23, 1942, in the area
between Sarajevo, Tuzla, Zvornik, and Visegrad in the NDH's south-
eastern corner.[4] The area was viewed by the 718th's intelligence section
as an "ethnic mishmash of a region." It consisted overwhelmingly of
Muslims and Orthodox Serbs, but also contained a Catholic Croatian
minority, generally hostile to "Old Serbia" and predominantly employed
on the land.[5] Serbia Command viewed it as a major center of hostile activity, in which the enemy had set up winter quarters and was endangering
important transport routes.[6] That enemy, it was reported, comprised up

to eight thousand Communist Partisans, some of whom were fugitives from Serbia, and—officially classed as the enemy, at least—about twenty thousand Bosnian Chetniks.[7] General Bader was clear about the operation's aims. He planned an encirclement with all persons encountered in the area to "be viewed as the enemy."[8]

During the operation the 718th fell under the temporary overall command of the 342d Infantry Division. Alongside the two divisions were seven Croatian infantry battalions and nine Croatian artillery batteries, while the Luftwaffe committed reconnaissance aircraft and a combat squadron.[9] The 718th was strengthened for the operation. The 738th Infantry Regiment, ordered to strike from Sarajevo through the Praca Valley towards Rogatica, received pioneer troops, four Croatian battalions, four Croatian artillery batteries, and two and a half German mountain artillery batteries sent from the Bosnian capital, Sarajevo. The 750th Infantry Regiment, moving out from southwest of Tuzla towards Olovo, was accompanied by a German artillery battery, and a Croatian infantry battalion and mountain battery.[10] But the extra forces allotted to the division would be of limited help. Indeed, the Croats would prove more of a hindrance.

The operation was called off on January 23, having failed to destroy the insurgents as planned. On its heels a few days later came Operation Ozren, which lasted until February 4. The 718th, advancing from Kladanj, was tasked with clearing the area between the Rivers Bosna and Spreca of the circa two-thousand-strong Partisan forces there.[11] The division had been further strengthened by the time of this operation. Alongside its core infantry and artillery regiments it was now allocated an armored train and five Panzer platoons. Sixteen territorial companies, meanwhile, reduced the pressure on the 718th, largely by assuming static security duties in its jurisdiction.[12] To the operation itself the 718th committed its full infantry and artillery strength, together with an Ustasha battalion. It was also loaned the 697th Infantry Regiment from the 342d Infantry Division.[13] Ten Croatian battalions and an unspecified number of Croatian artillery batteries were tasked with cordoning off the Spreca and the Bosna valley to prevent the Partisans from escaping, while the main body of the 718th advanced from the north and west.[14] In the event, however, the great majority of Partisans managed to escape.[15]

Mid-February, finally, brought Operation Prijedor. Here, in northwest Bosnia, the 718th committed the 750th Infantry Regiment, advancing from Dubica, to pulling Territorial Battalion 923 and numerous Croatian units out of trouble after they had been isolated in Prijedor following Partisan attacks on the surrounding railway lines. This operation achieved its limited aims, the 718th committing four battalions together with two artillery batteries, two additional artillery platoons, and pioneer and signals troops.[16] The Croatian army committed four infantry battalions, a gendarmerie battalion, four artillery batteries and two artillery sections, and a further twenty-nine companies of various types. Most of the Croatian units were assigned to guarding the roads and the cordon around the operational area. But the Croatian units' already limited effectiveness was further curtailed by the fact that five of the companies consisted of low-quality replacements or recruits.[17]

The orders the 718th issued during these operations, relayed in Southeast Croatia's case from the 342d Infantry Division, remained true to the German military's harsh counterinsurgency tradition and drew little distinction between combatant and noncombatant. On January 9, in advance of Operation Southeast Croatia, the 718th ordered its regiments to view as hostile anyone falling into one of the following, very much all-encompassing groups: all nonresidents and residents who had been absent from their localities until recently; all identifiable "Mihailović people" with or without weapons or ammunition; all identifiable Dangić Chetniks—a group with whom the Germans were not yet supposed to be officially dealing—with or without weapons or ammunition; all Communists who could be identified in any way, with or without weapons or ammunition; and, finally, anyone concealing, supplying, or informing the above groups. No distinction was to be made between members of the different ethnic groups.[18]

When it came to how to treat captured insurgents, the directives were predictably fierce. A brief interrogation or examination, followed by summary shooting, was to be the fate of all Communists, and of anyone who had participated in combat or been caught carrying ammunition or messages. Anyone resisting or fleeing was likewise to be shot. The 718th, though interestingly not the 342d, extended the same treatment to all "Serbian Chetniks"—a reference, one assumes, to Mihailović Chetniks. Finally, houses from which shots were fired, unless useful as accommodation, were to be burned down.[19] The division's orders for Operation Ozren were similarly merciless, sparing again neither Communist Partisans nor "Serbian Chetniks," and its regiments entered into the spirit of things. The 750th Infantry Regiment, for instance, ordered that villages from which shots had been fired, and that were not needed for accommodation, were to be burned down.[20]

Operation Prijedor, finally, was prefaced by one of the harshest directives of all. It being so difficult to identify the enemy, the operational orders declared that all male Serbian inhabitants between sixteen and sixty were to be treated as though they had been encountered in battle with a weapon in their hands. In other words, it can be presumed, all were to be shot. As with the inhabitants, so with their dwellings: just as in the previous operation, the Serbian villages on each side of the main route of march, unless they could be used as troop accommodation, were to be burned down.[21] Again, the 718th's subordinate units followed the brutal lead. For instance, Battle Group Wutte provided a lengthy list on March 7 of which groups of houses were to be burned down either side of its route of march.[22] Copious amounts of livestock were also seized during Prijedor: 667 cattle, 417 sheep, and eighty-five pigs.[23]

Yet ferocious as such ruthlessness was, it was of a different quality to the 342d Infantry Division's back in Serbia the previous autumn. None of the orders the 342d or the 718th issued for these winter operations were couched in racial terms. They did not invoke historic resentments against the enemy, but instead dispassionately labeled Chetniks as Serb and Partisans as Communist. One report referred to a Partisan leader's Jewish identity;[24] otherwise, all the orders and reports relating to the operations were racially "blind." What suffused the orders instead was the ruthlessly "pragmatic" doctrine of annihilating the enemy through maximum force and maximum terror. This different motivation would, of course, have been no comfort to the unarmed civilians whom the 342d and 718th were killing. But it does shed a different light on what was driving the division. The 718th for one seems particularly to have believed that such an obdurate doctrine would compensate for the difficulties it was bound to encounter when its substandard troops faced the operations' arduous conditions.

Indeed, sometimes the 718th Infantry Division and its regiments urged their troops to be brutal not just to the enemy, but to themselves also, if they were to best the obstacles they were facing. On January 17, at the outset of Operation Southeast Croatia, the 718th informed the 750th Infantry Regiment that its troops would need to dig deep within themselves in order to overcome the challenge ahead: "the troops' enthusiasm must overcome the major difficulties, the high snow levels, and the lack of mountain equipment, so as to ensure that all participating units make ruthless progress."[25] Likewise for Operation Ozren, in which the 718th's troops were similarly hampered by high snow levels and thickly forested, mountainous terrain,[26] the division directed that "just as the troops hammered the insurgents in South-East Croatia, so will they exterminate this enemy also, despite the difficulties of weather and terrain."[27] The 738th Infantry Regiment ordered that less capable men and horses be left behind during the operation, and urged the troops to "do their utmost," through their own self-reliance, "to fulfil the tasks with which the division has entrusted them."[28]

Such harsh exhortations certainly had plenty to compensate for. The forces committed to Operation Southeast Croatia in particular were set too ambitious a schedule within too limited a time frame. Prospects for bagging large numbers of insurgents were further diminished when atrocious weather held the Germans up. These problems were not encountered during the smaller-scale Operation Ozren, but the 718th Infantry Division still had to negotiate deep snow and thickly wooded terrain during that operation.[29]

Moreover, the 718th went into these operations in a seriously deficient state. The root problem was that both the 342d and the 718th were ill-equipped for winter mountain warfare.[30] The main division-level order for Operation Southeast Croatia virtually acknowledged this; it ordered that the 718th's patchy transportation facilities be utilized to their absolute limit. "All means of forward mobility (skis, trucks suited to the terrain, pack animals and so on . . .) are to be used to the point of exhaustion . . . All that matters is that transport is available whenever and wherever needed."[31]

Conditions during Southeast Croatia itself were execrable. The 698th Infantry Regiment operated under the 342d Infantry Division, but the conditions it experienced would have been familiar to all units involved in the operation: villages, and the supply and shelter contained within them, given the "scorched earth" treatment by retreating insurgents; areas practically devoid of human life, and frequently meter-high snow.[32] During Operation Prijedor the 718th's troops found it immensely difficult to ensure the flow of ammunition, and the troops' pack radios were unable to maintain contact by night. This caused especially acute problems whenever officers tried to direct artillery fire. And shortage of officers was preventing the division's units from authorizing leave.[33]

The 718th also expected little if any real help from its Croatian allies. Croatian army units assigned to the 718th during Operation Southeast Croatia, the division reported, possessed appalling levels of fighting power, and were blighted by constant supply problems and a complete lack of comradeship between officers and men.[34] The command of the division's armored train concurred that the Croatian troops were indeed useless. It regarded small-unit combined operations with the Croatian military as pointless, because the Croats always rapidly degenerated into a disorganized shambles. They also preferred to hang back rather than support German raiding parties actively.[35] During Operation Prijedor, meanwhile, the 750th Infantry Regiment, under the command of Colonel Rudolf Wutte, reported that "the Croatian mountain column . . . is more a hindrance than a help to the troops."[36]

Such excoriating reports, generated as they were by German army units anxious to cover up their own failures, must be approached cautiously. But given the manifold problems blighting the Croatian army, such reports clearly contained a substantial element of truth. And during Operation Ozren the 718th found that it could not always rely even on German units. On February 7 General Fortner reported that the 697th Infantry Regiment, loaned from the 342d Infantry Division, had failed to follow orders to extend the attack on its right as far as the River Spreca. The 750th Infantry Regiment had had to cover for it, but this had enabled the enemy to slip past the Germans' left flank. The 718th came under even more pressure when the 697th was relocated while the operation was still going on.[37]

None of this helped, of course, in trying to locate and vanquish an adversary who was proving increasingly elusive and resourceful. Operation Southeast Croatia set the tone. Only one regiment of the 342d Infantry Division was able to properly come to grips with the enemy, the majority of whom took advantage of a weak Italian cordon to escape over the Italian demarcation line.[38] During Southeast Croatia, Territorial Battalion 823 noted the speediness of the insurgents' communications system, a system aided substantially by the efforts of local villagers. It regularly enabled the enemy to anticipate the Germans' approach, disappear before it, and then resurface in the same place days later. Matters on this score grew worse during Operation Ozren. The heavy snow on the roads impeded the Germans' progress further.[39]

Especially vexing in Operation Ozren was the fact that the Germans thought they had thoroughly encircled the area beforehand. They had employed several artillery batteries and ten Croatian infantry battalions, and checked the cordon's impenetrability every night. But Serbia Command realized that the operation had overlooked the enemy's ability to escape in small groups through supposedly impassable terrain. It also believed that many other insurgents, even if they had not actually escaped, had been able to disappear into the mountains using the snow prints of the men in front to conceal their true numbers, and that they would resurface and reestablish themselves after the operation.[40]

The 718th lacked the sort of specialist mountain troops who might have been able to pursue escaping insurgents successfully. LXV Corps urged that each regiment convert and equip one of its companies as such troops. It also urged more time to prepare for operations in future, so that the Germans could ready specialist troops, properly assemble communications, and set smaller and more realistic daily targets. Otherwise, it asserted, such operations were pointless.[41]

Operation Prijedor, meanwhile, brought a further worrying development. The insurgents stopped trying merely to escape, and began to show not just themselves but their teeth also—not, however, in a way that enabled the Germans to get to grips with them. They frequently fired upon the Germans from skillfully concealed positions:

They often let our own troops approach to within 20 meters before opening fire. Single riflemen also often fire from great distances, with carefully targeted fire from very well concealed positions, whereby they avoid using even houses, but rather dig themselves into the landscape . . . The riflemen, scattered across the landscape, hide in their nests until they can escape under cover of darkness. These lone riflemen often fire for just a few minutes, and even then only with a few, carefully targeted shots. For this reason, locating these lone riflemen is very difficult.[42]

The 750th Infantry Regiment described the Partisans' appearance, as well as their very diverse composition:

According to an ethnic German whose property is next to the rail bridge on Height 127, and who allegedly spent a week as a hostage of the insurgents, the insurgents are, overall, well uniformed, with black-colored Yugoslavian uniforms, and equipped with rifles and hand grenades. They consist of fifteen to twenty per cent Communists, ten per cent Muslims and the rest Serbs and Croats. On their caps the Serbs wear Serbian national colors, the Croats their provincial colors, the Muslims the Crescent and the Communists the Soviet star.[43]

These winter operations whittled down the 718th's manpower alarmingly. During Operation Prijedor, for instance, the 750th Infantry Regiment's combat strength fell from 692 officers, NCOs, and men, to 564. Total losses for Prijedor were severe, the Germans suffering thirty-four dead and the Croats seventeen, for ninety-seven Partisan dead.[44] There were major gaps in the 738th Infantry Regiment's manpower also; according to its roll call of March 1, its second battalion now possessed 319 officers, NCOs, and men, as against the first battalion's 376.[45]

Yet the 718th Infantry Division, and its subordinate units, showed restraint as well as ruthlessness during these operations. In a display of moderation during Operation Southeast Croatia, the 718th relayed orders from the 342d Infantry Division declaring that "women and children will not be shot or carried off, unless they demonstrably have taken part in combat or message-carrying."[46] Perhaps it was this provision alone that led both divisions to proclaim, apparently without irony, that "Croatia is a country that is friendly to us. The troops must be aware of this, and avoid any exceeding of their duties."[47] For Operation Ozren, the division directed that Chetniks were to be treated as prisoners, not shot, if they surrendered unconditionally with their weapons.[48]

Much impetus for these particular measures seems to have come from General Bader. Bader, it appears, had begun to see the wisdom of some restraint even as he spurred his troops to ruthlessness. On January 21 he had ordered that, while armed opponents who resisted the Germans in the course of Operation Southeast Croatia were to be shot, those who gave themselves up were to be treated as prisoners of war. Villagers in whose houses weapons were found, but who had not themselves participated in the fighting, were to be treated similarly.[49] This order contrasts with Bader's ferocious exhortation of just days previously, when on January 8 he had announced that any person encountered in the area being cleansed was to be viewed as an enemy.[50] Bader's likeliest motive for the change was more calculating than enlightened. Deescalating the operation's violence would enable the Dangić Chetniks, whom Bader would be courting assiduously by the end of the month, to come out of it relatively unscathed. Dangić, for his part, ordered his followers to avoid encounters with the Germans during the operation, and to surrender themselves and their weapons immediately should such encounters prove unavoidable.[51]

Because the 718th Infantry Division found itself interspersing these more measured orders with much harsher ones, its troops may well have felt they were receiving conflicting signals. But the signs are that, overall, such orders were beginning to put at least some check on their troops' brutality. On January 20, during Operation South-East Croatia, the 738th Infantry Regiment secured the Rnovica-Podomanija railway line in the face of minor resistance, together with thirty prisoners—of whom only one was shot. Certainly, the 718th dealt out some dreadful brutality during Operation Ozren. On February 19, for instance, it ordered the annihilation of the villages of Jasenje, Celebinci, and Vlaskovici "by the strongest possible combat methods."[52] But the overall body count its troops inflicted in this operation was less fearful than it might have been. The division and its Croatian collaborator units suffered five dead and eleven wounded, together with over forty men reported frostbitten or sick. The enemy, by contrast, lost 206 dead and 347 wounded, from whom 106 rifles and one pistol were seized.[53] These figures indicate that many of the enemy, 107 of them at least, were genuine combatants, even though many clearly were not.

And in Operation Prijedor particularly, the ferocity of its orders notwithstanding, the 718th Infantry Division's troops did not kill large numbers of civilians. This may have been because the 750th Infantry Regiment, together with its affiliated and subordinate units, did not get the opportunity, but it may also have been because the 750th increasingly saw the sense in keeping the population on its side. For, though the regiment wrote in early March that the population felt intimidated by the Partisans and sometimes openly sympathized with them, it also reported that other villages were requesting German protection from them.[54]

All this fell far short of a comprehensive, conciliatory effort to secure the population's hearts and minds. But compared with the savagery the 342d Infantry Division had inflicted upon north-west Serbia in 1941, it was a step in a more conciliatory direction. It was a small step, certainly, but one the civilians on the receiving end would have appreciated.

Meanwhile, on January 25, Tito set up headquarters in the eastern Bosnian town of Foča, where he aimed to regroup and reorganize. The Partisans stepped up their military organization by forming growing numbers of select troops into disciplined and mobile "proletarian brigades." The first, founded on December 29, 1941, was followed by the formation of the 2nd Proletarian Brigade on March 1 1942.[55]

The Partisans also began announcing their presence in other ways. As early as February 20, Serbia Command was reporting that the groups scattered by the 342d and 718th in Operation Southeast Croatia had regrouped and were active once more. By early March the Tuzla-Doboj railway line in eastern Bosnia was threatened by the same Partisans whom the 718th had scattered during Operation Ozren. By late March, Partisan activity was threatening road and rail communications across much of eastern Bosnia, not least around Sarajevo.[56]

The Axis might yet have dealt the Partisans a killer blow in early 1942. Unfortunately for them, they were too busy falling out amongst themselves. In December 1941, Hitler had been intensely preoccupied with the protracted struggle against the Soviet Union. He had resolved to transfer the Wehrmacht's entire occupation force in Yugoslavia to the eastern front, and to hand over all occupation duties in Croatia to the Italians. Mussolini, Army Chief of Staff Roatta, and Second Army Commander Ambrosio—Ambrosio and Roatta having yet to swap commands at that point—all welcomed this proposal, seeing in it a swift means of extending Italian influence in the region. However, beseeched by both the Nedić and Pavelić regimes, Hitler then moderated his proposal. Rather than relinquish the Wehrmacht's Yugoslav commitment entirely, he now elected to scale it down. The incensed Italians, Mussolini in particular, suspected a German–Ustasha plot. They then essentially sulked for the next three months, further stymieing effective anti-Partisan operations in eastern Bosnia.[57] With hindsight, the breathing space this provided Tito's Partisans proved crucial. They used it to reorganize and replenish themselves to a point where they would be considerably harder to kill off completely when the Axis united against them once more.[58]

Amid all this, on February 18, the 718th Infantry Division was handed long-term occupation responsibility for eastern Bosnia. Its jurisdiction was bordered by the Rivers Sava and Bosna to the north, the River Drina to the east, and the Italian demarcation line to the south. A central principle of the occupation, Serbia Command directed, must be that "in German-influenced areas, Croats, Serbs, and Muslims can live quietly and securely next to one another as fully entitled citizens." To help ensure this, General Fortner was to be assigned command of all German and Croatian troops in eastern Bosnia.[59] But during March and April, following the departure of the more effective 342d Infantry Division at the end of January, the less formidable 718th was only able to mount limited, largely ineffective operations against the Partisans.[60] An NCO of the 717th Infantry Division could identify with this, describing in a letter how "we've been hunting the bandits in the mountains and forests and have had to exert ourselves a great deal in doing so. All winter, when it was cold, they crept off and hid themselves, (but) now the brothers are showing themselves again. God grant us the day when we wipe them all out, then we can have peace and quiet."[61]

Meanwhile, German–Italian relations grew ever more convoluted. In March 1942 General Roatta, in addition to arming the Chetniks, also announced that he wished to extend the German–Italian demarcation line up to and including Sarajevo. The general may simply have been airing this intention in order to increase his leverage over the Chetnik question, but it alarmed both Croats and Germans nevertheless. Were the Italians to extend their territory so far north, into an area with significant Croat and particularly Muslim populations, the Chetniks they brought with them were wont to cause precisely the kind of havoc from which ultimately only the Partisans could benefit.[62]

In late April, however, this particular problem was solved by an operation in which the 718th Infantry Division took part. Together with three Italian divisions—the Italo-German impasse of early 1942 having now been resolved—and Italian and Croatian gendarmerie forces and aircraft, the division was committed to relieving Rogatica and cleansing the surrounding area in Operation Trio I.[63] However, only a fraction of the manpower the Italians had originally pledged actually arrived in time to participate in the operation at all.[64] General Bader, anxious to exploit the window of opportunity created by the successful attack of the Ustasha's elite Black Legion against the region's Partisans, commenced the operation anyway. Trio I relieved Rogatica, but otherwise achieved little militarily. Politically, however, it would prove useful. Its successful conclusion would enable Bader to claim that Bosnian territory north of the demarcation line was now even more extensively cleansed than before, and in no need of Italian troop garrisons there.[65]

Trio I also enabled the 718th Infantry Division to further develop the more restrained approach that had taken embryonic form during its operations of January and February. By mid-April, according to Serbia Command, the Rogatica region contained ten thousand Partisans, some of whom were former Chetniks, well equipped with rifles, machine guns, and grenade launchers, but of uneven fighting value overall.[66] The 718th's combat strength was significantly boosted in time for Trio I. This eased the pressure it was under, and almost certainly helped it to contemplate more constructive measures.

The division still suffered weaknesses. At the end of March, for instance, it failed to provide sufficient clothing with which to equip one company per infantry regiment as a mountain company.[67] But by the end of April it commanded a core artillery section and two infantry regiments in their entirety, four Panzer platoons, four armored trains, and ten territorial companies. At one point, on April 10, it had commanded four entire Panzer companies. This was double the number commanded by each of the other three German army occupation divisions in Yugoslavia at that time.[68] The 718th was to commit the whole of its combat strength to Trio I. It was further buttressed by two Ustasha battalions; four additional tanks; four Croatian artillery batteries; and twelve infantry, rifle, and border guard companies from the Croatian army.[69] While not the most formidable host yet assembled, it was a reasonable fighting force for the purposes of the operation.

Trio I's overall commander, General Bader, also sought to ensure that the operation would be conducted on a saner basis than operations past. On April 10, he announced that the operations must "exterminate the insurgents in the Bosnian region, and pacify Bosnia through the establishment of public peace, order, and security." But Bader had drawn lessons from past operations. The aim for Trio I was to seal the areas to be cleansed, and then for each unit to rapidly overwhelm the sector assigned to it. In order to maintain close contact with one's neighbor and cleanse each area thoroughly, commands were urged to keep their daily targets as small and manageable as possible. In other words, the 718th was committing forces of similar strength to those it had used for Operation Southeast Croatia, within a comparable space of time, but over a much smaller area and in markedly better weather. Further, to reduce both communication problems and the danger of being bombarded by one's own side, the Italian aircraft committed to the operation were to go nowhere near German ground units. They were to assist only Italian troops, while German and Croatian troops would cooperate with German and Croatian airpower.[70]

The 718th advanced from its assembly points in Sarajevo, Olovo, and Tuzla on April 20. The operation ended on April 30 with all targets reached, even though many Partisans had escaped.[71] The Axis forces lost sixteen dead, the Partisans eighty, with eighty-seven rifles captured. Such figures indicate that the Axis forces had had a proper fight on their hands instead of just slaughtering civilians. Copious amounts of livestock were seized, but the vast majority was distributed among the peaceable sections of the population.[72] Reinforcements, realistic daily targets, and effective air-ground coordination all gave the operation an easier passage and relieved the pressure on the 718th. And a formation under less pressure was likely to exercise more restraint.

Orders from on high fostered such restraint further. General Roatta— no dove when it came to counterinsurgency—prevailed upon Bader to consent that all insurgents who gave themselves up in the course of the fighting be allowed to surrender as prisoners of war.[73] This countered a profoundly punitive order that General Kuntze, Wehrmacht Commander Southeast, had issued on March 19. Kuntze had directed that the troops conduct themselves more ruthlessly than the insurgents and thus make the population fear them more. Though Kuntze left the specifics to the commanders on the spot, he strongly indicated that the policy of shooting one hundred hostages for every German soldier killed, and fifty for every German soldier wounded, should be resumed. And in contrast with Bader and Roatta, he made no allowance for sparing captured rebels, declaring instead that "captured rebels are in principle to be hanged or shot. If they are to be used for intelligence purposes, this should only be a brief postponement of their death."[74]

In another considered move, General Bader also commanded that "*actual or attempted atrocities* by members of allied units (were) to be dealt with on the spot using the *sharpest measures*."[75] During Operation Trio II, Trio I's successor operation (also referred to as Operation Foča), the 718th apprehended seven Ustashe under the terms of this particular directive.[76] The 718th's divisional command, meanwhile, directed that the troops distinguish between those found guilty and those merely under suspicion, and that civilians who had aided the insurgents be interned rather than shot. It also stressed that it was essential to glean information from villagers rather than simply kill or terrorize them.[77]

Following on the heels of the combat troops was the Wehrmacht's own Field Gendarmerie, strengthened by the Croatian army and the Croatian gendarmerie. The Field Gendarmerie's operations, according to General Bader, went a considerable way towards quieting the population. After only a short time, the population was "placing limitless trust in the measures of the German Wehrmacht."[78] A large proportion of the inhabitants, who for fear of the Ustasha had fled into the woods, now returned. Leaflets and proclamations called on all inhabitants to return to their homes and work peacefully. When the livestock the 718th Infantry Division had gathered during the operations was redistributed among the population, including refugees, it had "a particularly beneficial effect upon the population's mood."[79] The 718th was confident that such measures could, among other things, counter some of the propaganda messages the Partisans were spreading. "The Partisan commissars," according to the division's intelligence section, "are telling their followers that the Germans will soon leave the country because Turkey has declared war on Germany. Our soldiers are easily able to dismiss these rumors as nonsense."[80]

And the 718th's own troops were following the lead from above. The 738th Infantry Regiment's second battalion, for example, burned down houses and settlements on the way to Borovrat and arrested their male inhabitants, but shot "only" five suspect civilians.[81] Brutal conduct indeed, but it might have been more brutal still. Battle Group Wüst went into detail over its tribulations, but showed that it too realized that lashing out in response was less sensible than seeking to win the population over:

> 4/24/42: The poorest progress by night, through heavy rain and on softened ground. The women and children left behind display great anxiety over the Ustasha. The area gradually becomes steeper and more lined with cliffs, the differences in altitude increase.

> 4/26/42: The differences in altitude on the route of march exceed anything hitherto encountered in this operation . . . The population claims that during the two days previously the Ustasha systematically plundered the villages, abducting people and cattle and laying houses to waste.

4/27/42: The population (of Rogatica) was cut off for months and has suffered massive hunger. There have been accounts from all sides that people have been eating grass. There was a heartfelt reception for the German troops, reflecting the hopes of a better future in the people's emaciated faces. All inhabitants turned out onto the streets to greet their liberators.[82]

Though this may be an overly rosy account of the reception the Germans received, the inhabitants' relief that the Germans' presence could prevent the Ustasha from slaughtering them was probably profound. Mindful of this, on April 25 the 718th Infantry Division ordered Battle Group Wüst to send out patrols to identify which Croatian units were burning down villages behind Axis lines.[83]

Operation Trio II/Foča—in which the 718th was also involved—finally put enough pressure on Tito's Partisans to push them into embarking on a "long march" from eastern to western Bosnia. The trek, beginning on June 24, involved four thousand Partisans. The leadership blamed the need for withdrawal not just on the military pressure from the operations, but also on the damage to morale caused by "Nedićite" fifth columnists.[84] Ultimately, however, the Trio operations, like the winter operations before them, failed to actually destroy Partisan forces to a decisive extent. Serbia Command admitted as much in a report that nevertheless tried to talk up the operations' success:

> Through the actions of Combat Group General Bader in "Trio I and Foča," the *uprising* in the German area of *eastern Bosnia* has been *smashed,* and is now limited only to small local attacks. The pursuit of the bandit remnants is in full swing. The pacification operations are beginning to take effect. The population is returning to its homes and has to an extent begun to work again. But only German leadership, the presence of German troops and the proper implementation of German administrative measures can ensure that the limited successes achieved so far can be fully exploited.[85]

In other words—reading between the lines—the Partisans had not been destroyed and were still active, and in trying to destroy them the Germans faced a colossal task they were unable to entrust to anyone else. The 718th conceded that the best it could do was either to try to prevent the Partisans from returning to the region or to hinder their attempts to slip away to the relative safety of the Italian zone.[86]

The operations' failure to achieve more had many other causes also: the Partisans' elusiveness and, increasingly, their combativeness; the defective state of the Croats' fighting power, and the paltry "assistance" rendered by the Italians.[87] To Trio II/Foča, for instance, the Italians committed three divisions, but they were too slow to close the ring around the Partisans as directed.[88]

But this time, the operations' shortcomings seem to have further energized German efforts to cultivate the population rather than rely entirely on military measures and terror measures.[89] Bader pleaded for more constructive policies. He wanted the German forces in the NDH to induce the Croatian government to ensure religious freedom, resettle refugees, prevent Ustasha attacks, and punish the perpetrators of the crimes the Ustasha had already committed.[90] Fortner, for the 718th, went even further; on at least one occasion he authorized the release of enemy deserters irrespective of which particular insurgent movement they belonged to.[91]

In June, the Italians struck a deal with the Croats whereby the Croats assumed responsibility for civilian and police administration in Zone II and for civilian and military administration in Zone III. The Italians' main aim, alongside a desire to placate the Croats, was to reduce their military commitment to more manageable levels.[92] This was symptomatic of an Italian anti-Partisan "campaign" marked by increasing caution, the abandonment of important strongpoints, and the arming of increasingly uncontrollable Chetnik groups. While the deal gave the Croats a freer hand in these areas initially, it ultimately created an administrative void that would eventually be filled by the Partisans. The Croatian civilian commissar in Glaise's office perceived that Roatta was simply trying to pacify his jurisdiction on the cheap, and spin it as some kind of success to his rival Italian generals.[93] Serbia Command reported that a vacuum ensued in these regions as soon as the Italians implemented their plan.[94]

But the Partisans' eventual triumph was still not assured. Quite apart from anything else, they still faced enormous obstacles to overcoming their Chetnik opponents. Chetnik propaganda, though disorganized, peddled what was for many Bosnian Serbs a potent as well as chauvinistic message.[95] Back in January, in a misguided attempt to entice wavering elements and split the Chetnik movement, the east Bosnian Partisans had resolved to form "volunteer units" of Chetniks, under Partisan command but with a degree of autonomy. Yet these units proved of dubious loyalty at best. Indeed, the Axis offensives of April to June 1942 emboldened some "volunteer" Chetniks to attempt coups in several Partisan formations.[96] Individual Partisan units, at odds with the more sensible line now directed by their central leadership, also weakened their support by continuing to commit the kinds of brutal sectarian excesses—purportedly against fifth columnists—that could cripple their wider appeal. In eastern Herzegovina in particular, all these factors eroded the Partisan movement's strength to such a degree that the Trio/Foča offensives merely provided the final push that destroyed it there.[97]

Yet, overall, the Partisans took more steps forward than backward during spring and summer 1942. Even the losses they had sustained in battle came to their aid. For the destruction of poorer-quality units enabled them to concentrate more committed fighters in elite units.[98] Proletarian brigades, as mobile forces without affiliation to any particular region, gave them an edge in combat, even though, as "outsiders," they were often viewed with hostility in Bosnian Serb areas. The Partisans also imported the NOOs onto Bosnian territory and intensified their propaganda campaign.[99]

One aim of the Partisans' propaganda effort was to wean their Serb rank and file off the Great Serbian idea. To this end, they also imported workers and students from the towns and thereby increased the element within the Partisans that harbored civic, multinational, "Bosnian" values. They also increasingly engaged with religious groups. In order to attract support from Croats, Muslims, and Serbs, the Partisans often employed language designed to pit the "working masses" against the bourgeoisie in all three ethnic groups. A further perennial theme of

Partisan propaganda was the treacherous and reactionary nature of the government-in-exile with which the Mihailović movement was so closely associated. Organization and control improved at the Partisans' lower levels also. From June 1942, they made ever greater use of "mobile" battalion- and detachment-level commissars. These were usually of considerably higher quality than the company-level commissars. The following month, in order to drive home the advantage that this measure created, the movement's Operational Staff decreed that all new recruits must undergo political instruction.[100]

Further, given that the Partisans' burgeoning combat effectiveness increasingly enabled them to protect the population against the Ustasha, the Ustasha's murderous persecution of the Serbs was increasingly likely to feed the flow of Partisan volunteers. The dire state of Croatian administration, and the Germans' own thinly-stretched manpower, made it harder still for the Germans to keep the Ustasha's barbaric conduct in check. In June and July's German-led Operation Kozara, for instance, the SS reported that the Ustasha was killing the old, orphaned, and chronically ill among the deportees. In August, the Ustasha was able to wage a campaign of mass killing in the Syrmian lowlands by taking advantage of the absence of German troops busily combating Partisans in the Fruška mountains.[101]

Meanwhile, German army commanders responded to the burgeoning Partisan threat by reasserting their faith in "systematic and organized" terror. Operation Kozara was executed by Combat Group West Bosnia, headed by General Stahl of the 714th Infantry Division. The immediate spur for the offensive was the Partisans' capture of Prijedor and its mine works, and the severe disruption to communications that had followed. Kozara saw thirty thousand German and Croatian troops, including four battalions of the 714th Infantry Division newly arrived from Serbia,[102] pitted against thirty-five hundred Partisans. But this was also an operation against civilians. No serious attempt was made to distinguish between "guilty" and "innocent," and in a new and unusual development for the Yugoslav campaign, all men over fourteen seized during the operation were to be held in camps or deported as labor to the Reich. In the event, the Ustasha murdered huge numbers of civilians seized in the operation in its concentration camp at Jasenovac.[103]

Operation Kozara, which also had support from the air and from the Hungarian Danube Flotilla, inflicted very heavy losses on the Partisans in western Bosnia.[104] But it failed to pacify the region permanently. Once the bulk of German and Croatian troops had been withdrawn after the operation, no effective attempt was made to keep the region pacified with comprehensive hearts and minds measures, a permanent German troop presence, or frequent and numerous hunter group patrols. Other operations which the Germans executed in western Bosnia that summer, even those which enjoyed some short-term success, similarly failed to achieve any long-term impact.[105]

But while the German forces in western Bosnia seem not to have fully grasped some of the fundamentals of successful counterinsurgency, the 718th Infantry Division's grasp of them was altogether surer.

For one thing, the 718th favored flexible hunter group tactics. In mountainous Bosnia such tactics could be more effective than large-scale operations that, though they might inflict mass butchery, failed to deal the Partisans decisive blows. The division employed hunter groups particularly prominently in June 1942. Between June 3 and 22 the 718th, supported again by Croatian units, sought to winkle out and destroy the Partisan group in the mountain forests east of Zenica and south of Zavidovići. The group was reportedly disrupting the railway line between Sarajevo and Brod, and terrorizing and plundering the local population.[106] The division was able to commit only four infantry battalions and one of its batteries to the operation. The remaining forces—four battalions and four batteries of various types—were provided by the Croatian army.[107] Experience had taught the 718th that it lacked enough troops for a comprehensive encirclement, something the terrain in the Zenica-Zavidovići region rendered harder still. Lieutenant Peter Geissler, now serving with the 714th Infantry Division, knew this situation only too well. "With us, sadly, it's usually a question of wearing down the Partisans and scattering them, not exterminating them," he wrote in July 1942. "In these loathsome mountains it's hard to do anything else."[108] But the 718th aimed to overcome this hurdle by ordering hunter groups into the area in a series of speedy, direct, independently operating attacks. The division hoped among other things that this would confuse the Partisans so much that they would think they were facing more German troops than they actually were.[109]

The division later judged such tactics vindicated, particularly when the units taking part also distributed propaganda material. "At present," the division declared, "such a hunter group stands ready within every company of the 718th Infantry Division. They stand ready for every eventuality. They will naturally be strengthened according to each eventuality."[110] A further advantage of the hunter group was that, small as it was, it was easier to equip more formidably.

The 718th Infantry Division submitted a fairly upbeat report at the close of the Zenica-Zavidovići operation. It declared that, though the insurgents, particularly the Partisans, were gaining ever more recruits and increasingly unsettling hitherto undisturbed areas elsewhere in the NDH, insurgent activity had fallen in its own operational area significantly.[111]

Mutual hatred between Partisans and Chetniks aided German pacification efforts considerably. The two movements' totally incompatible aims, and numerous truces struck between Chetnik and Ustasha units during 1942,[112] had now led the Partisans to identify the Chetniks as their principal enemy. Where the Partisans lacked the organization on the ground to properly dominate the country, they simply terrorized the Chetniks and their settlements as far as they could.[113] "The Chetniks are fighting (in Bosnia as elsewhere) for Greater Serbia, the Partisans for Bolshevik Russia," the 718th reported. "But Draža Mihailović depicts Communism as being as great an enemy of the Serbian idea as the occupiers."[114] Following bloody fighting between the two groups in the Majevica and Ozren regions, many Partisans had withdrawn over the River Sava, or southward into Italian-administered territory. Some Chetnik groups in the division's area had agreed to aid the Croatian authorities against the Partisans.[115] One German officer approvingly reported of one such agreement that "the Chetnik group in the Majevica region is in every respect committed to complying with the necessary terms as precisely as possible, and has ruthlessly eliminated those of its own people who have not complied."[116]

Yet there was no room whatsoever for complacency. For the Partisans' partial defeat in Operation Kozara left many areas, including Syrmia,

Samarica, and northern Herzegovina, where they remained active. In eastern Bosnia, the 718th Infantry Division's area of operations, a relative quiet descended, but it did not last.[117] During July and early August, the 718th tried to engage Partisan groups moving northwest from Montenegro, but were prevented by the failure of the Ustasha troops serving alongside them.[118] In early August, together with troops from the 714th and 717th Infantry Divisions, it was assigned to intensive border patrolling. The aim was to prevent the battle between the Chetniks and Ustasha from spilling over into Serbia, and also to prevent Chetnik groups from both sides of the Drina from linking up. Meanwhile, conditions across the NDH grew ever more alarming. On August 21 Serbia Command reported that the NDH administration had lost all influence north of the River Sava.[119]

But the 718th Infantry Division still sought to engage the population; indeed, it was striving to this end more than ever. In addition to the directives it had already issued, it now forbade its troops to burn down houses and farms from which shots had been fired or in which ammunition had been found. For, according to the 718th, this had led in the past to "sometimes pointless destruction on the greatest scale, and to the burning of all elements, including those who may have been innocent, in the troops' rear."[120] The division also stressed, in capital letters, that "THESE ORDERS ARE TO BE MADE CLEAR TO THE TROOPS BEFORE THE OPERATION BEGINS."[121] This directive illuminates the barbarism many rank-and-file troops must still have been practicing, despite their commanders' exhortations to the contrary. But it also highlights how conscientiously the division was seeking to rein in such barbarism.

Throughout the final week of August the 750th Infantry Regiment, with Croatian backup, conducted Operation S in the Šekovići region. This too was a small-scale affair. Few Partisans were killed or captured, and the Germans lost more men to illness than to the enemy.[122] The operation's only significant military effect was that heavy grenade launchers showed their worth during its course, boosting the men's morale particularly strongly when they were fired in unison. "For the Partisan war in eastern Bosnia it is our best weapon—we cannot have too many of them," the division declared.[123]

Operation S was more important for demonstrating the 718th's ongoing commitment to engaging the population. "Every opportunity must be taken," it declared on August 17,

> to make clear to the population, in word and deed, that this action is directed entirely against the Partisans, and that those who are willing to work will enjoy the protection of German and Croatian arms. It is therefore forbidden to burn down houses unless the battle makes it unavoidable, and also forbidden to deprive the population of its livestock or food supply.[124]

The 718th ordered the use of Chetniks who, before the fighting began, had declared themselves willing to fight the Partisans. It even ordered its troops to make use of those captured Partisans willing to help guide efforts to winkle out their former comrades.[125] Finally, in Operation S's aftermath, Battle Group Faninger embarked on a "propaganda march," aided by willing Majevica Chetniks who helped guard the propaganda troops against both Partisans and a hostile Chetnik group from Serbia.[126] The 718th observed in a report of August 2 that:

> although the inhabitants of Bosnia seem to lead a disinterested and lethargic life, they are very receptive to propaganda. Rumor propaganda has a particularly strong effect on them. With their own tendency to exaggerate, bad news and rumors are cultivated, blown out of proportion and disseminated in fantastical forms. The only way to combat this is through clear, simple, and insistent propaganda.[127]

The division also wanted the population to be granted the opportunity to listen to Wehrmacht reports and read placards in the Croatian language, view weekly German film newsreels, and have access to simple maps displaying the situation on the eastern front. Furthermore, specially appointed units should distribute both propaganda and food to the poor from field kitchens.[128] In the Rogatica area, the Field Gendarmerie distributed provisions to the population, and reported that it "soon enjoyed incredible trust in the eyes of the population . . . All were treated equally, be they Muslims, Pravoslavs or Catholics."[129] The 718th's rank-and-file troops played their part in these efforts also. "The sharp discipline and exemplary conduct of individual soldiers, and of units as a whole, strengthens and maintains the trust and regard which the German Wehrmacht enjoys," the division declared.[130]

With Operation Kozara heralding a hardening of the German counterinsurgency campaign in the NDH, then, the 718th Infantry Division's constructive engagement effort was now ahead of that of the campaign in general. Indeed, it seems clear from a number of divisional reports that General Fortner was actively seeking to promote hearts and minds measures not just within his division's jurisdiction, but also to his superiors.

The irregular warfare that convulsed much of the NDH during the first eight months of 1942, like the Serbian national uprising before it, pitted overstretched, often substandard German troops against an increasingly adroit insurgent enemy. The troops had good reason to blame the highest leadership levels of the Axis for this state of affairs. While the Nazi leadership, including senior generals, had effectively allowed the Ustasha free rein, its Italian counterparts had granted even freer and more murderous rein to the Bosnian Chetniks. The chaos both groups had unleashed had primarily benefited the Partisans, a group destined to eventually triumph over its rivals, and one that in the meantime proved a growing source of difficulty for German troops on the ground. Pressured as they were, and disposed to anti-Slavic ideology and harsh counterinsurgency doctrine, it would have been little surprise if German troops had resorted to unbridled terror as surely as their comrades had in Serbia in 1941.

Many indeed did. But there were differences with the Serbian situation that led some German army units, if only for a limited period, to temper their predilection for terror. That predilection was clearly on show during these months, in the directives for the 718th Infantry Division's operations as well as more widely. But those directives, and the 718th, also displayed restraint. The 718th's was not an enlightened, comprehensive campaign of constructive engagement. But from the start of 1942, the measures it practiced were less severe than the terrible extremes to which the

Wehrmacht had gone in Serbia in autumn 1941. The populations of the areas affected would certainly have appreciated the difference.

That a division might conduct itself more moderately was made more likely by key differences between the situation in the NDH in 1942 and the situation in Serbia the previous year. One, which German commanders stressed from the start, was that the NDH was an "allied" state. This, of course, overlooked the fact that the Nedić regime in Serbia was supposedly an ally also. But by fostering this perception among their units more actively, some German commanders undoubtedly helped to dilute the savagery with which their men might otherwise have conducted themselves towards the population. A very grim corollary to this is the fact that, whether because they had been murdered or incarcerated, or had escaped to the Italian occupation zone or to the Partisans, there were very few Jews on the ground for the Germans to kill.[131]

A second key difference was the situation in the field. In Serbia in autumn 1941 the Germans had been seeking desperately to regain ground against an opponent who, in the western part of the country at least, had threatened to overwhelm them. The fear this had engendered was one of the factors, albeit only one, that had spurred them to such terrible reprisals. But in the NDH in early 1942, neither Partisans nor Chetniks constituted the same level of mortal threat. There was no cause yet, then, for German troops to feel the degrees of fear and desperation that had assailed their comrades in Serbia. This too was likely to make some German army units conduct themselves somewhat less ferociously, at least for a time.

Bosnia's mountainous environment, meanwhile, was more remote and impenetrable than much of the landscape of Serbia. This clearly rendered the Germans' task more arduous, particularly given their own troops' deficiencies. But because the situation they faced was less directly perilous than the one they had faced in Serbia, some German army units were more likely to try employing more considered, imaginative solutions to the challenge confronting them. Overall, the Germans did not rely enough upon hunter group–size actions, or accordingly scale down their reliance upon massive operations of annihilation—operations of a sort far less certain to succeed amid such terrain. But some units did at least try to handle the civilian population with more restraint. Among

other things, the information they gained from a more responsive popu-
lace was bound to ease the herculean task of locating insurgent groups.

Finally, a more "enlightened" approach was further compelled by
the actions of the Ustasha. The Ustasha was the single greatest threat
to the NDH's stability during the early months of 1942. Many German
units on the ground recognized, even if higher command levels did not,
that combating that threat, not to mention the rival mayhem perpetrated
by the Chetniks, was essential. This meant among other things that
the Germans must offer the threatened sections of the population less
coercion and more protection. Granted, the Wehrmacht's condemnation of the havoc the Ustasha was wreaking was partly motivated by the
Wehrmacht's need to rationalize its own failure to maintain order. But
healthy skepticism should not blind one to the carnage and chaos the
Ustasha was inflicting in the NDH.

For all these reasons, German divisions were facing a situation that
called for more constructive, conciliatory forms of counterinsurgency
warfare.

Even so, German army units rose to the challenge in ways that were
fitful and uneven, and fell well short of a truly comprehensive hearts
and minds campaign. Commanders were still clearly influenced by
the German army's utilitarian, ideologically colored predilection for a
counterinsurgency campaign of maximum force and maximum terror.
Consequently neither the 718th Infantry Division nor its subordinate or
superior formations were subjecting the Wehrmacht's traditionally brutal way of operating to more fundamental questioning. And from Operation Kozara onward, higher-level commands again placed increasing
faith in maximum force and maximum terror. Underpinning much of
this conduct, probably, was the frustration felt by commanders whose
troops, due to higher-level dictates, were lacking in training, resources,
and numbers.

Yet the 718th Infantry Division, for one, still held to the more restrained
course it had started pursuing. It was left out of Operation Kozara, the
largest and bloodiest anti-Partisan operation of summer 1942. Instead,
it operated for much of the time in a region that, for a time at least, was
more pacified than many other parts of the NDH. The 718th's location,
and its now augmented order of battle, together reduced that pressure for

immediate and dramatic results that bore down on divisions participating in those larger operations. This enabled the 718th to pursue a more incremental, yet rather effective approach that combined constructive engagement with smaller-scale hunter group operations.

The 718th Infantry Division was probably also influenced by the attitudes of its commander, General Fortner. These attitudes, as with other commanders, may well have been shaped by the general's experiences earlier in his life. In complete contrast to General Hinghofer, who had directed the 342d Infantry Division's murderous conduct in Serbia in 1941, Fortner spent his entire Great War serving on the western front, a service cut short on his capture in 1916. Perhaps more importantly still, Fortner was born not in Austria but in central western Germany.[132] Neither aspect automatically imbued him with the character of a dove. But it was General Hinghofer's Austrian origins, and the lengthy duration and particular character of the service he had undergone on the eastern front during the Great War, which had distinguished him from his fellow divisional commanders in autumn 1941. And it was Hinghofer who, of all of them, had been counterinsurgency warfare's most savage practitioner. That Fortner's experience of the Great War had been markedly different to Hinghofer's may well help explain why he did not comport himself as brutally.[133]

Moreover, Hinghofer's Habsburg prejudice towards the Serbs is likely to have been the decisive factor that set the predominantly German-born troops of his division down a singularly ferocious path. Conversely, Fortner's non-Habsburg background may well have influenced his efforts to rein in the predominantly Austrian-born troops of his division. Fortner too, it seems, had no love for Serbs; after all, the 718th Infantry Division had been particularly merciless towards the Mihailović Chetniks during its January 1942 operations. But the relative restraint which Fortner's division increasingly showed to all the region's ethnic groups as the year progressed was the mark of a commander who, unlike Hinghofer, was able to place a check on his anti-Serb prejudice

But in autumn 1942 the 718th Infantry Division, like the German forces across the NDH, would face steeper challenges. The ethnic complexities within its jurisdiction became more labyrinthine, so much so that any measure of constructive engagement was no longer enough to

master them. And the Partisans themselves became an ever more formidable adversary. Now, such commitment to hearts and minds measures
as the 718th had displayed would be tested to destruction—and this at a
time when the German army command in the NDH continued to radi-
calise its general effort against the Partisans ever more brutally.

CHAPTER 9

The Morass

Attitudes Harden in the 718th Infantry Division

C ONSTRUCTIVE AS SOME of the 718th Infantry Division's counterinsurgency measures of 1942 were, there was a limit to what they
could achieve as long as the failings in the division's fighting power
remained. And of failings, irrespective of the division's bolstered battle order, there were plenty. They would prove increasingly telling as
summer turned to autumn and the 718th faced a resurgent, burgeoning Partisan movement across its jurisdiction. The frustration that
now increasingly gripped the division, and the welter of increasingly
severe directives emanating down to it from above, would harden its
conduct markedly.

Even though Operation S had showcased the success of the 718th
Infantry Division's hearts and minds measures, its aftermath also produced more unsettling conclusions. The 718th reported that there had
been ongoing communication problems during the operation,[1] and
that its pioneer company was severely stretched: "the mountainous
region of eastern Bosnia offers the enemy so many possibilities for sev-
ering roads, paths (and) railways, that one company is not enough to
get everything in order in the necessary time."[2]

The division also bemoaned its state of supply. Leaders of supply columns had had no point of contact with the quartermaster during operations, and supplies had often arrived too late.[3] The troops had frequently
had to seize hay and straw during an operation itself. This meant that no
payment was handed over to civilians, and no form made out. Clearly
the division preferred to requisition supplies from the population in an
orderly fashion, rather than plunder them. But what was happening was
that "(we) later receive a countless mass of bills. It can be months before
people receive payment. Such goings-on damage the image of the German Wehrmacht."[4] And as with supply, so with clothing and equipment,
which the 718th judged totally inadequate for mountain warfare.[5] Above
all, the division could not ignore the fact that most of the Partisans had
not been killed in its operations, but merely "expelled." In other words,
they had been able to regroup and fight another day. And the 718th was
fully aware that, so execrable was the fighting power of the Croatian army
and the Ustasha, combating the Partisans effectively would in future be
down to itself alone.[6]

The 718th believed that the only viable long-term solution was its
wholesale conversion into a proper mountain division, a process already
begun but far from finished.[7] But it would be months before the division would receive resources and equipment to anything like that standard. Meanwhile, the chagrin it felt would begin to seriously erode the
restraint it had shown in its operations.

Furthermore, even though the clash between Chetniks and Partisans
might bring dividends to the occupiers, it was only one face of a myriad
interethnic conflict that was growing ever more tortuous for the 718th to
negotiate. There were no fewer than four groups the division needed to
include in its calculations. The first was the Chetniks, the second the
Partisans, the third the Bosnian Muslims. The fourth, principal root of
so many of the evils bedeviling the occupiers and, much more lethally,
the population, was the Ustasha. Now that Tito's principal Partisan force
had retreated from eastern Bosnia, the Ustasha had been quick to reestablish itself in the region.

As early as June 20, the 718th Infantry Division acknowledged that its
pacification effort was still blighted by Ustasha outrages. "Undisciplined
Ustasha units robbed and murdered," it reported. "The Ustasha believes

it has the right to exterminate everything Pravoslavic. In several places Serbs were bestially murdered. One Ustasha company, found guilty of such attacks by the German Field Gendarmerie, was disarmed."[8] In July, in an attempt to exercise greater control over the Croats, the 718th sought for General Fortner to be granted power over all Croatian military courts in the German operational area. But the NDH War Ministry was able to block the move.[9] By August, nothing had changed:

> The question of a genuine pacification of eastern Bosnia is, in the division's opinion, only possible via a German military adminis-tration with many German police and gendarmerie. This must be strong enough also to maintain a constant vigil over the Ustasha. Our current strength is insufficient to prevent the constant flaring up of small-scale uprisings, and there can be no expectation of a genuine resolution to the current situation.[10]

Here as elsewhere, Catholic priests were working hand in glove with the Ustasha; "in the Brod district, Dr. Subolić's mob has unleashed a reli-gious witch hunt . . . The Pravoslavic population are being forced on pain of a concentration camp to convert to the Catholic faith."[11]

Again, even though Wehrmacht expressions of detestation for the Ustasha should be approached cautiously, the Ustasha undoubtedly had played a central part in creating a horrendous state of affairs. The 718th's view was shared by Serbia Command, which in September 1942 reported that "in Croatia, current conditions have led the function of state law and administration to practically cease in many parts of the land. The Usta-sha terror and the mass slaughter in Syrmia have heralded a new wave of unrest which has thrown into question all attempts at pacification."[12]

The Chetniks made great propaganda play of the ongoing Ustasha massacres. Serbia Command reported in October that "references to the innocent victims of the Serb ethnic group will unleash a vengefulness which can have an immensely powerful propagandistic effect upon the population."[13] Yet Serbia Command soon recognized that, ultimately, the Partisans stood to benefit from this even more than the Chetniks: "the cruel and unjust behavior of the Ustasha has turned the population towards Communist mastery."[14]

By now the Ustasha's depravities were increasingly rivaled by those of the Bosnian Muslim militias. Muslims had sought to found an armed movement for their own protection as early as autumn 1941. This was despite the fact that the Ustasha, rhetorically at least, made much of Muslim "equality" in the NDH. In fact, the Ustasha needed to depict the Bosnian Muslims in such terms if the idea that Bosnia was a prime NDH heartland was to have any credibility.[15] The stress on Bosnia may also have helped deflect the Croatian population's attention from the fact that the NDH had been forced to relinquish Dalmatia to the Italians.[16] Nevertheless, such was the Ustasha's fanaticism that many Muslims feared that what the Ustasha was doing to the Serbs it might do to them next.[17]

Italian support for the Chetniks gave Muslims a further incentive to look to their own protection. In August, the Chetniks entered Foča and massacred one thousand members of the Muslim population and the surviving Croatian garrison. It was unclear whether the Italians had simply stood by or actually aided the Chetniks with artillery fire. What was clear was that an Italian relief column had fraternized with the Chetniks on its arrival in the town.[18] The massacre led to calls for an independent armed Muslim force and Bosnian autonomy under the Reich. Neither would be forthcoming. But Bosnian Muslim personnel would be employed by Himmler in a Waffen-SS formation, the Handschar Division, in 1943.[19]

Meanwhile, particularly in the 718th Infantry Division's jurisdiction, the actions of Muslim militias were contributing to the ghastly reality on the ground. Already in 1941, Muslims had sometimes participated in Ustasha atrocities against Serbs.[20] In May 1942 the 718th reported that the militias were committing atrocities against Serbian villagers, women and children included, east of Tuzla.[21] By August the main Muslim militia, the Muslim Legion, was plundering the area enthusiastically. "Between 21 and 23 August," it was reported, "Muslims in the vicinity of Sapna, in cooperation with the local Ustasha and the (Muslim) Legion, burned down 300 Serbian houses in Jovin Han. The Muslims—be they the Legion, the Muslim militias, or just members of the general population—were responsible for most of the low-level disturbances to the peace of the land."[22]

Navigating the mutual hatreds that animated these different ethnic groups called for more subtlety than German army units on the ground had hitherto demonstrated. "If we hadn't arrived here in May of this year, this pitiful country would have been completely devastated," wrote Lieutenant Geissler of the 714th Infantry Division. Reflecting on the need to read the ethnic situation with the utmost care, he remarked that "we're the real Croats here, and have become proper Balkan politicians. Every division from Russia that was relocated here and tried to fight according to its old method and experiences would in no time at all suffer heavy losses, if not be destroyed altogether."[23]

In the face of such chaos, co-opting the Chetniks for security duties could seem an attractive solution. Yet its more enthusiastic advocates, the Italians particularly, failed to recognize its perils. For the Chetniks, of course, also actively participated in ethnic terror. Some of their actions were directed against the Partisans, others against Croats in areas where Serbs and Croats lived side by side and Serbs themselves were being massacred by the Ustasha. Others still were directed against Muslims in Bosnia and Herzegovina and in Sandjak. The worst massacres the Chetniks perpetrated were at Foča in January, February, and August 1942, and in Sandjak and southeast Bosnia in January and February 1943.[24] Arming the Chetniks, or excessively accommodating them in other ways, made such massacres and the destabilization they brought all the more likely.

The 718th Infantry Division, though it had dabbled in cooperation with the Chetniks, perceived the potential danger especially acutely. Divisional command claimed to have obtained documents indicating that the Chetnik leadership had ordered its people to cease fighting, hide their weapons, and prepare themselves for renewed battle. The division was deeply suspicious of the "sudden readiness for peace of Chetnik groups probably in contact with Draza Mihailović, which is probably just a ploy to buy time for reorganizing and equipping for a general uprising."[25]

The 718th was also highly averse, again for fear of exacerbating interethnic mayhem, to arming villagers against attack. On May 13, 1942, it requested of General Bader that it not be required to arm "so-called" village protection groups and militias. Allowing the population to possess weapons, divisional command argued, would destabilize the situation further, not least because of "the strongly defined religious and ethnic differences, the laws of blood vengeance which are still in force today," and also because of "the likelihood that arming people suffering from scarce provisions will prompt them to go 'wandering' into the forests to seek subsistence there."[26]

Divisional command also feared that, if it did arm civilians, those arms would simply fall into the hands of the Partisans—particularly if the Croatian gendarmerie was the only body there to prevent it.[27] It only partly got its wish. General Bader advised the division that, though he did not intend to arm villagers across the board, the weakness of the Croatian gendarmerie made some kind of "reliable" militia essential.[28]

By late September the 718th's jurisdiction extended to the southwest. This made matters worse because that jurisdiction now encompassed more Partisan groups. Meanwhile, the Muslim Legion was creating havoc as ever, and of the other three groups the 718th's intelligence section drily observed that "Ustasha, Partisans, and Chetniks are, as before, competing to carry off the Strife Cup."[29] More generally the division commented that "there is hardly a Serb, Croat, or Muslim in the whole of eastern Bosnia, who does not have some kind of blood feud to settle with another."[30]

The idea of arming the Chetniks to counter the Serbs' persecutors remained one that the 718th regarded with consternation. It still believed that, despite the increasingly mortal danger the Serbian population faced from the Ustasha and the Muslim militias, arming the Chetniks would only make matters worse—especially when the Italians seemed to indulge them so much.[31] More widely, there were even reports that the Italians were buying off the Partisans with weapons, sometimes even field guns, in exchange for the return of Italian prisoners. Glaise von Horstenau, the Wehrmacht's General in Agram, believed this practice too was being sanctioned from on high.[32]

The Chetniks in the 718th's area, divisional command drily observed, were essentially seeking to butter up the Germans to obtain peace and quiet, the Italians to obtain weapons, and the Croats to obtain both.[33] This local-level Chetnik-Croat accommodation was replicated more widely across the NDH during 1942, as both the Chetniks and the NDH regime increasingly grasped the need for some degree of co-operation against the burgeoning threat which the Partisans now posed to them both.[34] But the Chetniks within its jurisdiction, the 718th argued, were in a latent state of war with the Croatian army, as well as in a real state of war with the

Ustasha. The division argued that "the present, inconsistent treatment of the Chetniks (as firm friends by the Italians, as comrades-in-arms by the 714th Infantry Division, with refusal by the 718th Infantry Division, as mortal enemies by the Ustasha, as partners in cooperation by Croatian government representatives) holds massive dangers. Above all, it awakens in the Chetnik leadership the impression that German, Italian, and Croatian civil and military authorities are divided, and can be played off against one another." The 718th considered it essential that the Chetniks be disarmed and suppressed, even though a unified effort with the Italians would be needed in order to achieve this.[35] But the 718th also recognized that it needed to be evenhanded. As it opined to General Bader, once the Chetniks were disarmed, the Ustasha and the Muslim militias would need disarming also. Failure to do this would only cause a resurgence of the kind of chaos that would enable the Chetniks to renew themselves.[36]

It is clear from the 718th's comments that a fellow German army division, General Stahl's 714th Infantry, was much more open to the idea of cooperating militarily with the Chetniks than General Fortner's 718th was.[37] Given the relative restraint with which the 718th had been conducting itself for much of 1942, it is unlikely that Fortner was averse to arming Chetniks for anything other than pragmatic reasons. That said, it is only consistent with this study's approach to consider the possibility that something in Fortner's past might have instilled in him some hardened ideological objection to arming the Chetniks.

Between 1914 and his capture by the British in 1916, Fortner served as an infantry officer on the western front. This was perhaps a more brutalizing way to spend the Great War, even if it did only last two years rather than the entire four, than the service with the Imperial German Army's air wing which Stahl had undergone. Further, Fortner was a reactivated officer, reentering military service in 1935. During his service in the civilian police during the 1920s and early to mid-1930s, he had risen to the rank of colonel. The police service of the Weimar period, still more of the first two years of the Nazi dictatorship, rivalled the Reichswehr officer corps for authoritarian harshness.[38] On the other hand, both Fortner and Stahl hailed from central western Germany. This was not a birthplace that would have suffused either of them with anti-Serb contempt as extensively as an Austrian birthplace would have done.[39]

More telling than any biographical nugget is the pragmatic tone and considered wording, devoid of racist or ideological overtones, that the 718th employed to argue against arming the Chetniks. More telling still is the growing commitment to more measured forms of counterinsurgency that the 718th had been displaying throughout much of 1942. Clearly, this was a unit of which pragmatism was a more powerful driver than National Socialist values. The most likely reason why the 718th's divisional command recoiled from arming Chetniks during 1942, then, is also the most likely reason why it was so merciless towards the Mihailović Chetniks in its operations at the year's outset—not ideological hatred, but a firm intent to stamp on any threat it perceived to the region's security and stability.

And in eastern Bosnia, the threat the Chetniks posed to security and stability was particularly acute. For eastern Bosnia, unlike the regions further west in which the 714th Infantry Division was operating, contained a Muslim population that outnumbered the Serb population.[40] Far from stabilizing the region, then, giving armed Chetniks a prominent security role would have unleashed the Chetnik fox on the Muslim hen coop with all the havoc that would have entailed. Perhaps even more frightening were the possible consequences of an armed clash between the Chetniks and the Muslim Legion on the 718th's turf.

Conversely, the 714th had its own practical reason to be *open-minded* about arming the Chetniks. It was an especially hard-pressed formation operating in the particularly ferocious Partisan cauldron of western Bosnia. Operation Fruška Mountains, which the 714th headed in August 1942, was only its single largest operational commitment in a particularly unrelenting schedule that summer. A formation under considerably more immediate pressure than the 718th at this time may have been concerned to arm the Chetniks as a quick fix to its own problems.

This, then, was the serpentine ethno-political backdrop to the 718th Infantry Division's final operations of 1942.[41]

Meanwhile, over three months during spring and summer 1942, enduring harrowing conditions along the way, the four thousand Partisans accompanying Tito had completed the two-hundred-mile trek to the Bosanska

Krajina region of western Bosnia. By late September they had founded a liberated area of approximately twenty thousand square miles, centered on the town of Bihać.[42] After the loss of much liberated territory in Herzegovina, eastern Bosnia, Montenegro, and the Sandzak, this major new base provided the Partisans with safety and several considerable advantages. The region had long possessed a particularly strong Communist organization. It was also adjacent to the similarly robust Communist organization in Croatia. The Germans had greatly reduced their presence in Bosanska Krajina when they had transferred the 718th Infantry Division to eastern Bosnia in late 1941. The region's distance from the Serbian border largely dispelled the danger that Chetniks from Serbia might infiltrate it. Finally, so slaughterous had been the Ustasha persecutions that had taken place there in 1941 that Partisan combativeness appealed to the region's Bosnian Serb population much more than did the Chetniks' duplicitous waiting game.[43]

Above all, the new base enabled the Partisans to further consolidate their organization and propaganda. They impressed Bosanska Krajina's Serb population with their military effectiveness, and its Muslim population with their growing ability to protect it from Chetnik attacks. In August 1942, the Partisans liberated the Croatian town of Livno and its surrounding area. In doing so, they absorbed a large portion of the Croatian population into the Partisan movement for the first time. Even though they had to withdraw in October, they were to return two months later.[44]

Moreover, the actions of the Ustasha and the Chetniks were boosting Partisan support north as well as south of the River Sava. Tito therefore felt emboldened to expand his borders northward, as well as in the southerly direction into which the Partisans had been expanding hitherto. By October 1942 Tito would command ten times more experienced troops than he had a year previously.[45] By early November, the Partisan-liberated area centered on Bosanska Krajina had joined with smaller enclaves to form an area of about 250 kilometers long and forty to seventy kilometers wide, largely in what was supposedly still the Italian occupation zone.[46]

The summer had revealed just how destabilizing the ethnic rivalries within the NDH were becoming. By autumn, the Partisans were reaping the rewards. Serbia Command remarked that "the extent of the regions that need securing, in relation to the strength of available troops, gendarmerie, and police, makes any permanent occupation impossible. This creates for the insurgents, especially in Croatia, the opportunity to gather up escaped groups and form new ones."[47] Matters were made worse by problems with the harvest, which in turn were exacerbated by the scale of the requisitions which the Axis war economy was now demanding: "if a lack of provisions sets in, large parts of the population will go into the forests und exist on the fringes through robbery."[48] In time, the inundation would be further driven by many young Croat men anxious to escape conscription to the eastern front.[49]

The Partisans amassed the support of this multitude with the promise not just of protection, but also of a patriotic people's struggle that would abolish the country's destructive ethnic divisions. This process would culminate, in November, in the formation of the Anti-Fascist Council of the People's Liberation of Yugoslavia (AVNOJ) in Bihać. AVNOJ was an assembly of representatives of most of the core Yugoslav lands, with Communist and non-Communist figures at its head. It was intended to further coordinate the liberation struggle on a national level. Moreover, although Tito fell short of proclaiming it a government, AVNOJ was a further development in the administration both of the liberated areas and of the Partisan army. The region around Bihać became a showcase liberated area, with NOOs extended to its territory and new military commands and units founded also.[50]

By now, the NDH's inability to master the security situation was increasingly clear. A measure of its desperation was a directive issued by the Directorate for Public Order and Security of the Ministry of the Interior issued on 9 October 1942. This directive drew up—admittedly limited—guidelines for negotiations between Chetniks groups and the NDH civilian and military authorities.[51] Indeed, the fact that numerous Chetnik groups were willing to negotiate was a measure of their own mounting anxiety at the Partisan threat.

October and November also saw fundamental changes to the NDH's military structure. Glaise prevailed upon Pavelić to approve the division of the NDH north of the Italo-German demarcation line into a series of defensive areas. Each would have both a German and a Croatian com-mander, but the Croats were not to commence major operations on their own initiative. German troops would guard those transport and economic installations deemed essential to the Reich. Glaise was also empowered, unlike before, to provide the Croats with military advice even if he had not been asked for it first.[52] Important also was Pavelić's sacking of his Minister of Defense, Slavko Kvaternik, a figure whom many German officials reviled as corrupt, incompetent, and possibly defeatist.[53]

November 16, meanwhile, saw an end to the unsatisfactory situation whereby a German general in Belgrade had had operational command of German formations in the NDH. Lieutenant General Rudolf Lüters was appointed Wehrmacht Commander in Croatia. Under him were all German military forces in the NDH between the River Sava and the Italo-German demarcation line—the 718th Infantry Division in eastern Bosnia, the 714th to the west, the 187th Reserve Division in the area around Agram, and a regiment stationed in Syrmia that had been transferred from the 717th Infantry Division in Serbia.[54] On Glaise's request to Pavelić, Lüters also enjoyed extensive power over the deployment and organization of Croatian army units, over Croatian military appointments, and over Croatian military justice in cases dealing with actions that went against Wehrmacht regulations.[55] The Germans could now also take full operational command, whenever it was deemed necessary, of all Croatian army units north of the demarcation line. As a cosmetic concession to the Pavelić regime, Glaise and not Lüters would have formal command of those units.[56] But whilst all this made it harder for the Ustasha to commit atrocities against the Bosnian Serbs, it could not halt those atrocities completely. And Glaise's rather belated call for more stringent measures to rein in the Ustasha's corruption as well as its brutality came to nothing.[57]

The 718th's autumn operations demonstrated that the division, like the Germans across the NDH, faced in the Partisans an increasingly acute military threat—and this at a time when, following major Allied victories in North Africa, the threat of an Allied invasion of southeast Europe made overcoming the Partisans an increasingly urgent task. The Germans' response—including the 718th's this time—showed little appreciation of the need for restraint.

By now, the highest German command levels were responding increasingly ferociously to the burgeoning Partisan threat in both eastern and southeastern Europe. Hitler's Directive No. 46, which the dictator issued on August 18, made some nods to constructive engagement. But it also directed that the troops execute reprisals even more severely than before, and guard against any "misplaced confidence" in the population. Similarly, the Commando Order of October 18 declared that "only where the struggle against the partisan nuisance was begun and carried out with ruthless brutality have successes been achieved."[58] Glaise, together with the Austrian-born Luftwaffe general Alexander Löhr, who succeeded General Kuntze as Wehrmacht Commander Southeast in August 1942, mooted the idea of trying to open some kind of dialogue with the Partisans. But this suggestion found no support from Hitler. The Führer was already vexed by the fact that, as he put it, too many prisoners were being taken in counterinsurgency operations in the NDH already.[59]

But Hitler need not have worried, because Löhr, for one, generally subscribed even more strongly than his predecessor to the virtues of maximum terror and maximum concentrated force.[60] In late October he issued a Balkan-specific version of Hitler's Commando Order, with ruthless additions of his own. "All visible enemy groups are, under all circumstances, to be exterminated to the last man," Löhr decreed. "Only when every rebel realises that he will not escape with his life under any circumstances can the occupation troops expect to master the rebel movement . . . I expect every commander to commit his entire person to ensuring that this order, without exception and in a brutally harsh spirit, is executed by the troops. I will investigate every transgression and bring those responsible to account."[61]

And even before this, the ferocious tone being set by higher command was increasingly suffusing the directives of General Bader's Serbia Command also. So read its war diary on October 2:

In order to achieve an effective deterrent effect (sic), those punishable deeds . . . which are directed against the Wehrmacht are to be punished more severely, the punishment to be executed ruthlessly. Aiding and abetting the enemy and unauthorized possession of arms (are) to be paid for with death . . . The ideas of the (military) judges are much too clement for the fourth year of the war. In cases of suspected espionage most severe measures must be employed . . . Our divisions frequently seem to have a too pro-Serbian attitude. The SS will offer example.[62]

Then on October 10, Serbia Command issued an order, signed by General Bader himself, directing that "the established reprisal measures for dead and wounded may also be extended in the future in accordance with the situation to *missing* German soldiers."[63]

And General Löhr's efforts also undoubtedly made it harder still for units in the field to contemplate the kinds of measures that might de-escalate the campaign's brutality. The effect of the welter of harsh directives upon the 718th Infantry Division was unmistakable. It was probably also out of its own mounting alarm at the burgeoning Partisan threat, and its failure thus far to extinguish that threat through popular engagement and small-unit tactics, that the division now came increasingly to rely on brute force and terror. Its operations around the town of Jajce between October and December demonstrate this clearly.

Partisan units, in the course of Tito's northward expansion of his territory, captured Jajce on September 25; advance parties of the 718th moving on Jajce from the southeast the following day were met by withering machine-gun and rifle fire.[64] Jajce, it seems, had been ripe for a Partisan takeover for some time, and for a depressingly familiar reason. The division remarked that, "according to the reliable part of the population, the foremost cause of the situation in Jajce was the behaviour of the Ustasha."[65] The 718th aimed firstly to attack the Partisan group that had just crossed the River Vrbas, driving it back to Jajce. It would then combine with elements of the 714th Infantry Division advancing from the northwest to destroy the Partisans. This operational phase was to be completed by October 2.[66]

The Jajce Partisans presented a mixed picture to the 718th. The division considered their state of supply less than impressive. It also believed that the Partisans' commanders often plied their troops with alcohol before they attacked, and concealed the scale of their losses from them.[67] But they were organized to effective military standard. They were distributed across three battalions, each consisting of three companies of between sixty and one hundred men, and commanded by Communist

Party commissars. They usually attacked at night, especially when it was raining and the moon was hidden.[68] "(Partisan) raiding parties are sent in with hand grenades and Molotov cocktails," according to the 718th's intelligence section. "Firing lines follow behind them."[69] The Partisans also possessed penal battalions, antitank battalions, mining sections, and an excellent communications network utilizing "mostly beggars, adolescents, and Dalmatian peddlers" as its couriers.[70]

With all its other proliferating responsibilities, the 718th could only commit limited forces to the operations. The lineup of divisional forces for the first operation, assembled on September 28, included only two battalions each from the 738th and 750th Infantry Regiments, a battery and an additional platoon from the 668th Artillery Section, two platoons of Panzers, and an armored train. The rest comprised elements of three different Croatian infantry regiments, an Ustasha company, and Croatian artillery batteries of various types.[71] This was hardly the most formidable array the 718th had yet assembled.

In the event, the 718th only retook Jajce on October 4. Even then, it failed to encircle the Partisans properly.[72] By mid-October, Partisan forces were massing west and southwest of Jajce to attack the town again.[73] The 718th resolved to attack them first, conducting a preemptive operation between October 24 and November 5. Its main force was divided between Battle Group Suschnig, formed around the three battalions of the 738th Infantry Regiment, and Battle Group Wüst, formed around the three battalions (minus one company) of the 750th Infantry Regiment. Battle Group Wüst was only granted two German infantry battalions (plus an additional company) against Battle Group Suschnig's three, and three Croatian artillery batteries against Battle Group Suschnig's four. It was, however, assigned three full Croatian infantry battalions against Battle Group Suschnig's one. Wüst's group possessed only one German artillery battery, Suschnig's none, and no tanks were provided to either. Two smaller battle groups, however, were between them allocated three Panzer platoons, two German artillery batteries, a German infantry company, an Ustasha company, an armored train, and parts of two Field Gendarmerie companies.[74]

But matters were not helped by the reassignment elsewhere, on October 14, of most of the second company of the division's motorized 501st Field Gendarmerie Detachment,[75] and, nine days later, of four Panzer companies that had been temporarily assigned to the division.[76] All this when the division had to contend with mushrooming chaos elsewhere in its jurisdiction, particularly Chetnik attacks against Croatian patrols and transport.[77]

On November 26, the Partisans succeeded in retaking Jajce. "The heights along the Donje Vakuf–Jajce road were held by strong enemy forces," reported Battle Group Wüst, "4,000 men equipped with machine-guns . . . grenade launchers, artillery, and sufficient ammunition."[78] Throughout the first week of December, in an effort to wrest the town back again and destroy the Partisan forces in the vicinity, the 718th prosecuted Operation Jajce III. For this operation the division committed fewer forces than before. Though it was able to field all six battalions of the 738th and 750th Infantry Regiments, they were deprived of all but one Panzer platoon, and one platoon of the 668th Artillery Regiment. Aside from an anti-aircraft platoon and an armored train, the remaining forces committed to the operation were, again, Croatian—six infantry battalions, two Ustasha battalions, two platoons of pioneers, and seven artillery platoons of various types.[79]

And throughout the operations, the 718th continued to regard its Croatian army "allies" as a burden. It had not always been thus. In March 1942, for instance, Croatian army units had acquitted themselves well against Partisans in the 718th's jurisdiction.[80] But in mid-November divisional command damned the Croatian units in its area as poorly armed, "decadent, and disorganized."[81] There was no trust in their officers, "no connection between officers and men . . . Units down to battalion level are fragmented and leaderless, while the staff officers just wander around with nothing to do."[82] The Ustasha's units were better armed than the Croatian army's, but their discipline was worse. "Theft, murder, and plunder are the daily routine in the Serb areas . . . (The Ustasha) is hated by the population, including the Croatian."[83]

In view of the division's pillorying of the Croatian army and Ustasha, General Fortner's typewriter probably balked at having to produce the address he felt obliged to issue, presumably for the sake of cordial relations, to the Croatian troops on October 10:

> Comrades of the Ustasha and the Croatian Army! Side by side with
> the men of my division, you have attacked, scattered or exterminated

the Communist enemy. In so doing, you have proven that, when you are possessed of the true martial spirit and assail the enemy wherever you meet him, no enemy can stand against you, whatever his numbers. I extend my recognition and gratitude to all of you, from the oldest commander down to the youngest soldier![84]

The reality was that, while the 718th Infantry Division itself stood "ready, in the event of a general uprising, to defend its positions, the Croatian Army can only be partially trusted. In the event of an English landing in Dalmatia it must be reckoned that a general Chetnik uprising will break out and a large part of the Croatian Army will defect to the insurgents."[85] By the end of the year, matters within the Croatian army had improved not one iota.[86]

Not all elements of the 718th held the Croats in such contempt. The 750th Infantry Regiment, for instance, testified to their usefulness as patrol personnel.[87] It is of course possible that here, as elsewhere, the division was scapegoating the Croats for its own failings. But clearly, given the Croatian army's undoubted serial defects, there was much truth in the 718th's contemptuous assessment.

And the 718th was increasingly plagued by failings of its own. It again stressed its need for more air reconnaissance, more artillery, more specialist mountain gear, better communications, and small patrols that could observe the enemy from concealed positions.[88] But the division's own fighting power was now being whittled down from above, as well as being dispersed ever more thinly. In mid-November the 718th requested to be allowed to retain its tanks, pleading that their mere presence helped deter attacks on supply transports and routes. Four days later, Croatia Command refused this entreaty.[89]

The effect of all this on the division's combat performance in the operations was entirely predictable. The 738th Infantry Regiment's report for the third phase of the Jajce operations claimed that its own troops' self-belief was suffering in the face of an enemy who had grown increasingly self-confident, and whose troops had been driven from the villages only after heavy fighting.[90] On October 10, meanwhile, the 750th Infantry Regiment drew up a list of all the bitter experiences the Jajce operation was teaching it. The defects in its equipment were legion; it also requested smaller, more realistic daily targets for its advance.[91]

The operations themselves were drawn out and hard-fought.[92] During the first operation the troops endured difficult terrain, poor weather, and Partisan disruption to rear communications. The 714th Infantry Division, meanwhile, blamed the terrain and the lack of mountain equipment for its own failure to advance from Jezero-Pliva to Sarici in line with the operational plan.[93] The 714th's other commitments soon prevented it from assisting the 718th further in the operations.[94]

The 718th's Battle Group Annacker issued a report in late November that conveyed in detail just how fearsome a prospect the Partisans now were. On November 25 the battle group had been given the task of extricating the fifth company of the 738th Infantry Regiment from encirclement. Then, "on 26 November at 5.15am the battle group reached the southern exit of Jajce at Skela. After such a rapid forward movement, it was possible to surprise the Partisans in Skela. It was established that Partisans wearing nothing but their underclothes had fled into the neighboring woods and surrounding hills. Some even had to jump out of the window."[95]

But then the battle group attacked the Partisans in the factory district, and it became immediately apparent what it was up against:

> A heavy rifle and above all machine-gun fire set in at the moment the searching of the houses began. The commander of the first company, Lieutenant Steiner, fell immediately to machine-gun fire.[96] Several NCOs and men were wounded in the same way. The Partisans, who may well have been members of the intelligentsia, put up a particularly fierce resistance in these houses. Unobserved by them, the company was able after heavy fighting to break into one of the buildings and kill around 30 Partisans. Meanwhile the third company of the 738th Infantry Regiment . . . came under heavy enemy attack from the east, and it was established that around 3,000 Partisans were approaching Jajce from the north-west. Artillery and grenade launchers were observed being brought into position, and after a short while they were inflicting heavy fire on our battle group's positions. Aside from this, heavy machine-gun fire became noticeable. During the period of heavy grenade launcher and machine-gun fire, the enemy was bringing his troops up ever nearer to our own lines. It was coming to the point where our men would also be encircled

from behind, leading to the battalion's total destruction. Above all, many trucks would be lost. Because our battle group lacked artillery, it was not possible to take on the Partisans effectively. We held out for longer, and when it was clear that the enemy was about to break into our lines at Point 568, the third company pulled back to avoid destruction. Encirclement was at that point almost complete. Giving up Point 568 also increased the enemy pressure from the north, pressure which the first company could not withstand. The ferocity of the fire, from both artillery and grenade launchers, was turned with full force upon the battle group and battalion staffs . . . Decision then taken to try and pull back. Once in Vijenac, the troops were fired upon from all sides by rifles, machine guns and grenade launchers, particularly from the surrounding hills and houses.[97]

The column was unable to halt, but forced to fight its way through the Partisans to escape.[98]

By December 7, the 718th Infantry Division had failed to destroy the Partisans but had at least retaken Jajce.[99] But all the signs are that a great many civilians had perished in the process. And there is little evidence, in contrast with its conduct earlier in the year, that the division paid particular heed to avoiding heavy civilian casualties. Many of its troops, certainly, paid no heed at all. They seem to have been primarily concerned with driving the Partisans out of Jajce, irrespective of the civilian cost, and reasserting German military prestige.

The killing escalated as the operations unfolded. After the 718th's first (temporarily) successful attempt to retake the town, it reported killing eighty-three Partisans, taking seventy-four prisoners, and seizing a similar number of guns. The division and its Croatian allies lost thirty-eight dead and fifty-two wounded. This signifies that a real battle had taken place, one in which the division itself had suffered severely, and not the indiscriminate butchery of civilians.[100] But later the picture changed dramatically. On October 28, Battle Group Suschnig and Battle Group Wüst reported that, at a loss to themselves and their Croatian allies of three dead and six wounded, they had killed at least 145 Partisans—from whom just six rifles and one machine gun had been retrieved.[101] Worse, on October 30 the division reported that its units, primarily Battle Group Suschnig, had killed 257 Partisans (including *Flintenweiber*), for the loss of one German soldier wounded and two civilian auxiliaries killed.[102]

At the end of the second Jajce operation, the 718th Infantry Division claimed to have killed at least 747 Partisans. It reckoned, observing that the Partisans sought to bury their dead and carry off their wounded, that it had actually killed considerably more. There were 106 prisoners taken; 127 rifles, eight machine guns, and a heavy grenade launcher were seized. The Germans and Croats themselves had lost fifty-three dead, the vast majority of whom were Croats, and eighty-two wounded. The division announced, with a combination of pride and contempt, that "the proportion of our own dead to the enemy's was 1:14. The result would have been better still if the Croatian troops too had learned that one must fight off attacks instead of running away from them."[103]

Even though some "Partisan" losses probably were down to genuine combat, then, rather more of them were probably down to the killing of noncombatants. This time, in contrast to before, divisional command seems to have been unperturbed.

With the troops mired in miserable conditions and ferocious combat, and divisional and regimental commanders making no attempt to rein in their brutality, there was nothing to prevent that brutality's threshold from falling. Since the beginning of 1942 the 718th's troops had been committed to successive counterinsurgency operations that had been often fruitless, frequently savage, and increasingly costly. Add to this the increasingly severe counterinsurgency directives they were being issued, if not by the division itself then certainly by higher command, and it would be surprising if the troops' behavior had *not* become more ferocious.

The personal letters of Lieutenant Peter Geissler, of the 714th Infantry Division, illustrate the effects. Although soldiers' letters as a source should be approached cautiously,[104] Geissler's nevertheless provide vivid and unsettling insights. It would not be too hyperbolic to conclude that his experiences during the second half of 1942 progressively dragged him down into his own personal hell.

At the outset of the summer Geissler already loathed the region and everything about it: "Where we are, hell has broken loose!" he wrote on June 21. "There's nothing to buy here, no meat, no oil, towns for the most part abandoned, houses empty and ransacked—this is our operational area! Here the Bolshevik is at home . . . Croatia is much worse even than Serbia—a complete cess pit . . . In Bosnia, the devil is abroad! If we didn't have any tanks or Stukas with us, then things really would be grim. We'd've been done here a long time ago if it wasn't for these damned mountains."[105]

In a letter the following month, Geissler described how hard hit he was by comrades' deaths in this war: "Today our mood's well below par. Our battalion's first company suffered an awful tragedy. Some soldiers walked into a minefield, among them our best sergeant, who was due to get his commission in the next few days."[106] Geissler was well aware that he himself could be next. "The enemy, crafty fellow, sits mainly in the trees, but can also conceal himself behind a bush," he wrote in September. "You never know where to train your eyes. I like to experience everything in life, but not a guerrilla war!"[107]

In another letter that month, Geissler described the Partisans' silent and unseen methods, and their predilection for night attack: "Every night the enemy attacked with a Hurra (!!!) . . . You have to picture it, us in the mountains, in the dark—unfortunately the moon is no longer shining— the enemy slips in through the thick woods (!) until he's about 25 meters in front of us, throws hand grenades and then slips back." His hatred of the Partisans was further entrenched by what he saw the following morning: "This morning, on the strip of territory before our battle-line, we discovered the corpses of a load of uniformed women! Just like in Russia."[108] Geissler's revulsion at the thought of women fighting in the Partisan ranks also emerges in a letter of October 4: "Yesterday we had our second black day, we had to leave many dead and badly wounded on a bridge. And when you consider that we suffered these losses at the hands of a *female* Partisan company, it really makes you want to throw up."[109]

That same letter also found Geissler in more reflective mood, as he mused over the character of the country in which he found himself. "Our objective today was the most prettily situated town in the Balkans—which naturally is in the hands of the Partisans. The countryside here is the most romantic I've ever seen, apart from the Grossglockner and Semmering." But the reality of the Partisan war extinguished any aesthetic pleasure to be gained from such surroundings. "We've got no feel for such sentiments. These splendidly romantic wooded hills have been thoroughly infested by the bandits."[110]

From late November, and all through December, the Partisans assailed Geissler's unit unremittingly. The ever present fear of annihilation seems to have intensified in his mind. "We had a pretty black day again today," he wrote on November 27. "The tireless Partisans attacked our positions in huge numbers across a thirty-kilometer front. Among other things they took the town which we'd recaptured just before I went on leave. The enemy wrecked everything in his path. Just like in Tobruk we had to destroy our own weapons, supplies, ammunition, and accommodation. The enemy also wrecked important rail and military installations. Among other things we lost one of our company commanders. Yes, these are going to be very hard nuts to crack. And that's only the start of what awaits us here this winter."[111] A fortnight later he wrote that "today things were black, the Partisans surprised our battalion, there were six dead, sixteen wounded, two missing and 28 dead horses! Naturally this is again an enormous blow, of the sort we won't be able to withstand much longer. If we don't get German reinforcements soon then we will all be in the shit."[112]

Two days later, relief had still to arrive: "For two days . . . we've been on alarm level 1. This means I have to keep my clothes on at night and a weapon lying next to me. This time it really is damned serious. According to prisoner interrogations the enemy is going to try to retake Prijedor before Christmas, something which, with a big attack, he should have no trouble achieving, for 1) there are only staffs here, of hardly any combat value, and 2) the enemy has already tried this with other places, and successfully!"[113]

Throughout, Geissler's psychological stability was further shaken by his experience of Partisan atrocities. "On one of these photos," he wrote in May, "you can see my regimental commander talking with a Serbian captain. He was explaining how the Partisans had slaughtered his wife and son a few days before. Before it happened the son was forced to have sex with his mother. Simply awful!"[114] Such instances loomed large in Geissler's mind even when his unit had had the better of the fighting. "Yesterday . . . the battalion exterminated 650 Partisans in combat," he wrote on September 6. "The first time any battalion in West Bosnia achieved this! But we lost our best NCO, who the scum managed to capture. We found him that evening. They'd pulled his fingernails out while he was still alive, chopped his fingers and his genitals off, sawed off a leg, and then finally they shot him. I also told you a lieutenant had gone missing. The enemy had nailed him alive to a door and then tortured him to death with a red-hot iron!"[115] On December 22, finally, he wrote that "today more of our comrades were sadly lost, falling into the hands of the Partisans. The poor souls were stripped naked, bound and thrown into a running mountain river. They died a horrible watery death. This is how the enemy spares his ammunition! May the almighty one day let justice be done and give our worthy people the decisive victory!"[116]

Geissler's ghoulish account may have been a reflection of his fevered brain-state, or an attempt to justify his own brutal conduct, rather than an accurate report. That said, Partisan units' capacity for savagery towards their prisoners is well attested to.[117] But whether or not Geissler was exaggerating, his recounting of such atrocities indicates that he was slipping into a mind-frame that justified committing all manner of brutality in the fight against the Partisans.

Geissler's unit was still precariously holding on by this time, but its day-to-day losses were fearful as ever. Meanwhile, the impression that German units were now tiny islands beleaguered by pandemic Partisan savagery grew stronger in his mind. "We lose many of our best every day . . . fifteen again yesterday! That may not seem much relative to the whole regiment, but it's mounted up horribly over the past few days. This evening the enemy tried to encircle Prijedor. They burned the villages all around. Road bridges wrecked all around, road blocks laid down, mines laid, rail track destroyed, a travelling hospital train attacked (!!). All transport routes impassable! . . . That's our situation in the 'sunny' south-east!"[118]

Finally, Geissler was surrounded by death throughout the whole period. "Yesterday," he wrote in August, "we advanced down a road, where we came across bloody corpses in a ditch, wrapped in tablecloths (men, women, children, murdered!) There must have been about a hundred of them . . . Dreadful. Man becomes beast!"[119] Which of the manifold belligerent groupings in the 714th Infantry Division's jurisdiction actually perpetrated this particular atrocity is unclear. It may even have been another unit *from* the 714th. Irrespective of who the perpetrators were, however, this extract displays yet another facet of the execrable conditions in which Geissler found himself for a sustained period of several months.

The brutalized, embittered way in which Geissler came to regard the enemy is clear throughout these extracts. It is easy to imagine how such a perspective could, in turn, brutalize a soldier's behavior. It is also easy to see how the behavior of the 718th's troops could by now have been similarly affected. Of course, the National Socialist indoctrination to which they had already been subjected almost certainly eased the path to barbarization. But the extreme and often perilous conditions the troops were enduring would have profoundly hardened them nonetheless.

The third Jajce operation, which finally saw the Partisans properly expelled from Jajce, was the hardest fought of all. It commenced at the start of December.[120] The Germans suffered fifty-eight dead and ninety-three wounded, the Croats twenty-three dead and 135 wounded. One hundred and forty-nine Croats were also reported missing. The Partisans, meanwhile, lost 431 dead and sixty wounded.[121] By December 5 it was reported that the enemy had finally pulled out of Jajce and was headed north.[122] But the scale of Axis losses indicates just how hard-pressed the division's troops were by this time. Having retaken the town, the vulnerability of the rest of its jurisdiction, particularly around Tuzla and Zenica, thwarted the 718th's attempt to pursue the Partisans and complete their destruction.[123] Other divisions, such as the 714th, faced a similar situation by now.[124]

By the end of the year the 718th had gained no respite. Among other things, the division's intelligence section reported that the large Communist groups beyond its demarcation line continued to threaten its area's southwestern border. Their skill in propaganda, their practice of forced recruitment, and what divisional command termed the "natural tendency of some of the population to murder and plunder" were all aiding them.[125]

Even the changes to the NDH's military structure, which had taken place in October and November, failed to bring about a significant change in Axis fortunes. In late November Croatia Command reported that a reshuffle in the NDH government had not affected internal policy, and that Ustasha attacks continued to spawn chaos. The Partisan presence in Zone III had increased since the Italians had abandoned it.[126] And Croatia Command now conceded that, compared with the mayhem in those regions still "administered" by the NDH, the population of the Communist-controlled areas actually enjoyed considerable stability.[127] By December Croatia Command believed that 95 percent of the population was supporting the Partisans' communication network. It also noted that the Partisans, by treating captured Croatian soldiers humanely, were fueling mounting desertion from the Croatian army.[128]

The 718th Infantry Division's experience during the final four months of 1942 shows that there were now ever greater limits to how far any unit was prepared to pursue the kind of counterinsurgency campaign that placed constructive engagement at its center. For one thing, it was no longer just a question of whether the division should engage with the population, but also of which groups to engage with, and how far. Considering the increasingly acute threat the Partisans now posed, and the mayhem being dispensed not just by the Ustasha but, increasingly, by the Muslim militias also, it might at first have seemed that the obvious partner for the 718th to woo was the Chetniks. But because the Chetniks themselves rivaled and sometimes surpassed these other groups for brutality, arming them was a course of action that, the division recognized, was fraught with pitfalls of its own.

In such conditions, hearts and minds measures were likely to bring tenuous benefits if any. The sense of frustration this was bound to fuel was perhaps one reason why the 718th eschewed much of its earlier restraint during the Jajce operations. Perhaps an even more immediate reason was that the Partisans' burgeoning fighting power would inevitably lead to a furious engagement—a particularly daunting prospect for an occupation division blighted by so many failings—from which mass civilian deaths were likely to result.

By now, moreover, the effect that almost unremitting counterinsurgency warfare was having upon the troops was likely to barbarize their own behavior irrespective of any measures divisional and regimental commands took to check it. And if divisional and regimental commands were *not* seeking to check it, it is little wonder that the "Partisan" body counts the Jajce operations yielded were so horribly disproportionate. And the absence of any restraint by divisional and regimental commands indicates the mounting obduracy, further fueled by directives from higher command, which was by now coloring their own mind-set.

The 718th Infantry Division's command had not been a model of enlightened thinking during 1942. But for much of the year it had sought to infuse its counterinsurgency campaign with a considerable degree of constructive engagement. But towards the end of the year, what seems to have hardened its attitude most decisively was not National Socialist conviction, but the sheer intractability of the military, political, and environmental conditions its campaign was facing. The origin of this morass ultimately lay, as earlier in 1942, in the strategic priorities and political mistakes of the division's highest military and civilian masters.

In the opening months of 1943, the fortunes of the German occupation divisions in the NDH would decline further still. How the divisions responded would depend, again, not just upon the Wehrmacht's central doctrines and the orders issued by high command, but also upon the conditions the divisions faced and the sensibilities of the men who commanded them. The 718th Infantry Division was by no means the worst offender during this period. That distinction went to the German-led "Croatian Legion" formations of the 369th and 373d Infantry Divisions.

CHAPTER 10

The Devil's Division

The 369th Infantry Division in Bosnia, 1943

THE COMMANDER OF THE 369TH INFANTRY DIVISION was Brigadier General Fritz Neidholt. Neidholt had been born in 1887 in
Thuringia, central eastern Germany, to the family of a Protestant pas-
tor. He spent the majority of his Great War on the eastern front, though
he did experience both the 1914 advance and the 1918 retreat on the
western front. Throughout those four years he served variously as an
adjutant, a communications officer, a pioneer officer, and a staff officer.
It was in this latter capacity that Neidholt's career seems to have stalled.
According to his resume, in April 1917 he was appointed an "officer in
the field" with the army high command, but just over a year later he
was serving on the staff of a reserve division. On the inception of the
Reichswehr, Neidholt began serving with the infantry, with which he
largely remained until leaving military service in 1935. By the outbreak
of war Neidholt had returned to the Wehrmacht, briefly commanding
an infantry regiment in Poland before ending up on the army high command's officer reserve list. He was only appointed a brigadier general
in October 1942.[1]

Neidholt's, then, was not an especially distinguished career. Perhaps
appropriately, the only way in which the division he commanded in
Yugoslavia distinguished itself was in the number of civilians it killed.

Known in Croatia as the "Devil's Division," its nickname would prove grimly apposite.[2]

Formed in 1942, the 369th arrived in Yugoslavia at the end of that year. The 369th itself was a replacement for a forerunner unit destroyed on the eastern front.[3] Its main body of combat troops was divided into two infantry regiments, the 370th and the 969th, each comprising three battalions of four companies, together with an artillery regiment and an antitank section.[4] In other respects, its composition was unusual. Together with the later-formed 373d and 392d Infantry Divisions, it was a "legionnaire division." Its senior officers, and some of its junior officers and NCOs, were German- or Austrian-born, but its rank-and-file personnel consisted of former soldiers of the Croatian army. The Germans had set up a German- and Austrian-led "Croatian Legion" during 1942 because they believed that the presence of German army officers and NCOs would compensate for the growing lack of suitable officer and NCO personnel within the Croatian army itself.[5]

But for the 369th Infantry Division, the presence of German army officers and NCOs would not compensate for low morale, discipline, and fighting power. These debilitating conditions would help to brutalize the division's conduct during this period. Yet that conduct, as with the 342d Infantry Division's in 1941, can also be attributed to the biography of its commander, and in particular to his Great War experience.

By early 1943, the numerical strength of the Partisans' regular forces, forty-five thousand by German estimates, was still less than a third of the now hundred and fifty thousand-strong Chetnik movement. But the rate of growth—a ten-fold increase in twelve months—had been dramatic.[6] Among other things, the Partisans were benefiting from growing popular affront at the increasingly rapacious economic measures to which the Axis was subjecting occupied Yugoslavia, particularly in terms of the procurement of crops and labor.[7] Against them, the Axis was in increasing disarray. Relations between the Germans and the Italians plummeted further during winter 1942-1943; whether in Yugoslavia, the Soviet Union, or North Africa, the Italians were increasingly blamed for Axis failures. Only Hitler's fellow feeling with Mussolini, and his fear that any further weakening of the Duce's position might have dire political consequences for the Axis, prevented the Germans from undermining the Italian leader. In the NDH General Roatta, reflecting the Italians' deteriorating position, had in November 1942 announced his intention of initiating a further withdrawal. The purpose this time was not to concentrate on areas of particular interest to the Italians, but simply to better defend Italy itself against the threat of invasion the Axis defeats in North Africa portended.[8]

Fearing another power vacuum, the Germans managed to get this withdrawal delayed. But the episode was a measure of how burdensome German relations with the Italians now were. The Germans also remained intensely uneasy at how far the Italians were willing to go to accommodate the Chetniks. Any pretension that this was a cunning, credible divide-and-rule policy, rather than a recipe for mayhem, now looked even more threadbare than before. By now if not earlier, the Italians, as the German police attaché in Agram observed, might be good at dividing, but did not possess the strength for ruling.[9]

Immensely difficult also were German relations with the NDH. Yet despite the Ustasha regime's ongoing weakness, most senior German figures remained reluctant to abolish it. General Löhr was an exception. Counterinsurgency hard-liner though he was, he had the presence of mind to want the Ustasha regime replaced either by a government headed by the Croatian Peasants' Party, or by a Wehrmacht military commander. This did not happen, partly because of Hitler's ongoing sympathy with the Ustasha, and partly because of lack of sufficient support for Löhr from Glaise and Kasche. Hitler also feared how replacing the Ustasha regime with one headed by the Croatian Peasants' Party might be perceived externally. Elsewhere in German-occupied Europe, conservative-authoritarian collaborationist regimes had been replaced by more radical ones. But performing the operation in reverse might be perceived as a humiliating failure. Furthermore, for reasons of Italo-German diplomatic relations, overthrowing the Ustasha regime would only have been possible by granting more concessions to Mussolini. But this in turn would have made it harder to mobilize the Croatian national forces.[10]

And preserving the Pavelić regime at least kept German options open. As long as the Chetniks were not completely disarmed, they could be used as leverage against the Ustasha. And as long as the Pavelić regime and the Italians remained at loggerheads the Germans could continue presenting their own economic demands on the NDH as more reasonable. These were scarcely inspiring motives, but they helped ensure that retaining the Pavelić regime appeared marginally preferable to the alternative.[11]

Confronting the Partisans in the NDH were three German army infantry divisions—the 714th, the 718th, and from February 1943 the 717th—together with a menagerie of Croatian, Italian, and pro-Axis Chetnik forces of questionable if any reliability. Yet the condition of the German divisions, at least, was improving. Early in 1943, they were upgraded to the status of light divisions (*Jäger-Divisionen*), and received improved equipment and weaponry.[12] Their fighting power still left something to be desired. Though their quality had been raised in some respects, they were still denied an influx of younger, fitter personnel with the level of training enjoyed by frontline combat troops.[13] Their numbers remained static just as those of the Partisans were multiplying. But their new status was at least an improvement on before.

The Axis forces received a further boost to their campaign—the powerful Prinz Eugen Division of the Waffen-SS, a formation composed almost entirely of ethnic Germans. But this division's often barbaric conduct, and the odium it provoked among the population, went some way towards canceling out its military contribution.[14] Glaise sought a political solution involving curbing the Ustasha's outrages and offering better treatment to the NDH's Serb population.[15] But the arrival of the "Croatian Legion" infantry divisions would infuse the anti-Partisan campaign with yet more savagery. Unlike the Prinz Eugen Division, however, the legionnaire divisions did not couple their savagery with formidable fighting power.

The major operations the Axis executed in the NDH during the first half of 1943 were highly ambitious. By now, they needed to be. They were designed to achieve the stage-by-stage conquest of the whole of Bosnia, and the complete destruction of the Partisan forces based there. Following Axis defeats in North Africa, the real possibility of an Allied landing in southeast Europe—and with it the likely collapse of Italy—brought a new urgency to this task.[16] Against twenty-five to thirty thousand largely battle-experienced and well-equipped Partisans, the Axis committed a total of circa ninety thousands troops.[17] The operations themselves were titled White I, II, and III. In essence, White I was to destroy the Partisans in western Bosnia, White II the Partisans in central Bosnia. White III, finally, was intended not only to destroy the Partisans in Herzegovina, but also to conclusively disarm the national Chetnik units in that region. This provoked the ire of the Italians, who had of course sanctioned the use of thousands of such Chetniks in the MVAC. In the event, the Italians reneged on their initial pledge to cooperate in this part of the plan, and managed to further postpone a final reckoning on the matter.[18] At the same time, in fact, Mihailović was himself planning what he hoped would be the decisive Chetnik blow against the Partisans. He eventually concluded that the best opportunity to finish off the Partisans lay in attaching his forces to the Italian formations participating in the Axis offensive. This he would do in time for Operation White II—though not with the result he had hoped for.[19]

White I, which commenced on January 20, was the first major operation planned for the first half of 1943. At first sight, the forces assembled for it were formidable: it involved the 369th and 717th Infantry Divisions—together with the 714th in a mopping-up capacity—the Prinz Eugen Division, and three Italian divisions. The troops, many of whom were battle experienced and—among the Germans at least—well equipped, would be supported by Luftwaffe combat aircraft; in 1942 German operations had had to rely mainly, and often unhappily, on Italian and Croatian airpower. The German forces were to advance on western Bosnia from the north and east, the Italians from the south and from the Dalmatian coast to the west.

But each of the three Italian divisions committed forces only at battle group strength. The 717th Infantry Division could barely muster a regiment's worth of strength at the start of the operation, and only the Prinz Eugen Division possessed specialized mountain gear. Finally, the distances the troops were expected to cover were wholly unrealistic. The troops of the Prinz Eugen Division, for instance, were ordered to cover one hundred and fifty kilometers of difficult terrain and cut off the Partisan retreat, all in the space of forty-eight hours.[20] In the event, the Prinz

Eugen's divisional command objected and got the target drastically reduced to no more than three kilometers daily. But this was overcompensating in the extreme, as well as indicating that some commanders lacked faith in the entire operation, because it guaranteed that thousands of fleet-footed Partisans would escape the trap.[21] The 369th's task, with support from the 714th Infantry Division, was to advance to the line of Slumj and Bihać, cleanse the Samarica region, and link up with the Prinz Eugen's left wing.[22] Facing its initiation into combat of any kind, the division's shortcomings would be mercilessly exposed.

The operation's ferocity is conveyed by Milovan Djilas: "the fierceness of the offensive from the day it began in Banija on 16 January, and in Kordun on 20 January, left no doubt about Hitler's determination to squash the resistance movement in Yugoslavia. The Germans crushed our defenses with tanks and artillery, set our villages afire, and shot hostages and prisoners. From morning till night their aviation pounded everything in sight; from the very first days our bases at Bihać, Petrovac, etc., were constant targets."[23]

The initial higher-level directives Croatia Command issued for the first of the White operations again exuded the German military's longstanding counterinsurgency ruthlessness. Such ruthlessness was encouraged by the highest command level of all; on December 16, 1942, Hitler had issued an exceptionally ferocious directive. He had ordered "the most brutal means . . . against women and children also" in the conduct of the security campaign, and declared that any officer or man showing scruples in the matter was committing treason against the German people.[24] Before White I's launch, Croatia Command issued two major directives for its prosecution. One, dated January 12, stated that "*every* measure that ensures the security of the troops and appears to serve the purpose of pacification is justifiable . . . No-one should be held to account for conducting themselves with excessive harshness."[25] The order went on to direct that anyone taking up arms against the Axis forces was to be shot or hanged, and that "villages which are difficult to enter, as other places which have been identified as Partisan strong-points or would suitably serve as such . . . are to be destroyed."[26] But the directive Croatia Command issued five days before this one contained even more severe implications:

a) In unreliable areas, the male population between 15–50 is to be concentrated in transit camps, with a view to transportation to Germany.
b) Partisans and Partisan suspects, together with civilians, in whose homes weapons and munitions are found, are to be summarily shot or hanged and their homes burned down.
c) The local garrisons . . . can set curfews for the general population.
d) Contravention of German orders to be dealt with ruthlessly and extensively with an armed response.
e) Functionaries of the Croatian state who fail to cooperate sufficiently to be arrested for sabotage.[27]

Granted, the directive's harshness was diluted somewhat, apparently on Glaise's intervention, in time for the operation. Orders dated a few days later, which appear in the files of the divisions participating in the operation, make no mention of the mass deportations stipulated in the first point.[28] But the second and fourth points were still in force, and their implications were ominous. The second was emphasizing that mere suspicion, not proof, was sufficient to invite brutal retaliation. The fourth was not so much an order as a guideline. In both encouraging ruthlessness and giving the directive's recipients a completely free hand in practicing it, it was a textbook example of the National Socialist leadership principle. The barbarity the 369th Infantry Division dealt out during the operation, like the 342d Infantry Division's barbarity in 1941, was not, therefore, simply down to the need to "follow orders."

The directives the 369th itself issued for the operation were in the spirit of Croatia Command's. On December 29, 1942, the division's operations section issued an order for the handing over of nonresidents in villages. It declared that "all people denounced as Partisans are to be arrested and thoroughly interrogated. If it becomes clear that those denounced may be suspected of being Partisans, they are to be hanged or shot."[29] In other words, no distinction was to be made between captured Partisans and civilians whom the troops merely suspected of being

Partisans, and mere suspicion, not proof, was enough to warrant a bullet or a noose. And the order was certainly carried out. The division's intelligence section reported that, while three hundred Partisan suspects had been sent to a concentration camp over the course of January 1943, a further fifty had been shot merely on suspicion of cooperating with Partisans.[30] Around the same time, the division decreed that the civilian population must hand over all its weapons by a certain deadline. It also proclaimed that anyone caught aiding or sheltering nonresidents would receive an automatic death penalty. This was regardless, presumably, of whether such nonresidents were Partisans or not.[31]

In issuing these orders, the 369th Infantry Division was not just following higher-level directives. It was also expressing the perennial fear of irregular warfare that had so brutalized German conduct over the past two years. The intelligence section gave voice to it:

> Anyone approaching from the enemy's direction is always suspect and therefore to be arrested. The Partisans have mastered the art of infiltrating our lines disguised as harmless farmers, forest workers . . . etc. Another of their techniques is for men and women to hide themselves in snow holes near villages . . . After the troops have passed by, they return to retrieve their weapons from their hiding place and form up again in the troops' rear to attack communications and supply columns. Later, they form large groups which undermine the entire transport and supply network and attack the troops in the rear.[32]

The intelligence section concluded from all this that:

> there is no place for sympathy for Partisans, Partisan suspects, etc. . . . It is the duty of all units, supply troops and columns to comb these areas and seize all men of this age group (15 to 50). At all costs, the whereabouts of the Partisans' hiding places must be prised out of the inhabitants they have left behind.[33]

As a direct prelude to White I, the 369th issued a general directive on January 6, 1943, urging "ruthless measures against the Partisans and the population who pact with them."[34] Three weeks later, as White I reached the heights of ferocity, the division ordered that "villages, houses either side of the roads are to be burned down so as to deny the Partisans shelter."[35]

Such orders, as so often before, could only encourage the troops to violent excess. Between January 9 and February 15 the 369th Infantry Division recorded that, though its troops had sustained losses of thirty-six dead, they had killed 834 Partisans for certain and estimated killing 455 more.[36] Frank Deakin, an officer of the British Special Operations Executive attached to Tito's headquarters during 1943, conveys what such figures could mean in human terms in an anecdote from an operation later that year:

> In one cave, where ninety men, women, and children huddled together, a German patrol approached within ten yards, without perceiving the entrance. At that moment a new-born baby began crying, and the mother sought to calm the child. The wailing continued, and panic seized hold of the people. A voice whispered to kill the baby, and the mother held out the infant in silent resignation. Even in terror no one had the will to commit the act. The mother strangled the infant. The Germans appeared at the mouth of the cave, shot down some of the aged occupants, and moved on their way.
>
> A child's cradle has remained in the cave since that day.[37]

And as so often before, the contrast between "Partisan dead" and Partisan weapons captured was horribly disproportionate. From a reported nigh-on thirteen hundred Partisan dead, the division retrieved only 256 weapons.[38] Granted, the Partisans were retrieving some of their weapons themselves, some among their number would have been unarmed in any case, and the figures for Partisan dead were subject to other distortions also. Yet this was still the kind of massive shortfall that had hundreds of noncombatant deaths written all over it. Such shortfalls in 1943 raise even more suspicion than they would have done in previous years. For the increasingly professionalized and militarized Partisans of this period were much less likely than their predecessors to have allowed substandard Axis troops to slaughter them in such numbers.

If it had already been apparent during 1942 that German troops in the NDH were conducting themselves ever more brutally, it was more apparent still in early 1943. This was irrespective of whether those troops were German themselves or, in the 369th's case, German-led. Granted, high-level commanders stipulated that persons taken in White I were not to be shot immediately, but placed in a hostage reserve. But the operation still produced a massive contrast between the number of persons shot and the number of weapons seized. Women, children, and deserters were, it seems clear, frequently being killed for the troops' convenience.

The legacy of ruthless decades-old counterinsurgency doctrine must take much of the blame for this. So too must the hardening effect of National Socialist ideological indoctrination—even if said ideology, and said doctrine, were being conveyed within the 369th to Croatian troops by German- or Austrian-born officers and NCOs. The conditions the troops faced played a role also. Among other things, soldiers now felt insecure even in those Muslim or Croatian areas in which they had previously felt safe. And it is probably not too outrageous to suggest that, fighting as they were in a region that by now was essentially lawless, and seeing what Yugoslavs were capable of doing to each another, many of the 369th's junior German officers and NCOs would have had fewer qualms about behaving similarly and encouraging their troops likewise.[39] Many of their Croatian rank and file, of course, would have had fewer qualms still. Seeking to fully explain events of the kind Frank Deakin describes, however, should not detract from their harrowing nature.

But, as before, not all divisions were behaving as brutally as others. In late 1942, such restraint as the 718th Infantry Division had shown earlier that year had been supplanted by a gruesome lapse during its operations around Jajce. But in early 1943 it returned to something approaching its earlier form, form that contrasted markedly with the 369th Infantry Division's. The 718th's files for early 1943 do not contain ruthless directives of the sort which the 369th was so fond of issuing; if anything, they contain the opposite. On February 16, for instance, the 718th's divisional command decreed that "it is understandable that the soldier should be able to obtain extra provisions in the form of plundered livestock. But it has been established that some livestock have been slaughtered, one piece of meat taken, and the livestock left in the road. This is plunder and squandering to the detriment both of our own homeland and of the local land."[40] The same order, mindful perhaps of the slaughter the division's troops had inflicted during the Jajce operations, also directed that:

> Valuable individuals are not to be shot, so that some information can be prised out of them.

> Deserters with our own certification, who provided testimony, were shot, in some cases purely because they could not be escorted back. This attitude cannot be tolerated!

> Women and children, when not under suspicion, are to be left exactly where they are found.[41]

Nor was the need for measured treatment of the population lost on the 718th's subordinate units. In February 1943, for instance, Battle Group Annacker requested "the formation of propaganda units which will follow the troops and explain and justify their conduct to the population through the spoken and written word."[42] Because leaflets alone would have little effect upon the illiterate sections of the population, the group urged "skilful spoken propaganda, as practised recently by the Partisans."[43] It also recognized that "the propaganda troops must not consist of Ustasha people, for the population views the Ustasha and everything it stands for with hate and distrust. Rather, they should consist of members of the Croatian Army or civilians."[44] Free, at least for the moment, of the brutalizing pressure it had faced during the Jajce operations, the 718th Infantry Division seems to have been allowing saner counsel to prevail.

Furthermore, the body counts the 718th's troops inflicted during this period, high though they were, were less outrageous than those the 369th was dealing out. For the whole of January 1943 the 718th recorded killing 204 Partisans at a loss to itself of thirty-eight dead.[45] Against this was the 369th's recording of 834 reported Partisan dead, at a loss to itself of thirty-six dead, between mid-January and mid-February. The contrast does need qualifying. For one thing, the 718th's troops still seem to have been killing large numbers of civilians; as before, the very relative nature of their "restraint" needs keeping firmly in mind. Furthermore, if they still were not killing as many civilians as the 369th, this was partly because they had less opportunity; the "Partisan" dead they recorded were killed in the course not of major mobile operations, but of smaller-scale operations and general security duties. Even so, some of the contrast is surely due to the greater restraint the 718th exercised. For though the 369th and 718th suffered comparable losses during these periods, the 369th killed at least four times as many "Partisans" as the 718th.

Most strikingly, unlike the 369th, the 718th stood ready, immediately after White I and its follow-up operation, to exchange prisoners with the Partisans. There had been sporadic contact between Germans and Partisans from as early as spring 1942. The first significant prisoner exchange had taken place in Posusje, between Livno and Mostar, in September of that year. It is unclear who made the first move on that occasion; that it was Tito is suggested by reports from the Partisans, who, perhaps seeking a basis for prisoner negotiations with the Germans, were treating their German prisoners well at this particular time.[46]

One reason why a number of senior German officers stood ready to negotiate such exchanges was that they now believed Partisans should be granted the status of proper combatants. Major General Benignus Dippold, commander of the 717th Infantry Division, appeared to express admiration for the Partisans' fighting qualities when he declared that "one must view the enemy as poorly-equipped troops, but not as bandits."[47] There was undoubtedly a pragmatic motivation behind such professions of gallantry. Recognizing that they were facing a genuine military opponent, more astute officers realized that according the Partisans proper combatant status made it more likely that both sides would give quarter when taking prisoners. But this was still a profound about-face from the German military's usual view of insurgents. Some senior figures, at least, were forming a saner perception of the challenge their forces were facing.[48] Yet there is no sign that the 369th Infantry Division was contemplating similar measures at this time.[49]

Even higher command was reining in its subordinates to some extent. Although Croatia Command had on January 12 issued extremely harsh guidelines, the same directive also forbade attacks on women and children. This was a clear contrast with Hitler's order of December 16,

1942.[50] But much of the impetus, particularly for the 718th, came from divisional command. That the 369th and the 718th Infantry Divisions diverged so hugely on this score was down to three reasons.

It has already been established that a poor-quality unit, facing a hardy, dangerous opponent in a harsh environment, was more likely to feel vexed by its situation, and behave more ferociously in order to ease its frustration and reassure its superiors. The further down the command chain such a unit was, the sharper its experience of battle, and the more vicious its likely response. Given the poor quality of the 369th's units, it would have been surprising if such a brutalizing malaise had *not* infected its divisional command.

If Croatia Command's reports are to be believed, the 717th Infantry Division, despite having been officially upgraded to light division status, was even weaker than the 369th when it went in to Operation White I.[51] Yet the 369th gave ample cause for concern. A brace of reports issued during January and February 1943 testifies to its parlous manpower. On January 23, for instance, General Neidholt reported that "through borrowing and requisitioning the troops have acquired a huge amount of baggage. They make for an extremely unmilitary looking picture on the roads . . . (T)he troops are completely out of control."[52] Throughout February the situation grew worse: "(troops and non-commissioned officers) lie about uninterested on the trucks and give no salute. . . . The morale reports show that a large number of the Croatian troops are just fellow travellers without any understanding of the necessity of the battle against the Partisans."[53] Desertion became endemic.[54] The 369th's situation was not helped during White I by the fact that the Luftwaffe provided most of its assistance to other formations participating in the operation, particularly the Prinz Eugen Division, and not to the 369th.[55]

In August 1943 the 369th's intelligence section finally snapped out of its dejection over the troops' condition, and articulated some reasons for it. It identified problems born of national character; of the country's political and economic conditions; and of the ways in which the troops were led, used, and treated. On the last of these scores, it maintained that the troops' morale was worst in units where German personnel were less numerous. But it also maintained that, once the rot to morale had hit in, no amount of harsh German army discipline could arrest it.[56]

But perhaps the single main reason why the troops' performance was so afflicted was that the 369th was too slow to recognize and counter the symptoms of worsening morale. The fact that General Neidholt's prior career had been less than dazzling may indicate that here was a commander with an uncertain grip on the discipline and morale of his division. Certainly, there was nothing intrinsic in a Croatian legionnaire division's makeup that made poor morale inevitable, at least in early 1943. For as will shortly be seen, poor morale was a pitfall the 373d Infantry Division, the 369th's sister legionnaire formation, managed to avoid.

Whatever the reason, troops of such poor quality were clearly unable to fight a counterinsurgency campaign successfully. The frustration both the division and its troops doubtless felt can only have intensified when the White operations failed to achieve their objectives. Tito had had advance warning of White I ten days before the operation even started. He used this window of opportunity to systematically destroy roads and bridges in the region, and thus further hamper Axis attempts to encircle his forces effectively.[57]

By early 1943, in contrast, the 718th Infantry Division's troops were of considerably better quality than the 369th's. Of course, their equipment and manpower were still beset by deficiencies. In this they were no different to their comrades in any of the core German army counterinsurgency divisions in Yugoslavia.[58] But like its fellow "seven-hundred-number" divisions, the 718th had been converted into a light division in early 1943. In February the 718th's command described the division's fighting power as "extremely good given its current combat strength."[59] It had positive things to say about the division's training, artillery, pioneer companies, and supply, and about the morale of its troops. It was certainly overstating things when it described the division's ability to carry out its tasks as "limitless."[60] But, clearly, its fighting power was considerably higher than the 369th's. And just as poorer fighting power probably helped make the 369th more ferocious, so did the 718th's superior strength probably help make it less so.

But this is not the full explanation. For one thing, the 718th's situation was hardly comfortable either. Following a very brief pause in December,

Serbia Command reported in January that the pressure from the Partisans in the 718th's area was now greater than in any other German divisional area in the NDH. Even though White I brought it some respite, then, it was starting from a low base.[61] Moreover, the 718th Infantry Division's moderation had already been apparent—even though it was very relative, took time to develop, and dimmed for a time during Operation Jajce—before it became a light division. And even the ferocity of the 718th's troops during the Jajce operations was smoothed by divisional command's indifference, rather than driven by a conscious attempt to incite it. In other words, a division of poorer fighting power was not necessarily always going to deport itself more ruthlessly.

By the same token, divisions that enjoyed greater fighting power were not necessarily going to act with more restraint. This becomes clear when comparing the 369th Infantry Division with the 373d.

Between May and July 1943, the 373d's first three months in the NDH, the quality of its troops was considerably superior to that of the 369th's. Granted, they suffered shortages in specialist clothing and artillery for mountain warfare, pack animals, suitable trucks, and interpreters.[62] But troop discipline and morale in the 373d was significantly higher. An after-action report by the division's pioneer battalion commented on the men's "excellent" combat performance and their willingness to fight to the end.[63] At the end of June divisional command itself was similarly upbeat about the troops' mood.[64] And the 373d, it seems, had itself to thank. It credited itself with spotting the danger signs of sinking troop morale, and moving immediately to counter them: "a noticeable deterioration in discipline . . . was countered with appropriate measures. The troops' self-confidence has risen, particularly in comparison with Croatian (Army) units."[65] Not only was the troops' morale healthy, but their numbers also. In March the operations section reported that the division's roster of 10,730 men was actually fifty-six more than it was supposed to have.[66]

Yet if the 373d's approach to its men's discipline and morale was more rigorous than the 369th's, its approach to counterinsurgency was no less harsh than the 369th's. For an operation the division launched in the

Cardaci region of southern Bosnia in early July, it directed that "suspect persons are to be arrested. Those found with a weapon in their hands are to be shot . . . Settlements which have aided the Partisans . . . are to be razed to the ground. The bandits must be combated with ruthless harshness."[67] An order from mid-July, issued by the divisional commander himself, Major General Emil Zellner, expressed the hope that "all units under me or cooperating with me will continue to conduct themselves with such ruthlessness against the Partisans in the cause of pacifying the land . . . Our common struggle is against the disruption of order and the Bolshevik-infected bandits!"[68] Indeed, this directive contrasts not just with those the 717th and 718th Infantry Divisions were producing at this time, but even with those of the 369th. For ideological language as crude as this, with all its talk of "Bolshevik infection," is nowhere to be found even in the 369th's files during this period.[69]

Otherwise, though the condition of their troops was very different, there was little difference in the pitiless attitudes of the divisional commands of both the 369th and 373d. Whatever was hardening those attitudes so intensely, then, it was more than just the condition of the troops.

Firstly, unlike the officers of the 717th and 718th Infantry Divisions, the officers of the 369th and 373d Infantry Divisions were newcomers to the NDH, to Bosnia, to the region's labyrinthine interethnic relations, and to counterinsurgency generally. This meant they had had no experience of the complex reality on the ground. It also meant, by extension, that they were less likely to see the need for a balanced, restrained, and insightful approach, which engaged the population rather than terrorized it. Such, after all, is the loathing with which regular forces have so often regarded irregular forces, that the intricacies of cultivating a population caught between Partisans and Germans were particularly likely to be lost on a counterinsurgency unit that was "new to the game." Granted, given the interethnic mayhem besetting the region by this time, it is difficult to conceive of how a relatively restrained approach might have succeeded anyway. The point, however, is that some German army officers were inclined to attempt something at least resembling such an approach, while others were not.

And there was greater chance of such an attempt coming from a unit, such as the 718th Infantry Division, that had been stationed in one region for a longer period.[70] Following its experience of 1942, the 718th better understood that it was the survival pressures civilians were facing, and not any "Bolshevik infection," that were the most compelling reason why many were joining or aiding the Partisans. The 369th and 373d Infantry Divisions' officers were perhaps too new to the region for them to have fully learned these lessons yet.

And as before, the life influences and experiences that shaped a divisional commander's standpoint need considering also. The information the sources provide on the social origins of the commanders in question is too patchy for any conclusions to be drawn from it.[71] There is more information on the officers' military specialisms. Dippold, Neidholt, and Zellner had all, at some earlier time in their careers, served in one of the new, technocratic military branches, or had received or provided specialist training.[72] One might therefore expect them to have felt frustrated, perhaps to the point of brutalization, by the demodernized conditions many counterinsurgency units in the NDH endured. Fortner, on the other hand, did not undergo such specialist training. But the professional route he took during the interwar years possessed a hardening potential of its own.

Instead, important clues as to what separated more radical officers like Neidholt and Zellner from their more measured colleagues can be found in where these officers were born and the experiences they underwent during the Great War.

For one thing, both the 369th and 373d Infantry Divisions were commanded by men who had had considerable experience of the eastern front, both on the defensive and on the offensive into the territory of the Russian Empire, during the Great War.[73] Neidholt served in a variety of posts at army, divisional, brigade, and company level on the eastern front between March 1915 and April 1917. Zellner served on the eastern front against the Russian army from September 1914 until August 1916, first with the Austro-Hungarian 11th Field Gun Regiment and then with the 70th *Honvéd* Field Howitzer Regiment. He then served with the 16th Field Artillery Regiment in the campaign against Rumania from September 1916, before being transferred to the Italian front, presumably in early 1917, following that campaign's conclusion.[74] Two of the 373d's regimental commanders also saw extensive action on the eastern front, again in both defensive and offensive roles, during the Great War. One was Colonel Nikolaus Boicetta of the 384th Croatian Grenadier Regiment, the other Colonel Alois Windisch, who commanded the 383d Croatian Infantry Regiment.[75]

By contrast, neither Dippold nor Fortner spent any time on the eastern front during the Great War. Indeed Dippold, like Fortner, spent the entire duration of his Great War on the western front. Coincidentally, moreover, his experience of that battlefront was cut short, like Fortner's, after two years. He was captured by the British in September 1916, the exact same month as his colleague in the 718th.[76] Some of the 718th's regimental commanders likewise experienced the Great War in ways that were less brutalizing than they might have been. Colonel Joachim Wüst, for instance, fought entirely on the western front during the Great War. However, born as he was in 1900, Wüst spent only the last six months of the war in combat.[77] It was a similar picture with Colonel Rudolf Wutte. Wutte was born in Austria in 1897. He served on the eastern front, but only briefly, from October 1914 to February 1915. He then returned to his previous post in the military machinists' school at Pola. From September 1915, until the beginning of 1918, he served on the cruiser *Novara* in the Adriatic before taking up various technical posts on the home front until the end of the war.[78]

That extensive eastern front experience during the Great War helped to radicalize an officer's conduct during World War II was suggested by the case of the 342d Infantry Division in Serbia. It is suggested here also.

And General Zellner and Colonel Boicetta, both Austrian-born, had also participated in the invasion of Serbia during the Great War.[79] In Serbia in 1941, General Boehme had exploited the memory of the 1914 invasion to immensely brutal effect.[80] Bosnia in 1943 was not Serbia in 1941. But when Boehme invoked the Serbian atrocities of 1914 to justify his call for vengeance against the Serbs in 1941, he may also have been tapping into wider Austrian perceptions about the "backwardness and savagery" of southern Slavs generally. These were perceptions to which General Conrad had given voice in his memoirs decades before.[81] In any case, to many officers the interethnic slaughter that ravaged Bosnia in 1943 may have seemed another symptom of such savagery, alongside the Serbian "barbarism" of 1914. Officers faced with the latter, during a formative time of their lives, in 1914 may well have been more likely to lash out in response to the former in 1943. Indeed, any officer of Austrian origin was subject to such collective memory, even if he had not actually served in the Balkans during the Great War. And officers encountering ethnic Serbs in Bosnia during 1943 may have drawn a particularly strong connection with the purported Serbian savagery of 1914.

Habsburg origins and eastern front experience may well have also hardened another of the divisional commanders serving in the NDH in 1943. Lieutenant General Karl Eglseer was appointed commander of the 714th Infantry Division in March of that year. Eglseer served briefly on the eastern front in 1914, before being badly wounded and captured by the Russians at the end of that year. He was not to see action again until spring 1918, when he rejoined his old regiment on the Italian front.[82] But even though he was out of the action, his experience as a prisoner of war may well have affected him profoundly. Until the Bolshevik Revolution, captured officers of the Central powers, unlike their men, enjoyed privileged arrangements in line with the terms of the Geneva Convention. But the Bolshevik Revolution transformed their situation. The Bolsheviks' pronouncement of captured officers as class enemies, stoppage of their monthly allowance, and the terrible economic hardships ravaging Russia at this time all caused their conditions to deteriorate markedly.[83] It is likely that this experience contributed to Eglseer's own radicalization.

Eglseer's conduct at the time of the 1938 Anschluß certainly marks him out as a convinced follower of National Socialism.[84] Chief of staff of the Austrian 6th Infantry Division when the Anschluß took place, he quickly supplanted his non-Nazi superior, Brigadier General Szente, as divisional commander. Such was his buoyant mood that, twelve days after the Anschluß, he quashed pending disciplinary charges against two soldiers "in view of the enthusiasm which the reunification of Austria with Germany has released."[85]

On arriving in Bosnia as the new commander of the 714th Infantry Division, Eglseer issued directives that set him apart from commanders such as Fortner and Dippold. For he was singularly keen on issuing "why we fight"–type directives to the troops.[86] He also stressed, underlining the point for effect, that *there is no such thing as a non-combatant! Anyone who runs away or does not take part in the battle will come before a military court!*[87]

Eglseer's particularly acute concern for discipline may be attributed to his Great War experiences. He had seen discipline collapse among frontline troops just before his capture on the eastern front in 1914.[88] He had probably also seen it, though the available sources do not explicitly say so, among the disintegrating Habsburg armies on the Italian front in 1918. It may also be attributed to an ideological harshness forged by the personal indignities and hardships he had suffered as a captive of the Bolsheviks. It could be further attributed, finally, to a personal belief in driving the troops as hard as possible—a legacy, perhaps, of the extreme infantry training to which General Conrad had subjected the men of the Royal-Imperial Army before the Great War.

The hapless state of the 369th Infantry Division's manpower helps to explain why that division's propensity for brutality during Operation White I was so strong. It did, after all, have to contend with such a situation while also contending with severe overstretch, vast tracts of difficult terrain, and an at best ambivalent population. These conditions, as the 718th Infantry Division had discovered in 1942, might have been avoided had the Reich's military and political leadership resourced the anti-Partisan campaign properly from the start, asserted itself with the Italians, and above all taken a much firmer line against the Ustasha.

Nevertheless, the 369th's epidemic discipline problems indicate that its poor fighting power was to some degree self-inflicted. Yet it also becomes clear, by comparing the 369th with the 373d Infantry Division, that formations that possessed *different* levels of fighting power could respond to their situation in similarly extreme ways. That the two divisions were newcomers to the business of counterinsurgency warfare, whether in Yugoslavia or elsewhere, may have contributed to this. So too may the combat theaters in which both divisional commanders, and indeed two of their regimental commanders, saw service during the Great War. And in Bosnia in 1943, the effect for some commanders may well have been reinforced by their Austrian origins. This may also explain why the language employed by the 373d, commanded by the Austrian Zellner, was more ideological than that of the 369th under the German Neidholt. Both commanders, however, shared common ground with the 714th Infantry

Division's General Eglseer. And all three differ sharply from the more restrained divisional commanders whom this chapter has considered.

Operation White I itself was a failure. Not only did the forewarned Partisans resist with surprising ferocity; it eventually became clear to the Axis that the largest body of Partisans was located further south anyway. Sensing that the Axis were themselves about to realize this, Tito ordered his main force to move to the southeast, across the River Neretva, to escape encirclement. As the Partisans advanced on the Neretva during the first half of February, they also threatened the bauxite mines in the Mostar area. General Lüters canceled White I accordingly on February 15. Six days later, in an effort to destroy the main Partisan group, he initiated White II. A subsidiary Axis operation was also launched to protect the mines. The Italians barred the Partisans' way to the Neretva. And now Mihailović opportunistically threw his Chetniks into the struggle also. He committed between twenty thousand and twenty-six thousand Chetniks—the exact figures are unclear—with the aim of finishing off the Partisans once and for all.[89]

But Tito then destroyed the Neretva bridges and turned his forces around to attack the Germans advancing on his rear. This not only bought time in which to protect the Partisan wounded, but also made the Axis believe that the Partisans were not planning to cross the Neretva anyway. Thus, when Tito's forces eventually turned to face the Neretva again, successfully crossing it by makeshift means, only Mihailović's Chetniks stood in their way. Between March 9 and 15, 1943, the Partisans conclusively demonstrated their military superiority over the Mihailović Chetniks by routing them in a decisive battle from which they never recovered.[90]

During the months that followed, so badly did the Axis position against the Partisans deteriorate that all prospect of success for any kind of anti-Partisan campaign progressively dwindled to nothing.

Conclusion

THE WHITE OPERATIONS had shown how formidable a prospect the Yugoslav Partisans were becoming by early 1943. The operations the Axis conducted against them during the rest of 1943, and into 1944, increasingly demonstrated that defeating them decisively with the forces available was impossible. This book's main concern has not been why the Wehrmacht's counterinsurgency campaign in Yugoslavia ultimately failed, or whether it might have succeeded had it acted differently. Its main concern has been with what motivated German army commanders to conduct the campaign in the way that they did. But before returning to that central question, it is important to consider the main military and political reasons why ultimate success eluded the Wehrmacht's campaign during the period examined in this book, and the consequences during the period that followed from spring 1943 onward.[1]

There were manifold reasons why the Wehrmacht failed to destroy the Partisans before their strength reached its level of early 1943. The Wehrmacht, due primarily to the manpower demands of the eastern front and the rest of occupied Europe, never committed enough troops to enable it to pacify Yugoslavia enduringly. Even during 1943, when German military commitment to the Yugoslav theater peaked in response to fears of an Allied landing in south-east Europe, few of the divisions on the ground were of full frontline quality.[2] Similarly parsimonious was higher command's commitment of airpower to the campaign.

With the Germans' paucity of strength, the actions of the non-German Axis players acquired greater importance. Perhaps none were more important than the actions of the Pavelić regime. The ethnic chaos unleashed by the Ustasha's anti-Serb persecutions guaranteed a flood of support for both Partisans and Chetniks. Senior German commanders realized this too late, and even then, whether for political reasons or personal ones, they failed to act on the knowledge decisively. The Germans' consistent failure to take firmer action against the Pavelić regime, combined with their own minimal commitment to security on the ground, rendered it impossible for them to check the Ustasha's savagery decisively. Instead, the Germans' extensive reliance on NDH forces to provide longer-term "security" in regions recently cleansed of insurgents only made it more likely that such savagery would be visited upon the ethnic Serb populations of those regions. Nor, save a few exceptions, were the NDH forces themselves equal to the task of combating or suppressing Partisan groups.

Nor could the Germans rely upon their Italian allies to check the groundswell of insurgent support. The Italians persistently failed to prosecute the counterinsurgency campaign with the necessary rigor, and the Germans, too sensitive to Italy's great power pretensions in the region, failed to cajole them into doing so. Thus on different occasions the Italians conducted anti-Partisan operations with the utmost ineptitude, dragged their feet over committing to such operations in the first place, or failed to commit to them at all. Instead, they relied excessively upon the Chetniks to provide "security."[3] But in empowering that particular group, they ultimately made it even harder for the Axis to exercise control on the ground.

Co-opting the Chetniks might have yielded tangible long-term benefits had it been done in the right way. A fundamental political settlement that decisively curtailed the reach of the NDH's power and raised the status of the Serbian rump state might have provided a way forward. Such an arrangement might have strengthened the Nedić regime, and thus drawn more non-Communist Serbs to that surer base of Axis support, instead of to the Mihailović movement. But such a scenario was never a serious prospect: Hitler's support for the Pavelić regime, which abated too little and too late, and his thoroughly unabated Serbophobia both saw to that. So too did the failure of German diplomatic and military figures to argue with the Führer more assertively over such matters.[4] In the absence of fundamental political reorganization, the Chetniks aggravated the chaos on the ground. At the same time, they disappointed as an effective bulwark against the Partisans. The Partisans' readiness to take on the occupiers, their improving fighting power, and their ability to appeal to all ethnic groups, all enabled them to achieve increasingly formidable levels of support and strength at the expense of the prevaricating, disorganized, and chauvinistic Chetniks.

Had the Germans appreciated the true extent of the Partisan threat sooner, and committed more fully against it, they might yet have largely destroyed the movement by early 1943. Even then, however, the NDH's weakness and the Ustasha's resurgent depravity might well have spawned a Partisan revival anyway. In the event, however, the Germans failed to appreciate the threat sooner. In particular, disputes with their Italian allies in early 1942 stopped them from acting against the Partisan movement more decisively. This, together with the Italians' withdrawal from Zone III in summer 1942, gave the movement vital time in which to recover following the Serbian debacle of 1941.[5]

Yet even when the Partisans were the principal target, the Germans could not entirely pin the blame for failure upon their Croatian and Italian allies. Nor could they pin it upon the elusiveness of their enemy. Granted, the Partisans used classic irregular tactics whenever they could. However, particularly in autumn 1941's Operation Užice and again from 1943 onward, the Partisans also fought more as a conventional opponent would, and it was as a conventional opponent that the Germans so often failed to defeat them decisively.[6]

Too many German commanders, weaned on the long-standing practices of the military establishment to which they belonged, were excessively enamored of brutal reprisals and big encirclements. Here, they ignored the facts. Firstly, massive reprisals became increasingly unworkable as the counterinsurgency campaign in Yugoslavia unfolded. In

Serbia in 1941, they faced running out of victims. In the purportedly "allied" state of the NDH, they were politically impossible. Secondly, although a big encirclement had worked in Operation Užice, the Germans forgot that that operation had also succeeded because of particular environmental and political circumstances. Such encirclements repeatedly failed, even if they occasionally came close to success, amid the much more rugged terrain of Bosnia. Yet between January 1942's Operation Southeast Croatia and January 1943's Operation White I, German commanders drew none of the right lessons regarding either the harshness of the terrain, or what they might reasonably have expected of their so often substandard troops in the face of it.[7]

Conversely, many German commanders relied too little upon mobile, well-equipped hunter groups deployed in operations conducted on the insurgents' own terms.[8] Even when the Germans did employ them effectively, hunter groups were a local-level solution that could not have defeated the insurgency on their own. Had the Germans committed more troops on the ground generally, established a proper, permanent presence among the population, and shown a more imaginative political approach, hunter groups employed on a larger scale might yet have proved an effective element of a potentially winning, four-way combination. There is no way of knowing for sure, however, because the Germans did far too little to give such a combination of measures a decent prospect of success.[9] Such were the minimal troop numbers the high command was prepared to commit to Yugoslavia that few of the already small number of units operating in the NDH possessed the mobility, equipment, or resilience necessary for successful hunter group–type operations.[10] That same lack of manpower prevented the Germans from providing a stable long-term troop presence, partly to reassure and partly to coerce, among the civilian population. German army units similarly failed to impose such a permanent, predictable presence in the anti-partisan campaign in the Soviet Union.[11] Finally, most higher- and middle-level commanders alike failed to fully realize that force and terror needed balancing with, or even downgrading in favor of, an effective political approach. Had they realized it sooner, the senior-most among them might yet have sought more forcefully to check not only the destructive free rein granted the Pavelić regime, but also the increasingly rapacious Axis exploitation of the NDH economy.

Together, all these factors prevented the Germans from destroying the Partisan movement before early 1943. By then, even though the Germans were now committing greater air and land forces to the task, the Partisans had grown too strong, militarily and organizationally, for them to be defeated conclusively by those forces.

The Germans, reinforced on the ground and in the air, were still able to land blows on the Partisans in the months following the White operations. The fact that the Partisans increasingly resembled a regular army in form, size, and organization certainly reflected their growing strength. But it also made them a more visible target, particularly for air attack. In May 1943's Operation Black, a revised version of the postponed Operation White III, the Germans even came close to destroying Tito's main Partisan force. Yet even if they had succeeded, so beneficial was the NDH's chaotic state to the Partisan cause, and so incomplete the Germans' ability to station sufficient troops on the ground permanently, that the Partisans might well have been able to reconstitute themselves anyway. In any case, close as they came, the Germans did not succeed.[12] This was partly because, even by this stage, they failed to accord destroying the Partisan movement the proper importance, and sought instead to defeat decisively both Partisans and Mihailović Chetniks during the operation.[13]

Operation Black also saw German brutality towards civilians reach new heights of ferocity.[14] In addition, General Löhr successfully demanded that the region in which the White operations had taken place be taken out of the NDH and designated a German operational area. This enabled Himmler to build up the German police presence within the region, and call upon ethnic German manpower to fill the ranks of the Police and Waffen-SS. Himmler increased his power further in June 1943, when the entire NDH was declared a "bandit area."[15]

The Axis in general remained riven by dissension. The Croatian army continued to hemorrhage its personnel and weapons—both of which went over to the Partisans in increasingly large quantities—and the NDH its support. Within German–Italian relations, trust had broken down entirely; the Germans even concealed their plans for Operation Black from the Italians.[16] But Italy's capitulation to the Allies in summer 1943, far from unifying the Germans and the NDH, merely removed a buffer between them and set them at loggerheads even more.

The Germans exploited the NDH's economic resources ever more rapaciously. They antagonized the Pavelić regime by bypassing it in the decision-making process, recruiting Croats into the Wehrmacht and Waffen-SS en masse and, at the end of 1943, embarking on full-scale collaboration with the Mihailović Chetniks. Given the Chetniks' manifest indiscipline, incompetence, and military bankruptcy, this new alliance exemplified the increasing desperation of German efforts against the Partisans. The Pavelić regime also feared that German sponsorship of the NDH Muslims, which peaked when Himmler handed over Muslim-dominated northeast Croatia for the Muslim troops of the Waffen-SS Handschar Division to occupy, would prompt them to secede from the state. Relations hit a new low when the Prinz Eugen Division massacred two thousand Croats in early 1944.[17]

The Ustasha, meanwhile, entirely lost what remained of its grip, particularly after the loss of eastern Bosnia to the Partisans in October 1943. It violently reescalated its anti-Serb policy, yet also secretly negotiated with both the Partisans and the Allies. Yet when the Germans learned of the negotiations, it led merely to a reshuffle of the NDH leadership rather than the abolition of the regime itself. Hitler, disillusioned with the NDH at last, wanted it absorbed into the Reich or turned into a protectorate. But the increasingly precarious situation at the front precluded such radical surgery.[18]

It was also in 1943 that the western Allies, frustrated at Mihailović's inaction and his real or de facto collaboration with the Axis, formally switched their support to the Partisans.[19] Following Italy's fall, this support comprised not just material aid but also Allied airpower operating from southern Italian airfields. The Partisans were also well placed to seize vast quantities of abandoned Italian military equipment and hitherto Italian-controlled territory.[20] Thus were they able to expand and consolidate their territory, repel the Germans' ever more desperate offensives, and eventually take the offensive themselves. In early summer 1944, following earlier aborted attempts, they recommenced their advance into Serbia, linking up with the Red Army now advancing on the Balkans following the destruction of Germany's front in the East. This was yet another blow in a sequence that would eventually culminate in the loss of all Yugoslavia to Tito's Partisans and the Red Army.[21]

German army commanders' excessive reliance upon bludgeoning terror and force, then, was a major reason why the Axis campaign against the Partisans failed. It was not the most decisive reason; such were the overarching weaknesses of the Axis occupation edifice in Yugoslavia that, ultimately, no amount of restraint, moderation, or constructive engagement by individual units would have brought more than a temporary reprieve. Yet German army commanders' terroristic proclivities are still centrally important to this study's primary concern. For this study's primary concern has been not with outcomes, but with motives: why some German army units employed more constructive counterinsurgency measures, others employed them less extensively or eschewed them entirely, and others still employed terror and brutality on a scale surpassing even higher command's ruthless directives. It is to *that* central question that this conclusion now turns.

The social and institutional environment of the officer corps of the Imperial German Army, and of the Royal-Imperial Army of the Austro-Hungarian Empire, already provided a bedrock of harshness before and during the Great War. In some respects, particularly before 1914, this environment was relatively benign. In other respects, it emphatically was not. These respects were reinforced by the changing nature of warfare, politics, and society in Germany and Austria during the decades leading up to the Great War.

In the case of both officer corps, officer cadets were joining institutions that were deeply conservative and sought to instill a corresponding mentality among their personnel. But at the same time, both officer corps needed to reach some sort of accommodation with the forces of social and political change. Had they not done so, they would have failed to attract that larger, more socially diverse intake of officers that was essential to their viability. Yet by embarking on this course, they were absorbing larger numbers of men from milieus increasingly susceptible to new and radical social and political influences.

Foremost among these were Social Darwinism and its anti-Slavic and anti-Semitic corollaries—sentiments that were already making their presence felt in both officer corps. The suppression of colonial revolts by the German military saw Social Darwinism combine with terroristic counter-insurgency doctrine to terrible effect. Add to all this the fact that both officer corps, presaging the rise of the "specialist in mass destruction" during the interwar years, were increasingly preoccupied with the organizational and technological dimensions of the new industrialized warfare. A picture thus emerges of institutions whose personnel were increasingly susceptible to radical ideology, intellectually unsuited to countering its malign influence, and increasingly preoccupied with the devastating opportunities afforded by ominous trends in modern warfare.

But it would be wrong to exaggerate the strength of these phenomena during the years before the Great War. Some were not unique to Germany and Austria. Within the Habsburg officer corps in particular, officers were subjected to other influences that fostered open-mindedness instead of diminishing it. And the same institutional conservatism that, in many respects, eroded officers' ability to withstand the strengthening currents of destructive ideology, in other respects protected them against it. The stress both officer corps placed on good character, their aversion to notions of unquestioning, zombified obedience, and the ongoing prevalence of traditional Christian values were all more beneficial elements of such conservatism.

It was the Great War and its chaotic two-year aftermath that made the violent radicalization of both officer corps, and their eventual amalgamation with National Socialism, much more likely. It was not just the annihilative ferocity of so much of the fighting that played a part in this process. So too did the squalor and hardship of conditions in the field, and the manner in which the merciless, all-encompassing "total" nature of the Great War impressed itself upon officers and men.

And there were important respects in which the Great War was a battle not just against the enemy's armies, but against his culture also. This element was particularly strengthened when officers and men came into direct contact with ethnic groups who had long attracted disdain or animosity in military and societal circles in Germany and Austria—eastern Jews, eastern Slavs, and Serbs. As the war continued, moreover, many officers increasingly associated the first two of these groups with the emerging specter of Bolshevism. The odium with which officers regarded Bolshevism was fueled by what they perceived as Bolshevism's danger to social and moral order and, more directly, to the discipline and fighting power of their own troops. Meanwhile counterinsurgency warfare often, albeit not always, saw German and Austro-Hungarian troops perpetrate acts of utilitarian and ideologically colored brutality.

The obduracy all these influences collectively strengthened was further buttressed by the trauma of defeat, by the urge to blame it on perceived enemies internal and external, by the violent aftershock that followed defeat, and by the resolution to wage future wars in a more single-mindedly ruthless as well as technically superior manner.

Yet even then, neither the German nor the Austrian officer corps was firmly set on an irreversible path towards criminal complicity in the Nazi regime. Granted, the Reichswehr officer corps of the 1920s and early 1930s was an exclusive, elitist institution, contemptuous of democracy and set on restoring its prominence within a militarily resurgent Germany. Granted also, the Bundesheer was instrumental in crushing the Austrian political left and sustaining the Austrofascist dictatorship that abolished democracy during the early 1930s. But none of this, in itself, was synonymous with embracing Nazism. That particular endpoint was the result of a series of further developments—military, political, and diplomatic—that were in train throughout the 1930s.

Still further developments during the two years following the outbreak of war in 1939 cemented the process by which the two officer corps, now merged into the single officer corps of the German army, eventually became enmeshed in a war of conquest and annihilation in National Socialism's name. The moral degeneration that gathered pace after the fall of Poland; the hubris following the fall of France; and the ideologically, militarily, and economically determined readiness to wage a war of unparalleled ferocity against the Soviet Union all contributed to sealing the pact. And the invocation of much older enmities, enmities originating from before 1914 but radicalized during the Great War's course and aftermath, further ensured such a brutal endpoint. The ruthless, ideologically suffused mind-set that now characterized so much of the senior officer corps ensured that the army's counterinsurgency doctrine in Eastern and south-eastern Europe would be shaped less by relatively measured precedents such as the Germans' 1918 counterinsurgency in the Ukraine, than by precedents that were much more ruthless.

It is clear, then, that the Wehrmacht's higher command levels extolled a brand of counterinsurgency in Eastern and south-eastern Europe that was based primarily upon the pitiless exercise of terror. But it did not automatically follow that all commanders in the field would blindly adhere to it. After all the Wehrmacht, like other Reich agencies, often issued directives that were more guidelines for ruthless action, and thus open to some interpretation, rather than specific orders. Even where directives were more specific, commanders often had some freedom of action over how radically they implemented them. Some commanders followed the spirit of such directives closely. Others took ruthlessness to extremes. Others still tempered their ruthlessness with some restraint. How German army commanders and units behaved in the field also depended greatly upon the conditions in the field which they experienced. It was these that, along lines elucidated by the historian Jürgen Förster,[22] could create a bridge between the ideological beliefs that shaped the officers' mind-set, and how they then went on to conduct themselves.

In Serbia, such were the fairly sedate conditions occupation units faced during spring and early summer 1941 that they at first exercised considerable restraint. But there was no contradiction between this apparently benign picture and the ruthless mind-set that had taken root in the officer corps. For theirs was a selective restraint, one from which only the majority Serbian population could hope to benefit. There is almost no evidence of officers or units refusing to participate in the intensifying persecution of the country's Jews during this period. Moreover, even at this early stage, the moderation that occupation divisions exercised towards the Serbs—a moderation to which "demonstrative" harshness towards, Jews, Communists, and Sinti and Roma was an essential accompaniment—had its own limits. Yet moderation there was.

But once the Serbian national uprising was under way, restraint withered and terror intensified—not only against Serbia's Jews, but against the wider Serbian population also. Given that the escalating severity of

German reprisal policy eventually helped to discourage Mihailović from involving his Chetnik forces in the uprising any further, it can be seen that the policy in one sense possessed a terrible pragmatic logic—even though a policy reliant upon terror, and not upon more insightful solutions, could not hope to triumph in the long term. But the severity of the measures was not just due to the fact that commanders possessed a remarkably obdurate sense of "pragmatism." It was also because of their institutionally conditioned abhorrence of irregular warfare. More immediately, it was because of the mounting frustration and desperation felt by formations like the 704th Infantry Division and their substandard units, facing a security situation that daily grew more alarming. Such conduct was also apparent among German army anti-Partisan units in the Soviet Union.[23]

Further, though the need to "obey orders" should not be ignored, it should also be remembered that German army commanders, like Third Reich operatives more generally, often enjoyed considerable freedom of action when interpreting higher-level directives. Even where directives were more stringent, it was possible for individual commanders to speak out against them, or against the premise behind them. Despite this, not one of the divisional commanders examined in this study chose, as the national uprising escalated, to proceed with moderation. Instead, they chose to implement them with all their inherent harshness. One, for reasons of his own, behaved even more harshly. The Wehrmacht campaign against the Serbian national uprising showcases the explosion of violence that took place when decades of intensifying institutional harshness combined with the pressures and dangers of the campaign on the ground.

From the beginning of 1942, when the main center of the Yugoslav Partisan war shifted to the NDH, through to early 1943, German army counterinsurgency commanders found themselves in markedly different circumstances. During this period, in contrast to 1941, the Wehrmacht was not facing a desperate defensive situation. It spent much of the period on the offensive, even though the offensive action it took varied in scale and intensity. Their circumstances being less immediately alarming than those they had faced in Serbia the previous year, the Germans deescalated their reprisal policy somewhat. The unworkability of a policy that relied on an infinite supply of reprisal victims drawn from a finite population, not to mention the "allied" status of the NDH, made it foolhardy to pursue such a policy there.

Even so, German formations remained overstretched, underresourced, and pitted against an increasingly resourceful opponent amid extremely arduous terrain. The Germans therefore still faced onerous difficulties in their struggle to defeat the Partisans. This struggle was made no easier by the fact that their Italian and Croatian allies were unequal to the task. The Germans' solution again reflected not just reality on the ground but also the brutal, ideologically colored proclivities of their favored counterinsurgency doctrine. The "solution" was to accord maximum violence just as prominent a place in the NDH as it had been accorded in Serbia. The difference was that maximum violence assumed another form here. The largest offensives, such as Kozara and White I, spawned mass destruction and vast body counts that, though they purportedly comprised insurgents slain in combat, clearly included large numbers of civilians.

Yet the 718th Infantry Division's example shows that there were commanders who, unless their unit's position became so execrable as to close off all means of success, saw opportunities to do things differently. As well as relying more on small mobile units, they sought to erode Partisan strength by making potential deserters feel safe in crossing the line, and by cultivating a population that could provide vital information, manpower, and other practical support against the Partisans.

Thus, the situation facing the Germans in the NDH during 1942 was onerous, but not yet a life-or-death struggle. This fact helped foster cooler, more measured judgments by some—even if they were uneven, temporary, and often highly relative. German army anti-Partisan divisions serving in the Soviet Union during World War II could behave similarly. The 221st Security Division and Army Rear Area 532 are well-documented examples of units that were sane enough to realize that there were more sensible ways of trying to compensate for their own failings than just untrammeled terror.[24] One thing these units had in common with the 718th Infantry Division was their circumstances. All three units experienced periods in which their struggle against insurgents was not so urgent and intense as to prevent them from employing measures that, though more restrained and smaller in scale than massive encirclement operations, needed more time in which to bear fruit.

Yet, while small-unit tactics and constructive engagement could certainly bring dividends, two conditions were essential for them to work to their full effect. The first was sufficient troops of sufficient quality on the ground, and for sufficient duration. The second was a wider occupation policy properly geared towards the population's basic needs of personal security and economic stability. Axis occupation policy in the NDH met neither condition. The Pavelić regime itself *certainly* met neither condition. The eventual result was an inexorable swelling of Partisan support.

And by the time the Partisans' strength and influence had reached a certain level, neither destructive, maximum-force mobile operations nor more imaginative approaches could defeat them conclusively. In these circumstances, such were many commanders' terroristic proclivities that they opted for maximum destructive force as a panacea. Others, such as the 718th Infantry Division's General Fortner, may simply have opted for harsher action out of sheer frustration. Officers' anxiety at the growing Partisan threat, and the pressure from higher command for quick and spectacular results, could only drive them even more surely down such a path.

A similar example from the Soviet Union is that of the 201st Security Division. This formation carried out massive, bloody antipartisan operations in the Polotsk Lowland, in the northwestern portion of the Army Group Center Rear Area, during 1942 and 1943. The partisans it faced in this region were especially numerous and active. Moreover, the transport network that crisscrossed it, a network now under serious partisan threat, was of special importance to the German war effort in the East. Not only did the 201st face a singularly formidable foe on the ground, then; it also had to reckon with intense pressure from above for quick, tangible results.[25]

Moreover, even when German army units on the ground did aspire to cultivate the NDH's population, such was the situation they faced that cultivation was immensely difficult to implement. For the tortuous complexities of the ethnic situation rendered a straightforward wooing of the population increasingly impossible. Army commanders needed to consider not just whether to engage with the population, but also which particular population groups to engage with in preference to others, and how far. And there were periods even in 1942 in which the Wehrmacht already found itself facing powerful Partisan attacks. When Wehrmacht forces sought to counter a Partisan offensive, as happened with the 718th

Infantry Division at Jajce in late 1942, even units that had hitherto shown restraint began to display brutalized desperation instead. Brutality, then, remained a central component of counterinsurgency for all the German army divisions in the NDH. It seems that even units that were more inclined to cultivate felt compelled to terrorize instead if they felt driven to it by circumstances.

The 221st Security Division provides a similar example from the occupied Soviet Union. This division too sought to moderate its conduct and engage the population during the years 1942 and 1943. But its conduct during these years was also punctuated by periods in which, whether due to pressures on the ground or pressure from above for results, it ratcheted up its ruthlessness markedly.[26]

How long a division had actually been engaged in such warfare could also color its behavior. The longer ordinary soldiers spent in the field, the harder and more savage their conduct could become. The 718th Infantry Division at Jajce demonstrated this. But at command level, a lengthy tenure on the ground could, over time, lead a unit to exercise more restraint. Thus in early 1943, for instance, the newly arrived 369th Infantry Division meted out a great deal more brutality—at divisional command's behest—than the 717th and 718th Infantry Divisions. The commands of these latter units, by contrast, had had longer to adjust to the intricacies of Balkan politics and thus begin comporting themselves with more insight. The 221st Security Division again provides a similar example from the Soviet Union. Here too was a unit that, in general, behaved more moderately over time, partly because it increasingly saw the need to engage with the population it was occupying.[27] That said, passing time and mounting pressure could actually make rank-and-file troops less likely to follow their commanders' moderate lead.

Conditions on the ground, then, did indeed provide a bridge that transformed Wehrmacht doctrine into brutal behavior. But just as conditions could brutalize the behavior of German army commanders and their units, they could also moderate it.

Ultimately, however, German army counterinsurgency commanders were not just members of a particular institution. They were also individuals.

How far they followed the directives they had been issued could depend, therefore, not just upon the situation they faced, but also upon how they as individuals perceived it. Their perceptions could be colored, in turn, by influences and experiences they had undergone over the course of their lives. It is likely that this is why there were German army commanders in Yugoslavia whose behavior was markedly harsher and more brutal than that of others, even if they faced similar conditions or had been in the field for similar periods.

In autumn 1941, during the Wehrmacht's savage suppression of the Serbian national uprising, the suppression dealt out by the 342d Infantry Division was not only the most savage of all, but also exceeded even General Boehme's bloody dictates. The man primarily responsible was the division's commander, General Hinghofer. But the 342d did not hold a monopoly on extraordinary ruthlessness. In the NDH in 1943, it was Neidholt and Zellner, commanders of the 369th and 373d Infantry Divisions respectively, who exercised particular severity. Meanwhile, General Eglseer, commander of the 714th Infantry Division, stood apart from other divisional commanders also, if not for his actual brutality then certainly for the zeal with which he sought to harden and discipline his men.

These officers stand apart from other divisional commanders whose conduct this study has considered—General Borowski of the 704th Infantry Division; from the 714th General Stahl; from the 717th General Hoffmann (latterly of the 342d) and General Dippold; and from the 718th General Fortner.

This second group of officers was not particularly "enlightened," whether by today's standards or by those of seventy years ago. Some, such as General Fortner, were indeed capable of considerable moderation. But officers in this group were clearly capable of deeds that were anything but moderate. The 704th, 714th, and 717th Infantry Divisions in particular were unfailing in their obedience to General Boehme's orders for the ferocious suppression of the Serbian national uprising in 1941. Yet what distinguished the ruthlessness of these officers was that, although it was in line with the directives of higher command, it did not actually exceed them. Theirs was a "mainstream" ruthlessness, brutal as it was, rather than ruthlessness of a more exceptional kind.

By contrast, the ruthlessness of radical commanders like Hinghofer, Zellner, and Neidholt did indeed exceed those directives. Not the institutional harshness that permeated the officer corps, nor orders from above, nor conditions on the ground, then, can fully explain why these particular officers comported themselves thus.

Radical officers such as these also served in divisions fighting in the antipartisan campaign in the Soviet Union. One case, again, is that of the 221st Security Division, one of three such divisions that served in the Army Group Center Rear Area during 1941. In late 1942, the 221st was learning the virtues of greater restraint. But that was not only for the future, but also for a later, more enlightened divisional commander, Brigadier General Hubert Lendle. In 1941, the 221st was commanded by Major General Johann Pflugbeil. An incident from the early days of the invasion of the Soviet Union provides a telling insight into the particular strength of anti-Semitism that seems to have animated Pflugbeil's command. In late June 1941, the 221st's divisional command turned a blind eye when the Order Police battalion in its jurisdiction massacred the Jewish population of the town of Bialystok. Two grisly distinctions marked this atrocity out. Firstly, it preceded by several weeks the first mass shootings of Soviet Jews by the SS Einsatzgruppen, a key phase in the unfolding of the Final Solution that year. Secondly, though equally horrendous as those later killings in a moral sense, it lacked their cold and clinical precision; instead, it was atavistic and savage.[28]

The 221st's reaction to this massacre contrasts markedly with the attitude of German army units towards the Einsatzgruppe shootings. Army units allowed Einsatzgruppe shootings to take place in their jurisdictions. Yet they were anxious to distance the army from the killings, and counter any danger to their troops' discipline by forbidding them to witness or participate in the killings. But the 221st's divisional command, headed by Pflugbeil himself and operations officer Major Karl Haupt, appears to have been completely unperturbed by the unbridled, sadistic massacre which they and their troops witnessed. That these officers were apparently so unruffled says much about the likely strength of their own anti-Semitism.[29]

A second case is the 203d Security Division. During summer and early autumn 1942, under its commander Brigadier General Gottfried Barton, the 203d operated in the southwestern portion of the Army Group Center

Rear Area. It faced very similar fighting conditions to those of the 221st Security Division, now commanded by the more restrained General Lendle, directly to the 203d's southeast. But the directives the 203d issued for the treatment of the population were more severe than the 221st's at this time. Moreover, severity seem to have permeated the division further down. Its troops killed far more Partisans in excess of their own losses—largely unarmed civilians, in other words—than did the troops of the 221st.[30]

Such examples indicate that the radical officers who made their presence felt in Yugoslavia belonged to a wider group. It now remains to consider the influences and experiences that made that decisive difference in brutalizing their mind-set beyond even the German army's norms.

The first question to consider is where an officer was born. In Yugoslavia, it was officers born in the old Austro-Hungarian Empire whom the forces of historical enmity were most likely to drive towards particularly harsh conduct. Secondly, just as an officer's geographical background might shape him, so might his social background. Officers hailing from the "new" middle-class circles to which both the German and Austro-Hungarian officer corps were opening up before the Great War were more likely to be susceptible to the prejudices upon which National Socialist ideology would eventually build. Such prejudices could affect their prosecution of counterinsurgency also. One of the most pivotal phases in the process that shaped officers' worldview was the Great War. During its course, officers underwent experiences which could be both varied and brutalizing.

And there is one final respect in which an officer's experiences earlier in life may have hardened him particularly. Counterinsurgency warfare, it should be remembered, was widely seen as a particularly thankless and unglamorous form of soldiering. A German army officer would likely have felt additionally frustrated by the fact that it emphatically was not the kind of warfare that would have enabled him to demonstrate the technocratic, operational prowess for which the German military was renowned. His resentment at having instead been "dumped in a backwater" would probably have been considerable.[31] Those officers who, at some time, had served in technocratic or elite branches of the army may well have found the experience particularly galling, frustrating, and in turn brutalizing.[32]

The radical officers featured in this particular study, it appears, were not radicalized beyond the norm by their social class. On this score there are no startling contrasts with their less extreme colleagues. There is certainly every reason to suppose that officers' middle-class origins helped them to imbibe harsh ideological and military attitudes. Yet there is nothing to suggest that those origins were what took radical officers that decisive *further* step towards *extreme* ruthlessness.[33] Similarly, most of the officers featured in this study, however ruthlessly they conducted themselves, served at some time or other in technical or elite branches of the particular army to which they belonged.

More decisive, perhaps, were the experiences officers underwent during the Great War. Every European battlefront of the Great War influenced officers in ways that could mark them well into their lives. The lengthier an officer's service in a particular theater, the more deeply it might mark him. But what seems yet more apparent among the individuals in this study is that, of all such theaters, it was the East that could subject officers to a particularly potent combination of brutalizing experiences. The reasons why this may have been so are numerous. In the East, men underwent not only savage fighting—against frontline troops or insurgents—and miserable environmental hardship. They also had firsthand experience of groups who, under the Third Reich, would be singled out for special contempt or hatred—Jews, Bolsheviks, and eastern Slavs. For these reasons, Eastern Europe during the Great War and its immediate aftermath was arguably an especially potent incubator of the ideological harshness National Socialism would come to exploit in its military servants a quarter of a century later.[34] One might expect, then, that officers who served in the East during the Great War would behave particularly ferociously, in certain circumstances, during World War II.

Among such circumstances were those that were encountered by officers who found themselves waging a brutal, protracted, and often fruitless counterinsurgency campaign, amid hostile terrain and a population of dubious loyalties, with largely substandard units at their own disposal, against a resourceful, effective, and sometimes savagely ruthless opponent. Officers ferocity was likely to be heightened if that opponent was both Slavic—even if southern Slavs per se stood higher on the Nazi racial-ideological scale than their eastern brethren—and Communist. All these conditions applied to the Wehrmacht's campaign in Yugoslavia during World War II.

It follows from this, then, that officers' experience of the East during the Great War was likely to increase the brutality with which they responded to such conditions during World War II—even if they were serving in the southeast during World War II, rather than in the East proper.

Thus, the exceptionally ruthless General Hinghofer spent a particularly lengthy, uninterrupted stretch of the Great War on the eastern front; in this, he contrasted with his fellow divisional commanders in the Serbia of 1941. In the NDH, more radical divisional commanders such as Neidholt, Zellner, and Eglseer all spent significant amounts of time in the East during the Great War. The less radical commanders operating alongside them—Fortner and Dippold—spent none. In the Soviet Union, similarly, General Lendle of the 221st Security Division—a relatively enlightened divisional commander who spent no time on the eastern front during the Great War—was outdone for ruthlessness by his predecessor in 1941, General Pflugbeil, and by his neighbor in 1942, General Barton. Both commanders, again, spent considerable time on the eastern front between 1914 and 1918.[35]

It would be wrong, particularly given the small number of officers considered here, to judge such matters sweepingly. Soldiers of the Central powers were not always repelled and brutalized by their encounter with the eastern front and its peoples. Even if they were, this did not mean that officers who experienced the eastern front during the Great War would inevitably conduct themselves particularly ferociously in the conflagration of a quarter of a century later.[36] By the same token, the brutalizing effect of lengthy service in the trenches of the western front, or in another theater, should not be underestimated either. But the pattern that emerges among the radical officers whom *this* study has examined suggests that this group was particularly brutalized by its experience of the eastern front. And the case of General Hinghofer suggests that such experience could be even more brutalizing if it was of particularly lengthy duration and exposed an officer to insurgency.

Yet, though one must again be cautious with a sample of this size, the evidence appears most striking when considering the significance of where these officers were born. It was Austria-Hungary, not Germany, that experienced years of firsthand confrontation with Serbia in the run-up to the Great War. It was this confrontation that, in 1914, led directly to war between Austria-Hungary and Serbia, and infused that conflict with particular animosity. Habsburg troops' experience of Serbian irregulars during 1914, the humiliating defeats in the field at the hands of the Serbian army, and the collective memory of the death march to which Austro-Hungarian prisoners were subjected during the winter of 1915–1916 all served to exacerbate such bitterness. So too did the fact that the exiled Serbian army remained a rallying point, for the rest of the war, for disaffected southern Slavic soldiers of the Austro-Hungarian army— with all the peril to the Habsburg Empire's stability that this posed. So too, finally, did the Serbian army's central role in the autumn 1918 Balkan campaign that led directly to Austria-Hungary's collapse.

Austrian-born officers, then, were likelier than their German colleagues to be animated by Serbophobia. Granted, the Great War did not make it inevitable that this hate-filled instinct would one day find expression in such abominations as General Boehme's 1941 reprisal campaign. After all, the occupation regime to which the Austro-Hungarians subjected Serbia between 1916 and 1918, harsh and exploitative as it was, was more lenient than it might have been. Yet it was not this legacy that Boehme invoked in autumn 1941, but the more poisonous one that preceded it. The majority of those Austrian-born officers receptive to Boehme's pitiless exhortations had not actually fought in Serbia during the Great War. But this, apparently, mattered little; the toxic dissonance of embittered collective memory could color their behavior anyway.

It is also distinctly possible, though the link is less clear, that the Austrians' contempt for what they perceived as brutish Serbian savagery was part of a more general aversion to the "primitive" southern Slavs of the Balkans. This was perhaps a distant echo of General Conrad's contemptuous sentiments towards the Bosnian irregulars he encountered between 1878 and 1882. This may well help explain why Austrian-born officers, irrespective of the conditions their units faced or the duration of their prior experience of the Yugoslav campaign, could also comport themselves with particular harshness in the NDH—perhaps especially against its ethnic Serb inhabitants—as well as in Serbia.

The German army officers in this study belonged to an institution that favored a terroristic doctrine of counterinsurgency warfare. During World War II, German army units in Eastern and south-eastern Europe, and their commanders, applied this doctrine extensively in response to the resistance they faced. In time, some commanders acknowledged the folly of pursuing it at the expense of a more measured, insightful approach that appreciated the importance of winning hearts and minds. But this dawning realization was never enough to overturn the basic principles of Wehrmacht counterinsurgency warfare decisively—not least because too many commanders continued subscribing to those principles themselves.

But field commanders did not just behave according to the collective mind-set of their institution. Among other things, such was the nature of the directives emanating down to them that they often enjoyed considerable freedom of action. The ruthless thrust of many of these directives was unmistakable. But officers often chose to implement them with varying amounts of severity. The conditions in the field they and their units experienced could profoundly affect their conduct.

So too could the experiences officers had undergone earlier in their lives. The years between 1914 and 1945 may not have been a second Thirty Years' War in every respect. But officers who were subjected to the destructiveness of its earlier years could be enduringly affected by the experience. It seems that the legacy of those years was still marking officers' behavior, in sometimes immensely brutal ways, more than a quarter of a century later. Investigating this phenomenon, through both this study and others, is important for a fuller understanding of what motivated the agents of the Third Reich.

Appendixes

Abbreviations

Notes

Acknowledgments

Index

Source References
for Featured Officers

The full set of officer sample data that was obtained from the sources that follow is accessible via http://www.gcu.ac.uk/gsbs/staff/drbenshepherd/.

YUGOSLAVIA-BASED DIVISIONAL COMMANDERS

Heinrich Borowski: Militärishe Sammlungen, entry for Heinrich Borowski; United States War Department, *Histories of Two Hundred and Fifty-One Divisions of the German Army Which Participated in the War (1914–1918)* (Washington, DC: Government Printing Office, 1920), 33–35, 654–656.

Benignus Dippold: RH7, Heeresgeneralkartei. File on Benignus Dippold; PERS 6, file on Benignus Dippold. United States War Department, *Histories of Two Hundred and Fifty-One Divisions of the German Army Which Participated in the War (1914–1918)*, 101–103; Hans Jäger, *Das K. B. 19. Infanterie-Regiment König Viktor Emmanuel III. von Italien* (Munich; Schick, 1930), *passim.*

Karl Eglseer: RH7, Heeresgeneralkartei. File on Karl Eglseer; KA Vienna, Offiziers-Belohnungsanträge. Karton 328, Nr. 249.501. Karl Eglseer; KA Vienna. Nachlaß, Karl Eglseer. Lebenslauf; Edmund Glaise von Horstenau et al., *Österreich-Ungarns letzter Krieg,* vols. 1–7 (Vienna: Verlag der Militärwissenschaftlichen Mitteilungen, 1930–1938), order-of-battle entry for 87th Infantry Regiment, Vol. I, pp. 62–91; index entries for 87th Infantry Regiment and commanding formations, Vols. I and VII.

Johann Fortner: BA-MA, MSg 9. File on Johann Fortner; United States War Department, *Histories of Two Hundred and Fifty-One Divisions of the German Army Which Participated in the War (1914–1918)*, 101–103; *Das K.B. 5. Infanterie-Regiment Großherzog Ernst Ludwig von Hessen* (Munich: Schick, 1929; no author details).

Walter Hinghofer: RH7, Heeresgeneralkartei. File on Walter Hinghofer; Glaise von Horstenau et al., *Österreich-Ungarns letzter Krieg*, order-of-battle entries for 11th Field Artillery Regiment: Vol. I, pp. 62–91, Vol. II, Beilage 14; order-of-battle entries for 11th Field Artillery Brigade: Vol. III, Beilage 2, Vol. IV, Beilage 2, Vol. V, Beilage 7, Vol. VII, Beilage 3; index entries for 11th Field Artillery Regiment and commanding formations, Vols. I and II; for 11th Field Artillery Brigade and commanding formations, Vols. III–VII. The brigade's whereabouts during 1917 were traced via the documents contained in the KA Vienna, NFA, Karton 3703. Feld-Artillerie Brigade 11. Brigadebefehle, 1916–1918.

Paul Hoffmann: RH7, Heeresgeneralkartei. File on Paul Hoffmann; PERS 6, file on Paul Hoffmann. Personal-Nachweis; Hans Schöning, *Leib-Grenadier-Regiment König Friedrich Wilhelm III. (1. Brandenburgisches) Nr. 8 im Weltkrieg* (Oldenburg: Stalling, 1924), pp. 13–14, *passim*.

Fritz Neidholt: RH7 Heeresgeneralkartei. File on Fritz Neidholt; PERS 6, file on Fritz Neidholt. Personal-Nachweis; United States War Department, *Histories of Two Hundred and Fifty-One Divisions of the German Army Which Participated in the War (1914–1918)*, 59–61, 592–594.

Friedrich Stahl: RH7, Heeresgeneralkartei. File on Friedrich Stahl; PERS 6, file on Friedrich Stahl. Personal-Nachweis. Dienstlaufbahn.

Emil Zellner: RH7, Heeresgeneralkartei. File on Emil Zellner; AdR Vienna, Bundesheer-Akten. Personnel file on Emil Zellner. Volkswehr Bataillon Bruck a./d. Leitha. Vormerkblatt für die Qualifikationsbeschreibung; Glaise von Horstenau et al., *Österreich-Ungarns letzter Krieg*, order-of-battle entries for 11th Field Gun Regiment: Vol. I, pp. 62–91, Vol. II, Beilage 14; index entries for 11th Field Gun Regiment and 16th Field Artillery Regiment, and commanding formations: Vols. I–VII.

Nikolaus Boicetta: PERS 6, file on Nikolaus Boicetta. Personal-Nachweis; AdR Vienna, Bundesheer-Akten. Personnel file on Nikolaus Boicetta. [Bundesheer officer personnel files are arranged alphabetically rather than under any numerical system.] Bericht zur Dienstbeschreibung et al.; Otto Tumliz, *Waffengänge des IR 6: Skizzen aus dem großen Kriege* (regimental press, published in the field 1917); Glaise von Horstenau, *Österreich-Ungarns letzter Krieg*, order-of-battle entries for 6th Infantry Regiment: Vol. I, pp. 62–91, Vol. II, Beilage 14; index entries for 6th Infantry Regiment, 6th Bosnian Rifle Battalion, and commanding formations: Vols. I–IV.

Adalbert Lontschar: RH7, Heeresgeneralkartei. File on Adalbert Lontschar; KA Vienna, Offiziers-Belohnungsanträge. Karton 55, Nr. 63.331. Adalbert Lontschar; AdR Vienna, Bundesheer-Akten. Personnel file on Adalbert Lontschar. Bericht zur Dienstbeschreibung;

Glaise von Horstenau et al., *Österreich-Ungarns letzter Krieg,* order-of-battle entries for 24th Infantry Regiment: Vol. I, pp. 62–91, Vol. II, Beilage 14; index entries for 24th Infantry Regiment and commanding formations: Vols. I–VII.

Alois Windisch: RH7, Heeresgeneralkartei. File on Alois Windisch; KA Vienna, Nachlaß, Alois Windisch. Lebenslauf; AdR Vienna, Bundesheer-Akten. Personnel file on Alois Windisch. Personalblatt; Maximilian Ehnl, *Das X. Bataillon des oberösterreichischen k. u. k. Infanterie-Regimentes "Ernst Ludwig Großherzog von Hessen und bei Rhein" Nr. 14 im Weltkrieg* (Linz, 1932); Glaise von Horstenau et al., *Österreich-Ungarns letzter Krieg,* order-of-battle entries for 1st Infantry Regiment: Vol. I, pp. 62–91, Vol. II, Beilage 14; index entries for 14th Infantry Regiment and commanding formations: Vols. I–VII.

Joachim Wüst: Lebenslauf. PERS 6, file on Joachim Wüst. Lebenslauf.

Rudolf Wutte: AdR Vienna, Bundesheer-Akten. Personnel file on Rudolf Wutte. Bericht zur Dienstbeschreibung; Glaise von Horstenau et al., *Österreich-Ungarns letzter Krieg,* index entries for SMS Novara: Vol. III.

SOVIET UNION-BASED DIVISIONAL COMMANDERS:

Gottfried Barton: BA-MA, MSg 9. File on Gottfried Barton; Glaise von Horstenau et al., *Österreich-Ungarns letzter Krieg,* vols. 1–7 (Vienna: Verlag der Militärwissenschaftlichen Mitteilungen, 1930–1938), order-of-battle entries for 6th Lancer Regiment: Vol. I, pp. 62–91; for 8th Cavalry Division: Vol. II, Beilage 14, Vol. III, Beilage 2, Vol. IV, Beilage 2. Index entries for 6th Lancer Regiment, 8th Cavalry Division, and commanding formations: Vols. I–IV.

Hubert Lendle: BA-MA RH7, Heeresgeneralkartei. File on Hubert Lendle; BA-MA Pers 6. Personnel file on Hubert Lendle. Personal-Nachweis.

Johann Pflugbeil, BA-MA RH7, Heeresgeneralkartei. File on Johann Pflugbeil; BA-MA, Pers 6. File on Johann Pflugbeil. Personal-Nachweis, Lebenslauf.

Note on the Primary Sources

Except where stated, the primary source material presented in this study is housed in the Federal Military Archive (Bundesarchiv-Militärarchiv or BA-MA) in Freiburg-im-Breisgau. Endnote primary material belonging to the groupings RH, RW, or MSg was accessed in the form of original documents. Most of the primary material was, however, obtained from microfilmed copies belonging to the archive's MFB4 series. As BA-MA researchers usually work with original documents, the author has produced a conversion chart listing the MFB4 files against their designations as original document files. The chart is accessible via http://www.gcu.ac.uk/gsbs/staff/drbenshepherd/. MFB4 references are presented in the endnotes in the following order: film number, file number, frame number. For example: MFB4/56159 (film), 28326/16 (file), 442–443 (frame).

The study originally set out to examine what motivated German army officers serving in Yugoslavia at divisional and regimental levels, including how officers' behavior was shaped by influences and experiences earlier in their lives. Investigating this question involved examining both personal-level data and unit-level data.

Initially, personal-level data were collected for approximately forty officers, predominantly from various types of officer personnel file. Based on the author's previous research experience, it was anticipated at the study's outset that the main source types available—personal-level sources on particular officers, and unit-level sources generated by divisions, regiments, and other formations—would be unlikely to state officers' motivations explicitly. It would therefore be necessary in most cases to infer individual motivations by examining biographical details alongside the way in which a particular officer subsequently behaved. This approach distinguishes a divisional- or regimental-level study from studies focusing upon higher command levels, such as Johannes Hürter's *Hitlers Heerführer*, which, thanks to the available sources, are much better placed to utilize material such as private letters and diaries to provide a more explicit picture of the motivations of army-level and army group–level generals. Nevertheless, this author's previous monograph, *War in the Wild East: The German Army and Soviet Partisans,* had demonstrated the potential of a more inferential approach to studying officers at divisional and regimental levels. It was therefore anticipated that such an approach would be even more effective when applied to an officer sample considerably larger than that available for *War in the Wild East.*

In the event, the group of officers for whom data could be utilized meaningfully to illustrate personal motivations proved considerably smaller than had been anticipated. The main reason for this concerned the *quantity* and *quality* of divisional and regimental sources. The *quantity* of information will be compromised by a failure of any group to keep records or a willful destruction of those records by the group, enemy action, or other factors such as records being mislaid or lost. The *quality* of information is influenced by the extent to which officers were diligent, effective, and/or honest in recording their actions. Quality can vary with regard to how officers were instructed to record information and the circumstances in which they produced records.

All these concerns were apparent during the research for *War in the Wild East,* and it was anticipated that a similar pattern would be in evidence in the present study. In the event, the magnitude of these concerns was greater than anticipated. This meant that attempting to gather sufficient data was more time-consuming than anticipated. In cases where inadequate information prevented a more accurate picture it was necessary to draw more inferences from other available information.

A particular concern emerged in the case of regimental commanders. It was anticipated at the study's outset that, while regimental-level sources would be considerably less extensive than division-level sources, there would nevertheless be sufficient material to illuminate the individual motives of some regimental commanders. This was a reasonable expectation based on the author's experiences with the source material for *War in the Wild East.* Eventually, however, it became clear that the source material available for the current study contained much less of interest in this respect.

Why the regimental-level source material utilized for *War in the Wild East* was fuller than the equivalent material for the present study is not entirely clear. One possible explanation is that particularly hard-line officers serving in the relatively quiet sectors that were the focus of *War in the Wild East* felt they needed to go to extra effort to impose their will upon their troops. Many units serving in Yugoslavia, by contrast, faced more dangerous or more pressing circumstances. In these circumstances, it was more likely for harsher directives to be issued at divisional level or above anyway. Hard-line regimental commanders may therefore have felt no need to go to the extra effort of issuing such directives themselves.

It was also decided to exclude divisional operations officers (Ia officers) from the sample. This was because sufficient data could not be found on a meaningfully large number of Ia officers drawn from the divisions on which the study focused. However, given divisional *commanders'* central importance, excluding Ia officers still enables the study to produce important findings regarding influences on division-level behavior, and the importance of divisional commanders to that process.

In view of all these issues, it eventually became necessary to focus primary analysis on just nine officers, all of whom were divisional commanders serving in Yugoslavia. Nevertheless, it has proved possible to make select comparisons with certain regimental commanders, and with certain divisional commanders who served in the Soviet Union, in order to aid analysis of the core group of Yugoslavia-based divisional commanders.

Despite this unavoidable reduction in the amount of wholly satisfactory information available, the results that emerged make a significant contribution to incremental understanding of German army officers' motivations at the middle command level. As such, these results provide a useful basis on which further case studies can build in the future. Historians working on similar studies in the future should take note both of the limitations and opportunities inherent in the archival sources and how they might best be utilized accordingly.

Abbreviations

Abt.	Abteilung (section)
AdR	Archiv der Republik, Vienna
AK	Armeekorps (army corps)
Anl.	Anlage (supplement)
AOK	Armeeoberkommando (army command)
AVNOJ	Antifašističko Vijeće Narodnog Oslobođenja Jugoslavije (Anti-Fascist Council of the People's Liberation of Yugoslavia)
BA-MA	Bundesarchiv-Militärarchiv (Federal Military Archive), Freiburg-im-Breisgau
Bayr.	Bayerisch (Bavarian)
Betr.	Betrifft (regarding)
Der bevollm. Kdr. Gen. in Serbien / BKG Serbien	Der bevollmächtigte Kommandierende General in Serbien (Plenipotentiary Commanding General in Serbia)
Bf. dt. Tr. Kroatien	Befehlshaber der deutschen Truppen in Kroatien (Croatia Command)
BfZ	Bibliothek für Zeitgeschichte (Library of Contemporary History), Stuttgart
BKA	Bayerisches Kriegsarchiv (Bavarian War Archive), Munich
KG Serbien	Befehlshaber und Kommandierende General in Serbien (Serbia Command)

Div.-Kmdo.-Abfert.	Divisionskommando-Abfertigung (divisional command dispatch)
EOK	Etappenoberkommando (rear area command [Austro-Hungarian])
FABrig.	Feld-Artillerie-Brigade
Fmlt.	Feldmarschalleutnant (lieutenant general [Austro-Hungarian])
GM	Generalmajor (Brigadier General)
GR / Gren.-Rgt.	Grenadier-Regiment
ID / Inf.-Div.	Infanterie-Division
IR / Inf.-Rgt.	Infanterie-Regiment
IWM	Imperial War Museum, London
JD / Jäg.-Div.	Jäger-Division (light division)
JR / Jäg.-Rgt.	Jäger-Regiment (light regiment)
KA	Kriegsarchiv (War Archive, Vienna)
Kdr.	Kommandeur
Kp. / Komp.	Kompanie
Kpfgr.	Kampfgruppe (battle group)
Kpfw.	Kampfwagen (armored car)
KTB	Kriegstagebuch (war diary)
k. u. k. Heer	Das königliche und kaiserliche Heer ([Austro-Hungarian] Royal-Imperial Army)
LSB	Landesschützen-Bataillon (territorial battalion)
Ltn.	Lieutenant
MVAC	Milizia Volontaria Anti Comunista (Anti-Communist Volunteer Militia)
NARA	US National Archives and Records Administration, College Park, MD
NDH	Nezavisna Država Hrvatska (Independent State of Croatia)
NFA	Neue Feldakten (New Battlefield Files)
NHT	Nuremberg Hostage Trial
NOO	Narodno Oslobodilacki Odbor (people's liberation committee)
OKH	Oberkommando des Heeres (Army High Command)
OKW	Oberkommando der Wehrmacht (Armed Forces High Command)
P-Zug	Panzerzug (armored train)
Sch.-Div.	Schützen-Division (rifle division)

Notes

1. Throughout this study, the term *Wehrmacht* denotes the German armed forces generally, or at least more than one of the three armed services. It is frequently used in reference to German occupation of the Balkans because several senior Wehrmacht commanders who served in the region hailed from the air force (*Luftwaffe*) rather than the army (*Heer*). The term *Wehrmacht* is not used in this study to denote the army specifically, as is often the case in other studies.

2. While guerrillas seek simply to overthrow the established order, partisans see themselves as an adjunct to regular forces seeking to reestablish independent government. This is the meaning of the term as used in the title of this study, and applies to the main insurgent groups who were active in Yugoslavia during World War Two. In the study's text, however, the term is normally used with a capital *P*. This denotes the Yugoslav Communist Partisans, who took the term *Partisan* as the title of their movement as well as a general descriptive label. The term is occasionally used in the text with a small *p* where the partisan movement in the Soviet Union is referred to. The term *insurgent* is used in the text to denote irregular fighters generally, be they guerrillas, partisans or Partisans in the specific Yugoslav context.

3. Fred Singleton, *Twentieth-Century Yugoslavia* (London: Macmillan, 1976), 86.

4. Generals' ranks are translated into their World War II U.S. Army and British army equivalents at first mention, then simply as "general" thereafter. The translations (in order of rank) are as follows:

General = *Generaloberst*

Lieutenant General = *General der Infanterie/General der Artillerie/General der Gebirgsjäger* (mountain troops)

Major General = *Generalleutnant*

Brigadier General = *Generalmajor*

5. Walter Manoschek, "The Extermination of the Jews in Serbia" in *National Socialist Extermination Policies: Contemporary German Perspectives and Controversies*, ed. Ulrich Herbert (Oxford: Berghahn, 2000), 170.

6. See Geoffrey Best, *Humanity in Warfare* (London: Weidenfeld and Nicolson, 1980); Stephen C. Neff, *War and the Law of Nations: A General History* (Cambridge: Cambridge University Press, 2005).

7. See, for instance, Edward B. Westermann, *Hitler's Police Battalions: Enforcing Racial War in the East* (Lawrence: University Press of Kansas, 2005); Philip W. Blood, *Hitler's Bandit Hunters: The SS and the Nazi Occupation of Europe* (Washington, DC: Potomac, 2006).

8. On the historiography from the late 1940s to the mid-1980s, see the introduction in Theo J. Schulte, *The German Army and Nazi Policies in Occupied Russia* (Oxford: Berg, 1989).

9. For a historiographical overview up to the 2000s, see Rolf-Dieter Müller and Gerd R. Überschär, eds., *Hitler's War in the East 1941–1945: A Critical Assessment* (Oxford: Berg, 2000). Recent overview works, with further pointers to secondary literature, include Rolf-Dieter Müller and Hans-Erich Volkmann, eds., *Die Wehrmacht: Mythos und Realität* (Hamburg: Oldenbourg, 1999); Hannes Heer and Klaus Naumann, eds., *War of Extermination: The German Military in World War II 1941–1944* (New York: Berghahn, 2000); Christian Hartmann et al., eds., *Verbrechen der Wehrmacht: Bilanz einer Debatte* (Munich: C. H. Beck, 2005); Ben Shepherd, "The Clean Wehrmacht, The War of Extermination, and Beyond," *Historical Journal* 52 (2009): 455–473.

10. Klaus Schmider, *Partisanenkrieg in Jugoslawien 1941–1944* (Hamburg: E. S. Mittler, 2002), 547.

11. The fourth condition, that of being commanded by a superior responsible for his subordinates, was met. Aubrey C. Dixon, and Otto Heilbrunn, *Communist Guerrilla Warfare* (London: Allen and Unwin, 1954), 85.

12. Klaus Schmider, "Der jugoslawische Kriegsschauplatz," in *Das Deutsche Reich und der Zweite Weltkrieg, Band 8. Die Ostfront, 1943/44: Der Krieg im Osten und an den Nebenfronten*, ed. Karl-Heinz Frieser et al. (Stuttgart: Deutsche Verlags-Anstalt, 2007), 1072.

13. Ben Shepherd, "German Army Security Units in Russia, 1941–1943: A Case Study" (PhD diss., University of Birmingham, 2000), 7–10. See also Chapter 6.

14. On the need for a nuanced approach to the officer corps and the Wehrmacht generally, see Rolf-Dieter Müller, "Die Wehrmacht—Historische Last und Verantwortung: Die Historiographie im Spannungsfeld von Wissenschaft und Vergangenheitsbewältigung," in *Die Wehrmacht: Mythos und Realität*, ed. Rolf-Dieter Müller and Hans-Erich Volkmann (Hamburg: Oldenbourg, 1999), 3–35; Christian Hartmann, "Verbrecherischer Krieg—verbrecherische Wehrmacht? Überlegungen zur Struktur des deutschen Ostheeres 1941–1944," *Vierteljahreshefte für Zeitgeschichte* 52 (2004): 1–75.

15. Though for rank-and-file studies of great merit, see for example Omer Bartov, *The Eastern Front, 1941–45: German Troops and the Barbarization of Warfare* (Basingstoke: Macmillan, 1985); Omer Bartov, *Hitler's Army: Soldiers, Nazis, and War in the Third Reich* (New York: Oxford University Press, 1992); Christoph Rass, *Menschenmaterial: Deutsche Soldaten an der Ostfront* (Paderborn: Schöningh, 2003); Christoph Rass, "The Social Profile of the German Army's Combat Units, 1939–1945," in *Germany and the Second World War, Volume 9, Part 1. German Wartime Society 1939–1945: Politicization, Disintegration, and the Struggle for Survival*, Ralf Blank et al. (Oxford: Oxford University Press, 2008), 671–768. On source-related problems that studies of the motivations of NCOs and rank-and-file soldiers should consider, see Shepherd, "German Army Security Units in Russia, 1941–1943: A Case Study" 7–10.

16. In particular, the picture becomes less reliable and complete further down the command chain, especially at battalion and company level. On the source-related issues regarding German army divisional files, see Shepherd, "German Army Security Units in Russia, 1941–1943: A Case Study," 27–31. Two recent division-level studies of particular prominence are Hermann Frank Meyer, *Blutiges Edelweiss: Die 1. Gebirgs-Division im Zweiten Weltkrieg* (Berlin: Links, 2008); Christian Hartmann, *Wehrmacht im Ostkrieg: Front und militärisches Hinterland 1941/42* (Munich: Oldenbourg, 2009).

17. For more detail, see Shepherd, "German Army Security Units in Russia, 1941–1943: A Case Study," 7–10.

18. Records of the royal armies of Bavaria, Saxony, and Württemberg, which belonged to the Imperial German Army, have survived, but the central records in Potsdam, containing the records of the much more predominant Prussian units, were for the most part destroyed.

19. Edmund Glaise von Horstenau et al., *Österreich-Ungarns letzter Krieg*, vols. 1–7 (Vienna: Verlag der Militärwissenschaftlichen Mitteilungen, 1930–1938).

20. See also Appendix A.

21. On the leadership principle, see Ian Kershaw, *The Nazi Dictatorship: Problems and Perspectives of Interpretation*, 4th ed. (London: Edward Arnold, 2000), chap. 4. On the nature of rear area security directives as guidelines rather than clear orders, see Hannes Heer, "The Logic of the War of Extermination. The Wehrmacht and the Counter-Insurgency War," in *War of Extermination: The German Military in World War II 1941–1944*, ed. Hannes Heer and Klaus Naumann (New York: Berghahn, 2000), 99–103. Heer arguably overstates the degree to which "leadership principle"-type directives brutalized the Wehrmacht counterinsurgency campaign, but his observations as to *how* they worked are illuminating.

22. A flawed and dated, but nevertheless useful, introductory English-language overview of German counterinsurgency warfare in Yugoslavia between these dates is Paul N. Hehn, *The German Struggle against Yugoslav Guerrillas in World War II: German Counter-Insurgency in Yugoslavia 1941–1943* (New York: Columbia University Press, 1979).

23. Eric Hobsbawm, *Age of Extremes: The Short Twentieth Century 1914–1991* (London: Michael Joseph, 1994), 52.

1. BEFORE THE GREAT WAR

1. On the social composition of the German army officer corps under the Third Reich, see Bernhard R. Kroener, "Strukturelle Veränderungen in der Militärischen Gesellschaft des Dritten Reiches," in *Nationalsozialismus und Modernisierung*, ed. Michael Prinz and Rainer Zitelmann (Darmstadt: Wiss. Buchgesellschaft, 1994), 267–296; Bernhard R. Kroener, "Generationserfahrungen und Elitenwandel: Strukturveränderungen im deutschen Offizierkorps 1933–1945," in *Eliten in Deutschland und Frankreich im 19. Und 20. Jahrhundert: Strukturen und Beziehungen, Band 1*, ed. Rainer Hudemann and Georges-Henri Soutou (Munich: Oldenbourg, 1994), 219–233; Bernhard R. Kroener, "The Manpower Resources of the Third Reich in the Area of Conflict between Wehrmacht, Bureaucracy, and War Economy, 1939–1942," in *Germany and the Second World War, Volume 5. Organization and Mobilization of the German Sphere of Power. Part 1: Wartime Administration, Economy, and Manpower Resources 1939–1941*, Bernhard R. Kroener et al. (Oxford: Oxford University Press, 2000), 787–1154; Bernhard R. Kroener, "Management of Human Resources, Deployment of the Population, and Manning the Armed Forces in the Second Half of the War (1942–1944)," in *Germany and the Second World War, Volume 5. Organization and Mobilization in the German Sphere of Power. Part 2: Wartime Administration, Economy, and Manpower Resources 1941–1944/5*, Bernhard R. Kroener et al. (Oxford: Oxford University Press, 2003), 918–942.

2. On the social exclusivity of the German officer corps during this period, see Karl Demeter, *The German Officer Corps in Society and State, 1650–1945* (London: Weidenfeld and Nicolson, 1965), 1–73; Martin Kitchen, *The German Officer Corps, 1890–1914* (Oxford: Clarendon Press, 1968); Detlef Bald, *Der deutsche Offizier: Sozial- und Bildungsgeschichte des deutschen Offizierkorps im 20. Jahrhundert* (Munich: Bernard und Graefe, 1995), 38–100; Johannes Hürter, *Hitlers Heerführer: Die deutschen Oberbefehlshaber im Krieg gegen die Sowjetunion 1941/42* (Munich: Oldenbourg, 2006), 23–33.

3. On the officer corps' attitude towards the working class, see Kitchen, *The German Officer Corps, 1890–1914*, chap. 7.

4. Hürter, *Hitlers Heerführer: Die deutschen Oberbefehlshaber im Krieg gegen die Sowjetunion 1941/42*, 27.

5. István Deák, *Beyond Nationalism: A Social and Political History of the Habsburg Officer Corps 1848–1918* (Oxford: Oxford University Press, 1990), 86–88; Gunther E. Rothenburg, *The Army of Francis Joseph* (Lafayette, IN: Purdue University Press, 1998), 132, 145–146; Günther Kronenbitter, *"Krieg im Frieden": Die Führung der K. u. K. Armee und die Großmachtpolitik Österreich-Ungarns 1906–1914* (Munich: Oldenbourg, 2003), 26–33; Jonathan Gumz, *The Resurrection and Collapse of Empire in*

Habsburg Serbia, 1914–1918 (Cambridge: Cambridge University Press, 2009), 13–16, 30–34.

6. Rothenburg, The *Army of Francis Joseph*, 105–110, 125–127; Kronenbitter, *"Krieg im Frieden": Die Führung der K. u. K. Armee und die Großmachtpolitik Österreich-Ungarns 1906–1914* 521–531.

7. Rothenburg, The *Army of Francis Joseph*, 118; Deák, *Beyond Nationalism: A Social and Political History of the Habsburg Officer Corps 1848–1918*, 86–88.

8. Deák, *Beyond Nationalism: A Social and Political History of the Habsburg Officer Corps 1848–1918*, 90.

9. Ibid., 94–95; Kronenbitter, *"Krieg im Frieden": Die Führung der K. u. K. Armee und die Großmachtpolitik Österreich-Ungarns 1906–1914*, 44–45; Kitchen, The *German Officer Corps*, 1890–1914, 24; Hürter, *Hitlers Heerführer: Die deutschen Oberbefehlshaber im Krieg gegen die Sowjetunion 1941/42*, 47.

10. Deák, *Beyond Nationalism: A Social and Political History of the Habsburg Officer Corps 1848–1918*, 95–97.

11. Demeter, *The German Officer Corps in Society and State, 1650–1945*, 89–91.

12. Hürter, *Hitlers Heerführer: Die deutschen Oberbefehlshaber im Krieg gegen die Sowjetunion 1941/42*, 41, 50. See also John Moncure, *Forging the King's Sword: Military Education between Tradition and Modernization. The Case of the Royal Prussian Cadet Corps, 1871–1918* (New York: Peter Lang, 1993).

13. Kitchen, The *German Officer Corps*, 1890–1914, 29–31, 120–123; Heiger Ostertag, "Der soziale Alltag eines Offiziers im Kaiserreich 1913: Ein militärsoziologisches Zeitbild," *Zeitschrift für Geschichte* 38 (1990): 1069–1080; Hürter, *Hitlers Heerführer: Die deutschen Oberbefehlshaber im Krieg gegen die Sowjetunion 1941/42*, 50–53.

14. On relations between the German army and German society during the Wilhelmine period, see also Ute Frevert, *A Nation in Barracks: Modern Germany, Military Conscription, and Civil Society* (Oxford: Berg, 2004), chaps. 1–5.

15. Deák, *Beyond Nationalism: A Social and Political History of the Habsburg Officer Corps 1848–1918*, 86–88; Gumz, *The Resurrection and Collapse of Empire in Habsburg Serbia, 1914–1918*, 13–16, 30–34.

16. Rothenburg, The *Army of Francis Joseph*, 176.

17. A point Rothenburg himself makes.

18. See, for instance, David G. Herrmann, *The Arming of Europe and the Making of the First World War* (Princeton, NJ: Princeton University Press, 1996).

19. Hürter, *Hitlers Heerführer: Die deutschen Oberbefehlshaber im Krieg gegen die Sowjetunion 1941/42*, 54–60; Deák, *Beyond Nationalism: A Social and Political History of the Habsburg Officer Corps 1848–1918*, 166–169; Kronenbitter, *"Krieg im Frieden": Die Führung der K. u. K. Armee und die Großmachtpolitik Österreich-Ungarns 1906–1914*, 50–57.

20. Dennis Showalter, "From Deterrence to Doomsday Machine: The German Way of War, 1890–1914," *Journal of Military History* 64 (2000): 691; Hürter, *Hitlers Heerführer: Die deutschen Oberbefehlshaber im Krieg gegen die Sowjetunion 1941/42*, 58–60; Deák, *Beyond Nationalism: A Social and Political History of the Habsburg Officer Corps 1848–1918*, 112.

21. For an introduction to the backgrounds of the membership of the two movements, see Roger Chickering, *We Men Who Feel Most German: A Cultural Study of the Pan-German League 1886–1914* (London: George Allen and Unwin, 1984), 103–148; Andrew G. Whiteside, *The Socialism of Fools: Georg Ritter von Schönerer and Austrian Pan-Germanism* (Berkeley: University of California Press, 1975), 43–63. See also Michael Wladika, *Hitlers Vätergeneration: Die Ursprünge des Nationalsozialismus in der K. u. K. Monarchie* (Vienna: Böhlau Verlag, 2005); Peter Walkenhorst, *Nation—Volk—Rasse: Radikaler Nationalismus im Deutschen Kaiserreich 1890–1914* (Göttingen: Vandenhoeck & Ruprecht, 2007).

22. John W. Boyer, *Culture and Political Crisis in Vienna: Christian Socialism in Power, 1897–1918* (Chicago: University of Chicago Press), 445–446.

23. Deák, *Beyond Nationalism: A Social and Political History of the Habsburg Officer Corps 1848–1918,* 172–178.

24. Kronenbitter, *"Krieg im Frieden": Die Führung der K. u. K. Armee und die Großmachtpolitik Österreich-Ungarns 1906–1914,* 25.

25. Rothenburg, The *Army of Francis Joseph,* 151. See also Marsha Rozenblit, *Reconstructing a National Identity: The Jews of Habsburg Austria during World War I* (Oxford: Oxford University Press, 2001), chaps. 1, 2, and 4.

26. Kitchen, The *German Officer Corps, 1890–1914,* 46.

27. Ibid.

28. Michael Burleigh and Wolfgang Wippermann, *The Racial State: Germany 1933–1945* (Cambridge: Cambridge University Press, 1991), 23–28.

29. Mark Mazower, *Hitler's Empire: Nazi Rule in Occupied Europe* (London: Allen Lane, 2008), 19–23. See also William W. Hagen, *Germans, Poles and Jews: The Nationality Conflict in the Prussian East, 1772–1914* (Chicago: University of Chicago Press, 1980), esp. chaps. 5, 8.

30. William Mulligan, *The Origins of the First World War* (Cambridge: Cambridge University Press), 139, 152–154. Recent overviews of German attitudes towards the East include Gregor Thum, *Traumland Osten: Deutsche Bilder vom östlichen Europa im 20. Jahrhundert* (Göttingen: Vandenhoeck & Ruprecht, 2006); Wolfgang Wippermann, *Die Deutschen und der Osten: Feindbild und Traumland* (Darmstadt: Primus Verlag, 2007).

31. Holger R. Herwig, *The First World War: Germany and Austria-Hungary 1914–1918* (London: Hodder Arnold, 1997), 51.

32. Ibid.

33. Ibid., 20.

34. Wolfram Wette, *The Wehrmacht: History, Myth, Reality* (Cambridge, MA: Harvard University Press, 2006), 6–8.

35. Lawrence Sondhaus, *Franz Conrad von Hötzendorf: Architekt der Apokalypse* (Vienna: Neuer Wissenschaftlicher Verlag, 2003), 251–252. See also John R. Schindler, "Defeating Balkan Insurgency: The Austro-Hungarian Army in Serbia, 1878–1882," *Journal of Strategic Studies* 27 (2004): 528–552; Robin Okey, *Taming Balkan Nationalism: The Habsburg "Civilizing Mission" in Bosnia, 1878–1914* (Oxford: Oxford University Press, 2007).

36. Robert S. Wistrich, *Laboratory for World Destruction: Germans and Jews in Central Europe* (Lincoln: University of Nebraska Press, 2007), 7. See also Christian Promitzer, "The South Slavs in the Austrian Imagination: Serbs and Slovenes in the Changing View from German Nationalism to National Socialism," in *Creating the Other: Ethnic Conflict and Nationalism in Habsbgurg Central Europe*, ed. Nancy M. Wingfield (Oxford: Berghahn, 2003), 183–210.

37. On the Balkan situation during the years before the Great War, see Hew Strachan, *The First World War*, vol. 1, *To Arms* (Oxford: Oxford University Press, 2003), 35–64.

38. Promitzer, "The South Slavs in the Austrian Imagination: Serbs and Slovenes in the Changing View from German Nationalism to National Socialism," 193.

39. Sondhaus, *Franz Conrad von Hötzendorf: Architekt der Apokalypse,* 105.

40. Ibid., 91.

41. Herwig, *The First World War: Germany and Austria-Hungary 1914–1918* 9.

42. Sondhaus, *Franz Conrad von Hötzendorf: Architekt der Apokalypse,* 98–100.

43. Rothenburg, *The Army of Francis Joseph*, 127, 141–142; Kronenbitter, *"Krieg im Frieden": Die Führung der K. u. K. Armee und die Großmachtpolitik Österreich-Ungarns 1906–1914*, 121–144.

44. Kronenbitter, *"Krieg im Frieden": Die Führung der K. u. K. Armee und die Großmachtpolitik Österreich-Ungarns 1906–1914,* 121–144; Gumz, *The Resurrection and Collapse of Empire in Habsburg Serbia, 1914–1918*, 12–13; Arno Mayer, *The Persistence of the Old Regime: Europe to the Great War* (New York: Pantheon, 1981), 282–284.

45. See, for instance, Trutz von Trotha, "'The Fellows Can Just Starve': On Wars of 'Pacification' in the African Colonies of Imperial Germany and the Concept of 'Total War,'" in *Anticipating Total War: The German and American Experiences 1871–1914*, ed. Manfred F. Boemke, Roger Chickering, and Stig Förster (Cambridge: Cambridge University Press, 1999), 415–436; Sabine Dabringhaus, "An Army on Vacation? The German War in China," in Boemke et al., *Anticipating Total War: The German and American Experiences 1871–1914*, 459–476; John Horne and Alan Kramer, *German Atrocities 1914: A History of Denial* (New Haven, CT: Yale University Press, 2001); Isabel V. Hull, *Absolute Destruction: Military Culture and the Practice of War in Imperial Germany* (Ithaca, NY: Cornell University Press, 2006), chaps. 1–8.

46. Hull, *Absolute Destruction: Military Culture and the Practice of War in Imperial Germany,* 132–133.

47. Ibid., 106.

48. For more depth on this issue, see Ben Shepherd, *War in the Wild East: The German Army and Soviet Partisans* (Cambridge, MA: Harvard University Press, 2004), chap. 2.

49. On development of insurgency and counterinsurgency during the nineteenth and early twentieth centuries, see John Ellis, *From the Barrel of a Gun: A History of Guerrilla, Revolutionary, and Civil Warfare from the Romans to the Present* (London: Greenhill, 1995); Bruce Vandervort, *Wars of Imperial Conquest in Africa 1830–1914* (London: University College London Press, 1998); Ian F. W. Beckett, *Modern Insurgencies and Counter-Insurgencies: Guerrillas and their Opponents since 1750* (London: Routledge, 2001).

50. Charles D. Melson, "German Counter-Insurgency Revisited," *Journal of Slavic Military Studies* 24 (2011): 118–119.

51. Horne and Kramer, *German Atrocities 1914: A History of Denial,* 1.

52. See the essays by Stig Förster, Manfred Messerschmidt, and Thomas Rohkrämer, in Stig Förster and Jörg Nagler, eds., *On the Road to Total War: The American Civil War and the German Wars of Unification, 1861–1871* (Cambridge: Cambridge University Press, 1997); Geoffrey Wawro, *The Franco-Prussian War: The German Conquest of France in 1870–1871* (Cambridge: Cambridge University Press, 2005), chap. 11.

53. Robert M. Citino, *The German Way of War: From the Thirty Years' War to the Third Reich* (Lawrence: University Press of Kansas, 2008).

54. Hull, *Absolute Destruction: Military Culture and the Practice of War in Imperial Germany,* chaps. 1–8. On German military planning during the late nineteenth and early twentieth centuries, see also Arden Bucholz, *Moltke, Schlieffen, and Prussian War Planning* (New York: Berg, 1991). On the effect such doctrines had upon general German military planning during World War II, see Geoffrey P. Megargee, *Inside Hitler's High Command* (Lawrence: University Press of Kansas, 2000); and upon counterinsurgency warfare in particular, see Jonathan Gumz, "Wehrmacht Perceptions of Mass Violence in Croatia, 1941–1942," *Historical Journal* 44 (2001): 1015–1038; Philip W. Blood, *Hitler's Bandit Hunters: The SS and the Nazi Occupation of Europe* (Dulles, VA: Potomac, 2006).

55. Hans Umbreit, "Das unbewältigte Problem: Der Partisanenkrieg im Rücken der Ostfront," in *Stalingrad: Ereignis—Wirkung—Symbol,* ed. Jürgen Förster (Zurich: Piper, 1992), 133.

56. Hull, *Absolute Destruction: Military Culture and the Practice of War in Imperial Germany,* chap. 8.

57. Horne and Kramer, *German Atrocities 1914: A History of Denial,* 425.

58. Gumz, *The Resurrection and Collapse of Empire in Habsburg Serbia, 1914–1918,* 33–34.

59. Hürter, *Hitlers Heerführer: Die deutschen Oberbefehlshaber im Krieg gegen die Sowjetunion 1941/42,* 63–66.

2. FORGING A WARTIME MENTALITY

1. Stig Förster, "Dreams and Nightmares: German Military Leadership and the Images of Future Warfare 1871–1914," in *Anticipating Total War: The German and American Experiences 1871–1914,* ed. Manfred F. Boemke, Roger Chickering, and Stig Förster (Cambridge: Cambridge University Press, 1999), 362–376. See also Dennis Showalter, "From Deterrence to Doomsday Machine: The German Way of War, 1890–1914," *Journal of Military History* 64 (2000): 705–710.

2. Gunther E. Rothenburg, *The Army of Francis Joseph* (Lafayette, IN: Purdue University Press, 1998), 177.

3. Alan Kramer, *Dynamic of Destruction: Culture and Mass Killing in the First World War* (Oxford: Oxford University Press, 2007), 90.

4. Rudolf Jerabek, *Potiorek: General im Schatten von Sarajevo* (Graz: Verlag Styria, 1990), 162–165; Jonathan Gumz, *The Resurrection and Collapse of Empire in Habsburg Serbia, 1914–1918* (Cambridge: Cambridge University Press, 2009), 34–59.

5. Gumz, *The Resurrection and Collapse of Empire in Habsburg Serbia, 1914–1918,* 46.

6. Ibid.

7. Ibid., 58.

8. Jerabek, *Potiorek: General im Schatten von Sarajevo,* 162. On Habsburg ruthlessness towards occupied populations during the Great War, see also Anton Holzer, *Das Lächeln der Henker: Der unbekannte Krieg gegen die Zivilbevoelkerung 1914–1918* (Darmstadt: Primus, 2008).

9. Jerabek, *Potiorek: General im Schatten von Sarajevo,* 162–165; Kramer, *Dynamic of Destruction: Culture and Mass Killing in the First World War,* 132–134.

10. Gumz, *The Resurrection and Collapse of Empire in Habsburg Serbia, 1914–1918,* 52, 59–61.

11. John Horne and Alan Kramer, *German Atrocities 1914: A History of Denial* (New Haven, CT: Yale University Press, 2001). See also Jeff Lipkes, *Rehearsals: The German Army in Belgium, August 1914* (Leuven: Leuven University Press, 2007).

12. Förster, "Dreams and Nightmares: German Military Leadership and the Images of Future Warfare 1871–1914,"; Isabel V. Hull, *Absolute Destruction: Military Culture and the Practice of War in Imperial Germany* (Ithaca, NY: Cornell University Press, 2005), chap. 7.

13. Horne and Kramer, *German Atrocities 1914: A History of Denial,* 113–129, 425.

14. Ibid., 153–161.

15. For instance, for listings of Bavarian army units participating in the 1914 reprisals, see Horne and Kramer, *German Atrocities 1914: A History of Denial,* 600 (index).

16. Peter Lieb, "Aufstandsbekämpfung im strategischen Dilemma: Die deutsche Besatzung in der Ukraine 1918," in *Die Besatzung der Ukraine 1918: Historischer Kontext—Forschungsstand—Wirtschaftliche und Soziale Folgen,* ed. Wolfram Dornik and Stefan Karner (Graz: Ludwig Boltzmann-Institut, 2008), 111–139.

17. John Horne and Alan Kramer, "War between Soldiers and Enemy Civilians 1914–1915," in *Great War, Total War: Combat and Mobilisation on the Western Front 1914–1918,* ed. Roger Chickering and Stig Förster (Cambridge: Cambridge University Press, 2000), 159–160.

18. Horne and Kramer, *German Atrocities 1914: A History of Denial,* 402–403; Richard M. Fattig, "Reprisal: The German Army and the Execution of Hostages during the Second World War" (PhD thesis, University of California, 1980), 30–47, chap. 3.

19. On the German soldier's perspective, see Bernd Ulrich, "Feldpostbriefe im Ersten Weltkrieg: Bedeutung und Zensur," in *Kriegsalltag: Die Rekonstruktion des Kriegsalltags als Aufgabe der historischen Forschung und der Friedenszerziehung,* ed. Peter Knoch (Stuttgart: Metzler, 1989), 40–83; Bernd Ulrich, "Feldpostbriefe des Ersten Weltkrieges: Möglichkeiten und Grenzen einer alltagsgeschichtlichen Quelle," *Militärgeschichtliche Mitteilungen* 53 (1994): 73–84; Anne Lipp, "Friedenssucht und Durchhaltebereitschaft: Wahrnehumgen und Erfahrungen deutscher Soldaten im Ersten Weltkrieg," *Archiv für Sozialgeschichte* 36 (1996): 279–292; Gerhard

Hirschfeld et al., eds., *Kriegserfahrungen: Studien zur Sozial- und Mentalitätsge-schichte des Ersten Weltkrieges* (Essen: Klartext-Verlag, 1997); Philipp Witkop, ed., *German Students' War Letters*, trans. A. F. Wedd (Philadelphia: University of Pennsylvania Press, 2002); Bernd Ulrich and Benjamin Ziemann, eds., *Frontalltag im Ersten Weltkrieg: Ein Historisches Lesebuch* (Essen: Klartext Verlag, 2008).

20. Robert G. L. Waite, *Vanguard of Nazism: The Free Corps Movement in Postwar Germany 1918–1923* (Cambridge, MA: Harvard University Press, 1952), 23.

21. See in particular the sources in Ulrich and Ziemann, *Frontalltag im Ersten Weltkrieg: Ein Historisches Lesebuch.*

22. Tony Ashworth, *Trench Warfare, 1914–1918: The Live and Let Live System* (London: Pan Grand Strategy, 2004).

23. BKA. I Bayr. AK, 11/21/15. Korps-Befehl. Betr.: Verkehr mit dem Feind. The file listings in this endnote and in some other endnotes in this chapter are incomplete. At the time of writing it was not possible to re-check the relevant listings. The complete listings for these endnotes can instead be accessed via http://www.gcu.ac.uk/gsbs/staff/drbenshepherd/. The other relevant endnotes are: 49, 65, 75, 77, 83, 84, 89–92, 96, 119.

24. On the western front as a multifaced experience, see David Englander, "Mutinies and Military Morale," in *The Oxford Illustrated History of the First World War*, ed. Hew Strachan (Oxford: Oxford University Press, 2000), 191–203; Hew Strachan, *The First World War: A New History* (London: Simon and Schuster, 2003), chap. 6.

25. For a balanced appraisal of the extent to which Germany's wartime generation was "brutalized," see Kramer, *Dynamic of Destruction: Culture and Mass Killing in the First World War,* 304–313.

26. Alon Rachamimov, *POWs and the Great War: Captivity on the Eastern Front* (Oxford: Berg, 2002), 43.

27. John Schindler, "Disaster on the Drina: The Austro-Hungarian Army in Serbia, 1914," *War in History* 9 (2002): 159–195. On the Royal-Imperial Army's 1914 Serbian campaigns, see also Günther Rothenburg, "The Austro-Hungarian Camapaign against Serbia in 1914," *Journal of Military History* 53 (1998): 127–146; Hew Strachan, *The First World War*, vol. 1, *To Arms* (Oxford: Oxford University Press, 2003), 335–347.

28. Kramer, *Dynamic of Destruction: Culture and Mass Killing in the First World War,* 142–143. "[*Sic*]" pointed out by Kramer.

29. Ibid.

30. Geoffrey Wawro, "Morale in the Austro-Hungarian Army: The Evidence of Habsburg Army Campaign Reports and Intelligence Officers," in *Facing Armageddon: The First World War Experience*, ed. Hugh Cecil and Peter Liddle (Basingstoke: Pen and Sword, 1996), 399–412; Mark Cornwall, "Morale and Patriotism in the Austro-Hungarian Army, 1914–1918," in *State, Society and Mobilization in Europe during the First World War*, ed. John Horne (Cambridge: Cambridge University Press, 1997), 184ff.; Mark Cornwall, *The Undermining of Austria-Hungary: The Battle for Hearts and Minds* (London: Macmillan, 2000).

31. Andrej Mitrović, *Serbia's Great War 1914–1918* (London: C. Hurst and Co., 2007), 312–326.

32. See also Walter Manoschek, "The Extermination of the Jews in Serbia" in *National Socialist Extermination Policies: Contemporary German Perspectives and Controversies*, ed. Ulrich Herbert (Oxford: Berghahn, 2000), 170–171.

33. Fred Singleton, *Twentieth-Century Yugoslavia* (London: Macmillan, 1976), 10; Tim Judah, *The Serbs: History, Myth and the Destruction of Yugoslavia* (New Haven, CT: Yale, 1997), 99. See also Mitrović, *Serbia's Great War 1914–1918*.

34. Mitrović, *Serbia's Great War 1914–1918*, 221–244.

35. Gumz, The *Resurrection and Collapse of Empire in Habsburg Serbia, 1914–1918*, 231–248. See also review by Matthew Stibbe in *German History* 28, no. 3 (2010): 379–380.

36. Gumz, The *Resurrection and Collapse of Empire in Habsburg Serbia, 1914–1918*, 134, 215–230.

37. Judah, *The Serbs: History, Myth and the Destruction of Yugoslavia*, 99.

38. Mark Thompson, *The White War: Life and Death on the Italian Front, 1915–1919* (London: Faber and Faber, 2008). For an overview of the war on the Italian front from the Austro-Hungarian viewpoint, see Holger R. Herwig, *The First World War: Germany and Austria-Hungary 1914–1918* (London: Hodder Arnold, 1997), 149–154, 336–350, 365–373.

39. Thompson, *The White War: Life and Death on the Italian Front, 1915–1919*, 108, 194.

40. Ibid., 108.

41. Holger R. Herwig, *The First World War: Germany and Austria-Hungary 1914–1918*, 365.

42. Kriegsarchiv, Vienna (KA Vienna). Neue Feldakten (NFA) series 24, box 156 (24/156). 43. Sch.-Div. Kommando Truppendivisionskommandobefehl Nr. 111, 5/9/17, p. 3; ibid., 43. Sch.-Div. Kommando Reservat-Truppendivisionskommandobefehl Nr. 63, Feldpost 643, 6/5/17.

43. KA Vienna, NFA 195/1. K. u. k. Infanterie-Regiment Nr. 87, Feldpost 304, 8/1/18.

44. Thompson, *The White War: Life and Death on the Italian Front, 1915–1919*.

45. Rothenburg, *The Army of Francis Joseph*, 187; István Deák, *Beyond Nationalism: A Social and Political History of the Habsburg Officer Corps 1848–1918* (Oxford: Oxford University Press, 1990), 192; Norman Stone, *The Eastern Front, 1914–1917*, 2nd ed. (London: Penguin, 1998), 243; Kramer, *Dynamic of Destruction: Culture and Mass Killing in the First World War*, 54–68.

46. Kramer, *Dynamic of Destruction: Culture and Mass Killing in the First World War*, 55–56.

47. Ibid., 55–57.

48. On the food situation in Austria-Hungary during the Great War, see Herwig, *The First World War: Germany and Austria-Hungary 1914–1918*, 272–283; Maureen Healy, *Vienna and the Fall of the Habsburg Empire: Total War and Everyday Life in World War I* (Cambridge: Cambridge University Press), chap. 1. On the situation in Germany, see Herwig, *The First World War: Germany and Austria-Hungary 1914–1918*, 283–295; Belinda Davis, *Home Fires Burning: Food, Politics, and Everyday Life in World War I Berlin* (Chapel Hill: University of North Carolina Press, 2000).

49. KA Vienna, NFA. 11. Inf.-Div., 5/-9/15. K. u. k. 4. Armeekommando. Etappenkommando, 8/6/15. Behandlung italienischer kriegsgefangener Offiziere.

50. On the military course of the war on the eastern front, see Stone, *The Eastern Front, 1914–1917*; Herwig, *The First World War: Germany and Austria-Hungary 1914–1918*,

81–96, 135–149, 204–227, 333–335. For more recent detailed treatment of German and Austro-Hungarian combat performance on the eastern front during 1914 and 1915, see Dennis E. Showalter, *Tannenberg: Clash of Empires, 1914* (Oxford: Brassey's, 2004); Gerhard P. Groß, ed., *Die vergessene Front: Der Osten 1914/15* (Paderborn: Schöningh, 2006), 29–146; Timothy C. Dowling, *The Brusilov Offensive* (Bloomington: Indiana University Press, 2008); Graydon A. Tunstall, *Blood on the Snow: The Carpathian Winter War of 1915* (Lawrence: University Press of Kansas, 2010).

51. Michael Geyer, "Gewalt und Gewalterfahrung im 20. Jahrhundert: Der Erste Weltkrieg," in *Der Tod als Maschinist: Der industrialisierte Krieg 1914–1918*, ed. Rolf Spilker and Bernd Ulrich (Osnabrück: Bramsche, 1998), 248ff.

52. Rothenburg, The *Army of Francis Joseph*, 177.

53. Herwig, *The First World War: Germany and Austria-Hungary 1914–1918*, 137.

54. Ethnic Italian troops serving in the Austro-Hungarian army.

55. KA Vienna, Akten der Truppenkörper, box 684. K. u. k. Infanterie-Regiment Nr. 87, 12/24/14. Kriegstagebuch, 8/1–12/31/14.

56. See Tunstall, *Blood on the Snow: The Carpathian Winter War of 1915*.

57. Herwig, *The First World War: Germany and Austria-Hungary 1914–1918*, 145. On environmental conditions in the East, see also Vejas Gabriel Liulevicius, *War Land on the Eastern Front: Culture, National Identity, and German Occupation in World War I* (Cambridge: Cambridge University Press, 2000), 28–29.

58. Hans-Erich Volkmann, "Der Ostkrieg 1914/15 als Erlebnis- und Erfahrungswelt des deutschen Militärs," in *Die vergessene Front: Der Osten 1914/15*, ed. Gerhard P. Groß (Paderborn: Schöningh, 2006), 292; Eva Horn, "Im Osten nichts Neues: Deutsche Literatur und die Ostfront des Ersten Weltkriegs," in *Die vergessene Front: Der Osten 1914/15*, ed. Gerhard P. Groß (Paderborn: Schöningh, 2006), 217–230.

59. Liulevicius, *War Land on the Eastern Front: Culture, National Identity, and German Occupation in World War I*, 29–30.

60. Volkmann, "Der Ostkrieg 1914/15 als Erlebnis- und Erfahrungswelt des deutschen Militärs," 272.

61. Lothar Höbelt, "'So wie wir haben nicht einmal die Japaner angegriffen': Österreich-Ungarns Nordfront 1914/15," in *Die vergessene Front: Der Osten 1914/15*, ed. Gerhard P. Groß (Paderborn: Schöningh, 2006), 108–113.

62. KA Vienna, NFA 201/1. K. u. k. 57. Inf.-Div. Kommando, Feldpost 304, 8/4/18.

63. Liulevicius, *War Land on the Eastern Front: Culture, National Identity, and German Occupation in World War I*, 22.

64. Peter Hoeres, "Die Slawen. Perzeptionen des Kriegsgegners bei den Mittelmächten. Selbst- und Feindbild," in *Die vergessene Front: Der Osten 1914/15*, ed. Gerhard P. Groß (Munich: Schöningh, 2006), 190–199.

65. KA Vienna, NFA, box 305. III AK, 8/-11/14. K. u. k. III Korpskommando, Abfertigung, 10/20/14.

66. KA Vienna, NFA, 24/156. 43. Sch.-Div., 2/15–5/17. K. u. k. 43. Sch.-Div. Kommando. Abfertigung, 1/29/15

67. KA Vienna, NFA, C026/41. 11. Inf.-Div., 5/-9/15. K. u. k. XVII AK. Korpskommando, 8/28/15.

68. KA Vienna, NFA, C026/41. AK XVII, 5/15–6/18. K. u. k. 17. Korpskommando. Abfertigung, 2/12/16.

69. KA Vienna, NFA, C026/41. AK XVII, 5/15–6/18. K. u. K. 17. Korpskommando. Abfertigung, 4/23/17.

70. On German soldiers' impressions of Russian primitiveness during World War I, see Peter Jahn, "Russenfurcht und Antibolschewismus. Zur Entstehung und Wirkung von Feindbildern," in *Erobern und Vernichten: Der Krieg gegen die Sowjetunion 1941–1945: Essays*, ed. Peter Jahn and Reinhard Rürup (Berlin: Argon, 1991), 51; Liulevicius, *War Land on the Eastern Front: Culture, National Identity, and German Occupation in World War I*, 151–156; Hoeres, "Die Slawen. Perzeptionen des Kriegsgegners bei den Mittelmächten. Selbst- und Feindbild;" Volkmann, "Der Ostkrieg 1914/15 als Erlebnis- und Erfahrungswelt des deutschen Militärs."

71. Volkmann, "Der Ostkrieg 1914/15 als Erlebnis- und Erfahrungswelt des deutschen Militärs," 266.

72. Johannes Hürter, *Hitlers Heerführer: Die deutschen Oberbefehlshaber im Krieg gegen die Sowjetunion 1941/42* (Munich: Oldenbourg, 2006), 81.

73. Hoeres, "Die Slawen. Perzeptionen des Kriegsgegners bei den Mittelmächten. Selbst- und Feindbild," 187.

74. Johannes Hürter, "'Freischärler'—'Banden'—'Horden': Erfahrungen späterer Wehrmachtsgeneräle mit irregulärer Kriegführung 1914–1920" (paper presented at conference of German Committee for the Study of the Second World War, Dresden, June 29, 2001).

75. KA Vienna, NFA, box 305. III AK, 8/-11/14. K. u. k. III Korpskommando, 11/27/14.

76. KA Vienna, NFA, 24/156. 43. Sch.-Div., 2/15–5/17. K. u. k. 43. Sch.-Div. Kommando. Abfertigung, 1/21/15. Aus dem Armeekommandobefehl Nr. 55 vom 1/15/15.

77. KA Vienna, NFA, box 305. III AK, 8/-11/14. K. u. k. 3. Korpskommando, Abfertigung, 10/7/14, p. 1.

78. KA Vienna, NFA, 24/156. 43. Sch.-Div., 2/15–5/17. K. u. k. 43. Sch.-Div. Kommando. Abfertigung, 7/2/15. Ad. Res. Nr. 1281 der Gruppe Fmlt. SZURMAY, 6/29/15.

79. KA Vienna, NFA, 24/156. 43. Sch.-Div., 2/15–5/17. Gruppe Fmlt. Szurmay E Nr. 300/JR. Abschrift. Beilage zur Abfertigung vom. . . . Juni 1915 (date illegible).

80. KA Vienna, NFA, C026/41. AK XVII, 5/15–6/18. K. u. k. Korpskommando. Abfertigung. Feldpost 200, 2/14/16.

81. Ibid., 2/13/16.

82. Volkmann, "Der Ostkrieg 1914/15 als Erlebnis- und Erfahrungswelt des deutschen Militärs," 277–278.

83. BKA, Generalkommando II Bayr. AK, 9/24/14. Korpstagesbefehl.

84. BKA, Generalkommando I Bayr. AK, 2/8/15. Bestimmungen für die Ernährung der Zivilbevölkerung.

85. Hull, *Absolute Destruction: Military Culture and the Practice of War in Imperial Germany*, 230–242, 248–262; Kramer, *Dynamic of Destruction: Culture and Mass Killing in the First World War*, 41–46. For greater depth, see Larry Zuckerman, *The Rape of Belgium: The Untold Story of World War I* (New York: New York University Press, 2004); Gerhard Hirschfeld, ed., *Die Deutschen an der Somme 1914–1918:*

Krieg, Besatzung, Verbrannte Erde (Essen: Klartext Verlag, 2006); Jens Thiel, *"Men-schenbassin Belgien": Anwerbung, Deportation und Zwangsarbeit im Ersten Welt-krieg* (Essen: Klartext Verlag, 2007).

86. A. Polonsky, "The German Occupation of Poland during the First and Second World Wars: A Comparison," in *Armies of Occupation*, ed. Roy A. Prete and A. Hamish Ion (Waterloo, Ontario: Wilfrid Laurier University Press, 1981), 97–142.

87. Liulevicius, *War Land on the Eastern Front: Culture, National Identity, and German Occupation in World War I*, chaps. 2–4; Vejas Gabriel Liulevicius, "Von 'Ober Ost' nach 'Ostland'?" in *Die vergessene Front: Der Osten 1914/15*, ed. Gerhard P. Groß (Paderborn: Schöningh, 2006), 295–312; Hull, *Absolute Destruction: Military Culture and the Practice of War in Imperial Germany*, 243–248; Kramer, *Dynamic of Destruction: Culture and Mass Killing in the First World War*, 47–49.

88. Hürter, *Hitlers Heerführer: Die deutschen Oberbefehlshaber im Krieg gegen die Sow-jetunion 1941/42*, 83–85; Hull, *Absolute Destruction: Military Culture and the Practice of War in Imperial Germany*, 257–262.

89. BKA, Generalkommando II Bayr. Armeekorps, 8/28/14. Korpstagesbefehl, p. 1.

90. KA Vienna, NFA, box 305. III AK, 8/-11/14. Abfertigung 9/26/14.

91. BKA, Generalkommando I Bayr. AK, 8/31/16. Korpstagesbefehl.

92. BKA, Generalkommando II Bayr. AK, 12/20/16. Korpstagesbefehl II.

93. KA Vienna, NFA, C026/41. 11. FABrig., 11/16–12/17. K. u. k. 11. FA Brigadekom-mando. Reservatbefehl Nr. 20, 12/21/17. Disziplin.

94. KA Vienna, NFA, 24/156. K. u. k. IR Nr. 14. Regimentskommandobefehl Nr. 114, 5/2/18, p. 3. Alois Windisch, a future regimental commander in Yugoslavia, served with the 14th.

95. Gerald F. Feldman, *Army, Industry, and Labor in Germany 1914–1918* (Princeton, NJ: Princeton University Press, 1966); Robert J. Wegs, *Die Österreichische Krieg-swirtschaft 1914–1918* (Vienna: A. Schendl, 1979); Lothar Burchardt, "The Impact of the War Economy on the Civilian Population in Germany during the First and Second World Wars," in *The German Military in the Age of Total War*, ed. Wilhelm Deist (Leamington Spa: Berg, 1985); Herwig, *The First World War: Germany and Austria-Hungary 1914–1918*, chaps. 6, 7; David Welch, *Germany, Propaganda & Total War, 1914–1918* (London: Athlone Press, 2000), chap. 4.

96. KA Vienna, NFA. K. u. k. 11. Inf.-Div., Res. Nr. 950. Beilage zur Div.-Kmdo.-Abfert. Nr. 252, 10/9/18.

97. Liulevicius, *War Land on the Eastern Front: Culture, National Identity, and German Occupation in World War I*, 195–197.

98. Cornwall, "Morale and Patriotism in the Austro-Hungarian Army, 1914–1918," 183; Liulevi-cius, *War Land on the Eastern Front: Culture, National Identity, and German Occupation in World War I*, 212; Welch, *Germany, Propaganda & Total War, 1914–1918*, 225–227, 238.

99. Hew Strachan, "The Morale of the German Army 1917–18," in *Facing Armageddon: The First World War Experience*, ed. Hugh Cecil and Peter Liddle (Basingstoke: Pen and Sword, 1996), 393.

100. Cornwall, "Morale and Patriotism in the Austro-Hungarian Army, 1914–1918," 183; Rachamimov, *POWs and the Great War: Captivity on the Eastern Front*, 120–122, 193–195.

101. Peter Lieb, "Aufstandsbekämpfung im Strategischen Dilemma. Die deutsche Besatzung in der Ukraine 1918," in *Die Besatzung der Ukraine 1918: Historischer Kontext—Forschungsstand—Wirtschaftliche und Soziale Folgen*, ed. Wolfram Dornik and Stefan Karner (Graz: Ludwig Boltzmann-Institut, 2008), 122–129; Wolfram Dornik, "Die Besatzung der Ukraine 1918 durch österreichisch-ungarische Truppen," in *Die Besatzung der Ukraine 1918: Historischer Kontext—Forschungsstand—Wirtschaftliche und Soziale Folgen,* ed. Wolfram Dornik and Stefan Karner (Graz: Ludwig Boltzmann-Institut, 2008), 166–172. On reasons for the Austrians' greater brutality, see chap. 6.

102. On the Central powers' 1918 occupation of the Ukraine generally, see Mark von Hagen, *War in a European Borderland: Occupations and Occupation Plans in Galicia and Ukraine, 1914–1918* (Seattle: University of Washington Press, 2007), chap. 5; Dornik and Karner, *Die Besatzung der Ukraine 1918: Historischer Kontext—Forschungsstand—Wirtschaftliche und Soziale Folge*n.

103. Christian Streit, *Keine Kameraden: Die Wehrmacht und die sowjetischen Kriegsgefangenen*, 2nd ed. (Bonn: Dietz, 1997), 50–59; Manfred Messerschmidt, "Harte Sühne am Judentum: Befehlslage und Wissen in der deutschen Wehrmacht," in *"Niemand war dabei und keiner hat's gewußt": Die deutsche Öffentlichkeit und die Judenverfolgung 1933–1945*, ed. Jörg Wollenberg (Munich: Piper, 1989), 113–128; Jonathan Steinberg, *All or Nothing: The Axis and the Holocaust 1941–1943* (London: Routledge, 1990), 236–241.

104. Hans-Heinrich Wilhelm, *Rassenpolitik und Kriegführung: Sicherheitspolizei und Wehrmacht in Polen und der Sowjetunion* (Passau: Wissenschaftsverlag Rother, 1991), 147–148.

105. Liulevicius, *War Land on the Eastern Front: Culture, National Identity, and German Occupation in World War I*, 192.

106. Volkmann, "Der Ostkrieg 1914/15 als Erlebnis- und Erfahrungswelt des deutschen Militärs," 279.

107. Ibid., 278–280; Hoeres, "Die Slawen. Perzeptionen des Kriegsgegners bei den Mittelmächten. Selbst- und Feindbild," 199–200.

108. Wolfram Wette, *The Wehrmacht: History, Myth, Reality* (Cambridge MA: Harvard University Press, 2006), 42. See also Werner T. Angress, "Das deutsche Militär und die Juden im Ersten Weltkrieg," *Militärgeschichtliche Mitteilungen* 19 (1976): 77–146.

109. Wette, *The Wehrmacht: History, Myth, Reality*, 38.

110. Ibid., 34–37; Christhard Hoffmann, "Between Integration and Rejection: The Jewish Community in Germany 1914–1918," in *State, Society and Mobilization in Europe during the First World War*, ed. John Horne (Cambridge: Cambridge University Press, 1997), 98–99.

111. Bruce F. Pauley, *Prejudice to Persecution: A History of Austrian Anti-Semitism* (Chapel Hill: University of North Carolina Press, 1992), 62–64.

112. Ibid., 68.

113. Mark Mazower, *Hitler's Empire: Nazi Rule in Occupied Europe* (London: Allen Lane, 2008), 29.

114. Ibid., 94.

115. Robert Asprey, *The German High Command at War: Hindenburg and Ludendorff and the First World War* (London: Warner, 1994), chap. 21ff.; Welch, *Germany, Propaganda & Total War*, chaps. 6, 7.

116. Herwig, *The First World War: Germany and Austria-Hungary 1914–1918*, 410.

117. See Wilhelm Deist, "The Military Collapse of the German Empire: The Reality behind the Stab-in-the-Back Myth," *War in History* 3 (1996): 186–207; Wilhelm Deist, "The German Army, the Authoritarian Nation State and Total War," in *State, Society and Mobilization in Europe during the First World War*, ed. John Horne (Cambridge: Cambridge University Press, 1997), 161–171; Alexander Watson, *Enduring the Great War: Combat, Morale and Collapse in the German and British Armies 1914–1918* (Cambridge: Cambridge University Press, 2008).

118. On the fighting performance of the German army on the western front in 1918, see Rod Paschall, *The Defeat of Imperial Germany, 1917–18* (Chapel Hill, NC: Da Capo Press, 1989), chap. 6; Asprey, *German High Command,* chaps. 34, 35, 37–42; Herwig, *The First World War: Germany and Austria-Hungary 1914–1918*, chap. 10.

119. BKA, I Bayr. AK, 10/21/18. Tagesbefehl.

120. Peter Fiala, *Die letzte Offensive Altösterreichs: Führungsprobleme und Führerverantwortlichkeit bei der öst.-ung. Offensive in Venetian, Juni 1918* (Boppard: H. Boldt, 1967).

121. Herwig, *The First World War: Germany and Austria-Hungary 1914–1918*, 433–437; Cornwall, "Morale and Patriotism in the Austro-Hungarian Army, 1914–1918," 188–190.

122. Rothenburg, *The Army of Francis Joseph*, 203–204. On the Royal-Imperial Army's relationship with internal politics during the Great War, see Christoph Führ, *Das K. u. K. Armeeoberkommando und die Innenpolitik in Österreich, 1914–1917* (Graz: Böhlau, 1968).

123. KA Vienna, NFA, 24/156. K. u. k. IR Nr. 14. Regimentskommandobefehl Nr. 244, 10/8/17, p. 3. Verlautbarung über die Bestrafung der Desertion.

124. Herwig, *The First World War: Germany and Austria-Hungary 1914–1918*, 438. See also Thompson, *The White War: Life and Death on the Italian Front, 1915–1919*, 352–368.

125. See Appendix A.

126. For a brief overview of the collapse, see Steven Beller, *A Concise History of Austria* (Cambridge: Cambridge University Press, 2006), 191–200.

127. Pauley, *Prejudice to Persecution: A History of Austrian Anti-Semitism*, 80, 172–173; Michael Mann, *Fascists* (Cambridge: Cambridge University Press, 2004), 227; Robert Gerwarth, "The Central European Counter-Revolution: Paramilitary Violence in Germany, Austria and Hungary after the Great War," *Past and Present* 200 (2008): 198–201.

128. Christian Streit attaches particular importance to anti-Bolshevism as an "integrating factor" in officers' support for the Nazis. Christian Streit, *Keine Kameraden: Die Wehrmacht und die sowjetischen Kriegsgefangenen*, 2nd ed. (Bonn: Dietz, 1997), 50–59; Christian Streit, "Ostkrieg, Antibolschewismus, und 'Endlösung,'" *Geschichte und Gesellschaft* 17 (1991): 242–255.

129. On Germany's collapse in autumn 1918, see Jörg Duppler and Gerhard P. Groß, eds., *Kriegsende 1918: Ereignis, Wirkung, Nachwirkung* (Munich: 1999), Section V.

130. Wette, *The Wehrmacht: History, Myth, Reality,* 43.

131. On the Free Corps, see Robert G. L. Waite, *Vanguard of Nazism: The Free Corps Movement in Postwar Germany 1918–1923*; Hagen Schulze, *Freikorps und Republik 1918–1920* (Boppard am Rhein: Boldt Verlag, 1969); Nigel H. Jones, *Hitler's Heralds: The Story of the Freikorps 1918–1923* (London: John Murray, 1987); Klaus Theweleit, *Männerphantasien,* vols. 1 and 2 (Zürich: Piper, 2009).

132. Jones, *Hitler's Heralds: The Story of the Freikorps 1918–1923,* 114–115.

133. Hürter, *Hitlers Heerführer: Die deutschen Oberbefehlshaber im Krieg gegen die Sowjetunion 1941/42,* 86–96.

134. Gerwarth, "The Central European Counter-Revolution: Paramilitary Violence in Germany, Austria and Hungary after the Great War." See also C. Earl Edmondson, *The Heimwehr and Austrian Politics, 1918–1936* (Athens: University of Georgia Press, 1982); John T. Laurisden, *Nazism and the Radical Right in Austria 1918–1934* (Copenhagen: Museum Tusculanum Press, 2007).

3. BRIDGING TWO HELLS

1. For more detail on several themes in this chapter, see Ben Shepherd, *War in the Wild East: The German Army and Soviet Partisans* (Cambridge, MA: Harvard University Press, 2004), chap. 1.

2. Karl Demeter, *The German Officer Corps in Society and State, 1650–1945* (London: Weidenfeld and Nicolson, 1965), 189; Johannes Hürter, *Hitlers Heerführer: Die deutschen Oberbefehlshaber im Krieg gegen die Sowjetunion 1941/42* (Munich: Oldenbourg, 2006), 98–99. On Reichswehr relations with the Weimar Republic, see Demeter, *The German Officer Corps in Society and State, 1650–1945,* chap. 24; Hürter, *Hitlers Heerführer: Die deutschen Oberbefehlshaber im Krieg gegen die Sowjetunion 1941/42,* 96–111; Jürgen Förster, *Die Wehrmacht im NS-Staat: Eine strukturgeschichtliche Analyse* (Munich: Oldenbourg, 2007), chap. 1.

3. Bernhard R. Kroener, "Strukturelle Veränderungen in der Militärischen Gesellschaft des Dritten Reiches," in *Nationalsozialismus und Modernisierung,* ed. Michael Prinz and Rainer Zitelmann (Darmstadt: Wissenschaftliche Buchgesellschaft, 1994), 277–278; Hürter, *Hitlers Heerführer: Die deutschen Oberbefehlshaber im Krieg gegen die Sowjetunion 1941/42,* 108–109.

4. Hürter, *Hitlers Heerführer: Die deutschen Oberbefehlshaber im Krieg gegen die Sowjetunion 1941/42,* 96–111.

5. Ibid., 105–106; Wolfram Wette, *The Wehrmacht: History, Myth, Reality* (Cambridge, MA: Harvard University Press, 2006), 17–21.

6. Michael Geyer, *Aufrüstung oder Sicherheit: Die Reichswehr in der Krise der Machtpolitik 1924–1936* (Wiesbaden: Steiner, 1980); Michael Geyer, "Professionals and Junkers: German Rearmament and Politics in the Weimar Republic," in *Social Change and Political Development in Weimar Germany,* ed. Richard Bessel and E. J.

Feuchtwanger (London: Croom Helm, 1981), 77–133; Michael Geyer, "Traditional Elites and National Socialist Leadership," in *The Rise of the Nazi Regime: Historical Reassessments*, ed. Charles S. Maier (Boulder, CO: Westview Press, 1986), 57–73; Kroener, "Strukturelle Veränderungen in der Militärischen Gesellschaft des Dritten Reiches," 277–278; Hürter, *Hitlers Heerführer: Die deutschen Oberbefehlshaber im Krieg gegen die Sowjetunion 1941/42*, 111–122.

7. Demeter, *The German Officer Corps in Society and State, 1650–1945*, 190.

8. Hürter, *Hitlers Heerführer: Die deutschen Oberbefehlshaber im Krieg gegen die Sowjetunion 1941/42*, 100–105. Two of the officers featured in this study—Hoffmann and Stahl—served within the ministry for a period during the interwar years. See Appendix A.

9. Manfred Messerschmidt, "The *Wehrmacht* and the *Volksgemeinschaft*," *Journal of Contemporary History* 18 (1983): 719–744; Förster, *Die Wehrmacht im NS-Staat: Eine strukturgeschichtliche Analyse*, chap. 1.

10. Hürter, *Hitlers Heerführer: Die deutschen Oberbefehlshaber im Krieg gegen die Sowjetunion 1941/42*, 99.

11. Klaus-Jürgen Müller, *The Army, Politics and Society in Germany, 1933–45: Studies in the Army's Relation to Nazism* (Manchester: Manchester University Press, 1987), 19–35.

12. Francis Ludwig Carsten, *Fascist Movements in Austria: From Schoenerer to Hitler* (London: Sage, 1977), 327–336.

13. Martin Kitchen, *The Coming of Austrian Fascism* (London: Croom Helm, 1980), 4, 30, 97–106.

14. Franz Ludwig Carsten, *The First Austrian Republic, 1918–38: A Study Based on British and Austrian Documents* (London: Ashgate, 1986), 151–154; Barbara Jelavich, *Modern Austria: Empire and Republic, 1815–1986* (Cambridge: Cambridge University Press, 1987), 185–191.

15. On the electoral success of the Austrian Nazis during the early 1930s, see especially Dirk Hänisch, *Die österreichischen NSDAP-Wähler: Eine empirische Analyse ihrer politischen Herkunft und ihres Sozialprofils* (Vienna: Böhlau, 1998).

16. For assessment of Dollfuss and pointers to secondary literature, see Gunther Bischof et al., eds., *The Dollfuss/Schuschnigg Era in Austria: Contemporary Austrian Studies Volume 11* (New Brunswick, NJ: Transaction Publishers, 2003).

17. Ludwig Jedlicka, *Ein Heer im Schatten der Parteien: Die militaerpolitische Lage Österreichs 1918–1938* (Graz: Verlag Hermann Boehlaus, 1955), 89–90.

18. Carsten, *The First Austrian Republic, 1918–38: A Study Based on British and Austrian Documents*, 173.

19. Ibid., 162; Erwin A. Schmidl, *März 38: Der deutsche Einmarsch in Österreich* (Vienna: Österreichsicher Bundesverlag, 1988), 49.

20. Kroener, "Strukturelle Veränderungen in der Militärischen Gesellschaft des Dritten Reiches," 277–278.

21. Hürter, *Hitlers Heerführer: Die deutschen Oberbefehlshaber im Krieg gegen die Sowjetunion 1941/42*, 124.

22. Kroener, "Strukturelle Veränderungen in der Militärischen Gesellschaft des Dritten Reiches," 277–278.

23. Martin Broszat, "Soziale Motivation und Führer-Bindung im Nationalsozialismus," *Vierteljahreshefte für Zeitgeschichte* 18 (1970): 392–409; Messerschmidt, "The *Wehrmacht* and the *Volksgemeinschaft*."

24. Joachim C. Fest, *The Face of the Third Reich* (London: Weidenfeld and Nicolson, 1970), 237.

25. For recent work on the German army officer corps' development and its evolving relationship with National Socialism between 1933 and 1939, see Hürter, *Hitlers Heerführer: Die deutschen Oberbefehlshaber im Krieg gegen die Sowjetunion 1941/42*, 123–155; Förster, *Die Wehrmacht im NS-Staat*, chap. 2.

26. Hürter, *Hitlers Heerführer: Die deutschen Oberbefehlshaber im Krieg gegen die Sowjetunion 1941/42*, 136.

27. Wette, *The Wehrmacht: History, Myth, Reality*, 84–85.

28. Manfred Messerschmidt, "Harte Sühne am Judentum. Befehlslage und Wissen in der deutschen Wehrmacht," in *"Niemand war dabei und keiner hat's gewußt": Die deutsche Öffentlichkeit und die Judenverfolgung 1933–1945*, ed. Jörg Wollenberg (Munich: Piper, 1989), 113–128; Christian Streit, *Keine Kameraden: Die Wehrmacht und die sowjetischen Kriegsgefangenen*, 2nd ed. (Bonn: Dietz, 1997), 50–59.

29. Hürter, *Hitlers Heerführer: Die deutschen Oberbefehlshaber im Krieg gegen die Sowjetunion 1941/42*, 134.

30. See Conan Fischer, *The Rise of the Nazis* (Manchester: Manchester University Press, 1995).

31. For an introduction to the debate on Nazi foreign policy, see Ian Kershaw, *The Nazi Dictatorship: Problems and Perspectives of Interpretation*, 4th ed. (London: Arnold, 2000), chap. 6.

32. Alexander Lassner, "The Foreign Policy of the Schuschnigg Government 1934–1938: The Quest for Security," in *The Dollfuss/Schuschnigg Era in Austria: Contemporary Austrian Studies Volume 11*, ed. Gunther Bischof et al. (New Brunswick, NJ: Transaction Publishers, 2003), 163–186.

33. Mark Mazower, *Hitler's Empire: Nazi Rule in Occupied Europe* (London: Allen Lane, 2008), 47.

34. Schmidl, *März 38: Der deutsche Einmarsch in Österreich*, 48–50.

35. Ibid., 47–48.

36. Peter Broucek, "Heereswesen," in *Geschichte der Ersten Republik 1*, ed. Erika Weinzierl and Kurt Skalnik (Graz: Styria, 1983), 218–222.

37. Schmidl, *März 38: Der deutsche Einmarsch in Österreich*, 49, 57.

38. Ibid., 50. See also Kitchen, *The Coming of Austrian Fascism*, 105–106.

39. Schmidl, *März 38: Der deutsche Einmarsch in Österreich*, chap. 6.

40. Kitchen, *The Coming of Austrian Fascism*, p. 234. On the purging of non-Nazi officers, see Richard Germann, "'Österreichische' Soldaten in Ost- und Südosteuropa 1941–1945: Deutsche Krieger—Nationalsozialistische Verbrecher—Österreichische Opfer?" (PhD thesis, University of Vienna, 2006), chap. 2.

41. Alexander B. Rossino, *Hitler Strikes Poland: Blitzkrieg, Ideology, and Atrocity* (Lawrence: University Press of Kansas, 2003), 5–8.

42. Hürter, *Hitlers Heerführer: Die deutschen Oberbefehlshaber im Krieg gegen die Sowjetunion 1941/42*, 158.

43. Rossino, *Hitler Strikes Poland: Blitzkrieg, Ideology, and Atrocity*, 1, chaps. 2–4, 234.

44. Omer Bartov, *Hitler's Army: Soldiers, Nazis and War in the Third Reich* (New York: Oxford University Press, 1992), 66.

45. Rossino, *Hitler Strikes Poland: Blitzkrieg, Ideology, and Atrocity*, 86–87, 126–129, 203–216; Charles D. Melson, "German Counter-Insurgency Revisited," *Journal of Slavic Military Studies* 24 (2011): 121.

46. Jürgen Förster, "Hitlers Entscheidung für den Krieg gegen die Sowjetunion," in *Der Angriff auf die Sowjetunion*, Horst Boog et al. (Frankfurt am Main: Fischer, 1991), 27–68.

47. Wette, *The Wehrmacht: History, Myth, Reality*, 17–24. On the importance of anti-Bolshevism within the generals' mind-set, and the connection with their anti-Semitism, see also Messerschmidt, "Harte Sühne am Judentum. Befehlslage und Wissen in der deutschen Wehrmacht;" Steinberg, *All or Nothing: The Axis and the Holocaust 1941–1943*, 236–241; Christian Streit, "Ostkrieg, Antibolschewismus, und 'Endlösung,'" *Geschichte und Gesellschaft* 17 (1991), 242–255; Streit, *Keine Kameraden: Die Wehrmacht und die sowjetischen Kriegsgefangenen*, 2nd ed., 50–59.

48. Bartov, *Hitler's Army: Soldiers, Nazis, and War in the Third Reich*, 129.

49. For overviews and guidance on further literature regarding the German military planning for Barbarossa, the criminal aspects of the invasion, and the subsequent military campaign, see Rolf-Dieter Müller and Gerd R. Ueberschär, eds., *Hitler's War in the East 1941–1945: A Critical Assessment* (Oxford: Berghahn, 2000); Evan Mawdsley, *Thunder in the East: The Nazi-Soviet War, 1941–1945* (London: Bloomsbury, 2006).

50. OKW WFSt. / Abt. L (IV/Qu.), 5/19/41, Anlage 3. Richtlinien für das Verhalten der Truppe in Russland. Reprinted in Wolfram Wette and Gerd R. Ueberschär, eds., *Der deutsche Überfall auf die Sowjetunion 1941: Berichte, Analyse, Dokumente* (Frankfurt am Main: Fischer, 1991), 258–259.

4. INVASION AND OCCUPATION: YUGOSLAVIA, 1941

1. On the Italian army's failings, see MacGregor Knox, *Hitler's Italian Allies: Royal Armed Forces, Fascist Regime, and the War of 1940–1943* (Cambridge: Cambridge University Press, 2000), 23–67; Richard L. Dinardo, *Germany and the Axis Powers: From Coalition to Collapse* (Lawrence: University Press of Kansas, 2005), 28–36; Mark Mazower, *Hitler's Empire: Nazi Rule in Occupied Europe* (London: Allen Lane, 2008), 341.

2. Detlef Vogel, "German Intervention in the Balkans," in Gerhard Schreiber et al., *Germany and the Second World War, Volume III: The Mediterranean, South-East Europe, and North Africa 1939–1941* (Oxford: Clarendon Press, 1995), 479–485.

3. Fred Singleton, *Twentieth-Century Yugoslavia* (London: Macmillan, 1976), 68.

4. Jozo Tomasevich, *War and Revolution in Yugoslavia, 1941–1945: Occupation and Collaboration* (Stanford, CA: Stanford University Press, 2001), 337–338.

5. Stevan K. Pavlowitch, *Yugoslavia* (London: Ernest Bevin, 1971), 76, 83–84; Stevan K. Pavlowitch, *Serbia: The History behind the Name* (London: Hurst, 2002), 135–136; Singleton, *Twentieth-Century Yugoslavia*, 3; Gerhard Schreiber, "Germany, Italy, and South-East Europe: From Political and Economic Hegemony to Military Aggression," in *Germany and the Second World War, Volume 3: The Mediterranean, South-East Europe, and North Africa 1939–1941*, Gerhard Schreiber et al. (Oxford: Clarendon Press, 1995), 316–321. On interwar Yugoslavia generally, see Tomasevich, *War and Revolution in Yugoslavia, 1941–1945: Occupation and Collaboration*, chap. 1; Dejan Djokić, *Elusive Compromise: A History of Interwar Yugoslavia* (London: Hurst, 2007).

6. Pavlowitch, *Yugoslavia*, 83–84.

7. Pavlowitch, *Serbia: The History behind the Name*, 128.

8. Tomasevich, *War and Revolution in Yugoslavia, 1941–1945: Occupation and Collaboration*, chap. 1; Djokić, *Elusive Compromise: A History of Interwar Yugoslavia*, chaps. 1 and 2.

9. Tomasevich, *War and Revolution in Yugoslavia, 1941–1945: Occupation and Collaboration,* 39–46; Pavlowitch, *Serbia: The History behind the Name*, 131–132; Djokić, *Elusive Compromise: A History of Interwar Yugoslavia*, chap. 5.

10. Djokić, *Elusive Compromise: A History of Interwar Yugoslavia*, 280.

11. Marko Attila Hoare, "Whose Is the Partisan Movement? Serbs, Croats and the Legacy of a Shared Resistance," *Journal of Slavic Military Studies* 15 (2002): 25.

12. Schreiber, "Germany, Italy, and South-East Europe: From Political and Economic Hegemony to Military Aggression," 316–325, 362–372.

13. Vogel, "German Intervention in the Balkans," 479–481; Ian Kershaw, *Hitler: Nemesis, 1936–1945* (London: Penguin, 2000). On German policy towards Yugoslavia in 1941, see also Klaus Olshausen, *Zwischenspiel auf dem Balkan: Die deutsche Politik gegenüber Jugoslawien und Griechenland von März bis Juli 1941* (Stuttgart: Deutsche Verlags-Anstalt, 1973).

14. Vogel, "German Intervention in the Balkans," 480–485. On Hitler's Serbophobia, see also Klaus Schmider, *Partisanenkrieg in Jugoslawien 1941–1944* (Hamburg: E. S. Mittler, 2002), 43.

15. Vogel, "German Intervention in the Balkans," 493–526; Mark Wheeler, "Pariahs to Partisans to Power: The Communist Party of Yugoslavia," in *Resistance and Revolution in Mediterranean Europe 1939–1948*, ed. Tony Judt (London: Routledge, 1989), 123–125.

16. Klaus Schmider, "Der jugoslawische Kriegsschauplatz," in *Das Deutsche Reich und der Zweite Weltkrieg, Band 8. Die Ostfront, 1943/44: Der Krieg im Osten und an den Nebenfronten,* Karl-Heinz Frieser et al. (Stuttgart: Deutsche Verlags-Anstalt, 2007), 1010–1011.

17. Ibid., 1009–1010.

18. On the partition of Yugoslavia in spring 1941 and its immediate effects, see for overviews Mazower, *Hitler's Empire: Nazi Rule in Occupied Europe*, 132–133, 340–354;

Schmider, *Partisanenkrieg in Jugoslawien 1941–1944*, 28–53; Stevan K. Pavlowitch, *Hitler's New Disorder: The Second World War in Yugoslavia* (London: Hurst, 2008), chap. 2. For more detailed treatment, see Tomasevich, *War and Revolution in Yugoslavia, 1941–1945: Occupation and Collaboration*, chaps. 2–6.

19. Matteo Milazzo, *The Chetni Movement and the Yugoslav Resistance* (Baltimore, MD: The Johns Hopkins University Press, 1975), 3; Mazower, *Hitler's Empire: Nazi Rule in Occupied Europe*, 340–341.

20. Milazzo, *The Chetni Movement and the Yugoslav Resistance*, 10.

21. Ibid., 11.

22. On the NDH, see Ladislaus Hory and Martin Broszat, *Der Kroatische Ustasha-Staat 1941–1945* (Stuttgart: Deutsche Verlags-Anstalt, 1964); Tomasevich, *War and Revolution in Yugoslavia, 1941–1945: Occupation and Collaboration*, chaps. 6–11.

23. Schmider, *Partisanenkrieg in Jugoslawien 1941–1944*, 28–33.

24. Milazzo, *The Chetni Movement and the Yugoslav Resistance*, 6; Schmider, *Partisanenkrieg in Jugoslawien 1941–1944*, 49–51.

25. Tomasevich, *War and Revolution in Yugoslavia, 1941–1945: Occupation and Collaboration*, 4, 30–39, 336–342; Marko Attila Hoare, *Genocide and Resistance in Hitler's Bosnia: The Partisans and the Chetniks 1941–1943* (Oxford: Oxford University Press, 2005), 21–23.

26. On the Ustasha's anti-Semitic beliefs, see Tomasevich, *War and Revolution in Yugoslavia, 1941–1945: Occupation and Collaboration*, 43, 348–349, 370, 593.

27. Hoare, *Genocide and Resistance in Hitler's Bosnia: The Partisans and the Chetniks 1941–1943*, 22–23.

28. Tomasevich, *War and Revolution in Yugoslavia, 1941–1945: Occupation and Collaboration*, 335.

29. On NDH-Italian-German relations and the state of the NDH economy, see Tomasevich, *War and Revolution in Yugoslavia, 1941–1945: Occupation and Collaboration*, 241–294, 617–706.

30. Ibid., 387.

31. On Catholic support for the Ustasha, see Tomasevich, *War and Revolution in Yugoslavia, 1941–1945: Occupation and Collaboration*, 369–372. On priests' abhorrence of Ustasha crimes, see ibid., 400.

32. Ibid., 343.

33. Ibid., 380–387.

34. Pavlowitch, *Hitler's New Disorder: The Second World War in Yugoslavia*, 32.

35. Walter Manoschek, *"Serbien ist judenfrei": Militärische Besatzungspolitik und Judenvernichtung in Serbien 1941/42* (Munich: Oldenbourg, 1995), 49; Schmider, *Partisanenkrieg in Jugoslawien 1941–1944*, 594.

36. Manoschek, *"Serbien ist judenfrei,"* 28; Schmider, *Partisanenkrieg in Jugoslawien 1941–1944*, 573; BA-MA, RW 40/2. Militärbefehlshaber Serbien, 5/1/41, 5/4/41. Unterstellung. All further archival references are BA-MA unless otherwise stated. On Turner, see in particular Christopher R. Browning, "Harald Turner und die Militärverwaltung in Serbien 1941–1942," *Verwaltung contra Menschenführung im*

Staat Hitlers, ed. Dieter Rebentisch and Karl Topper (Göttingen: Vandenhoek & Ruprecht, 1986), 351–373

37. Walter Manoschek, "The Extermination of the Jews in Serbia," in *National Socialist Extermination Policies: Contemporary German Perspectives and Controversies,* ed. Ulrich Herbert (Oxford: Berghahn, 2000), 167.

38. For an overview of the general structure of the German occupation in Serbia and the individuals who headed it, see Schmider, *Partisanenkrieg in Jugoslawien 1941–1944,* 573–575, 590–608.

39. Georg Tessin, *Verbände und Truppen der Deutschen Wehrmacht und Waffen-SS im Zweiten Weltkrieg 1939–1945* (Osnabrück: Biblio Verlag, 1972–1997), 6:193, 272; 12:149, 188; Richard Germann, "'Österreichische' Soldaten in Ost- und Südosteuropa 1941–1945: Deutsche Krieger—Nationalsozialistische Verbrecher—Österreichische Opfer?" (PhD thesis, University of Vienna, 2006), 120–122.

40. Albert Seaton, *The German Army 1933–1945* (London: Weidenfeld and Nicolson, 1982), 159–160; Bernhard R. Kroener, "The Manpower Resources of the Third Reich in the Area of Conflict between Wehrmacht, Bureaucracy, and War Economy, 1939–1942," in *Germany and the Second World War, Volume 5. Organization and Mobilization of the German Sphere of Power. Part 1: Wartime Administration, Economy, and Manpower Resources 1939–1941,* Bernhard R. Kroener et al. (Oxford: Clarendon, 2000), 810–816, 964–1000; Germann, "'Österreichische' Soldaten in Ost- und Südosteuropa 1941–1945: Deutsche Krieger—Nationalsozialistische Verbrecher—Österreichische Opfer?," 120–122.

41. Schmider, "Der jugoslawische Kriegsschauplatz," 1013.

42. RW 40/2. Kriegstagebuch, 5/11, 5/16 and 5/20/41.

43. Charles D. Melson, "German Counter-Insurgency Revisited," *Journal of Slavic Military Studies* 24 (2011): 124–125.

44. Manoschek, "The Extermination of the Jews in Serbia," 164.

45. Germann, "'Österreichische' Soldaten in Ost- und Südosteuropa 1941–1945: Deutsche Krieger—Nationalsozialistische Verbrecher—Österreichische Opfer?," 120–122.

46. In this and later chapters, the term *insurgent* is used to denote the Germans' Partisan *and* Chetnik opponents combined. For an introduction to the 1941 Serbian uprising and the German response, see Pavlowitch, *Hitler's New Disorder: The Second World War in Yugoslavia,* 49–72. For greater depth, see Walter R. Roberts, *Tito, Mihailović and the Allies, 1941–1945* (New Brunswick, NJ: Rutgers University Press, 1973), chaps. 1, 2; Milazzo, *The Chetni Movement and the Yugoslav Resistance,* chaps. 2, 3; Jozo Tomasevich, *War and Revolution in Yugoslavia, 1941–1945: The Chetniks* (Stanford, CA: Stanford University Press, 1975), chap. 5; Milovan Djilas, *Wartime: With Tito and the Partisans* (London: Martin Secker and Warburg, 1977), 3–121; Wheeler, "Pariahs to Partisans to Power: The Communist Party of Yugoslavia," 123–144; Schmider, *Partisanenkrieg in Jugoslawien 1941–1944,* chap. 3; Hoare, *Genocide and Resistance in Hitler's Bosnia: The Partisans and the Chetniks 1941–1943,* chaps. 1, 2; Geoffrey Swain, *Tito: A Biography* (London: I. B. Tauris, 2011), 33–41.

5. ISLANDS IN AN INSURGENT SEA

1. See Appendix A.

2. Georg Tessin, *Verbände und Truppen der Deutschen Wehrmacht und Waffen-SS im Zweiten Weltkrieg 1939–1945* (Osnabrück: Biblio Verlag, 1972–1997), 6:193, 12:149, 202, 222.

3. MFB4/72350, 20294/3, 1229–1230. 704. Inf.-Div. Ia, 6/13/41. Betr.: Personelle und materielle Ausstattung der Division, p. 3; MFB4/72350, 20294/3, 1241. 704. Inf.-Div. Ib/Ic, 6/13/41. Gesundheitszustands-Meldung nach dem Stande vom 10. Juni 1941.

4. MFB4/72350, 20294/3, 1317–1318. 704. Inf.-Div. Ic, 5/29/41. Betr.: Stimmungsberichte, p. 1.

5. Ibid., p. 2.

6. MFB4/72350, 20294/3, 1279. 704. Inf.-Div. Ia, 6/5/41. Divisionsbefehl, p. 1.

7. Ibid.

8. RW 40/2. Befehlshaber Serbien Ic. Tätigkeitsbericht, 5/25–6/8/41.

9. RW 40/2. Befehlshaber Serbien Ic. Tätigkeitsbericht, 4/24–5/24/41, p. 2.

10. For the 704th see MFB4/72350, 20294/3, 1317–1318. 704. Inf.-Div. Ia, 5/29/41. Betr.: Stimmungsberichte, p. 2.

11. MFB4/72350, 20294/3, 1248–1249. OKH Hauptquartier, 4/21/41. Merkblatt über Plünderung und Beutemachen zu Belehrungszwecken.

12. MFB4/72350, 20294/3, 1271–1272. 704. Inf.-Div. Ia, 6/6/41. Betr.: Ausbildung, p. 2.

13. The German army was not uniformly chivalrous during the 1940 campaign. See Raffael Scheck, *Hitler's African Victims: The German Army Massacres of French Black Soldiers in 1940* (New York: Cambridge University Press, 2006).

14. On the role national and regional "initiatives" across Nazi-occupied Europe played in the emergence of the Final Solution, see Ulrich Herbert, ed., *National Socialist Extermination Policies: Contemporary German Perspectives and Controversies* (Oxford: Berg, 2000).

15. Walter Manoschek, *"Serbien ist judenfrei": Militärische Besatzungspolitik und Judenvernichtung in Serbien 1941/42* (Munich: Oldenbourg, 1995), 26.

16. Walter Manoschek, "The Extermination of the Jews in Serbia," in *National Socialist Extermination Policies: Contemporary German Perspectives and Controversies*, ed. Ulrich Herbert (Oxford: Berghahn, 2000), 165–166.

17. Ibid.

18. Manoschek, *"Serbien ist judenfrei": Militärische Besatzungspolitik und Judenvernichtung in Serbien 1941/42,* 40; Manoschek, "The Extermination of the Jews in Serbia," 165–166. On the Wehrmacht campaign against the Serbian Jews in 1941, see Manoschek, *"Serbien ist judenfrei": Militärische Besatzungspolitik und Judenvernichtung in Serbien 1941/42,* 35–49, 62–66, 91–108; Christopher R. Browning, "Harald Turner und die Militärverwaltung in Serbien 1941–1942," *Verwaltung contra Menschenführung im Staat Hitlers,* ed. Dieter Rebentisch and Karl Topper (Göttingen: Vandenhoek & Ruprecht, 1986), 351–373; Christopher R. Browning, "The Final Solution in Serbia. The Semlin Judenlager—A Case Study," *Yad Vashem Studies* 15 (1983): 55–90; Christopher R. Browning, "Wehrmacht Reprisal

Policy and the Mass Murder of Jews in Serbia," *Militärgeschichtliche Mitteilungen 33* (1983): 31–47. The best English-language overview is Manoschek, "The Extermination of the Jews in Serbia."

19. Manoschek, *"Serbien ist judenfrei": Militärische Besatzungspolitik und Judenvernichtung in Serbien 1941/42*, 39.

20. Though the Serbian government then made allowances for Sinti and Roma whose forefathers had been of fixed abode since 1850 (ibid., 39).

21. Manoschek, *"Serbien ist judenfrei": Militärische Besatzungspolitik und Judenvernichtung in Serbien 1941/42*, 26, 38, 62. On the refugees' murderous treatment later in 1941, see ibid., 62–69, 75–79.

22. MFB4/72350, 20294/3, 1305. Standortkommandantur Valjevo, 5/19/41.

23. BfZ, Sammlung Sterz. Corporal Gerhard Reichert, tenth company, 70th Infantry Regiment, 111th Infantry Division, 4/27/41. Reichert is a pseudonym; federal German data protection laws prevent the naming of individuals (a) who are still alive, (b) who died within the last thirty years, or (c) for whom no date of death or proof that they are still alive could be found, but who were born within the last 110 years. For this study, individuals for whom no date of birth could be established are also anonymized. Nor are photographs of anonymized individuals reprinted for this study.

24. RW 40-3. Befehlshaber Serbien, Kommandostab 6/27/41. Betr.: Juden in deutschen Wehrmachtsquartieren.

25. BfZ, Sammlung Sterz. Corporal Ludwig Bauer, 3. Kp. Nachsch. Btl. 563, 4/6/41. Bauer is a pseudonym.

26. MFB4/72350, 20294/3, 1295–1296. Anlage 2 zum Befehl 704. Inf.-Div. Ic, 6/2/41.

27. MFB4/72350, 20294/3, 1306–1308. 704. Inf.-Div. Ia, 6/1/41. Betr.: Heeresstreifen. Throughout this book, the term *divisional command* is taken to mean the divisional operations section. This section was subordinate to the divisional commander and would have liaised closely with him. Cases of a divisional commander directly issuing orders himself are indicated in the text.

28. MFB4/72350, 20294/3, 1202–1205. 704. Inf.-Div. Ia/Ic, 6/14/41. Divisionsbefehl, p. 2.

29. Manoschek, *"Serbien ist judenfrei": Militärische Besatzungspolitik und Judenvernichtung in Serbien 1941/42*, 31–32; Stevan K. Pavlowitch, *Hitler's New Disorder: The Second World War in Yugoslavia* (London: Hurst, 2008), 60.

30. Philip W. Blood, *Hitler's Bandit Hunters: The SS and the Nazi Occupation of Europe* (Washington, DC: Potomac Books, 2006), 76.

31. MFB4/72350, 20294/3, 1184. 704. Inf.-Div. Ia, 6/20/41. Divisionsbefehl.

32. MFB4/72350, 20294/3, 1137. IR 724 Ia, 6/21/41. Betr.: Banden- und Freischärler-Umtriebe.

33. MFB4/72350, 20294/3, 1110. Höheres Kommando LXV, 6/14/41; Charles D. Melson, "German Counter-Insurgency Revisited," *Journal of Slavic Military Studies* 24 (2011): 129–132.

34. Tim Judah, *The Serbs: History, Myth and the Destruction of Yugoslavia* (New Haven, CT: Yale University Press, 1997), 117. On the armistice arrangements of April 1941, see Jozo Tomasevich, *War and Revolution in Yugoslavia, 1941–1945: The Chetniks* (Stanford, CA: Stanford University Press, 1975), 73–74.

35. In April 1942 the Pećanac Chetniks' strength stood at 8,745 men. Tomasevich, *War and Revolution in Yugoslavia, 1941–1945: The Chetniks*, 110.

36. Ibid., 122.

37. Matteo J. Milazzo, *The Chetni Movement and the Yugoslav Resistance* (Baltimore, MD: The Johns Hopkins University Press, 1975), 14–19; Tomasevich, *War and Revolution in Yugoslavia, 1941–1945: The Chetniks*, 115–132.

38. MFB4/72350, 20294/3, 1256. Generalkommando XI Armeekorps Ia, 5/28/41. Betr.: Bewachungsaufgaben.

39. MFB4/72350, 20294/3, 1234. 704. Inf.-Div. Ib, 6/13/41. Fehlbestand-Meldung nach dem Stand vom 10. Juni 1941 für Waffen und Gerät; MFB4/72350, 20294/3, 1233. 704. Inf.-Div. Ib, 6/13/41. Munitionsbestands-Fehlmeldung nach dem Stand vom 10. Juni 1941.

40. Manoschek, *"Serbien ist judenfrei": Militärische Besatzungspolitik und Judenvernichtung in Serbien 1941/42*, 26, 30.

41. MFB4/72350, 20294/3, 1312. 704. Inf.-Div. Ia, 5/31/41. Betr.: Personal für die Aufstellung einer Tragtierstaffel.

42. MFB4/72350, 20294/3, 1185–1187. 704. Inf.-Div., 6/19/41. Betr.: Nachrichtenmittel der Division.

43. MFB4/72350, 20294/3, 1200–1201. 704. Inf.-Div. Ia, 5/31/41. Divisions-Tagesbefehl Nr. 2.

44. MFB4/72350, 20294/3, 886–888. 704. Inf.-Div. Ia, 7/21/41. Divisionsbefehl, p. 2.

45. MFB4/72350, 20294/3, 841–842. 704. Inf.-Div. Ia, 7/30/41. Divisionsbefehl, p. 2.

46. MFB4/72350, 20294/3, 1200–1201. 704. Inf.-Div. Ia, 5/31/41. Divisions-Tagesbefehl Nr. 2.

47. MFB4/72350, 20294/3, 1168–1170. 704. Inf.-Div. Ia, 6/21/41. Divisionsbefehl, p. 3.

48. MFB4/72350, 20294/3, 1183. Höheres Kommando LXV Ia, 6/20/41. Emphasis in original.

49. Ibid.

50. Geoffrey Swain, *Tito: A Biography* (London: I. B. Tauris, 2011), 27.

51. Marko Attila Hoare, *Genocide and Resistance in Hitler's Bosnia: The Partisans and the Chetniks 1941–1943* (Oxford: Oxford University Press, 2005), 42–43; Swain, *Tito: A Biography*, 15–26.

52. M. R. D. Foot, *Resistance: An Analysis of European Resistance to Nazism 1940–1945* (London: Eyre Methuen, 1976), 192. On the general beginnings of the Yugoslav Partisan movement in 1941, see Milovan Djilas, *Wartime: With Tito and the Partisans* (London: Martin Secker and Warburg, 1977), 3–58; Mark Wheeler, "Pariahs to Partisans to Power: The Communist Party of Yugoslavia," in *Resistance and Revolution in Mediterranean Europe 1939–1948*, ed. Tony Judt (London: Routledge, 1989), 128–136; Richard West, *Tito and the Rise and Fall of Yugoslavia* (London: Sinclair Stevenson, 1996), chaps. 3, 4; Schmider, *Partisanenkrieg in Jugoslawien 1941–1944*, 54–59; Hoare, *Genocide and Resistance in Hitler's Bosnia: The Partisans and the Chetniks 1941–1943*, 28–92; Swain, *Tito: A Biography*, 27–36.

53. Swain, *Tito: A Biography*, 29–30.

54. Wheeler, "Pariahs to Partisans to Power: The Communist Party of Yugoslavia," 130.

55. Marko Attila Hoare, "Whose Is the Partisan Movement? Serbs, Croats and the Legacy of a Shared Resistance," *Journal of Slavic Military Studies* 15, no. 4 (2002):

25–27; Schmider, *Partisanenkrieg in Jugoslawien 1941–1944*, 64–65; Swain, *Tito: A Biography*, 34–35.

56. Klaus Schmider, "Der jugoslawische Kriegsschauplatz," in *Das Deutsche Reich und der Zweite Weltkrieg, Band 8. Die Ostfront, 1943/44: Der Krieg im Osten und an den Nebenfronten*, Karl-Heinz Frieser et al. (Stuttgart: Deutsche Verlags-Anstalt, 2007), 1013.

57. On the Catholic Church in the NDH, see Jozo Tomasevich, *War and Revolution in Yugoslavia, 1941–1945: Occupation and Collaboration* (Stanford, CA: Stanford University Press, 2001), 372–368, 522–568.

58. Wheeler, "Pariahs to Partisans to Power: The Communist Party of Yugoslavia," 129; Judah, *The Serbs: History, Myth and the Destruction of Yugoslavia*, 126; Hoare, *Genocide and Resistance in Hitler's Bosnia: The Partisans and the Chetniks 1941–1943*, 21–22.

59. The three hundred thousand figure closely corresponds with those offered by recent scholarly research. See Hoare, *Genocide and Resistance in Hitler's Bosnia: The Partisans and the Chetniks 1941–1943*, 23–25. On the problems in accurately identifying the scale and composition of Yugoslav population losses during World War II, see Tomasevich, *War and Revolution in Yugoslavia, 1941–1945: Occupation and Collaboration*, chap. 17. On the Ustasha's campaign of persecution and killing in 1941 generally, see Tomasevich, *War and Revolution in Yugoslavia, 1941–1945: Occupation and Collaboration*, chap. 9; Hoare, *Genocide and Resistance in Hitler's Bosnia: The Partisans and the Chetniks 1941–1943*, 19–28. For an examination of the role local-level factors played in fueling the campaign, see Tomislav Dulić, *Utopias of Nation: Local Mass Killing in Bosnia and Herzegovina, 1941–42* (Uppsala: Uppsala University Press, 2005).

60. Tomasevich, *War and Revolution in Yugoslavia, 1941–1945: Occupation and Collaboration*, 85–91, 392–397; Mark Mazower, *Hitler's Empire: Nazi Rule in Occupied Europe* (London: Allen Lane, 2008), 203–204.

61. Tomasevich, *War and Revolution in Yugoslavia, 1941–1945: The Chetniks*, 132–134. On the Montenegrin case, see Milazzo, *The Chetni Movement and the Yugoslav Resistance*, 43–48; Schmider, "Der jugoslawsiche Kriegsschauplatz," 1011–1012.

62. Tomasevich, *War and Revolution in Yugoslavia, 1941–1945: Occupation and Collaboration*, 401.

63. Schmider, *Partisanenkrieg in Jugoslawien 1941–1944*, 45.

64. Hoare, *Genocide and Resistance in Hitler's Bosnia: The Partisans and the Chetniks 1941–1943*, 23.

65. Schmider, *Partisanenkrieg in Jugoslawien 1941–1944*, 49.

66. See especially Peter Broucek, ed., *Ein General im Zwielicht. Die Erinnerungen Edmund Glaises von Horstenau. Band III: Deutscher Bevollmächtiger General in Kroatien und Zeuge des Untergangs des "Tausendjährigen Reiches"* (Vienna: Böhlau, 1988).

67. Schmider, *Partisanenkrieg in Jugoslawien 1941–1944*, 46–48.

68. Dulić, *Utopias of Nation: Local Mass Killing in Bosnia and Herzegovina, 1941–42*, 283.

69. Schmider, *Partisanenkrieg in Jugoslawien 1941–1944*, 46; Ruth Bettina Birn, *Die Höheren SS- und Polizeiführer: Himmlers Vertreter im Reich und den besetzten Gebieten* (Düsseldorf: Droste, 1986), 261; Mazower, *Hitler's Empire: Nazi Rule in Occupied Europe*, 347.

70. RW 40/4. Befehlshaber Serbien Verwaltungsstab, 7/23/41. Betr.: Politische Lage in Serbien, p. 1.

71. West, *Tito and the Rise and Fall of Yugoslavia*, 110–111; Schmider, *Partisanenkrieg in Jugoslawien 1941–1944*, 57.

72. Swain, *Tito: A Biography*, 36.

73. Manoschek, *"Serbien ist judenfrei": Militärische Besatzungspolitik und Judenvernichtung in Serbien 1941/42*, 125.

74. Melissa K. Bokovoy, *Peasants and Communists: Politics and Ideology in the Yugoslav Countryside, 1941–1953* (Pittsburgh, PA: University of Pittsburgh Press, 1998), 9–10; Hoare, *Genocide and Resistance in Hitler's Bosnia: The Partisans and the Chetniks 1941–1943*, 83–92; Swain, *Tito: A Biography*, 37–40.

75. Milazzo, *The Chetni Movement and the Yugoslav Resistance*, 15; Manoschek, *"Serbien ist judenfrei": Militärische Besatzungspolitik und Judenvernichtung in Serbien 1941/42*, 115; West, *Tito and the Rise and Fall of Yugoslavia*, 110–111. For detailed treatment of the activities of the Chetnik movement in Serbia in 1941, see Milazzo, *The Chetni Movement and the Yugoslav Resistance*, chap. 2; Tomasevich, *War and Revolution in Yugoslavia, 1941–1945: The Chetniks*, chap. 5.

76. Schmider, *Partisanenkrieg in Jugoslawien 1941–1944*, 99–100.

77. Ibid., 100.

78. Tomasevich, *War and Revolution in Yugoslavia, 1941–1945: The Chetniks*, 141–142.

79. Manoschek, *"Serbien ist judenfrei": Militärische Besatzungspolitik und Judenvernichtung in Serbien 1941/42*, 116.

80. Ibid., 124.

81. Milazzo, *The Chetni Movement and the Yugoslav Resistance*, 21; Tomasevich, *War and Revolution in Yugoslavia, 1941–1945: Occupation and Collaboration*, 177–180.

82. RW 40/4. Befehlshaber Serbien Kommandostab, 8/5/41. Tätigkeitsbericht, Juli 1941, p. 1.

83. Manoschek, *"Serbien ist judenfrei": Militärische Besatzungspolitik und Judenvernichtung in Serbien 1941/42*, 124.

84. MFB4/72351, 20294/4, 439–440. Höheres Kommando LXV, 8/8/41, p. 1; RW 40/4. Befehlshaber Serbien Ia, no date. Lagebericht, 8/21–8/31/41, p. 1.

85. Stevan K. Pavlowitsch, *Yugsolavia* (London: Ernest Bevin Ltd., 1971), 127; Swain, *Tito: A Biography*, 37.

86. Tomasevich, *War and Revolution in Yugoslavia, 1941–1945: Occupation and Collaboration*, 177–180.

87. Ibid., 180–183; Schmider, *Partisanenkrieg in Jugoslawien 1941–1944*, 60–62.

88. Schmider, *Partisanenkrieg in Jugoslawien 1941–1944*, 61; Browning, "Harald Turner und die Militärverwaltung in Serbien 1941–1942," 357.

89. MFB4 72351, 20294/4, 439–440. Höheres Kommando LXV, 8/8/41, p. 2.

90. RW 40/4. Militärbefehlshaber Serbien 7/26/41. Propaganda-Abteilung "S." Lage und Tätigkeitsbericht, 6/26–7/25/41, p. 1.

91. RW 40/4. Befehlshaber Serbien Verwaltungsstab, 7/23/41. Betr.: Politische Lage in Serbien, p. 1.

92. NARA T-175, 233. Der Chef der Sicherheitspolizei und des SD Amt IV, 6/25/41, p. 3.

93. Browning, Harald Turner und die Militärverwaltung in Serbien 1941–1942," 357.

94. Hermann Frank Mayer, *Von Wien nach Kalavryta: Die blutige Spur der 117. Jäger-Division durch Serbien und Griechenland* (Mannheim: Peleus, 2001), 42.

95. RW 40/5. Befehlshaber Serbien, no date. Lagebericht, 8/21–8/31/41, p. 2.

96. Schmider, *Partisanenkrieg in Jugoslawien 1941–1944*, 59.

97. RW 40/4. Befehlshaber Serbien Ia. Kriegstagebuch, 7/24/41.

98. Ibid., 35.

99. Manoschek, "The Extermination of the Jews in Serbia," 167.

100. Manoschek, *"Serbien ist judenfrei": Militärische Besatzungspolitik und Judenvernichtung in Serbien 1941/42*, 44.

101. Ibid., 41–42.

102. Ibid., 52–53.

103. Ibid., 53–54; Schmider, *Partisanenkrieg in Jugoslawien 1941–1944*, 63.

104. Manoschek, *"Serbien ist judenfrei": Militärische Besatzungspolitik und Judenvernichtung in Serbien 1941/42*, 45. Restraint towards the general population, coupled with "demonstrative" terror against such targeted sections of it, was a tactic also practiced by many army units in the occupied Soviet Union during summer 1941. See Jürgen Förster, "Die Sicherung des Lebensraumes," in *Der Angriff auf die Sowjetunion*, Horst Boog et al. (Frankfurt am Main: Fischer, 1991), 1234–1235; Jürgen Förster, "The Relationship between Operation Barbarossa as an Ideological War of Extermination and the Final Solution," in *The Final Solution: Origins and Implementation*, ed. David Cesarani (London: Routledge, 1994), 94; Jörg Friedrich, *Das Gesetz des Krieges: Das deutsche Heer in Rußland 1941 bis 1945* (Munich: Piper, 1993), 412–444.

105. Manoschek, *"Serbien ist judenfrei": Militärische Besatzungspolitik und Judenvernichtung in Serbien 1941/42*, 46.

106. Ibid., 45.

107. MFB4/72350, 20294/3, 1044. IR 724, 7/9/41. Meldung (Fernspruch); MFB4/72350, 20294/3, 939. Abschrift. 1. Kp. / IR 724, 7/14/41. Betr.: Razzia in Guca am 7/13/41.

108. Manoschek, *"Serbien ist judenfrei": Militärische Besatzungspolitik und Judenvernichtung in Serbien 1941/42*, 48, 52.

109. MFB4/72350, 20294/0, 100. 704. Inf.-Div. Ia. Tätigkeitsbericht, 7/20/41; MFB4/72350, 20294/3, 911. IR 724 Ia, 7/19/41. Betr.: Feuerüberfall auf der Fahrt von Valjevo nach Užice auf den Wagen des General Lomtschar [*sic*]; Manoschek, *"Serbien ist judenfrei": Militärische Besatzungspolitik und Judenvernichtung in Serbien*, 52.

110. MFB4/72351, 20294/4, 357. JR 724 Ia, 8/25/41. Nachtrag zur Meldung über den Einsatz des I/IR 724 bei Gorjani am 8/17/41.

111. Manoschek, *"Serbien ist judenfrei": Militärische Besatzungspolitik und Judenvernichtung in Serbien*, 39–50; Manoschek, "The Extermination of the Jews in Serbia," 167; RW 40/4. Befehlshaber Serbien Verwaltungsstab, 7/23/41. Betr.: Politische Lage in Serbien, p. 3; RW 40/5. Höheres Kommando LXV, 8/13/41. Betr.: Bekämpfung kommunistischer Banden, p. 1.

112. MFB4/18729, 16150/6, 447–453. Höheres Kommando LXV, 10/10/41. Betr.: Jagdkommandos.

113. Manoschek, *"Serbien ist judenfrei": Militärische Besatzungspolitik und Judenvernichtung in Serbien,* 46.

114. MFB4/18729, 16150/6, 278. Befehlshaber Serbien Ia, 9/8/41. Abschrift (v. Kaisenberg); MFB4/18729, 16150/6, 330–331. Befehlshaber Serbien Ia, 9/15/41. Tagesmeldung; MFB4/18729, 16150/6, 437. Serbien Kommandostab, 9/29/41.

115. See chap. 6.

116. RW 40/4. Befehlshaber Serbien, Kriegstagebuch, 7/12/41, 7/24/41.

117. MFB4/72351, 20294/4, 644–645. Reserve-Polizei-Bataillon 64, 7/30/41. Erfahrungsbericht der 2. Kompanie über den Einsatz zur Bekämpfung von Raüberbanden. The general unreliability of the locals' reports was also commented on by LXV Corps. MFB4/72350, 20294/3, 888. Höheres Kommando LXV, 7/16/41. Betr.: Bekämpfung von Unruheherden.

118. MFB4/72351, 20294/4, 222. I/IR 724, 8/25/41. Meldung über den Einsatz des I/IR 724 vom 8/22–8/24/41 in Mokra Gora und Kaluderska Bara. The 714th Infantry Division also commented on the insurgents' effective communication system. MFB4/56147, 18861/3, 256–257. 714. Inf.-Div. Ia, 7/28/41. Geheim!

119. MFB4/72351, 20294/4, 387. Höheres Kommando LXV Ia, 8/12/41. Betr.: Straßenkontrolle.

120. RH 20–12/109. Wehrmachtbefehlshaber Südost Ia, 7/7/41.

121. MFB4/72351, 20294/4, 358. IR 724, 8/20/41. Betr.: Kommunistischer Überfall auf Guča.

122. MFB4/72351, 20294/4, 647–648. Der Führer der Waldgenossen Stefan Singer-Marcović.

123. MFB4/72351, 20294/5, 819–821. Anlage 3 zu 704. Inf.Div. Ia 407/41g, 9/12/41. Abschrift: Leutnant Klemm, 12. Kp. IR 724, 9/10/41. Bericht, p. 3.

124. MFB4/72352, 20294/6, 674–678. IR 724 Ia, 9/20/41, p. 1.

125. MFB4/72351, 20294/4, 409–411. Höheres Kommando LXV Ia, 8/13/41. Betr.: Bekämpfung kommunistischer Banden, p. 1.

126. MFB4/72351, 20294/4, 526–530. 704. Inf.-Div. Ia, 8/9/41. Betr.: Erfahrungen in der Bekämpfung kommunistischer Banden, p. 4.

127. MFB4/72353, 20294/8, 1092–1094. I/IR 724 Ia, 11/25/41. Bericht über das Unternehmen nach Ljubić am 11/23/41, p. 3.

128. Ibid.

129. For a more positive divisional report on the Serbian gendarmerie, see MFB/72352, 20294/6, 734–735. I/IR 724, 9/17/41. Meldung über den Einsatz des I/JR 724 bei Tripkova am 9/16/41.

130. RW 40/11. Major i. G. Jersak, 9/12/41. Beurteilung der mil. Lage in Serbien, p. 2. Jersak is a pseudonym.

131. BA ZStL, B 162 / 25110. Vernehmung Max Koehler, 10/18/72, p. 4. Koehler is a pseudonym.

132. For a further example, see MFB4/72350, 20294/3, 774. Major König, I/JR 724, 8/3/41. Meldung über Verlauf des Unternehmens "Viktoria."

133. MFB4/72351, 20294/4, 583–588. 714. Inf.-Div. Ia, 8/11/41. Betr.: Kosmaj-Unternehmen, pp. 3–4.

134. Ibid., p. 6.

135. MFB4/72351, 20294/4, 218–219. 12. Kp. IR 724, 8/24/41. Bericht über Unternehmen Geier am 8/23 und 8/24/41. Emphasis in original.

136. MFB4/72351, 20294/4, 179. I/JR 724, 8/27/41. Meldung über den Einsatz des I/JR 724 bei Miskovici am 8/25/41.

137. Mayer, *Von Wien nach Kalavryta: Die blutige Spur der 117. Jäger-Division durch Serbien und Griechenland*, 42.

138. MFB4/72350, 20294/3, 808–820. Befehlshaber Serbien Ia, 7/29/41. Betr.: Verbeugung und Sühnemaßnahmen bei Sabotageakten, p. 2; MFB4/72352, 20294/6, 523–525. Befehlshaber Serbien Kommandostab Ia, 9/16/41. Betr.: Aufstandsbewegung, p. 1.

139. MFB4/72351, 20294/4, 381. Anlage 3 zum Divisionsbefehl Ia/Ic 704. Inf.-Div., 8/16/41. Fortführung der V-Aktion.

140. MFB4/72351, 20294/4, 218–219. IR 734 Ia, 8/23/41. Betr.: Bericht über das Unternehmen Geier am 8/23/41.

141. MFB4/72350, 20294/3, 1042. Komp. / IR 724, 7/9/41. Bericht des 2. Zuges Ltn. Lange.

142. MFB4/72352, 20294/6, 736. 704. Inf.-Div. Ia/Ic, 9/16/41. Divisionsbefehl, p. 3.

143. MFB4/72350, 20294/0, 100. 704. Inf.-Div. Ia. Tätigkeitsbericht, 7/20/41; MFB4/72350, 20294/3, 911. IR 724 Ia, 7/19/41. Betr.: Feuerüberfall auf der Fahrt von Valjevo nach Užice auf den Wagen des General Lomtschar [*sic*]; Manoschek, *"Serbien ist judenfrei": Militärische Besatzungspolitik und Judenvernichtung in Serbien*, 46.

144. MFB4/72351, 20294/4, 357. JR 724 Ia, 8/25/41. Nachtrag zur Meldung über den Einsatz des I/IR 724 bei Gorjani am 8/17/41.

145. Ibid.

146. MFB4/72351, 20294/4, 343–348. 8/IR 750, 8/19/41. Gefechtsbericht über das Gefecht der 8/750 am 8/19/41.

147. MFB4/72351, 20294/4, 376–378. 704. Inf.-Div. Ia/Ic, 8/16/41. Divisionsbefehl.

148. MFB4/72351, 20294/4, 125. Höheres Kommando LXV Ia, 8/23/41.

149. Ibid.

150. Ibid.

151. RW 40/11. Der Wehrmachtbefehlshaber im Südosten, 9/5/41. Betr.: Niederkämpfen der serbischen Aufstandsbewegung, p. 2.

152. On accommodation between the Chetniks and the Partisans during 1941, see Milazzo, *The Chetni Movement and the Yugoslav Resistance*, 25–27; Tomasevich, *War and Revolution in Yugoslavia, 1941–1945: The Chetniks*, 132–145; Wheeler, "Pariahs to Partisans to Power: The Communist Party of Yugoslavia," 133–136; Hoare, *Genocide and Resistance in Hitler's Bosnia: The Partisans and the Chetniks 1941–1943*, 108–117.

153. See, for instance, RW 40–11, Kriegstagebuch, September 1941, entries for 9/9 and 9/17/41.

154. MFB4/72352, 20294/6, 716. 704. Inf.-Div. Ia, 9/17/41.

155. RW 40/11. Major i. G. Jersak, 9/12/41. Beurteilung der mil. Lage in Serbien, p. 2.

156. MFB4/72351, 20294/5, 1101–1104. 11/724, 9/6/41. Bericht über den Aus- und Durchbruch in Krupanj am 9/4/41, p. 4.

157. MFB4/72351, 20294/5, 1105–1111. 10/724, 9/6/41. Bericht über die Ereigniße in Krupanj während der Zeit vom 9/1–9/4/41, pp. 6–7.

158. Ibid., p. 7.

159. All three names are pseudonyms.

160. MFB4/72351, 20294/5, 1105–1111. 10/724, 9/6/41. Bericht über die Ereigniße in Krupanj während der Zeit vom 9/1–9/4/41, p. 1.

161. Ibid., p. 3.

162. MFB4/72351, 20294/5, 1101–1104. 11/724, 9/6/41. Bericht über den Aus- und Durchbruch in Krupanj am 9/4/41, p. 1.

163. Ibid.

164. Tellingly, the next sentence—"Due to the absence of the promised reinforcements, over-fatigue and lack of sleep, the men were in a nervous and overstrained state"— was crossed out in the final version of the report.

165. Volmer and Ulrich are pseudonyms.

166. MFB4/72351, 20294/5, 1105–1109. 10/724, 9/6/41. Bericht über die Ereigniße in Krupanj während der Zeit vom 9/1/-4/9/41, pp. 3–4. For the sequence of events to make sense, the reference to "02.00 on 9/3" can be assumed to mean "02.00 on 9/4."

167. MFB4/72351, 20294/5, 1105–1109. 10/724, 9/6/41. Bericht über die Ereigniße in Krupanj während der Zeit vom 9/1/-4/9/41, p. 5. Kreidel is a pseudonym.

168. MFB4/72351, 20294/5, 1101–1104. 11/724, 9/6/41. Bericht über den Aus- und Durchbruch in Krupanj am 9/4/41, p. 3.

169. Ibid.

170. MFB4/72351, 20294/5, 1101–1104. 11/724, 9/6/41. Bericht über den Aus- und Durchbruch in Krupanj am 9/4/41, p. 3.

171. MFB4/72351, 20294/5, 1105–1109. 10/724, 9/6/41. Bericht über die Ereigniße in Krupanj während der Zeit vom 9/1/-9/4/41, p. 6. Höhne and Seifert are pseudonyms.

172. MFB4/72351, 20294/5, 1101–1104. 11/724, 9/6/41. Bericht über den Aus- und Durchbruch in Krupanj am 9/4/41, p. 3.

173. Ibid., p. 4.

174. BfZ, Sammlung Sterz. Lt. Peter Geissler, Kommando Höh. Kommando z b V LXV Belgrad, 9/12/41. Geissler is a pseudonym. It is not entirely clear whether Geissler is referring to the same incident, but the date of the letter strongly suggests that he is.

175. MFB4/72351, 20294/5, 1101–1104. 11/724, 9/6/41. Bericht über den Aus- und Durchbruch in Krupanj am 9/4/41, p. 4.

176. MFB4/72351, 20294/5, 1105–1111. 10/724, 9/6/41. Bericht über die Ereigniße in Krupanj während der Zeit vom 9/1–9/4/41, p. 7.

177. Ibid.

178. NARA T-175/233. Der Chef der Sicherheitspolizei und des SD Amt IV, 9/14/41, pp. 2–4.

179. MFB4/72352, 20294/6, 695–696. Leutnant Döderlein, AA der 704. Inf.-Div., 9/19/41. Bericht, p. 2. Dollmann is a pseudonym.

180. On security troops' feeling of having been "dumped in a backwater," see Ben Shepherd, *War in the Wild East: The German Army and Soviet Partisans* (Cambridge, MA: Harvard University Press, 2004), 81.

181. See chap. 6.

6. SETTLING ACCOUNTS IN BLOOD

1. On the Central powers' 1915 offensive on the eastern front, see Holger R. Herwig, *The First World War: Germany and Austria-Hungary 1914–1918* (London: Hodder Arnold, 1997), chap. 4.

2. See Appendix A. On the Habsburg army of occupation in the Ukraine, see Mark von Hagen, *War in a European Borderland: Occupations and Occupation Plans in Galicia and Ukraine, 1914–1918* (Seattle: University of Washington Press, 2007); Wolfram Dornik, "Die Besatzung der Ukraine 1918 durch österreichisch-ungarische Truppen," in *Die Besatzung der Ukraine 1918: Historischer Kontext—Forschungsstand—Wirtschaftliche und Soziale Folgen*, ed. Wolfram Dornik and Stefan Karner (Graz: Ludwig Boltzmann-Institut, 2008), 141–182.

3. Klaus Schmider, *Partisanenkrieg in Jugoslawien 1941–1944* (Hamburg: Verlag E. S. Mittler GmbH, 2002), 64.

4. Ibid., 67–69, 594.

5. Ibid., 63–65; Geoffrey Swain, *Tito: A Biography* (London: I. B. Tauris, 2011), 36.

6. Christopher R. Browning, "Harald Turner und die Militärverwaltung in Serbien 1941–1942," in *Verwaltung contra Menschenführung im Staat Hitlers,* ed. Dieter Rebentisch and Karl Topper (Göttingen: Vandenhoek & Ruprecht, 1986), 359–360; Schmider, *Partisanenkrieg in Jugoslawien 1941–1944*, 60–61, 75–77, 102–103. Serbia Command commented on the gendarmerie's growing efficacy at the end of September. RW 40/12. Der Bevollm. Kdr. General in Serbien (Bfh. Serbien-Kdo. Stab), 10/29/41. 10–Tagesmeldung.

7. Browning, "Harald Turner und die Militärverwaltung in Serbien 1941–1942," 358.

8. Walter Manoschek, "The Extermination of the Jews in Serbia," in *National Socialist Extermination Policies: Contemporary German Perspectives and Controversies*, ed. Ulrich Herbert (Oxford: Berghahn, 2000), 170.

9. MFB4/72333, 15365/8, 650–651. BKG Serbien, 10/10/41. Betr.: Niederwerfung kommunistische Aufstandsbewegung.

10. Manoschek, "The Extermination of the Jews in Serbia," 169.

11. The main newspaper of the Yugoslav Communists. Milovan Djilas, *Wartime: With Tito and the Partisans* (London: Martin Secker and Warburg, 1977), 4.

12. Ibid., 93–94.

13. Christian Gerlach, *Kalkulierte Morde: Die deutsche Wirtschafts- und Vernichtungspolitik in Weißrußland 1941 bis 1944* (Hamburg: Hamburger Edition, 1999), 802.

14. Manoschek, "The Extermination of the Jews in Serbia," 45, 172–173; Richard Germann, "'Österreichische' Soldaten in Ost- und Südosteuropa 1941–1945: Deutsche Krieger—Nationalsozialistische Verbrecher—Österreichische Opfer?" (PhD thesis, University of Vienna, 2006), 141.

15. Walter Manoschek, *"Serbien ist judenfrei": Militarische Besatzungspolitik und Judenvernichtung in Serbien 1941/42*, 2nd ed. (Munich: Oldenbourg, 1995), 80–83.

16. Ibid., 105–106.

17. Manoschek, *"Serbien ist judenfrei": Militarische Besatzungspolitik und Judenvernichtung in Serbien 1941/42*, 96–102.

18. MFB4/72353, 20294/1, 250–251. I/IR 724, 10/27/41. Bericht über den Einsatz des I/IR 724, 10/17–10/25/41, pp. 1–2.

19. NARA T-175/2262, 18951, frame no. illegible. 717. Inf.-Div. Ia, 10/14/41. Tätigkeitsbericht, Oktober 1941.

20. Michael Zimmerman, "The National Socialist 'Solution of the Gypsy Question'," in *National Socialist Extermination Policies: Contemporary German Perspectives and Controversies,* ed. Ulrich Herbert (Oxford: Berghahn, 2000), 199.

21. Manoschek, *"Serbien ist judenfrei": Militarische Besatzungspolitik und Judenvernichtung in Serbien 1941/42,* 169–184; Manoschek, "The Extermination of the Jews in Serbia," 178–181.

22. Georg Tessin, *Verbände und Truppen der Deutschen Wehrmacht und Waffen-SS im Zweiten Weltkrieg 1939–1945* (Osnabrück: Biblio Verlag, 1972–1997), 6: 225–226, 228, 12:134, 136, 138.

23. MFB4/72332, 15365/7, 1197–1202. 342. Inf.-Div. Ia, 9/28/41. Unterkunftsübersicht.

24. Albert Seaton *The German Army 1933–45* (London: Weidenfeld and Nicolson, 1982), 159–160; Bernhard R. Kroener, "The Manpower Resources of the Third Reich in the Area of Conflict between Wehrmacht, Bureaucracy, and War Economy, 1939–1942," in *Germany and the Second World War, Volume 5. Organization and Mobilization of the German Sphere of Power. Part 1: Wartime Administration, Economy, and Manpower Resources 1939–1941*, Bernhard R. Kroener et al. (Oxford: Clarendon, 2000), 810–816, 964–1000. On the Category Fifteen divisions specifically, see ibid., 987. See also MFB4 72332, 15365/6, 436–442. 342. Inf.-Div. Ia, 9/11/41. Unterkunftsübersicht.

25. NARA T-175/233. "Der Chef der Sicherheitspolizei und des SD Amt IV, 9/27/41, pp. 7–8.

26. Schmider, *Partisanenkrieg in Jugoslawien 1941–1944,* 70.

27. MFB4/72332, 5365/7, 1022–1023. BKG Serbien Abt. Qu. Merkblatt für die wirtschaftliche Nutzung des Gebietes zwischen Save und Drina.

28. Ibid. On ethnic Germans in Yugoslavia, see Valentin Oberkirsch et al., *Die Deutschen in Syrmien, Slawonien, Kroatien und Bosnien: Geschichte einer deutschen Volksgruppe in Südosteuropa* (Stuttgart: Donauschwäbische Kulturstiftung, 1989).

29. Walter Manoschek, *"Serbien ist judenfrei": Militarische Besatzungspolitik und Judenvernichtung in Serbien 1941/42,* 61.

30. RH 24-15/3. Höheres Kommando LXV Ia, 9/18/41. Befehl für Saüuberung des Save-Bogens westlich Sabac und die Einschliessung des Cer-Gebirges.

31. Manoschek, *"Serbien ist judenfrei": Militarische Besatzungspolitik und Judenvernichtung in Serbien 1941/42,* 57–58; Schmider, *Partisanenkrieg in Jugoslawien 1941–1944,* 70.

32. NARA T-175/233. Der Chef der Sicherheitspolizei und des SD Amt IV, 9/27/41, pp. 7–8.

33. MFB4/72332, 15365/7, 1191–1193. BKG Serbien, 9/22/41, p. 1.

34. Ibid.

35. Ibid., p. 2.

36. MFB4/72332, 15365/7, 1102–1103. BKG Serbien, 9/23/41. Betr.: Gerichtliches Verfahren gegen Freischärler, p. 2.

37. MFB4/72332, 15365/7, 1098–1101. Der Gerichtsherr und Kommandeur der 342. Inf.-Div., 25/9/41. Betr.: Behandlung der Freischärler, p. 1. Emphasis in original.

38. Manoschek, *"Serbien ist judenfrei": Militarische Besatzungspolitik und Judenvernichtung in Serbien 1941/42*, 69–70.

39. MFB4/72332, 15365/7, 997. 342. Inf.-Div. Ia, 9/29/41.

40. Manoschek, *"Serbien ist judenfrei": Militarische Besatzungspolitik und Judenvernichtung in Serbien 1941/42*, 70.

41. MFB4/72332, 15365/7, 1154. BKG Serbien, 9/23/41.

42. Ibid., emphasis in original.

43. MFB4/72332, 15365/7, 1077–1078. 342. Inf.-Div. Ia, 9/27/41. Tagesmeldung, 9/26/-9/27/41.

44. Manoschek, *"Serbien ist judenfrei": Militarische Besatzungspolitik und Judenvernichtung in Serbien 1941/42*, 63–66. On the more general internment and brutal treatment of the male population of Šabac, and of the Jews of the "Kladowo Transport," see idem., 60–66, 75–79, 91–96.

45. MFB4/72332, 15365/7, 997. 342. Inf.-Div., 9/29/41.

46. MFB4/72332, 15365/7, 969–970. 342. Inf.-Div. Ia, 9/30/41. Tagesmeldung, 9/29/-9/30/41.

47. MFB4/72332, 15365/7, 1000. 9/30/41. Betr.: Kroatische Sicherung an der Drina.

48. MFB4/72332, 15365/7, 916–917. 342. Inf.-Div. Ia, 9/30/41. Betr.: 10-Tagesberichte und Monatsberichte.

49. Schmider, *Partisanenkrieg in Jugoslawien 1941–1944*, 71.

50. Ibid., 71–72.

51. MFB4/72332, 15365/7, 767. 342. Inf.-Div. Ia, 10/8/41. Einsatz-Gruppen.

52. MFB4/72332, 15365/7, 746–757. 342. Inf.-Div. Ic, no date. Gliederung und Führer der Aufständischen.

53. MFB4/72332, 15365/7, 767. 342. Inf.-Div. Ia, 10/8/41. Einsatz-Gruppen; MFB4/72333, 15365/8, 355–357. 342. Inf.-Div. Ia, 10/20/41. Betr.: 10-Tagesbericht; MFB4/72332, 15365/7, 758–763. 342. Inf.-Div. Ia, 10/8/41. Div. Befehl für den Angriff auf Feind im Cer-Gebirge.

54. MFB4/72333, 15365/8, 630–632. 342. Inf.-Div. Ia, 10/13/41. Divisionsbefehl für den 10/14/ und 10/15/41, pp. 2–3.

55. MFB4/72332, 15365/7, 758–763. 342. Inf.-Div. Ia, 10/8/41. Div. Befehl für den Angriff auf Feind im Cer-Gebirge, pp. 3-4; MFB4/72332, 15365/7, 702. Div. Gef. St., 10/10/41. Lage JR 697; MFB4/72332, 15365/7, 686. Div. Gef. St., 10/11/41. Zusammenfassung der Befehle für den 10/11/41; MFB4/72332, 15365/7, 677–678, 10/11/41. Tagesmeldung, 10/10/-10/11/41; MFB4/72332, 15365/7, 657. Div. Gef. St., 10/12/41.

56. MFB4/72333, 15365/8, 522–524. Tagesmeldung vom 10/14/-10/15/41; MFB4/72333, 15365/8, 481–488. 342. Inf.-Div. Ic, 10/17/41. Betr.: Feindnachrichten, p. 5.

57. MFB4/72333, 15365/8, 522–524. Tagesmeldung vom 10/14/-10/15/41, p. 2.

58. MFB472333, 15365/8, 481–88. 342. Inf.-Div. Ic, 10/17/41. Betr.: Feindnachrichten, p. 5.

59. MFB4/72333, 15365/8, 627–629. 342. Inf.-Div. Ia, 13/10/41. Divisionsbefehl für Unternehmen auf Krupanj.

60. MFB4 72333, 15365/8, 402–405. 342. Inf.-Div. Ia, 10/19/41. Div. Befehl für Unternehmen Krupanj, p. 2.

61. MFB4/72333, 15365/8, 348. 342. Inf.-Div. Ia, 10/21/41. Abendmeldung; MFB4/72333, 15365/8, 33-37. 342. Inf.-Div. Ia, 10/30/41. Betr.: 10-Tagesbericht vom 10/20/-10/30/41, p. 1.

62. MFB4/72333, 15365/8, 630-632. 342. Inf.-Div. Ia, 10/13/41. Divisionsbefehl für den 10/14/ und 10/15/41, pp. 2-3.

63. MFB4/72333, 15365/8, 671. 342. Inf.-Div. Ia, 10/12/41.

64. MFB4/72333, 15365/8, 663-666. 342. Inf.-Div. Ia, 10/12/41. Divisionsbefehl für Fortsetzung des Angriffs auf Feind in Cer-Gebirge, p. 3.

65. MFB4/72333, 15365/8, 33-37. 342. Inf.-Div. Ia, 10/30/41. Betr.: 10-Tagesbericht vom 10/20/-10/30/41, p. 5.

66. MFB4/72333, 15365/8, 355-357. 342. Inf.-Div. Ia, 10/20/41. Betr.: 10-Tagesbericht, p. 3.

67. On the ambiguities involved in interpreting numbers of "insurgent" dead in Wehrmacht counterinsurgency operations, see Lutz Klinkhammer, "Der Partisanenkrieg der Wehrmacht 1941-1944," in *Die Wehrmacht: Mythos und Realität*, ed. Rolf-Dieter Müller and Hans-Erich Volkmann (Munich: Oldenbourg, 1999), 819-831; Schmider, *Partisanenkrieg in Jugoslawien 1941-1944*, 253-254; Christian Hartmann, "Verbrecherischer Krieg—verbrecherische Wehrmacht? Überlegungen zur Struktur des deutschen Ostheeres 1941-1944," *Vierteljahreshefte für Zeitgeschichte* 52 (2004): 24-30; Ben Shepherd, *War in the Wild East: The German Army and Soviet Partisans* (Cambridge, MA: Harvard University Press, 2004), 240-242; Peter Lieb, *Konventioneller Krieg oder NS-Weltanschauungskrieg? Kriegführung und Partisanenbekämpfung in Frankreich 1943/44* (Munich: Oldenbourg, 2006), 567-573. See also Introduction.

68. MFB4/72333, 15365/8, 522-524. Tagesmeldung vom 10/14/-10/15/41, pp. 2-3.

69. MFB4/72334, 15365/9, 188. 342. Inf.-Div. Ia, 11/11/41. Betr.: Meldungen über Erschießungen, Festnahmen und Sühnemaßnahmen.

70. Ibid.

71. Manoschek, *"Serbien ist judenfrei": Militarische Besatzungspolitik und Judenvernichtung in Serbien 1941/42*, 77; Schmider, *Partisanenkrieg in Jugoslawien 1941-1944*, 71-72.

72. MFB4/72333, 15365/8, 522-524. Tagesmeldung vom 10/14/-10/15/41, p. 1.

73. Ibid.

74. MFB4/72333, 15365/8, 481-488. 342. Inf.-Div. Ic, 10/17/41. Betr.: Feindnachrichten, p. 2.

75. MFB4/72332, 15365/7, 1028-1029. 342. Inf.-Div. Ia, 9/27/41. Tagesmeldung, 9/27-9/28/; MFB4/72332, 15365/7, 705. 342. Inf.-Div. Ia, 10/10/41.

76. MFB4/72334, 15365/9, 179-180. 342. Inf.-Div. Ia, 11/12/41. Betr.: Einsatzwert der Truppe, pp. 1-2.

77. MFB4/72332, 15365/7, 1025. 342. Inf.-Div. Ia, 9/28/41. Betr.: Panzer-Einsatz Sabac; MFB4/72334, 15365/9, 115-116. 342. Inf.-Div. Ia (offen), 11/16/41. Betr.: Erfahrungsbericht der I/Pz. Rgt. 202.

78. MFB4/72332, 15365/7, 1046-1047. 342. Inf.-Div. Ia, 9/27/41, Anlage 2. Kampfanweisung; MFB4/72332, 15365/7, 952. 342. Inf.-Div. Ia, 9/30/41. Betr.: Tagesziel für

9/30/41; MFB4/72333, 15365/8, 572. 342. Inf.-Div. Ia, 10/14/41. Befehl für die Div.; MFB4/72333, 15365/8, 566–571. Der Gerichtsherr und Kommandeur der 342. Inf.-Div., 10/14/41. Betr.: Freischärler und ähnlichen Verbrechen; MFB4/72332, 15365/7, 891. 342. Inf.-Div. Ia (offen), 10/2/41.

79. BA ZStL, B 162 / 29141. Amtsgericht Bremen, 4/7/71. Vernehmung, Oberstleutnant Bernd P., p. 3; idem., 10. Kommissariat, Andernach, 12/16/71. Vernehmung, Gunther S.

80. MFB4/72332, 15365/7, 905–907. 342. Inf.-Div. Ib, 10/2/41. Wirtschaftliche Ausnützung des Gebietes in Save-Drina Bogen, p. 2.

81. Ibid., p. 1.

82. MFB4/72333, 15365/8, 481–488, 342. Inf.-Div. Ic, 10/17/41. Betr.: Feindnachrichten, p. 4.

83. MFB4/72332, 15365/7, 1028–1029. 342. Inf.-Div. Ia, 9/27/41. Tagesmeldung 9//27–9/28, p. 1; MFB4/72332, 969–70. 342. Inf.-Div. Ia, 9/30/41. Tagesmeldung 9/29/-9/30/41, p. 1; MFB4 72332, 825. 342. Inf.-Div. Ia, 10/5/41. Befehl für den 10/6/41.

84. MFB4/72333, 15365/8, 481–488. 342. Inf.-Div. Ic, 10/17/41. Betr.: Feindnachrichten, p. 4.

85. Ibid.

86. MFB4/72334, 15365/9, 148–158. 342. Inf.-Div. Kommandeur, 11/14/41.

87. Ibid.

88. Imperial War Museum (IWM), Nuremberg Hostage Trial (NHT), Document 907 (translation). Plenipotentiary Commanding General in Serbia, 10/25/41; Schmider, *Partisanenkrieg in Jugoslawien 1941–1944*, 73–74.

89. MFB4/72335, 15365/11, 756–757. 342. Inf.-Div. Ia / op. Nr. 951/41 geh. vom 12/14/41. Anlage 2. Befriedung.

90. MFB4/72335, 15365/11, 729–730. 342. Inf.-Div. Ia, 12/15/41. Betr.: Unternehmen Mihailović.

91. MFB4/72335, 15365/11, 855. 342. Inf.-Div. Ia, 12/9/41. Verluste und Beute während Unternehmen Mihailović, 12/5/-12/7/41.

92. MFB4/72335, 15365/11, 550–551. Panzerjägerabteilung 342. Ia, 12/22/41. Betr.: Fernspruch Nr. 32 vom 12/17/41. Erfahrungsbericht über Unternehmen Užice und Mihailović, p. 2.

93. MFB4/72335, 15365/11, 523–524. 342. Inf.-Div. Ia Nr. 927/41 geh. vom 11/27/41. Anweisung für die Zusammenarbeit zwischen militärischen Führer und Betriebsführer.

94. MFB4/72335, 15365/11, 496. 342. Inf.-Div. Ia, 12/30/41. Betr.: Überfall auf Lt. Friedrich 2/699. Friedrich is a pseudonym.

95. RW 40/14. Befehlshaber Serbien. Kriegstagebuch, 12/11/41.

96. See Appendix A.

97. See Appendix A.

98. See Appendix A.

99. See Appendix A.

100. Borowski served on the eastern front between August 1914 and January 1915, spent seven months in Germany with his regiment's replacement section after being wounded, then served with the German military administration in Warsaw between

September 1915 and January 1917, and on the western front between February and November 1918. His location during 1917 is unclear from the sources that could be accessed for this study. See Appendix A.

101. See Appendix A.
102. See AppendixA.
103. From the sources that could be accessed for this study it is not entirely clear whether Hinghofer was stationed in the East between July and November 1918, or whether he was transferred to the Italian front or elsewhere.
104. Wolfram Dornik, "Die Besatzung der Ukraine 1918 durch österreichisch-ungarische Truppen," 179–180.
105. Von Hagen, *War in a European Borderland: Occupations and Occupation Plans in Galicia and Ukraine, 1914–1918*, 89; Dornik, "Die Besatzung der Ukraine 1918 durch österreichisch-ungarische Truppen," 179–180. On the Austrian occupation of the Ukraine, see also Tamara Scheer, *Zwischen Front und Heimat: Österreich-Ungarns Militärverwaltungen im Ersten Weltkrieg* (Frankfurt am Main: Peter Lang, 2007), 49–54.
106. Von Hagen, *War in a European Borderland: Occupations and Occupation Plans in Galicia and Ukraine, 1914–1918*, 96–98.
107. RH7, file on Paul Hoffmann. Der Wehrmachtbefehlshaber Ukraine, 9/13/43.
108. See Appendix A.
109. Walter Manoschek and Hans Safrian, "717./117. Inf.-Div.: Eine Infanterie-Division auf dem Balkan," in *Vernichtungskrieg: Verbrechen der Wehrmacht, 1941 bis 1944*, ed. Hannes Heer and Klaus Naumann (Hamburg: Hamburger Edition, 1995)," 362–363; Hermann Frank Meyer, *Von Wien nach Kalavryta: Die blutige Spur der 117. Jäger-Division durch Serbien und Griechenland* (Mannheim: Peleus, 2002), 44–49; Germann, "'Österreichische' Soldaten in Ost- und Südosteuropa 1941—1945: Deutsche Krieger—Nationalsozialistische Verbrecher—Österreichische Opfer?," 145–149. Grisly but necessary distinctions need making between the 717th's conduct on these occasions, and that of the 342d, if the exceptional nature of the 342d's brutality is to be properly understood. At Kragujevac, the third battalion of the 749th Infantry Regiment (717th Infantry Division) and the first battalion of the 724th Infantry Regiment (704th Infantry Division) shot twenty-three hundred civilians in reprisal for ten dead and twenty-six wounded Wehrmacht soldiers. This reprisal was in line with General Boehme's 1:100 and 1:50 ratios.

Some of the killings at Kraljevo were not in response to particular attacks in which Wehrmacht soldiers had been killed or wounded. On October 15, soldiers of the 717th shot three hundred civilians simply because they had been fired upon from houses in the town. On October 16 the town commandant (not directly subordinate to the 717th) ordered that the *families* of hostages, as well as hostages themselves, be killed and their homes destroyed.

However, at the close of the operation, the 717th recorded losing fifty dead and ninety-two wounded to enemy action during its course. Both the "grand total" of enemy dead the division recorded (5,037) as well as of reprisal victims specifically (forty-three hundred), were actually far lower than the ninety-six hundred hostages who would have been shot had Boehme's reprisal ratios been followed. The shortfall was almost certainly due not to "restraint," but to lack of sufficient victims. Dreadful as this conduct clearly was, however, it remained within the boundaries set by Boehme. Manoschek, *"Serbien ist judenfrei"*: *Militarische Besatzungspolitik und Judenvernichtung in Serbien 1941/42*, chap. 4.

110. RH7, files on Walter Hinghofer, Paul Hoffmann and Erich Stahl; MSg 109, file on Heinrich Borowski.

111. Germann, "'Österreichische' Soldaten in Ost- und Südosteuropa 1941–1945: Deutsche Krieger—Nationalsozialistische Verbrecher—Österreichische Opfer?," 129–133.

112. The 342d's divisional files are not sufficiently detailed to enable a meaningful comparison of the different levels of brutality, in terms of numbers of "insurgents" reported killed, displayed by each of the division's three subordinate regiments.

113. Manoschek, *"Serbien ist judenfrei"*: *Militarische Besatzungspolitik und Judenvernichtung in Serbien 1941/42* 48–49.

114. Ibid., 161.

115. Theo J. Schulte makes a similar point regarding officers in German-occupied Russia. Theo J. Schulte, The *German Army and Nazi Policies in Occupied Russia* (Oxford: Berg, 1989), 290.

116. RW 40/12. Der Bevollm. Kdr. General in Serbien (Bfh. Serbien-Kdo. Stab), 10/29/41. 10-Tagesmeldung, p. 1.

117. NARA T-175/234. Der Chef der Sicherheitspolizei und des SD Amt IV, 10/21/41, pp. 1, 5–7.

118. On the course of Operation Užice, see Schmider, *Partisanenkrieg in Jugoslawien 1941–1944*, 78–80.

119. IWM, NHT Document 1051 (translation). 342. Inf.-Div. Ia, 11/24/41. Divisional Order for the Annihilation of the Enemy in the area of Užice.

120. Matteo J. Milazzo, *The Chetni Movement and the Yugoslav Resistance* (Baltimore, MD: The Johns Hopkins University Press, 1975), 31.

121. Jozo Tomasevich, *War and Revolution in Yugoslavia, 1941–1945: The Chetniks* (Stanford, CA: Stanford University Press, 1975), 145; Tim Judah, *The Serbs: History, Myth and the Destruction of Yugoslavia* (New Haven, CT: Yale University Press, 1997), 118; Schmider, *Partisanenkrieg in Jugoslawien 1941–1944*, 74–75.

122. Tomasevich, *War and Revolution in Yugoslavia, 1941–1945: The Chetniks*, 145; Schmider, *Partisanenkrieg in Jugoslawien 1941–1944*, 102.

123. Djilas, *Wartime: With Tito and the Partisans*, 94.

124. Manoschek, *"Serbien ist judenfrei"*: *Militarische Besatzungspolitik und Judenvernichtung in Serbien 1941/42*, 117–122, 126–131.

125. On plans for "Great Serbia," see Tomasevich, *War and Revolution in Yugoslavia, 1941–1945: The Chetniks*, 167–175; Marko Attila Hoare, *Genocide and Resistance in Hitler's Bosnia: The Partisans and the Chetniks 1941–1943* (Oxford: Oxford University Press, 2005), 144.

126. Melissa K. Bokovoy, *Peasants and Communists: Politics and Ideology in the Yugoslav Countryside, 1941–1953* (Pittsburgh, PA: University of Pittsburgh Press, 1998), 9–10; Swain, *Tito: A Biography*, 38.

127. Mark Wheeler, "Pariahs to Partisans to Power: The Communist Party of Yugoslavia," in *Resistance and Revolution in Mediterranean Europe 1939–1948*, ed. Tony Judt (London: Routledge, 1989), 134–135.

128. Milazzo, *The Chetni Movement and the Yugoslav Resistance*, 40–41; Schmider, *Partisanenkrieg in Jugoslawien 1941–1944*, 82.

129. Milazzo, *The Chetni Movement and the Yugoslav Resistance*, 36–38.

130. Ibid., 36.

131. Ibid., 41; Tomasevich, *War and Revolution in Yugoslavia, 1941–1945: The Chetniks*, 155; Wheeler, "Pariahs to Partisans to Power: The Communist Party of Yugoslavia," 136. On contact between Mihailović and the Axis during autumn 1941, see also Tomasevich, *War and Revolution in Yugoslavia, 1941–1945: The Chetniks*, 148–150.

132. Schmider, *Partisanenkrieg in Jugoslawien 1941–1944*, 102–103.

133. Ibid., 80.

134. Ibid., 78, 80.

135. Swain, *Tito: A Biography*, 40.

136. Schmider, *Partisanenkrieg in Jugoslawien 1941–1944*, 103.

137. Ibid., 81–83. Bader's actual title was *Kommandierende General und Befehlshaber in Serbien*, as distinct from Danckelmann's *Befehlshaber in Serbien*. The title reflects the fact that Bader, unlike Danckelmann, also retained command of the "seven-hundred-number" occupation divisions under LXV Corps, as well as holding theatre command over the 342d and 113th Infantry Divisions. However, as Bader's new title translates into English as the unwieldy "Commanding General and Commander in Serbia," this work instead refers to him as "Commander in Serbia."

138. Swain, *Tito: A Biography*, 40.

7. STANDING DIVIDED

1. On the Partisan movement in 1942, see Milovan Djilas, *Wartime: With Tito and the Partisans* (London: Martin Secker and Warburg, 1977), 101–212; Richard West, *Tito and the Rise and Fall of Yugoslavia* (London: Sinclair Stevenson, 1996), chaps. 6, 7; Marko Attila Hoare, *Genocide and Resistance in Hitler's Bosnia: The Partisans and the Chetniks 1941–1943* (Oxford: Oxford University Press, 2005), chaps. 3–5; Geoffrey Swain, *Tito: A Biography* (London: I. B. Tauris, 2011), 41–55.

2. Marko Attila Hoare, "Whose Is the Partisan Movement? Serbs, Croats and the Legacy of a Shared Resistance," *Journal of Slavic Military Studies* 15, 4 (2002): 27–28; Hoare, *Genocide and Resistance in Hitler's Bosnia: The Partisans and the Chetniks 1941–1943*, 242.

3. Hoare, *Genocide and Resistance in Hitler's Bosnia: The Partisans and the Chetniks 1941–1943*, 46.

4. Ibid., 47.

5. Ibid., 43–44.

6. Ibid. 53–62.

7. Ibid., 34–39.

8. Ibid., 98.

9. Hoare, "Whose Is the Partisan Movement? Serbs, Croats and the Legacy of a Shared Resistance," 26–28.

10. Hoare, *Genocide and Resistance in Hitler's Bosnia: The Partisans and the Chetniks 1941–1943*, 98.

11. Swain, *Tito: A Biography*, 42.

12. Tomislav Dulić, *Utopias of Nation: Local Mass Killing in Bosnia and Herzegovina, 1941–42* (Uppsala: Uppsala University Library, 2005) 117.

13. On the collapse of Partisan–Chetnik cooperation in eastern Bosnia, see Hoare, *Genocide and Resistance in Hitler's Bosnia: The Partisans and the Chetniks 1941–1943*, 119–126.

14. Dulić, *Utopias of Nation: Local Mass Killing in Bosnia and Herzegovina, 1941–42*, 117.

15. Matteo J. Milazzo, *The Chetni Movement and the Yugoslav Resistance* (Baltimore, MD: The Johns Hopkins University Press, 1975), 50; Klaus Schmider, "Der jugoslawische Kriegsschauplatz," in *Das Deutsche Reich und der Zweite Weltkrieg, Band 8. Die Ostfront, 1943/44: Der Krieg im Osten und an den Nebenfronten*, Karl-Heinz Frieser et al. (Stuttgart: Deutsche Verlags-Anstalt, 2007), 1012; Mark Mazower, *Hitler's Empire: Nazi Rule in Occupied Europe* (London: Allen Lane, 2008), 345.

16. Mark Wheeler, "Pariahs to Partisans to power: the Communist Party of Yugoslavia," in *Resistance and Revolution in Mediterranean Europe 1939–1948*, ed. Tony Judt (London: Routledge, 1989), 561.

17. Hoare, *Genocide and Resistance in Hitler's Bosnia: The Partisans and the Chetniks 1941–1943*, 96–97; Tim Judah, *The Serbs: History, Myth and the Destruction of Yugoslavia* (New Haven, CT: Yale University Press, 1997), 98.

18. Milazzo, *The Chetni Movement and the Yugoslav Resistance*, 48–55.

19. Dulić, *Utopias of Nation: Local Mass Killing in Bosnia and Herzegovina, 1941–42*, 180–186.

20. Ibid., 120; Hoare, *Genocide and Resistance in Hitler's Bosnia: The Partisans and the Chetniks 1941–1943*, 142–162.

21. West, *Tito and the Rise and Fall of Yugoslavia*, 118; Dulić, *Utopias of Nation: Local Mass Killing in Bosnia and Herzegovina, 1941–42*, 112.

22. Hoare, *Genocide and Resistance in Hitler's Bosnia: The Partisans and the Chetniks 1941–1943*, 176, 278.

23. Ibid., 170–171.

24. Melissa K. Bokovoy, *Peasants and Communists: Politics and Ideology in the Yugoslav Countryside, 1941–1953* (Pittsburgh, PA: University of Pittsburgh Press, 1998), 11–14; Swain, *Tito: A Biography*, 41–43.

25. Bokovoy, *Peasants and Communists: Politics and Ideology in the Yugoslav Countryside, 1941–1953*, 15–16; Hoare, *Genocide and Resistance in Hitler's Bosnia: The Partisans and the Chetniks 1941–1943*, 91; Swain, *Tito: A Biography*, 43–46.

26. Bokovoy, *Peasants and Communists: Politics and Ideology in the Yugoslav Countryside, 1941–1953*, 15–17.

27. Swain, *Tito: A Biography*, 44.

28. Jozo Tomasevich, *War and Revolution in Yugoslavia, 1941–1945: The Chetniks* (Stanford, CA: Stanford University Press, 1975), 183; Hoare, *Genocide and Resistance in Hitler's Bosnia: The Partisans and the Chetniks 1941–1943*, 291–293.

29. Hoare, *Genocide and Resistance in Hitler's Bosnia: The Partisans and the Chetniks 1941–1943*, 309.

30. Stevan K. Pavlowitch, *Yugoslavia* (London: Ernest Bevin, 1971), 131; Tomasevich, *War and Revolution in Yugoslavia, 1941–1945: The Chetniks*, 183.

31. Tomasevich, *War and Revolution in Yugoslavia, 1941–1945: The Chetniks*, 169, 177, 188–195.

32. Ibid., 230.

33. Klaus Schmider, *Partisanenkrieg in Jugoslawien 1941–1944* (Hamburg: E. S. Mittler, 2002), 442–448.

34. In November 1941 the Croatian Foreign Ministry estimated that the Italians had two hundred thousand troops stationed in Zones II and III. Jozo Tomasevich, *War and Revolution in Yugoslavia, 1941–1945: Occupation and Collaboration* (Stanford, CA: Stanford University Press, 2001), 249.

35. Schmider, *Partisanenkrieg in Jugoslawien 1941–1944*, 36.

36. MacGregor Knox, *Hitler's Italian Allies: Royal Armed Forces, Fascist Regime, and the War of 1940–1943* (Cambridge: Cambridge University Press, 2000), 23–67; Richard L. Dinardo, *Germany and the Axis Powers: From Coalition to Collapse* (Lawrence: University Press of Kansas, 2005), 28–36; Mazower, *Hitler's Empire: Nazi Rule in Occupied Europe*, 341. On German–Italian relations in the Balkans during World War II, see also Jonathan Steinberg, *All or Nothing: The Axis and the Holocaust 1941–1943* (London: Routledge, 1990).

37. MFB4 56156, 250–1. 718. Inf.-Div. Gef. St., 1/23/42. Lagebericht, 1/23/42 abends; RW 40–16; Luftwaffenverbindungsoffizier, 1/23/42. Betr.: Einsatz der ital. Bomber. Bombenangriff auf eigene Truppe bei Loznica.

38. BfZ, Sammlung Sterz. Lt. Peter Geissler, Kommando Höh. Kommando z b V LXV Belgrad, 9/8/41.

39. Schmider, *Partisanenkrieg in Jugoslawien 1941–1944*, 590, 605.

40. Ibid., 343–345; Schmider, "Der jugoslawische Kriegsschauplatz," 1075; Mazower, *Hitler's Empire: Nazi Rule in Occupied Europe*, 349–353.

41. Schmider, *Partisanenkrieg in Jugoslawien 1941–1944*, 341, 346.

42. Tomasevich, *War and Revolution in Yugoslavia, 1941–1945: Occupation and Collaboration*, 135.

43. Mazower, *Hitler's Empire: Nazi Rule in Occupied Europe*, 349–353. For more detail on Italian policy in the NDH, see Tomasevich, *War and Revolution in Yugoslavia, 1941–1945: Occupation and Collaboration*, 241–268; Schmider, *Partisanenkrieg in Jugoslawien 1941–1944*, 343–350.

44. Milazzo, *The Chetni Movement and the Yugoslav Resistance*, 50.

45. Stevan K. Pavlowitch, *Hitler's New Disorder: The Second World War in Yugoslavia* (London: Hurst, 2008), 135.

46. Djilas, *Wartime: With Tito and the Partisans*, 198.

47. Dulić, *Utopias of Nation: Local Mass Killing in Bosnia and Herzegovina, 1941–42*, 285–286; Hoare, *Genocide and Resistance in Hitler's Bosnia: The Partisans and the Chetniks 1941–1943*, 294.

48. On the build-up of Partisan support during 1942, see West, *Tito and the Rise and Fall of Yugoslavia*, chaps. 7–9; Hoare, *Genocide and Resistance in Hitler's Bosnia: The Partisans and the Chetniks 1941–1943*, 174–192, 268–279; Swain, *Tito: A Biography*, 41–55.

49. On NDH-Italian-German relations and the state of the NDH economy, see Tomasevich, *War and Revolution in Yugoslavia, 1941–1945: Occupation and Collaboration*, 241–294, 617–706. The brief account that follows is based on these sections.

50. For a highly critical study of Italian occupation policy in Axis Europe, see Davide Rodogno, *Fascism's European Empire: Italian Occupation during the Second World War* (Cambridge: Cambridge University Press, 2006).

51. Schmider, *Partisanenkrieg in Jugoslawien 1941–1944*, 200.

52. Tomasevich, *War and Revolution in Yugoslavia, 1941–1945: Occupation and Collaboration*, 355.

53. According to Jozo Tomasevich, information on the size of the Croatian armed forces is "far from satisfactory." The most reliable figures, from autumn 1943, give a total of 262,326 men. Tomasevich, *War and Revolution in Yugoslavia, 1941–1945: Occupation and Collaboration*, 423.

54. Ibid., 352–353.

55. The plural term for the Ustasha's members.

56. Tomasevich, *War and Revolution in Yugoslavia, 1941–1945: Occupation and Collaboration*, 424–434.

57. Schmider, *Partisanenkrieg in Jugoslawien 1941–1944*, 109–110.

58. Ibid., 257.

59. There is debate over the precise relationship between Mihailović and Dangić, and how far the two men's agendas differed or converged. See Dulić, *Utopias of Nation: Local Mass Killing in Bosnia and Herzegovina, 1941–42*, 189–192. On the "Dangić Affair," see also Milazzo, *The Chetni Movement and the Yugoslav Resistance*, 62–73; Tomasevich, *War and Revolution in Yugoslavia, 1941–1945: The Chetniks*, 160, 206–209; Schmider, *Partisanenkrieg in Jugoslawien 1941–1944*, 95–98, 104–105, 110, 114–117, 121, 125; Hoare, *Genocide and Resistance in Hitler's Bosnia: The Partisans and the Chetniks 1941–1943*, 111, 125, 154–156, 174.

60. Schmider, *Partisanenkrieg in Jugoslawien 1941–1944*, 135–136.

61. Ibid., 597.

62. Charles D. Melson, "German Counter-Insurgency Revisited," *Journal of Slavic Military Studies* 24 (2011): 137–146.

63. Jonathan Gumz, "Wehrmacht Perceptions of Mass Violence in Croatia, 1941–1942," *Historical Journal* 44 (2001): 1030.

64. Gumz, "Wehrmacht Perceptions of Mass Violence in Croatia, 1941–1942."

8. GLIMMERS OF SANITY

1. Georg Tessin, *Verbände und Truppen der Deutschen Wehrmacht und Waffen-SS im Zweiten Weltkrieg 1939–1945* (Osnabrück: Biblio Verlag, 1972–1997), 6: 272, 12:75–76,

188, 230, 254. An artillery section (*Artillerie-Abteilung*) was smaller than an artillery regiment, usually comprising two or three batteries. George F. Nafziger, *The German Order of Battle: Panzers and Artillery in World War II* (London: Greenhill, 1999), 361.

2. See Appendix A.

3. Tomislav Dulić, *Utopias of Nation: Local Mass Killing in Bosnia and Herzegovina, 1941–42* (Uppsala: Uppsala University Library, 2005), 211–212.

4. Klaus Schmider, *Partisanenkrieg in Jugoslawien 1941–1944* (Hamburg: Verlag E. S. Mittler GmbH, 2002), 110–112.

5. MFB4/56155, 28326/2, 982. 342. Inf.-Div. Ic, 1/10/42. Feindnachrichtenblatt Nr. 4/42 (Ostbosnien), p. 1.

6. MFB4/56155, 28326/2, 945–948. KG Serbien, 1/3/42. Kampf gegen Aufständische in Kroatien.

7. MFB4/56155, 28326/2, 982. 342. Inf.-Div. Ic, 1/10/42. Feindnachrichtenblatt Nr. 4/42 (Ostbosnien).

8. Schmider, *Partisanenkrieg in Jugoslawien 1941–1944*, 109.

9. MFB4/18730, 28328/1, 677–680. KG Serbien, 1/3/42. Kampf gegen Aufständische, pp. 1, 3.

10. MFB4/56155, 28326/2, 1030–1032. 718. Inf.-Div. Ia, 1/7/42. Operationsbefehl Nr. 2.

11. MFB4/56156, 28326/5, 624. 718. Inf.-Div. Ia, 1/25/42. Operationsbefehl Nr. 3, p. 1.

12. MFB4/56156, 28326/4, 359–361. 718. Inf.-Div. Ia, 1/28/42. Betr.: Unterkunftsverzeichnis. Anlage.

13. MFB4/56156, 28326/5, 612. Höheres Kdo LXV Ia, 1/25/42.

14. MFB4/56156, 28326/4, 425–432. Höheres Kdo LXV Ia, 2/19/42. Beurteilung und Ergebnis des Ozren-Unternehmens, pp. 2, 6; MFB4/56156, 28326/5, 619–620. Höheres Kommando z b V LXV Ia, 1/24/42. Befehl für die Säuberung des Ozren-Gebietes; MFB4/56156, 28326/5, 624–628. 718. Inf.-Div. Ia, 1/25/42. Operationsbefehl Nr. 3.

15. MFB4/56156, 28326/4, 425–432. Höheres Kdo LXV Ia, 2/19/42. Beurteilung und Ergebnis des Ozren-Unternehmens, pp. 1–2.

16. MFB4/56156, 28326/5, 973–975. 718. Inf.-Div. Ia, 2/13/42. Operationsbefehl Nr. 4; MFB4/56156, 28326/5, 982–983. 718. Inf.-Div. Ia, 2/20/42. Zu Operationsbefehl Nr. 4.

17. MFB4/18733, 33552/19, 821–822. Der deutsche General in Agram Ia, 2/12/42; MFB4/56156, 28326/6, 1024–1025. Der deutsche General in Agram Ia, 2/22/42.

18. MFB4/56155, 28326/2, 1037. 718. Inf.-Div. Ia, 1/9/42. Kampfanweisung (zur Belehrung der Truppe), p. 1; MFB4/72335, 15365/11, 358. Zu 342. Inf.-Div. Ia, op. Nr. 42 geh. vom 1/6/42, Anlage 2. Kampfanweisungen, p. 1.

19. MFB4/56155, 28326/2, 1037. 718. Inf.-Div. Ia, 1/9/42. Kampfanweisung (zur Belehrung der Truppe), p. 2; MFB4/72335, 15365/11, 358. Zu 342. Inf.-Div. Ia, op. Nr. 42 geh. vom 1/6/42, Anlage 2. Kampfanweisungen, p. 2.

20. MFB4/56156, 28326/5, 630. Anlage 2 zur Nr. 718 ID 310/42 geheim vom 1/25/42. Kampfanweisung (zur Belehrung der Truppe); MFB4/56156, 28326/5, 657. IR 750, 1/28/42. Regiments-Befehl für den Einsatz.

21. MFB4/56156, 28326/6, 982–983. 718. Inf.-Div. Ia, 2/20/42. Zu Operationsbefehl Nr. 4, p. 2.

22. MFB4/56156, 28326/6, 1097. Abt. Wutte, 3/7/42. Regimentsbefehl.

23. MFB4/56156, 28326/6, 1112. Divisionsveterinär, 4/3/42. Betr.: Beute im Einsatz Dubica-Prijedor.

24. MFB4/56155, 28326/2, 982. 342. Inf.-Div. Ic, 1/10/42. Feindnachrichtenblatt Nr. 4/42 (Ostbosnien), p. 5.

25. MFB4/56156, 28326/3, 71. 718. Inf.-Div., 1/17/42.

26. Schmider, *Partisanenkrieg in Jugoslawien 1941–1944*, 110, 112.

27. MFB4/56156, 28326/5, 624. 718. Inf.-Div. Ia, 1/25/42. Operationsbefehl Nr. 3, p. 1.

28. MFB4/56156, 28326/5, 644–646. IR 738 Kommandeur, 1/26/43. Regimentsbefehl Nr. 6, p. 3.

29. Schmider, *Partisanenkrieg in Jugoslawien 1941–1944*, 109–113.

30. Ibid., 109.

31. MFB4/56155, 28326/2, 1030–1032. 718. Inf.-Div. Ia, 1/7/42. Operationsbefehl Nr. 2.

32. MFB4/56156, 28326/3, 203–207. 342. Inf. Div. Ia, 1/21/42. Lagebericht, pp. 1, 3.

33. MFB4/56156, 28326/6, 1045–1048. Abt. Wutte, 3/5/42. Allgemeiner Lagebericht, pp. 2–3.

34. MFB4/56156, 28326/4, 351. 718. Inf.-Div. Kdr., 1/19/42. Betr.: Erfahrungen mit kroatischer Wehrmacht.

35. MFB4/56156, 28326/6, 1055–1057. Dienststelle Eisenbahn-Panzerzug 24, 3/10/42. Betr.: Einsatzbericht, 3/1–3/8/42.

36. MFB4/56156, 28326/6, 1045–1048. Abt. Wutte, 3/5/42, Allgemeiner Lagebericht, pp. 2–3. Examination of the 718th Infantry Division's files, and of the relevant officers' Wehrmacht personnel files, produces some confusion as to who commanded which of the 718th's two infantry regiments at which times during 1942. To cut a very long story short, there seems to have been some alternation in command between Wutte, Colonel Joachim Wüst, and a Colonel Suschnig. MFB4/56155–56159; PERS 6, files on Joachim Wüst and Rudolf Wutte. Personal-Nachweise.

37. MFB4/56156, 28326/5, 726–729. Kdr., 2/7/42. Bericht über die Säuberung im Ozren-Gebiet, 1/29/-2/4/42, p. 1; MFB4/56156, 28326/4, 425–432. Höheres Kdo LXV Ia, 2/19/42. Beurteilung und Ergebnis des Ozren-Unternehmens, p. 4.

38. Schmider, *Partisanenkrieg in Jugoslawien 1941–1944*, 110.

39. MFB4/56156, 28326/4, 354–355. LSB 823, 1/20/42. Betr.: Einsatz der 1. Kp. (Sisak) und 3. Kp. (Novska) am 1/19/-1/20/42 im Abschnitt Sisak-Sunja, p. 2; MFB4/56156, 28326/4, 425–432. Höheres Kommando LXV Ia, 2/19/42. Beurteilung und Ergebnis des Ozren-Unternehmens, p. 2; Anlage 89 2/20. Kommandierende General in Serbien (KG Serbien), 2/20/42. Betr.: Zehn-Tagesmeldung, p. 2.

40. Anlage 89 2/20. Kommandierende General in Serbien (KG Serbien), 2/20/42. Betr.: Zehn-Tagesmeldung, p. 2.

41. Ibid., pp. 6–9.

42. MFB4/56156, 28326/6, 1045–1048. Abt. Wutte, 3/5/42. Allgemeiner Lagebericht, p. 2.

43. MFB4/56156, 28326/6, 1049–1050. JR 750, 3/6/42. Betr.: Allgemeiner Lagebericht, p. 1.

44. MFB4/56156, 28326/6, 1030. Unternehmen Prijedor—Verluste und Beute (no date).

45. MFB4/56156, 28326/6, 1031–1032. Gefechtsstärken, 3/1/42; MFB4/56156, 28326/6, 1072. Abt. Wutte, 3/14/42. Gefechtsstärken am Beginn und Ende des Einsatzes.

46. MFB4/56155, 28326/2, 1037. 718. Inf.-Div. Ia, 1/9/42. Kampfanweisung (zur Belehrung der Truppe), p. 2; MFB4/72335, 15365/11, 358. Zu 342. Inf.-Div. Ia, op. Nr. 42 geh. vom 1/6/42, Anlage 2. Kampfanweisungen.

47. MFB4/56155, 28326/2, 1037. 718. Inf.-Div. Ia, 1/9/42. Kampfanweisung (zur Belehrung der Truppe), p. 2; MFB4/72335, 15365/11, 358. Zu 342. Inf.-Div. Ia, op. Nr. 42 geh. vom 1/6/42, Anlage 2. Kampfanweisungen.

48. MFB4/56155, 28326/5, 630. Anlage 2 zur Nr. 718. Inf.-Div. 310/42 geheim vom 1/25/42. Kampfanweisung (zur Belehrung der Truppe).

49. MFB4/56156, 28326/3, 201. Edelweiss II 50, 1/21/42.

50. Schmider, *Partisanenkrieg in Jugoslawien 1941–1944*, 109.

51. Ibid., 110.

52. MFB4/56156, 28326/3, 53. 718. Inf.-Div., 2/19/42.

53. MFB4/56156, 28326/5, 699–701. Ergebnis und Berichte Ib 2/7/42. Fernschreiben; Verluste und Beute des Ustasen-Btl., Major Francetić; Verluste und Beute der Sperrgruppe Vareš beim Ozren-Unternehmen.

54. MFB4/56156, 28326/5, 1045–1048. Abt. Wutte, 3/5/42. Allgemeiner Lagebericht, pp. 1–2.

55. Marko Attila Hoare, *Genocide and Resistance in Hitler's Bosnia: The Partisans and the Chetniks 1941–1943* (Oxford: Oxford University Press, 2005), 165–166; Geoffrey Swain, *Tito: A Biography* (London: I. B. Tauris, 2011), 41, 51–52.

56. MFB4/18730, 28328/2, 862–864. KG Serbien 2/20/42. Betr.: Zehn-Tagesmeldung, p. 1; MFB4/18730, 28328/3, 929–932. KG Serbien Ia, 3/1/42. Betr.: Zehn-Tagesmeldung, p. 1; MFB4/18730, 28328/3, 1026–1028. KG Serbien Ia, 3/20/42. Betr.: Zehn-Tagesmeldung, p. 1; MFB4/18730, 28328/3, 1067–1070. KG Serbien Ia, 3/31/42. Betr.: Zehn-Tagesmeldung, pp. 1–2.

57. Matteo J. Milazzo, *The Chetni Movement and the Yugoslav Resistance* (Baltimore, MD: The Johns Hopkins University Press, 1975), 68–69.

58. Schmider, *Partisanenkrieg in Jugoslawien 1941–1944*, 569.

59. MFB4/18730, file no. and frame illegible. Anlage 83, Februar 1942. KG Serbien, 2/18/42. Betr.: Befugnisse des deutschen Div Kdrs im kroatischen Operationsgebiet, p. 1.

60. MFB4/18730, file no. and frame illegible. Anlage 2, März 1942. KG Serbien Ia, 3/1/42. Betr.: Zehn-Tagesmeldung, p. 2.

61. BfZ, Sammlung Sterz. Sergeant Alfred Meyer, second company, IR 749, 717. Inf.-Div., 4/16/42. Meyer is a pseudonym.

62. Schmider, *Partisanenkrieg in Jugoslawien 1941–1944*, 119–120, 137.

63. MFB4/56157, 28326/10, 938–949. Führungsstab Kampfgruppe General Bader, 4/10/42. Richtlinien für die Operationen in Bosnien; MFB4/56157, 28326/10, 1078–1079. 718. Inf.-Div. Ia, 4/14/42. Gruppen-Einteilung; MFB4/56157, 28326/10, 1105–1107. 718. Inf.-Div. Ia, 4/11/42. Betr.: Unternehmen Trio I.

64. MFB4/56157, 28326/10, 1021–1025. Führungsstab Kampfgruppe General Bader Ia, 5/4/42. Betr.: Abschlußbericht "Säuberung des Raumes um Rogatica," pp. 4–5.

65. Schmider, *Partisanenkrieg in Jugoslawien 1941–1944*, 119–120, 126.

66. MFB4/18733, 33552/15, 374–376. KG Serbien, 4/14/42. Feindlage.

67. MFB4/56156, 28326/4, 590–591. 718. Inf.-Div. Ia, 3/27/42. Betr.: Ausrüstung mit Gebirgs-Bekleidung-Ausrüstung.

68. MFB4/56157, 28326/9, 735. 718. Inf.-Div. Ia. Anlage, 4/30/42. Unterkunftsverzeichnis der 718. Inf.-Div., Stand 4/30/42; MFB4/56157, 28326/9, 687. KG Serbien Ia, 4/10/42. Betr.: Panzer-Kompanie z b V 12.

69. MFB4/56157, 28326/10, 1105–1107. 718. Inf.-Div. Ia, 4/11/42. Betr.: Unternehmen Trio I, p. 1.

70. MFB4/56157, 28326/10, 938–949. Führungsstab KG Bader, 4/10/42. Richtlinien für die Operationen in Bosnien, pp. 4–5.

71. MFB4/56157, 28326/10, 1021–1025. Führungsstab KG Bader Ia, 5/4/42. Betr.: Abschlußbericht "Säuberung des Raumes um Rogatica," pp. 6–7.

72. MFB4/56157, 28326/10, 1033. Anlage 6 zu KG Bader Ia Nr. 130/42 g.Kdos. Abschlußmeldung über die Versorgungslage während der Säuberungsaktion im Bezirk Rogatica.

73. Stevan K. Pavlowitch, *Hitler's New Disorder: The Second World War in Yugoslavia* (London: Hurst, 2008), 119.

74. RH 20–12/218. Der Wehrmachtbefehlshaber im Südosten und Oberbefehlshaber der 12. Armee, 3/19/42. Betr.: Bekaempfung der Aufständischen in Serbien und Kroatien, p. 2.

75. MFB4/56157, 28326/10, 938–949. Führungsstab Kampfgruppe General Bader, 4/10/42. Richtlinien für die Operationen in Bosnien, p. 10. Emphasis in original.

76. MFB4/56157, 28326/10, 1273. Anlage 17 zum Bericht Unternehmen Trio I u. II. Eigene Verluste.

77. MFB4/56157, 28326/10, 1081–1083. Anlage 3 zu Nr. 1323/42 geh. der 718 Inf.-Div. Ia vom 4/14/42, pp. 1–2.

78. MFB4/56157, 28326/10, 1033–1034. Anlage 6 zu KG Bader Ia Nr. 130/42 g. Kdos. Abschlußmeldung über die Versorgungslage während der Säuberungsaktion im Bezirk Rogatica.

79. Ibid., p. 2.

80. MFB4/56157, 28326/10, 1175. 718. Inf.-Div. Ic, 5/9/42. Feindnachrichtenblatt Nr. 4 für diese Räume südlich und südwestl. Praca—westlich Goražde.

81. MFB4/56158, 28326/11, 172. II/IR 738, Abschrift, 4/17/42.

82. MFB4/56157, 28326/10, 1232–1234. Gruppe Wüst, 5/20/42. Bericht über das Unternehmen Trio I u. II, pp. 6–8.

83. MFB4/56158, 28326/12, 390. 718. Jäg.-Div., 4/25/42.

84. Swain, *Tito: A Biography*, 46–48.

85. MFB4/56157, 28326/9, 778–780. KG Serbien Ia, 5/23/42. Betr.: Operationen in Bosnien, p. 1.

86. MFB4/56157, 28326/10, 1135–1136. 718. Inf.-Div. Ia, 4/26/42.

87. MFB4/56157, 28326/10, 1190. 718. Inf.-Div. Kommandeur, 5/17/42. Tagesbefehl; MFB4/56157, 28326/10, 1045–1050. Führungsstab KG Bader Ia, 5/20/42. Betr.: Abschlußbericht "Unternehmen Foča."

88. Schmider, *Partisanenkrieg in Jugoslawien 1941–1944*, 129.

89. An inference Schmider also makes (*Partisanenkrieg in Jugoslawien 1941–1944*, 131–132).

90. MFB4/56158, 28326/14, 1021–1025. Führungsstab KG Bader Ia, 5/4/42. Betr.: Abschlußbericht, Säuberung des Raumes um Rogatica, pp. 3–4, 9–10.

91. Schmider, *Partisanenkrieg in Jugoslawien 1941–1944*, 132.

92. For an overview of the June 1942 agreement, see Jozo Tomasevich, *War and Revolution in Yugoslavia, 1941–1945: Occupation and Collaboration* (Stanford, CA: Stanford University Press, 2001), 250–252.

93. Schmider, *Partisanenkrieg in Jugoslawien 1941–1944*, 136.

94. MFB4/17200, file no. illegible, 1039–1042, KG Serbien Ia, 7/1/42, Lagebericht, p. 1.

95. Hoare, *Genocide and Resistance in Hitler's Bosnia: The Partisans and the Chetniks 1941–1943*, 176.

96. Ibid., 181–184, 201–208.

97. Ibid., chap. 4. Similar "left errors" were also committed in western Bosnia. See Milazzo, *The Chetni Movement and the Yugoslav Resistance*, 76–81.

98. Hoare, *Genocide and Resistance in Hitler's Bosnia: The Partisans and the Chetniks 1941–1943*, 238.

99. Ibid., 165, 279.

100. Ibid., 34–39, 142, 189, 275–276; Swain, *Tito: A Biography*, 52–53.

101. On the Ustasha killings during Kozara and its aftermath, see Schmider, *Partisanenkrieg in Jugoslawien 1941–1944*, 151; Dulić, *Utopias of Nation: Local Mass Killing in Bosnia and Herzegovina, 1941–42*, 243–281. On the Ustasha campaign in Syrmia, see Alexander Korb, "Integrated Warfare? The Germans and the Ustasha Massacres: Syrmia 1942," in *War in a Twilight World: Partisan and Anti-Partisan Warfare in Eastern Europe, 1939–45*, ed. Ben Shepherd and Juliette Pattinson (London: Palgrave Macmillan, 2010), 210–232. At time of writing, a monograph by Alexander Korb on Ustasha violence is shortly to be published. See Alexander Korb, *Im Schatten des Weltkriegs: Massengewalt der Ustaša gegen Serben, Juden und Roma in Kroatien, 1941–45* (Hamburg: Hamburger Edition 2012, forthcoming).

102. Schmider, *Partisanenkrieg in Jugoslawien 1941–1944*, 150. By the beginning of August the entire 714th had been transferred from Serbia to the NDH. Schmider, *Partisanenkrieg in Jugoslawien 1941–1944*, 154.

103. Tomasevich, *War and Revolution in Yugoslavia, 1941–1945: Occupation and Collaboration*, 398–401; Dulić, *Utopias of Nation: Local Mass Killing in Bosnia and Herzegovina, 1941–42*, chap. 13.

104. Schmider, *Partisanenkrieg in Jugoslawien 1941–1944.* 148.

105. Ibid., 155; Tomasevich, *War and Revolution in Yugoslavia, 1941–1945: Occupation and Collaboration*, 275–276; Marko Attila Hoare, *Genocide and Resistance in Hitler's Bosnia: The Partisans and the Chetniks 1941–1943* (Oxford: Oxford University Press, 2005), 272.

106. MFB4/56159, 28326/15, 4–5. 718. Inf.-Div. Ia, 5/28/42. Divisionsbefehl Nr. 11 für den Aufmarsch zur Säuberung des Raumes ostw. Zenica und südlich Zavidovići; MFB4/56159, 28326/15, 824. 718. Inf.-Div. Verbindungsoffizier, 6/11/42.

107. MFB4/56159, 28326/15, 4–5. 718. Inf.-Div. Ia, 5/28/42. Divisionsbefehl Nr. 11 für den Aufmarsch zur Säuberung des Raumes ostw. Zenica und südlich Zavidovići, p. 1.

108. BfZ, Sammlung Sterz. Lt. Peter Geissler, 11. Kp. / IR 721, 714. Inf.-Div., 7/16/42.

109. MFB4/56159, 28326/15, 8–9. 718. Inf.-Div. Ia, 5/29/42. Besondere Anordnungen zum Divisionsbefehl Nr. 11 für Kampfführung und Behandlung Aufständischer, p. 1.

110. MFB4/56159, 28326/16, 442–443. 718. Inf.-Div. Ia, 8/28/42. Betr.: Erfahrungsberichte, pp. 2–3.

111. MFB4/56157, 28326/9, 847–851. 718. Inf.-Div. Ic, 6/20/42. Lagebericht, 6/1–6/15/42, p. 1.

112. See chap. 9.

113. Hoare, *Genocide and Resistance in Hitler's Bosnia: The Partisans and the Chetniks 1941–1943*, 266–267.

114. MFB4/56157, 28326/9, 847–851. 718. Inf.-Div. Ic, 6/20/42. Lagebericht, 6/1/6/15/42, p. 1.

115. Ibid., pp. 1–2.

116. MFB4/56159, 28326/16, 392–395. Gruppe Oberstleutnant Faninger, 9/3/42. Betr.: Erfahrungsbericht über Einsatz bei Unternehmen "S," p. 2.

117. MFB4/17200, file no. illegible, 1140–1143. KG Serbien 7/20/42, Lagebericht, p. 1.

118. MFB4/17200, file no. illegible, 1095–1099. KG Serbien 7/10/42, Lagebericht, p. 3.

119. MFB4/18731, 28328/8, 513–517. KG Serbien, 8/21/42, Lagebericht.

120. MFB4/56159, 28326/15, 8–9. 718. Inf.-Div. Ia, 5/29/42. Besondere Anordnungen zum Divisionsbefehl Nr. 11 für Kampfführung und Behandlung Aufständischer, p. 2.

121. Ibid.

122. MFB4/56159, 28326/16, 382–385. Gruppe Oberstleutnant Faninger, 8/31/42. Bericht über die Säuberung im Raume Šekovići im Unternehmen S.

123. MFB4/56159, 28326/16, 442–443. 718. Inf.-Div. Ia, 8/28/42. Betr.: Erfahrungsberichte, p. 3.

124. MFB4/56159, 28326/16, 380. 718. Inf.-Div. Ia, 8/17/42. Besondere Anordnungen zum Divisionsbefehl Nr. 26 für die Behandlung der Bevölkerung und der Aufständischen während des Unternehmens S.

125. Ibid.

126. MFB4/56159, 28326/16, 392–395. Gruppe Oberstleutnant Faninger, 9/3/42. Betr.: Erfahrungsbericht über Einsatz bei Unternehmen "S."

127. MFB4/56159, 28326/16, 442–443. 718. Inf.-Div. Ia, 8/2/42. Betr.: Erfahrungsberichte, p. 5.

128. Ibid.

129. Ibid.

130. Ibid.

131. For an overview of the fate of the Jews in the NDH, see Tomasevich, *War and Revolution in Yugoslavia, 1941–1945: Occupation and Collaboration,* chap. 13. According to Tomasevich, over four and a half thousand Jews were members of the Yugoslav Partisan forces, but the largest influx did not come until September 1943, when Partisans released large numbers of Jews from former Italian internment camps. Ibid., 605.

132. See Appendix A.

133. Fortner was in fact executed by the Yugoslav government for war crimes in 1947, In this regard, the brutal nature of much of his conduct earlier in 1942 should be noted. See Appendix A.

9. THE MORASS

1. MFB4/56159, 28326/16, 442–443. 718. Inf.-Div. Ia, 8/28/42. Betr.: Erfahrungsberichte, p. 3.

2. Ibid., p. 4.

3. Ibid.

4. Ibid.

5. Ibid.

6. MFB4/56157, 28326/9, 847–851. 718. Inf.-Div. Ic, 6/20/42. Lagebericht, 6/1–6/15/42.

7. MFB4/56159, 28326/16, 442–443. 718. Inf.-Div. Ia, 8/28/42. Betr.: Erfahrungsberichte, p. 6.

8. MFB4/56157, 28326/9, 847–851. 718. Inf.-Div. Ic, 6/20/42. Lagebericht, 6/1/-6/15/42, p. 3. "Pravoslavic" means Eastern Orthodox—in this context, Serbs.

9. MFB4/17200, 1178. KG Serbien Ia, 7/28/42. Betr.: Deutsche Gerichtsherren für kroat. Kriegsgerichte.

10. MFB4/56158, file 28326/16. 718. Inf.-Div. Ia, 8/28/42. Betr.: Erfahrungsberichte, p. 5.

11. MFB4/56160, 34404/1, 120–123. 718. Inf.-Div. Ic. Lagebericht, 9/21/-10/6/42 (no date).

12. MFB4/17201, 28328/9, 128–141. KG Serbien Ia, 9/20/42. Lagebericht, 9/11–9/20/42 pp. 1–2.

13. MFB4/17201, 28328/10, 357–363. KG Serbien Ia, 10/20/42, Lagebericht 10/11–10/20/42, p. 2.

14. MFB4/17201, 28328/10, 426–431. KG Serbien Ia 10/31/42, Lagebericht, 10/21–10/31/42, pp. 1–2.

15. Jozo Tomasevich, *War and Revolution in Yugoslavia, 1941–1945: Occupation and Collaboration* (Stanford, CA: Stanford University Press, 2001), 377.

16. Marko Attila Hoare, *Genocide and Resistance in Hitler's Bosnia: The Partisans and the Chetniks 1941–1943* (Oxford: Oxford University Press, 2005), 21.

17. Marko Attila Hoare, *The History of Bosnia from the Middle Ages to the Present Day* (London: Saqi, 2007), 267.

18. Klaus Schmider, *Partisanenkrieg in Jugoslawien 1941–1944* (Hamburg: E. S. Mittler, 2002), 156–157.

19. Hoare, *The History of Bosnia from the Middle Ages to the Present Day*, 200–204, 226–230, 267–273. For a detailed examination of the Handschar Division, see George Lepre, *Himmler's Bosnian Division: The Waffen-SS Handschar Division 1943–1945* (Atglen, PA: Schiffer, 2004).

20. Jozo Tomasevich, *War and Revolution in Yugoslavia, 1941–1945: The Chetniks* (Stanford, CA: Stanford University Press, 1975), 257.

21. MFB4/56157, 28326/9, 743. LSB 923, 5/4/42. Lagebericht, 5/3/-5/4/42.

22. MFB4/56159, 28326/16, 392–395. Gruppe Oberstleutnant Faninger, 9/3/42. Betr.: Erfahrungsbericht über Einsatz bei Unternehmen "S," p. 3.

23. BfZ, Sammlung Sterz. Lt. Peter Geissler, 11. Kp. / IR 721, 714. Inf.-Div., 9/25/42.

24. Tomasevich, *War and Revolution in Yugoslavia, 1941–1945: The Chetniks*, 256–261; Hoare, *Genocide and Resistance in Hitler's Bosnia: The Partisans and the Chetniks 1941–1943*, 143–148; Hoare, *The History of Bosnia from the Middle Ages to the Present Day*, 254; Dulić, *Utopias of Nation: Local Mass Killing in Bosnia and Herzegovina, 1941–42*, 213–214.

25. MFB4/56157, 28326/8, 847–851. 718. Inf.-Div. Ic, 6/20/42. Lagebericht, 6/1/-6/15/42, pp. 1–2.

26. MFB4/56158, 28326/14, 1094. 718. Inf.-Div. Ia, 5/13/42. Betr.: Aufstellung von Dorf-wehergemeinschaften, Einstellung von Miliz.

27. Ibid.

28. MFB4/56158, 28326/14, 1096. Führungsstab KG Bader Qu., 5/19/42. Betr.: Aufstel-lung von Dorfwehrgemeinschaften, Einstellung von Miliz.

29. MFB4/56160, 34404/1, 86–89. 718. Inf.-Div. Ic, 9/22/42. Lagebericht, 9/1/-9/20/1942; MFB4/56160, 34404/1, 120–123. 718. Inf.-Div. Ic Lagebericht, 9/21/-10/6/1942 (no date).

30. MFB4/56158, 28326/14, 1094. 718. Inf.-Div. Ia, 5/13/42. Betr.: Aufstellung von Dorf-wehergemeinschaften, Einstellung von Miliz.

31. MFB4/56159, 28326/17, 652–656. 718. Inf.-Div. Ia, 10/13/42. Betr.: Verhältnis zu den Chetniks, pp. 3–4.

32. Schmider, *Partisanenkrieg in Jugoslawien 1941–1944*, 157.

33. MFB4/56159, 28326/17, 652–656. 718. Inf.-Div. Ia, 10/13/42. Betr.: Verhältnis zu den Chetniks, p. 1.

34. On Chetnik-NDH co-operation, see Hoare, *Genocide and Resistance in Hitler's Bos-nia: The Partisans and the Chetniks 1941–1943*, 233–234, 262, 274.

35. MFB4/56159, 28326/17, 652–656. 718. Inf.-Div. Ia, 10/13/42. Betr.: Verhältnis zu den Chetniks, pp. 3–4.

36. MFB4/56159, 28326/17, 811–812. 718. Inf.-Div. Ia, 11/13/42, p. 2.

37. MFB4/56159, 28326/17, 652–656. 718. Inf.-Div. Ia, 10/13/42. Betr.: Verhältnis zu den Chetniks, p. 3.

38. Edward B. Westermann, *Hitler's Police Battalions: Enforcing Racial War in the East* (Lawrence: University Press of Kansas, 2005), 1–19.

39. See Appendix A.

40. The 1931 census returns of four eastern Bosnian districts in 1931 record 79,738 Mus-lims as opposed to 59,939 Orthodox Serbs. By contrast, the 1931 census records of four districts in the vicinity of Mount Kozara record 32,665 Muslims as opposed to 119,850 Orthodox Serbs. Dulić, *Utopias of Nation: Local Mass Killing in Bosnia and Herzegovina, 1941–42*, 177, 216.

41. In addition, two movements might temporarily coalesce to fight another that they con-sidered a greater mutual threat at the time. See Hoare, *Genocide and Resistance in Hit-ler's Bosnia: The Partisans and the Chetniks 1941–1943*, 208–212 (Partisans and Ustasha against Chetniks), 233–234, 262, 274 (Chetniks and Ustasha against Partisans).

42. Geoffrey Swain, *Tito: A Biography* (London: I. B. Tauris, 2011), 46–48.

43. Hoare, *Genocide and Resistance in Hitler's Bosnia: The Partisans and the Chetniks 1941–1943*, 239–246.

44. Ibid., 278, 283–284.

45. Schmider, *Partisanenkrieg in Jugoslawien 1941–1944*, 190–192.

46. Tomasevich, *War and Revolution in Yugoslavia, 1941–1945: Occupation and Collabo-ration*, 279.

47. MFB4/17201, 28328/10, 241–247. KG Serbien Ia, 10/1/42. Betr.: Lagebericht, 9/21–9/30/42, p. 5.

48. MFB4/17201, 28328/10, 426–431. KG Serbien Ia 10/31/42, Lagebericht, 10/21–10/31/42, p. 5.

49. Stevan K. Pavlowitch, *Yugoslavia* (London: Ernest Bevin, 1971), 136.

50. Hoare, *Genocide and Resistance in Hitler's Bosnia: The Partisans and the Chetniks 1941–1943*, 320–325; Stevan K. Pavlowitch, *Hitler's New Disorder: The Second World War in Yugoslavia* (London: Hurst, 2008), 128–131; Swain, *Tito: A Biography*, 49–55.

51. Tomasevich, *War and Revolution in Yugoslavia, 1941–1945: The Chetniks*, 229.

52. Tomasevich, *War and Revolution in Yugoslavia, 1941–1945: Occupation and Collaboration*, 274–279.

53. Tomislav Dulić, *Utopias of Nation: Local Mass Killing in Bosnia and Herzegovina, 1941–42* (Uppsala: Uppsala University Library, 2005), 288–292.

54. Schmider, *Partisanenkrieg in Jugoslawien 1941–1944*, 176.

55. Tomasevich, *War and Revolution in Yugoslavia, 1941–1945: Occupation and Collaboration*, 277–278.

56. Schmider, *Partisanenkrieg in Jugoslawien 1941–1944*, 176.

57. Tomasevich, *War and Revolution in Yugoslavia, 1941–1945: Occupation and Collaboration*, 278–279.

58. Timothy P. Mulligan, *The Politics of Illusion and Empire: German Occupation Policy in the Soviet Union, 1942–1943* (New York: Praeger, 1988), 139. On the Commando Order, see also Philip W. Blood, *Hitler's Bandit Hunters: The SS and the Nazi Occupation of Europe* (Washington, DC: Potomac, 2006), 81–83.

59. Schmider, *Partisanenkrieg in Jugoslawien 1941–1944*, 165–166.

60. See, for example, Löhr's orders of October 18 and December 7, 1942 (ibid., 174, 182).

61. MFB4/17201, 28328/11, 466–467. Der Wehrmachtbefehlshaber im Südosten zugl. mit der Führung der 12. Armee beauftragt, 10/28/42; Schmider, *Partisanenkrieg in Jugoslawien 1941–1944*, 174.

62. IWM, NHT Document 1722 (translation). War Diary of the Commanding General and Commander in Serbia Ia, 10/2/42. Captured German documents used at the Nuremberg Trials were translated into English; sometimes, as is the case here, the translations were not of the highest quality.

63. IWM, NHT Document 1722 (translation). Commanding General and Commander in Serbia Ia, 10/10/42. Subject: Precautionary measures against enemy attacks.

64. MFB4/56159, 28326/17, 509–510. 718. Inf.-Div. Ia, 9/26/42. Divisionsbefehl Nr. 29 für Versammlung der Kampfgruppe Suschnig zur Entsetzung von Jajce, p. 1.

65. MFB4/56159, 28326/17, 569–570. 718. Inf.-Div. Ia, 10/5/42. Betr.: Bericht über Zustände in Jajce nach Einnahme durch deutsche Truppen, p. 2.

66. MFB4/56159, 28326/17, 538. 718. Inf.-Div. Ia, 9/30/42. Divisionsbefehl Nr. 31 für Vorstoß auf Jajce.

67. MFB4/56159, 28326/17, 529–531. 718. Inf.-Div. Ic, 9/30/42. Feindnachrichtenblatt Nr. 7 für das Unternehmen "Jajce," pp. 1–2.

68. Ibid.

69. Ibid., p. 1.

70. Ibid.

71. MFB4/56159, 28326/17, 524. 718. Inf.-Div. Ia, 9/28/42. Divisionsbefehl Nr. 30 zur Bildung der Kampfgruppe Suschnig und Wüst und Versammlung für Unternehmen Jajce.

72. Schmider, *Partisanenkrieg in Jugoslawien 1941–1944*, 170.

73. MFB4/56159, 28326/17, 660–661. 718. Inf.-Div., 10/18/42. Divisionsbefehl Nr. 34 für Zerschlagung der Partisanengruppen im Raum Jajce.

74. MFB4/56159, 28326/17, 669–670, 718. Inf.-Div. Ia, 10/18/42. Divisionsbefehl Nr. 34, p. 1.

75. MFB4/56159, 28326/17, 676. KG Serbien O. Qu., 10/14/42.

76. RW40/34. KG Serbien Ia. KTB, 10/23/42, 10/29/42, 10/31/42.

77. MFB4/17201, 28328/10, 312–321. KG Serbien Ia, 10/11/42. Betr.: Lagebericht, 10/1–10/10/42.

78. MFB4/56159, 28326/18, 938–948. Kampfgruppe Wüst, 12/23/42. Abschlußbericht über Unternehmen Jajce III, p. 1.

79. MFB4/56159, 28326/18, 897. 718. Inf.-Div. Ia, 11/30/42. Divisionsbefehl Nr. 49 für Unternehmen Jajce III. From this order of battle, it is clear that the 668th Artillery Section had now been re-designated as a regiment.

80. MFB4/18730, 28328/3, 929–932. KG Serbien Ia, 3/1/42. Betr.: Zehn-Tagesmeldung, pp. 2–3.

81. MFB4/56159, 28326/17, 692–695. 718. Inf.-Div. Ia, 11/14/42. Beurteilung der Lage im Sicherungsbereich der 718. Inf.-Div., p. 1.

82. Ibid.

83. Ibid.

84. MFB4/56159, 28326/17, 633. 718. Inf.-Div. Kommandeur, 10/10/42. Kameraden der Ustasa und des kroatishen Heeres!

85. MFB4/56159, 28326/17, 692. 718. Inf.-Div. Ia, 11/14/42. Beurteilung der Lage im Sicherungsbereich der 718. Inf.-Div., p. 2.

86. MFB4/56159, 28326/18, 1102–1104. 718. Inf.-Div. Ia, 12/31/42. Betr.: Bemerkungen zur Ausbildung und Betreuung der Truppe.

87. MFB4/56159, 28326/18, 991–993. Anlage Nr. 1 zu GR 750 Br. B. Nr. 1102/42 geh. . Erfahrungsbericht über Einsatz Jajce vom 11/23–12/11/42, p. 3.

88. MFB4/56159, 28326/17, 585–595. 718. Inf.-Div. Ia, 10/12/42. Abschluß- und Erfahrungsbericht über das Unternehmen gegen Jajce im Okt. 42.

89. MFB4/56159, 28326/18, 830. 718. Inf.-Div. Ia, 11/16/42. Betr.: Zuteilung von Pzkpfwg., Zügen; MFB4/56159, 28326/18, 832. Bf. dt. Tr. Kroatien, 11/20/42.

90. MFB4/56159, 28326/18, 963–964. GR 738. Erfahrungsbericht über das Unternehmen Jajce III (no date).

91. MFB4/56159, 28326/17, 622–623. IR 750, 10/10/42. Betr.: Erfahrungen beim Jajce-Unternehmen.

92. Ibid.; MFB4/56159, 28326/17, 628–629. Kampfgruppe Wüst, 10/10/42. Anlage 17, 18 zum Bericht über Unternehmen Jajce.

93. RW 40/34. KG Serbien, Kriegstagebuch, 10/4/42.

94. Ibid., 10/6/42.

95. MFB4/56159, 28326/18, 950–953. Gruppe Annacker, 11/26/42. Bericht über die Aktion vom 11/25/-11/26/42, p. 1.

96. Steiner is a pseudonym.

97. MFB4/56159, file 28326/18, 950–953. Gruppe Annacker, 11/26/42. Bericht über die Aktion vom 11/25/-11/26/42, pp. 1–2.

98. Ibid., pp. 2–3.

99. Schmider, *Partisanenkrieg in Jugoslawien 1941–1944*, 184.

100. MFB4/56159, 28326/17, 585–595. 718. Inf.-Div. Ia, 10/12/42. Abschluß- und Erfahrungsbericht über das Unternehmen gegen Jajce im Okt. 42, pp. 10–11.

101. MFB4/56159, 28326/17, 690–691. 718. Inf.-Div., 10/28/42. Fernschreiben. Tagesmeldung von 10/27/-10/28/42.

102. MFB4/56159, 28326/17, 700. 718. Inf.-Div. Ia, 10/30/42. Tagesmeldung vom 10/29/-10/30/42. For other major casualty disparities, see MFB4/56159, 28326/17, 701. 718. Inf.-Div. Ia, 10/31/42. Tagesmeldung von 10/30/-10/31/42; MFB4/56159, 28326/17, 713. 718. Inf.-Div. Ia, 11/2/42. Tagesmeldung vom 11/1/-11/2/42.

103. MFB4/56159, 28326/17, 757. 718. Inf.-Div. Ia, 11/19/42. Betr.: Unternehmen I u. II.

104. Methodological studies of German soldiers' letters include Klaus Latzel, "Tourismus und Gewalt: Kriegswahrnehmungen in Feldpostbriefen," in *Vernichtungskrieg. Verbrechen der Wehrmacht, 1941 bis 1944*, ed. Hannes Heer and Klaus Naumann (Hamburg: Hamburger Edition, 1995), 447–459; Klaus Latzel, "Vom Kriegserlebnis zur Kriegserfahrung. Theoretische und methodische Überlegungen zur erfahrungsgeschichtlichen Untersuchung von Feldpostbriefen," *Militärgeschichtliche Mitteilungen* 56 (1997), 1–30.

105. BfZ, Sammlung Sterz. Lt. Peter Geissler, 11. Kp. / IR 721, 714. Inf.-Div., 6/21/42.

106. Ibid., 7/24/42.

107. Ibid., 9/13/42.

108. Ibid., 9/10/42.

109. Ibid., 10/4/42. Emphasis in original.

110. Ibid.

111. Ibid., 11/27/42.

112. Ibid., 12/13/42.

113. Ibid., 12/15/42.

114. Ibid., 5/2/42.

115. Ibid., 9/6/42.

116. Ibid., 12/22/42.

117. See, for instance, Richard West, *Tito and the Rise and Fall of Yugoslavia* (London: Sinclair Stevenson, 1996), 146; Hermann Frank Meyer, *Blutiges Edelweiß: Die 1. Gebirgs-Division im Zweiten Weltkrieg* (Berlin: Ch. Links Verlag, 2008), 124–125.

118. BfZ, Sammlung Sterz. Lt. Peter Geissler, 11. Kp. / IR 721, 714. Inf.-Div., 12/20/42.

119. Ibid., 8/17/42.

120. MFB4/56159, 28326/18, 897. 718. Inf.-Div. Ia, 11/30/42. Divisionsbefehl Nr. 49 für Unternehmen Jajce III.

121. MFB4/56159, 28326/18, 968. Verluste "Jajce III" (no date).

122. MFB4/56159, 28326/18, 917. 718. Inf.-Div. Ia, 12/5/42. Divisionsbefehl Nr. 51.

123. RH 24–15/2. Bf. dt. Tr. Kroatien. Beurteilung der Lage, 11/26–12/6/42, p. 2; Schmider, *Partisanenkrieg in Jugoslawien 1941–1944*, 184.

124. RH 24–15/2. Bf. dt. Tr. Kroatien. Beurteilung der Lage, 12/7–12/16/42, p. 3.

125. MFB4/56160, 34404/1, 165–169. 718. Inf.-Div. Ic, 12/26/42. Lagebericht, 12/17–12/25/1942, p. 1.

126. RH 24–15/2. Bf. dt. Tr. Kroatien. Beurteilung der Lage, 11/15–11/25/42, p. 1.

127. Ibid.

128. RH 24–15/2. Bf. dt. Tr. Kroatien. Beurteilung der Lage, 11/26–12/6/42, p. 2; KG Serbien, Beurteilung der Lage, 12/7–12/16/42, p. 1.

10. THE DEVIL'S DIVISION

1. See Appendix A.
2. Jozo Tomasevich, *War and Revolution in Yugoslavia, 1941–1945: Occupation and Collaboration* (Stanford, CA: Stanford University Press, 2001), 267.
3. Ibid.
4. MFB4/72341, 30581/3, 558. Order of battle for 369th Infantry Division, 1/14/43.
5. Tomasevich, *War and Revolution in Yugoslavia, 1941–1945: Occupation and Collaboration*, 267–268. See also Franz Schraml, *Kriegsschauplatz Kroatien: Die deutsch-kroatischen Legionsdivisionen—369., 373., 392. Inf.-Div. (kroat.)—Ihre Ausbildungs- und Ersatzformationen* (Neckargemünd: Vowinckel, 1962).
6. Marko Attila Hoare, *Genocide and Resistance in Hitler's Bosnia: The Partisans and the Chetniks 1941–1943* (Oxford: Oxford University Press, 2005), 320, 330; Geoffrey Swain, *Tito: A Biography* (London: I. B. Tauris, 2011), 49.
7. Tomasevich, *War and Revolution in Yugoslavia, 1941–1945: Occupation and Collaboration*, 658–659, 711; Hoare, *Genocide and Resistance in Hitler's Bosnia: The Partisans and the Chetniks 1941–1943*, 317–325.
8. Klaus Schmider, *Partisanenkrieg in Jugoslawien 1941–1944* (Hamburg: Verlag E. S. Mittler, 2002), 179–180.
9. Ibid., 201–202.
10. Ibid., 50–51.
11. Ibid., 51.
12. MFB4/56160, 34404/3, 743. 718. Inf.-Div. Ia/Org, 2/13/43. Betr.: Umgliederung der Div. in Jägerdivision.
13. In April 1943, for instance, 53 percent of the 718th Infantry Division's troops were aged thirty or over. MFB5/42177, 37733/2, 402. Anlage I zu 118. Jäg.-Div. Ia Nr. 43, 4/17/43. On their upgrading to light division status, all four divisions received redesignated numbers as the 104th, 114th, 117th, and 118th Light Divisions. To avoid confusion, all such divisions are referred to in the text by their original numbers.
14. Tomasevich, *War and Revolution in Yugoslavia, 1941–1945: Occupation and Collaboration*, 321–322, 746; Schmider, *Partisanenkrieg in Jugoslawien 1941–1944*, 257. See also Thomas Casagrande, *Die volksdeutsche SS-Division "Prinz Eugen"* (Frankfurt am Main: Campus Verlag, 2006).
15. Tomasevich, *War and Revolution in Yugoslavia, 1941–1945: Occupation and Collaboration*, 291.
16. Jozo Tomasevich, *War and Revolution in Yugoslavia, 1941–1945: The Chetniks* (Stanford, CA: Stanford University Press, 1975), 252; Richard West, *Tito and the Rise and Fall of Yugoslavia* (London: Sinclair Stevenson, 1996), 142–143; Stevan K. Pavlowitch, *Hitler's New Disorder: The Second World War in Yugoslavia* (London: Hurst, 2008), 151–152.
17. Schmider, *Partisanenkrieg in Jugoslawien 1941–1944*, 215; Hoare, *Genocide and Resistance in Hitler's Bosnia: The Partisans and the Chetniks 1941–1943*, 330.
18. Tomasevich, *War and Revolution in Yugoslavia, 1941–1945: The Chetniks*, 237, 239; Schmider, *Partisanenkrieg in Jugoslawien 1941–1944*, 206–207.

19. The Chetniks' involvement in the operations was complicated both militarily and politically. For more detail, see Matteo J. Milazzo, *The Chetni Movement and the Yugoslav Resistance* (Baltimore, MD: The Johns Hopkins University Press, 1975), chap. 6; Tomasevich, *War and Revolution in Yugoslavia, 1941–1945: The Chetniks*, 231–243.

20. Schmider, *Partisanenkrieg in Jugoslawien 1941–1944*, 214–219. On the unrealistic planning for White I, see also Gaj Trifkovic, "A Case of Failed Counter-Insurgency: Antipartisan Operations in Yugoslavia 1943," *Journal of Slavic Military Studies* 24 (2011): 314–336.

21. Trifkovic, "A Case of Failed Counter-Insurgency: Antipartisan Operations in Yugoslavia 1943," 325.

22. MFB4/72341, 30581/3, 551–554. Bf. dt. Tr. Kroatien, 1/12/43. Operationsbefehl für das Unternehmen "Weiss," p. 2.

23. Milovan Djilas, *Wartime: With Tito and the Partisans* (London: Martin Secker and Warburg, 1977), 216.

24. Reproduced in Norbert Müller, ed., *Deutsche Besatzungspolitik in der UdSSR 1941–1944: Dokumente* (Cologne: Pahl-Rugenstein, 1980), 138–139.

25. MFB4/56160, 34404/2, 407–409. Bf. dt. Tr. Kroatien, 1/12/43. Befehl für die Kampfführung im kroatischen Raum, p. 1. Emphasis in original.

26. Ibid., p. 2.

27. MFB4/56160, 34404/2, 396–397. Bf. dt. Tr. Kroatien, 1/7/43. Betr.: Ausübung der vollziehenden Gewalt.

28. Schmider, *Partisanenkrieg in Jugoslawien 1941–1944*, 207–208.

29. MFB4/72341, 30581/3, 515–516. 369. Inf.-Div. Ia, 12/29/42. Divisionsbefehl Nr. 11.

30. MFB4/72341, 30581/3, 674–677. 369. Inf.-Div. Ic. Tätigkeitsbericht, Januar 1943, p. 3. Date illegible.

31. MFB4/72341, 30581/3, 678–679. Aufruf an die Bevölkerung!

32. MFB4/72341, 30581/3, 583. 369. Inf.-Div. Ic, 1/22/43. Nachrichtenblatt Nr. 2.

33. Ibid.

34. MFB4/72341, 30581/3, 531. 369. Inf.-Div. Ia, 1/6/43. Divisionsbefehl Nr. 14.

35. MFB4/72341, 30581/3, 585. 369. Inf.-Div. Ia, 1/29/43. Divisionsbefehl Nr. 20.

36. MFB4/72341, 30581/3, 652–658. 369. Inf.-Div. Ia, 3/12/43. Einsatz der 369. Inf.-Div. vom 1/9/-2/15/43, p. 5.

37. F. W. D. Deakin, *The Embattled Mountain* (Oxford: Oxford University Press, 1971), 30.

38. MFB4/72341, 30581/3, 652–658. 369. Inf.-Div. Ia, 3/12/43. Einsatz der 369. Inf.-Div. vom 1/9/-2/15/43, p. 5.

39. A point Schmider makes about the Germans in the NDH generally during 1943. Schmider, *Partisanenkrieg in Jugoslawien 1941–1944*, 257.

40. MFB4/56160, 34404/3, 769–771. Betr.: Div. Kdr. Besprechung in Sanski Most am 2/16/43, p. 1.

41. Ibid., p. 2.

42. MFB4/56160, 34404/2, 496–498. Kampfgruppe Annacker, 2/14/43. Betr.: Erfahrungsbericht zum Einsatz Teslic, p. 2.

43. Ibid.

44. Ibid.

45. MFB4/56160, 34404/3, 670–673. 718. Inf.-Div. Ia, 2/6/43. Lagebericht, 1/27/-2/6/43, p. 4.

46. Schmider, *Partisanenkrieg in Jugoslawien 1941–1944*, 158–159.

47. Ibid., 255–256.

48. It is interesting to compare Dippold's approach with that of one of his predecessors, General Hoffmann, and that of his immediate successor, Lieutenant General Karl le Suire. Under each of these two men—even though Hoffmann in his turn was a *relatively* less brutal successor to *his* forerunner as commander of the 342nd Infantry Division, General Hinghofer—the 717th carried out what were arguably the two most infamous mass killings that the Wehrmacht perpetrated in southeast Europe. Walter Manoschek and Hans Safrian, "717./117. Inf.-Div.: Eine Infanterie-Division auf dem Balkan," in *Vernichtungskrieg: Verbrechen der Wehrmacht, 1941 bis 1944*, ed. Hannes Heer and Klaus Naumann (Hamburg: Hamburger Edition, 1995), 359–373; Hermann Frank Meyer, *Von Wien nach Kalavryta: Die blutige Spur der 117. Jäger-Division durch Serbien und Griechenland* (Mannheim: Peleus, 2002). See also chap. 6.

49. High-level Partisan–German contacts went deeper than this in early 1943. Although nothing came of them, the Partisans used the respite to help win time in which to attack the Chetniks successfully in March. For more detail, see Djilas, *Wartime: With Tito and the Partisans*, 229–245; West, *Tito and the Rise and Fall of Yugoslavia*, 148–153; Schmider, *Partisanenkrieg in Jugoslawien 1941–1944*, 243–253; Swain, *Tito: A Biography*, 57–60.

50. MFB4/56160, 34404/2, 407–409. Bf. dt. Tr. Kroatien, 12/1/43. Befehl für die Kampfführung im kroat. Raum, p. 1.

51. RH 24–15/2. Bf. dt. Tr. Kroatien, 2/22/43. Erfahrungen bei Unternehmen Weiss I, pp. 1–2; ibid., Anlage 2, p. 1.

52. MFB4/72341, 30581/3, 584. 369. Inf.-Div. Kommandeur, 1/23/43.

53. MFB4/72341, 30581/3, 591–592. 369. Inf.-Div. Kommandeur, 2/1/43. MFB4/72341, 30581/3, 615–616. 369. Inf.-Div. Ia, 2/13/43. Divisionsbefehl Nr. 27, p. 2.

54. MFB4/72341, 30581/2, 674–677. 369. Inf.-Div. Ic. Tätigkeitsbericht, Januar 1943, p. 2; MFB4/72342, file 45652/1, 4–5. 369. Inf.-Div. Ia. Tätigkeitsbericht, 7/1/-12/31/43, p. 1.

55. MFB4/72341, 30581/3, 551–554. Bf. dt. Tr. Kroatien, 1/12/43. Operationsbefehl fuer das Unternehmen "Weiss," p. 3.

56. MFB4/72342, 45652/1, 37–41. 369. Inf.-Div. Ic, 8/22/43. Betr.: Unerlaubte Entfernungen. To a large extent, these causes tally with causes of poor morale and desertion amongst Croatian army units generally, as identified in Tomasevich, *War and Revolution in Yugoslavia, 1941–1945: Occupation and Collaboration*, 425–428.

57. Schmider, *Partisanenkrieg in Jugoslawien 1941–1944*, 215.

58. In particular, divisional reports point to the fact that its levels of weaponry were frequently below full strength. MFB5/42177, 37733/2, 398. 118. Jäg.-Div. Ia, 4/17/43;

MFB5/42177, 37733/3, 672–676. 118. Jäg.-Div. Ia, 5/18/43. Betr.: Ausbau der 718. Inf.-Div. zur Jäger-Division.

59. MFB4/56160, 34404/3, 743. 718. Inf.-Div. Ia/Org., 2/13/43. Betr.: Umgliederung der Div. in Jägerdivision.

60. Ibid. For qualifications to this rosy picture, see MFB5/42178, 37733/4, 513–514. 118. Jäg.-Div. Ia, 6/19/43. Betr.: Ausbau der 718. Inf.-Div. zur Jäger-Division. Bericht Nr. 7 über den Stand der Aufstockung der 118. Jäg.-Div.; MFB5/42178, 37733/4, 549–552. 118. Jäg.-Div. Ia, 6/25/43. Betr.: Ausbau der 718. Inf.-Div. zur Jäger-Division. Bericht Nr. 8 über den Stand der Aufstockung der 118. Jäger-Division.

61. RH 24–15/2. Bf. dt. Tr. Kroatien. Beurteilung der Lage, 1/7–1/16/43, p. 1.

62. MFB4/72346, 37165/1, 123–130. 373. Inf.-Div. Ia, 6/14/43. Betr.: Lagebeurteilung, p. 8.

63. MFB4/72346, 37165/1, 91–92. 373. Inf.-Div. Ia, 6/21/43. Betr.: Pioneer-Bataillon 373, p. 2.

64. MFB4/72346, 37165/1, 61. 373. Inf.-Div. Ia, 6/30/43. Tagesmeldung.

65. MFB4/72346, 37165/1, 142–143. 373. Inf.-Div. Ia, 6/10/43. Betr.: Stimmung und Haltung der Truppe, Mai 1943, p. 1.

66. MFB4/72346, 37165/1, 343. 373. Inf.-Div. Ia, 3/25/43. Anlage 1 zu Ia Nr. 55/43.

67. MFB4/72346, 37165/1, 678. 373. Inf.-Div. Ia, 7/2/43. Divisionsbefehl für das Unternehmen im Raum Cardaci, p. 2.

68. MFB4/72346, 37165/1, 615. 373. Inf.-Div. Kommandeur, 7/15/43. Zellner was promoted to the rank of major general on April 1, 1943. RH7, file on Emil Zellner.

69. A similarly extreme example, one that again contrasts with its neighboring units, is the 45th Security Regiment, which fought under the 221st Security Division in the rear area of Army Group Center during 1943. Ben Shepherd, *War in the Wild East: The German Army and Soviet Partisans* (Cambridge, MA: Harvard University Press, 2004), 208–216.

70. Shepherd, *War in the Wild East: The German Army and Soviet Partisans*, 160–161. The same process did eventually affect the 369th Infantry Division to an extent. See Ben Shepherd, "With the Devil in Titoland: A Wehrmacht Anti-Partisan Division in Bosnia-Herzegovina, 1943," *War in History* 16 (2009): 77–97.

71. Neidholt was from the family of a Protestant priest, Dippold from that of a Bavarian royal forester, but there is no information on the social origins of Fortner or Zellner. See Appendix A.

72. Neidholt underwent "secret training" with the Reichswehr in 1921. Zellner was an artillery officer during the Great War and a tactical instructor at the Austrian Military Academy in 1930. Dippold underwent military-scientific training with the Reichswehr in 1926. See Appendix A.

73. See Appendix A.

74. After this date, Zellner also served for an unspecified period in the Bukovina on the eastern front, western Ukraine. The Honvéd was the Hungarian home army of the pre-1918 Austro-Hungarian Empire. See Appendix A.

75. In a previous publication, it was mistakenly stated that the 384th was subordinate to the 369th Infantry Division. See Shepherd, "With the Devil in Titoland: A Wehrmacht Anti-Partisan Division in Bosnia-Herzegovina, 1943."

76. Though Dippold, unlike Fortner, was interned in Switzerland and returned to the western front as a company commander, presumably following a prisoner exchange, in July 1918. See Appendix A.

77. See Appendix A

78. See Appendix A

79. See Appendix A

80. Walter Manoschek, *"Serbien ist judenfrei": Militärische Besatzungspolitik und Juden-vernichtung in Serbien 1941/42* (Munich: Oldenbourg, 1995); Walter Manoschek, "The Extermination of the Jews in Serbia," in *National Socialist Extermination Policies: Contemporary German Perspectives and Controversies*, ed. Ulrich Herbert (Oxford: Berghahn, 2000), 163–185; Walter Manoschek and Hans Safrian, "717./117. Inf.-Div.: Eine Infanterie-Division auf dem Balkan," in *Vernichtungskrieg: Verbrechen der Wehrmacht, 1941 bis 1944*, ed. Hannes Heer and Klaus Naumann (Hamburg: Hamburger Edition, 1995).

81. Christian Promitzer, "The South Slavs in the Austrian Imagination: Serbs and Slovenes in the Changing View from German Nationalism to National Socialism," in *Creating the Other: Ethnic Conflict and Nationalism in Habsburg Central Europe*, ed. Nancy M. Wingfield (Oxford: Berghahn, 2003), 183–210.

82. See Appendix A.

83. Alon Rachamimov, *POWs and the Great War: Captivity on the Eastern Front* (Oxford: Berg, 2002), 54–58, 87–107. See also Reinhard Nachtigal, *Rußland und seine öster-reichisch-ungarischen Kriegsgefangenen (1914–1918)* (Remshalden: Greiner, 2003); Reinhard Nachtigal, "Die Kriegsgefangenen-Verluste an der Ostfront. Eine Übersicht zur Statistik und zu Problemen der Heimatfronten 1914/15," in *Die vergessene Front: Der Osten 1914/15*, ed. Gerhard P. Groß (Paderborn: Schöningh, 2006), 202–216.

84. Richard Germann identifies Eglseer as having belonged to an "Austrian network," a small coterie of National Socialist–minded former Bundesheer officers who flourished in the Wehrmacht. Richard Germann, "'Österreichische' Soldaten in Ost- und Südosteuropa 1941—1945: Deutsche Krieger—Nationalsozialistische Verbrecher—Österreichische Opfer?" (PhD thesis, University of Vienna, 2006), 347.

85. AdR Vienna, Bundesheer-Akten. Personnel file on Karl Eglseer. Staatssekretär Angelis, 3/13/38. Betr.: GM Adalbert Szente, Inf. Brig. Der 6. Division. Beurlaubung; ibid., Kommando der 6. Division, 3/25/38.

86. MFB4/56147, 37291/2, 299. 714. Inf.-Div. Ia, 3/26/43. Geheim! Betr.: Verhalten deutscher und kroatischer Soldaten bei Überfälle; MFB4/56147, 37291/4, 425–427. 114. Jäg.-Div. Kommandeur, 4/6/43. Geheim! Richtlinien (Nr. 1) für einheitliche Anschauungen und Arbeit in der Div.

87. MFB4/56147, 37291/2, 247–248. 714. Inf.-Div. Ia, 3/28/43. Merkblatt für Verhalten von Versorgungskolonnen im bandengefährdeten Raum. Emphasis in original.

88. See chap. 2.

89. Hoare, *Genocide and Resistance in Hitler's Bosnia: The Partisans and the Chetniks*, 330, 335.

90. On these phases of the White operations, see Milazzo, *The Chetni Movement and the Yugoslav Resistance*, 118–131; Tomasevich, *War and Revolution in Yugoslavia, 1941–1945: The Chetniks*, 237–256; Schmider, *Partisanenkrieg in Jugoslawien 1941–1944*, 219–239.

CONCLUSION

1. For the best general discussion of why the Axis failed militarily against the Partisans, see Klaus Schmider, *Partisanenkrieg in Jugoslawien 1941–1944* (Hamburg: Verlag E. S. Mittler, 2002), ch. 8.

2. Ibid., 535–541, 553.

3. Ibid., 525, 548.

4. Ibid., 525, 529–534.

5. Ibid., 568–569.

6. Ibid., 547.

7. Ibid., 550–552.

8. Ibid., 552–553.

9. Ibid., 541–542.

10. In 1944 units under Artur Phleps, commander of the Prinz Eugen Division, employed hunter group–type tactics on a larger scale, in the form of rapid pursuit operations rather than encirclement operations. However, the source base is too small to enable the drawing of firm conclusions as to how successful these operations were. Schmider, *Partisanenkrieg in Jugoslawien 1941–1944*, 553.

11. Ben Shepherd, *War in the Wild East: The German Army and Soviet Partisans* (Cambridge, MA: Harvard University Press, 2004), 163.

12. On German anti-Partisan operations in 1943, see Schmider, *Partisanenkrieg in Jugoslawien 1941–1944*, ch. 5; Gaj Trifkovic, "A Case of Failed Counter-Insurgency: Antipartisan Operations in Yugoslavia 1943," *Journal of Slavic Military Studies* 24 (2011): 314–336.

13. On Operation Black see Schmider, *Partisanenkrieg in Jugoslawien 1941–1944*, 261–288, 543; Trifkovic, "A Case of Failed Counter-Insurgency: Antipartisan Operations in Yugoslavia 1943."

14. Schmider, *Partisanenkrieg in Jugoslawien 1941–1944*, 282–283; Trifkovic, "A Case of Failed Counter-Insurgency: Antipartisan Operations in Yugoslavia 1943," 334–336.

15. Ruth Bettina Birn, *Die Höheren SS- und Polizeiführer: Himmlers Vertreter im Reich und den besetzten Gebieten* (Düsseldorf: Droste, 1986), 260–274.

16. Klaus Schmider, "Der jugoslawische Kriegsschauplatz," in *Das Deutsche Reich und der Zweite Weltkrieg, Band 8. Die Ostfront, 1943/44: Der Krieg im Osten und an den Nebenfronten*, Karl-Heinz Frieser et al. (Stuttgart: Deutsche Verlags-Anstalt, 2007), 1021.

17. Ibid., 1028–1030; Schmider, *Partisanenkrieg in Jugoslawien 1941–1944*, 545–547.

18. Schmider, *Partisanenkrieg in Jugoslawien 1941–1944*, 52–53; Schmider, "Der jugoslawische Kriegsschauplatz," 1028. On relations between the Germans and the NDH during late 1943 and 1944, see Schmider, *Partisanenkrieg in Jugoslawien 1941–1944*, 362–378, 397–413.

19. On the Partisans' increasingly impressive military performance during 1943 and increasing Allied support for them, see, for example, F. W. D. Deakin, *The Embattled Mountain* (Oxford: Oxford University Press, 1971); Milovan Djilas, *Wartime: With Tito and the Partisans* (London: Martin Secker and Warburg, 1977), 215–363; Michael McConville, *A Small War in the Balkans: British Military Involvement in Wartime*

Yugoslavia 1941–1945 (London: Macmillan, 1986); Richard West, *Tito and the Rise and Fall of Yugoslavia* (London: Sinclair Stevenson, 1996), chaps. 8, 9; Marko Attila Hoare, *Genocide and Resistance in Hitler's Bosnia* (Oxford: Oxford University Press, 2005), 329–349. On Chetnik–Axis collaboration, see Jozo Tomasevich, *War and Revolution in Yugoslavia, 1941–1945: The Chetniks* (Stanford, CA: Stanford University Press, 1975), chaps. 7, 9; on the eventual Chetnik–Allied break, see ibid., 359–372. For a detailed treatment of British–Chetnik relations, see Simon Trew, *Britain, Mihailović, and the Chetniks, 1941–42* (London: St. Martin's Press, 1997).

20. Schmider, "Der jugoslawische Kriegsschauplatz," 1024–1025. For more detail on the Italian capitulation's impact upon German efforts in Yugoslavia, see Schmider, *Partisanenkrieg in Jugoslawien 1941–1944*, 288–316.

21. On anti-Partisan operations in 1944 and the campaign's final phase, see Schmider, *Partisanenkrieg in Jugoslawien 1941–1944*, 378–397, 413–417.

22. Jürgen Förster, "The Relation between Operation Barbarossa as an Ideological war of Extermination and the Final Solution," in *The Final Solution: Origins and Implementation*, ed. David Cesarani (London: Routledge 1994), 90–97; Jürgen Förster, "Wehrmacht, Krieg und Holocaust," in *Die Wehrmacht: Mythos und Realität*, ed. Rolf-Dieter Müller and Hans-Erich Volkmann (Munich: Oldenbourg, 1999), 953.

23. See the example of Security Battalion 242. Shepherd, *War in the Wild East: The German Army and Soviet Partisans*, 203–207, 211.

24. Theo J. Schulte, *The German Army and Nazi Policies in Occupied Russia* (Oxford: Berg, 1989); Shepherd, *War in the Wild East: The German Army and Soviet Partisans*.

25. Shepherd, *War in the Wild East: The German Army and Soviet Partisans*, 147–149.

26. Ibid., chap. 6.

27. Ibid.

28. Ibid., 66–70.

29. Ibid., chap. 2.

30. Ibid., 155–157, 227–228.

31. Ibid., 81–82.

32. Three additional motivational factors to which previous secondary literature ascribes importance are omitted:

    1. *Direct experience of armed confrontation during the Time of Struggle (1918–1920)*, omitted because available sources rarely indicate whether or not a particular officer was engaged so actively.

    2. *Pursuit of civilian career during the interwar years.* This may have been a radicalizing factor, given that there was, from 1935 onward, a predominance within the German army officer corps of men who came from the middle-class civilian circles from whom the Nazis drew their most extensive electoral support. However, any impact this factor may have had is obscured by the fact that most of the sample served as continuing officers during the interwar years in any case.

    3. *Prior service in the East (Poland or the Soviet Union) during World War II.* This may have been a brutalizing factor for reasons similar to service on the eastern front during the Great War. It is omitted because the sample officers

who served in Yugoslavia from 1941 onward—a large portion of the entire sample—would have been unable to serve in the Soviet Union beforehand, because their occupation of Yugoslavia preceded the invasion of the Soviet Union.

33. See Appendix A.

34. On the 221st Security Division, see Shepherd, *War in the Wild East: The German Army and Soviet Partisans*, 129–218. On comparison between the 221st and the more hard-line 203d Security Division during the second half of 1942, see ibid., 155–157.

35. See Appendix A.

36. On continuities and discontinuities between the eastern front experience of the Great War and the Third Reich's prosecution of World War II, see Rüdiger Bergien, "Vorspiel des 'Vernichtunsgkrieges'? Die Ostfront des Ersten Weltkrieges und das Kontinuitätsproblem," in *Die vergessene Front: Der Osten 1914/15*, ed. Gerhard P. Groß (Paderborn: Schöningh, 2006), 393–408.

Acknowledgments

Grateful thanks are due to:

The School of Law and Social Sciences, Glasgow Caledonian University, for providing me with such a supportive environment in which to carry out this study.

Kathleen McDermott at Harvard University Press, and HUP's external reviewers, for helpful advice on writing the book.

Andrew Kinney at HUP, and Marianna Verturro and her colleagues at IBT Global, for helping put the book together in its later stages;

The British Academy and the Carnegie Foundation for providing extra research funding.

The following individuals, who freely provided either valuable advice, practical help, excellent company during my archival visits, or a combination: Alex Bangert, Sonja Bernhard, Heiko Brendel, John Breuilly, Peter Broucek, Caro Buchheim, Philip Cooke, Tomislav Dulić, Yvonne Ewen, Alex Flucker, Jürgen Förster, Richard Germann, Jonathan Gumz, Chris Haag, Christian Hartmann, Mike Hierholzer, Marko Hoare, Lothar Höbelt, Patrick Hoolahan, Ke-chin Hsia, Johannes Hürter, Maria Knight, Alexander Korb, Bernd Lemke, Peter Lieb, Walter Manoschek, Alex Marshall, Evan Mawdsley, Mark Mazower, Charles D. Melson, Timm C. Richter, Felix Römer, Klaus Schmider, Peter Steinkamp, Geoffrey Swain, Wolfram Wette, and Martina Winkelhofer.

The staff of the following institutions: Bavarian State Archive, Munich; Federal Archive, Berlin-Lichterfelde; Federal Archive, Koblenz (images department); Federal Archive, Ludwigsburg; German Historical Institute, London; Imperial War Museum, London; Library of Contemporary History, Stuttgart; Military History Research Institute, Potsdam; Süddeutscher Verlag, Munich (images department). Special thanks are due to the staff at the Federal Military Archive, Freiburg-im-Breisgau, and at the Austrian State Archive, Vienna, for their unfailing patience and help.

A note on the maps: the maps provided in the book are based extensively on copies of original German Army maps, which varied widely in cartographical consistency. They are intended to convey only a general idea of the scale and location of the events discussed.

Ultimately, the responsibility for the final work is, of course, my own.

Index

attempts to deescalate counterinsurgency brutality, 170, 175–176, 178; and Trio operations, 173–175, 177; and militias in eastern Bosnia, 194–195, 196. *See also* German army (1939–1945), corps: LXV; German army (1939–1945), regional commands: Serbia Command

Balkan Wars 1912–1913, 21, 30

Baltic States, 54, 138

Barton, Gottfried, 251, 254

Belgium, German invasion of 1914, 29, German atrocities in 1914, 31–32, 55, 68; German occupation of during Great War, 45

Boehme, Franz, radicalizes counterinsurgency campaign in Serbia, 1–3, 120–127, 143, 232, 255; engages with Nedić regime, 120–121, 123; manoeuvres against Danckelmann, 120; outdone for ruthless by 342d Infantry Division, 128, 131–133, 140, 250, 306–307; attempts to deescalate counterinsurgency brutality, 135; biographical details, 141; and Operation Uzice, 146; leaves Serbia, 147. *See also* German army (1939–1945), corps: XVIII

Boicetta, Nikolaus, 232

Bolsheviks, 39, 46–49, 138–139, 233–234. *See also* anti-Bolshevism; Communists, Yugoslavia

Borowski, Heinrich, 110, 117; biographical details, 83, 137–138, 141, 305–306; effect on troops' conduct, 90, 141, 142, 250. *See also* German army (1939–1945), infantry divisions, 704th

Brauchitsch, Walther von, 67

Britain. *See* Great Britain

Bulgaria, 35, 37, 76, 78, 81

Bundesheer, 57, 60–61, 64–65

Catholicism, anti-Catholicism in German military, 31–32, 62; in Bundesheer officer corps, 64; Catholic relations and cooperation with Ustasha, 78–79, 93, 192; among Croats generally, 162

Chetniks (Bosnia), support levels of, 148–149, 152, 153, 216, 237–238; initial coexistence with Partisans, 149; breakdown in

relations with Partisans, 150; relations with Italians, 150, 155, 173, 193–194, 196, 217–219, 235, 237–238; ethnic cleansing campaigns of, 150–151, 155, 185, 187, 193–198, 213; and "Great Serbia", 151; organizational weaknesses, 152–153, 238, 241; in combat against Axis, 153, 163, 165, 170, 188, 204; under Dangić, 158, 164, 170; poor military performance against Partisans, 158, 218, 235, 238, 241; relations with Germans, 158–159, 170, 184, 196–197, 218–219, 241; conflict with Partisans, 158, 179, 182, 184, 191, 198; propaganda of, 179, 192; relations with NDH, 182, 196, 199; 718th Infantry Division's view of, 184, 194–197, 205, 213; in 1943 counterinsurgency operations, 218–219, 240, 325. *See also* Chetniks (Mihailović movement, Serbia)

Chetniks (Mihailović movement, Serbia), formation and early support, 89, 95–96, 98; initial weakness of, 96–97; alliance with Partisans, 110; and Serbian national uprising, 112, 120, 125; against 342d Infantry Division, 128, 132–136, 143; split with Partisans, 143–145, 246; contacts with Nedić regime, 145; operations against Axis 1942, 153. *See also* Chetniks (Pecanac movement, Serbia); Mihailović, Draza

Chetniks (Pecanac movement, Serbia), 89, 98, 121, 294. *See also* Chetniks (Mihailović movement, Serbia)

Clausewitz, Carl von, 25

Commissars, 96, 176, 180, 202–203. *See also* Communists, Yugoslavia

Communists, Yugoslavia, and Serbian national uprising, 82, 91–92, 95–97, 104–105, 108, 109, 128, 134, 143; pre-1941 development of, 91–92; organization of Serbian Partisan movement by, 96–97; German measures against, 98, 100–103, 117, 118, 122–123, 136, 142–143, 164–165, 169, 245; support among Serbian population summer 1941, 99; German identification of Jews with, 100–103, 122; support in Bosnia for, 148–149, 154, 198; organization of Bosnian Partisan